Lee's Adjutant

Portrait of Taylor, posed in his uniform as lieutenant colonel, C.S. Army. Painted by Thomas C. Cole. (Original in the Virginia Historical Society, Richmond, Va. Reproduced with permission.)

Lee's Adjutant

The Wartime Letters of
Colonel Walter Herron Taylor,
1862–1865

Edited by R. Lockwood Tower
with John S. Belmont

University of South Carolina Press

©1995 by the University of South Carolina

Published in Columbia, South Carolina by the
University of South Carolina Press

Manufactured in the United States of America

Library of Congress Cataloging-in-Publication Data

Taylor, Walter Herron, 1838–1916.
 Lee's adjutant : the wartime letters of colonel Walter Herron
Taylor, 1862–1865 / edited by R. Lockwood Tower with John S.
Belmont.
  p. cm.
 Includes bibliographical references and index.
 ISBN 1-57003-021-9
 1. Virginia—History—Civil War, 1861–1865—Campaigns—Sources.
2. United States—History—Civil War, 1861–1865—Campaigns—
Sources. 3. Lee, Robert E. (Robert Edward), 1807–1870—Friends and
associates. 4. Taylor, Walter Herron, 1838–1916—Correspondence.
5. Soldiers—Confederate States of America—Correspondence.
I. Tower, R. Lockwood. II. Belmont, John S. III. Title.
E470.2.T28 1994
973.7'3'092—dc20   94–18751

To Mia

Contents

Illustrations and Maps

Illustrations

Frontispiece
Portrait of Taylor as lieutenant colonel

Maps

Preface

In his monumental biography of Robert E. Lee, Douglas Southall Freeman referred to the papers of Colonel Walter H. Taylor in these words: "These precious MSS. constitute the most important source of collateral manuscript material on the military career of General Lee."[1] To Clifford Dowdey the collection of Taylor's correspondence was "priceless."[2] These distinguished Confederate historians were in agreement that the most valuable items were the letters Taylor wrote from Lee's headquarters to the young lady to whom he was to be married under dramatic circumstances the night Richmond fell to the Northern army in April 1865, as well as those addressed to other members of his family in the early years of the war. Written without reserve by a highly intelligent young officer with an unparalleled opportunity to observe Lee on a daily basis and to know what was going on in the upper echelons of the Army of Northern Virginia, these letters constitute a unique historical record.

Taylor was an intensely private person and despite repeated urgings during his lifetime he refused to permit the letters to go beyond his immediate family. Sometime apparently around the turn of the century, he transcribed in his decorative and distinguished hand a portion of the letters that he rather grandly entitled "Flash-lights from Headquarters of the Army of Northern Virginia, C.S.A." Frequent deletions from the originals were made, references to his lady love were omitted, and a perceptible softening in his attitude toward the other side became evident. What he had previously described as Grant's "whipping" in the Wilderness now became the latter's "discomforture," and pejorative use of the term "Yankees" was abandoned. But this was of small account, for "Flash-lights" was never published.

Freeman was the first historian of note to have access to the wartime letters, and he characterized them as "frankness itself."[3] Indeed they were, for Taylor wrote for the eyes of the recipients only. Freeman's statement that "only about half" the letters were printed even partially in Taylor's *Four Years with General Lee*, however, is wide of the mark.[4] In fact, excerpts from scarcely one letter in five, often toned down for publication, were quoted therein. Typically reticent, Taylor alluded to these quotations as "notes taken by me at the time."[5] To refer to them as excerpts from letters to his sweetheart was more than his strong sense of privacy would permit. It was not until almost fifty years after his death that the originals were made available to public scrutiny, when in 1964 his granddaughter, Janet Fauntleroy Taylor, presented them to the Norfolk Public Library in Norfolk, Virginia, where they now repose.

For purposes of clarity and ease of comprehension, modern punctuation has been employed in certain instances to replace the dashes so frequently used in mid-nineteenth-century correspondence, and particularly lengthy passages have been divided into paragraphs where appropriate. Otherwise the letters are reproduced as Taylor wrote them, save for the omission, indicated by ellipses, of some social gossip and repetitious expressions of affection and religious sentiment that would add nothing of historical or human interest. Such editing has been held to a minimum. If the style at times seems turgid, one must keep in mind that life a hundred and twenty odd years ago moved at a slower pace than now and modes of expression were more elaborate. Should it be noted that Taylor habitually looked on the bright side of things, this may be attributed to his unswerving faith in eventual Southern victory and the unquenchable optimism of a young man in love.

A word of explanation is in order regarding the staff organization of the Army of Northern Virginia, and the distinction between Lee's personal staff, on which Taylor served, and the much larger general staff of the army. The latter consisted of a chief of artillery, chief of ordnance, chief commissary, chief quartermaster, chief engineer, medical director, judge advocate general, and a number of assistant inspectors general. These men, in turn, had numerous assistants. Lee's personal staff, on the other hand, was kept to a minimum in accordance with the general's wishes and the pressing need for qualified officers in the ranks. When he took command of the Army of Northern Virginia on June 1, 1862, it consisted of a chief of staff, a military secretary, an assistant adjutant general, four aides-de-camp, of whom Taylor was one, five clerks, a mess steward, and the general's body servant.

The lines between the staffs were not clearly drawn. For example, A. L. Long, while serving on Lee's personal staff as military secretary, often discharged many of the duties of chief of artillery of the army. Conversely, Major H. E. Young, army advocate general, came increasingly to serve as a member of the personal rather than the general staff.

Taylor was unique in that he served as a member of the personal staff from the beginning to the very end of the conflict, first as aide-de-camp, then "acting" and finally assistant adjutant general of the Army. Lee came to depend on him more and more as the war progressed, and in 1864–65 he served as chief of staff in all but name only. Never adequate in number, Lee's personal staff was overworked, furloughs were few, and promotion slow. On July 16, 1861, Taylor was commissioned a first lieutenant infantry in the Army of the Confederate States and ordered to report to General Lee. Transferred to the adjutant general's department, he was made a captain on December 10, 1861. On March 6, 1863, he attained his majority and in December of that year was promoted to lieutenant colonel, a rank he was to hold for the remainder of the war. Lest there be confusion as to why Taylor's title was *assistant* adjutant general, be it noted that there was only one adjutant and inspector general in the Confederate armed forces, namely Samuel Cooper, the ranking full general of the army. A host of assistant adjutants general served on the staffs of army, corps, division, and brigade commanders, their relative importance depending on the headquarters to which they were assigned.

Acknowledgments

Above all, I am indebted to the Norfolk Public Library of Norfolk, Virginia, for making available its vast collection of Walter Herron Taylor Papers and authorizing the publication in full or in part of the Taylor letters and other original documents contained therein. Permission has also been granted to reproduce for publication photographs from the Taylor Papers. I express my deep appreciation to Peggy A. Haile, Archivist, who has continued to be most gracious and helpful well beyond the call of duty, especially in replying to innumerable requests for information and assistance.

I express my gratitude and appreciation to the late Janet Fauntleroy Taylor, granddaughter of Walter H. Taylor, for her encouragement and assistance in recalling anecdotes of the Taylor family; to Stuart Symington Taylor, grandson, for providing important documents and letters formerly in his possession and now in the library at Stratford Hall, birthplace of Robert E. Lee, and for making available the original endorsement of Robert E. Lee on a recommendation for Taylor's promotion to major (see fig. 4); to Powell H. Taylor, grandson, for the gift of a daguerreotype of Taylor as a cadet at the Virginia Military Institute (V.M.I.) (see fig. 1).

Others whose kind assistance I would like to acknowledge include Lucille B. Portlock, predecessor of Peggy Haile in the Sargeant Memorial Room of the Kirn Library, a branch of the Norfolk Public Library; Nelson Langford, Virginius C. Hall, Howson W. Cole, and Patricia Thompson of the staff of the Virginia Historical Society; Diane B. Jacobs, Archivist of the Preston Library at the Virginia Military Institute, who made available Taylor's class records at V.M.I. and a number of interesting letters from him and his father; Corrine P. Hudgins, Curator of Photographic Collections of the Museum of the Confederacy in Richmond, Virginia; Anne Rosebrock, for typing the manuscript; and the staffs of the South Carolina Historical Society and the Library Society in Charleston, South Carolina.

Last, but by no means least, I gratefully acknowledge the inestimable contribution of my stepson, John S. Belmont, in the organization and research involved in preparing Taylor's letters for publication. Without his invaluable assistance it would have been impossible to complete the task.

Lee's Adjutant

Introduction

Biographical Sketch of Walter Herron Taylor, 1838–1916

Of all those who served with Robert E. Lee in the headquarters of the Army of Northern Virginia no one was as close to him personally as Walter Taylor. This remarkable young man, only twenty-two when hostilities broke out in the spring of 1861, was at Lee's side, virtually without interruption, during the entire four years of the Civil War. Perhaps never before or since has it been the good fortune of so youthful a soldier to find himself in such intimate relationship with one of the truly great figures of American history.

It is not surprising that Lee was drawn to his young adjutant, for in Taylor he found the traits of character that appealed to him most—honesty, hard work, deep religious conviction, and, above all, devotion to duty. On a personal level an increasingly strong bond of affection grew up between the two men despite the disparity in age and station. Years later George Washington Custis Lee, eldest son of Robert E. Lee and his successor as president of the college that would become Washington and Lee University, wrote Taylor that he looked upon him "as a member of his father's family."[1] Taylor, in turn, was to name one of his sons for Robert E. Lee.

"It was my particular privilege," wrote Taylor, "to occupy the position of a confidential staff-officer with General Lee during the entire period of the War for Southern Independence."[2] He was, in fact, the only officer who could lay claim to such a distinction. He remained with Lee to the very end at Appomattox, ate at his mess and was in almost daily contact with him, serving first as aide-de-camp (ADC) and subsequently as assistant adjutant general (AAG) of the Army of Northern Virginia.

Douglas Southall Freeman commented:

Of all the personal staff at Army headquarters, the best known to visitors and on the most intimate terms with the aides of other general officers was Walter Taylor. He was the youngest of Lee's official family and much against his wishes had to serve as 'inside man' because of his skill and accuracy in handling the official correspondence that Lee detested. Of unassuming personality was Taylor but magnetic from youth, friendly and understanding. Possessed of a memory as notable as his industry, his one weakness was an impulse to steal off during a battle and to participate in a charge.[3]

Of English stock on both sides, Walter Herron Taylor was born on June 13, 1838, into a prominent, well-connected Norfolk family. His parents were Walter Herron Taylor, Sr., and Cornelia Wickham Cowdery. When of an age to leave home he was enrolled in the Norfolk Military Academy, where he distinguished himself by winning a medal for the outstanding pupil in the Lower Form.[4] One of his classmates later recalled that "he entered into all our sports with spirit and zest, being equally popular with boys and girls."[5]

In August 1854, at sixteen, he was sent to the Virginia Military Institute in Lexington. That institution, modeled after the United States Military Academy at West Point, had been founded in 1839 under the direction of Colonel Claude Crozet, a graduate of the Ecole Politechnique in Paris and a veteran of Napoleon's army in its retreat from Moscow. In Taylor's day it was headed by Colonel Francis H. Smith, superintendent for half a century, from 1839 to 1889.[6]

The class of 1857 at V.M.I., which Taylor entered with advanced standing as a third classman or sophomore, consisted of fifty-eight members of whom only twenty-three were to graduate in course. He was not to be among them, having been compelled to withdraw from the Institute in the autumn of 1855 due to the death of his father in one of those recurrent epidemics of yellow fever that ravaged Southern cities in the nineteenth century. In recognition of his distinguished war record, however, he was made the only honorary graduate of his class in 1870.[7]

By the time Taylor left Norfolk's tidewater for the mountains of Rockbridge County, where V.M.I. was located, he had fallen head over heels in love with Miss Elizabeth Selden "Bettie" Saunders, daughter of Commander John L. Saunders of the United States Navy (USN). This estimable young woman cast a spell over her admirer the intensity of which never abated from their first acquaintance in 1850 until death intervened some sixty-six years later.

At its inception, however, the course of true love was by no means smooth. Not long after arriving at V.M.I., Taylor's hopes were jolted by a crushing letter from his Norfolk friend, Duncan Robertson. Dated November 8, 1854, it read in part: "This letter will convey the answer to the question you asked me concerning Miss Bettie. She desired that I would leave the locket unclasped as a token of a broken engagement. . . . Lizzie Barron told me Sunday that Bettie didn't give a fig for you some time before you left here but did not let you know it. Now she says she hates you."[8]

As might have been anticipated, Taylor was a conscientious student and by the end of his first full academic year had compiled an enviable record. In General Merit, as in Mathematics, he stood at the head of his class. In Latin and Drawing his rank was number two out of thirty-one. Even in Composition and Declaration, which evidently caused him some difficulty, he was a respectable tenth.[9] All of this elicited from his father the comment in a letter to the superintendent that his parents were "much gratified by the 'stand' taken by Walter in his last report on 'merit' as well as his studies." The hope was expressed that he would "make strenuous efforts to maintain his ground."[10]

Equally outstanding was Walter's conduct, for he received only 21 demerits for the year in comparison with 74 for the cadet next most amenable to discipline and a prodigious 194 amassed by a more venturesome lad from Orange County.[11] That he was not averse to kicking over the traces on occasion, however, is revealed by his embroilment in July 1855 in an episode involving the hazing of a lower classman, for which breach of discipline he was threatened with a court martial. Fortunately for him Colonel Smith interceded, and at an "unofficial" interview with the superintendent, Taylor made a clean breast of it, confessing all he had done. With a stern warning, the matter was disposed of.[12]

On his withdrawal from V.M.I. Taylor was urged to continue his father's business as a commission merchant, but the prospect of a steady salary was more appealing than the uncertainty of an enterprise in which he had no previous experience, and he found employment at the Norfolk branch of the Bank of Virginia. A few years later he put in a stint as auditor of the recently completed Norfolk and Petersburg Railroad, later to be absorbed by the Norfolk and Western, of which he subsequently served as a director for over thirty years. This connection, however, proved temporary. Offered a promotion at the Bank of

Virginia, he accepted and was working there when war broke out in the spring of 1861.[13]

On March 15, 1857, along with seventeen others, he was confirmed in the Episcopal faith at Christ Church in Norfolk, and thus was formalized one of the enduring and pervasive influences of his life. "Having given the matter prayerful and serious consideration," he wrote at the time, "being convinced of the vast importance of embracing religion, of leading a different life & of the danger of delay, I hesitated no longer to take the step, thoroughly convinced as I was of my duty, & not withstanding my exceeding sinfulness, I was not deterred, re-solved, desired & left the rest to my Father."[14] Bettie Saunders followed his lead and "decided for Christ" in April 1858.

Walter's relationship to Bettie had resumed on New Year's Day, 1858. They later remembered this as a happy period, but it was not without contretemps. Bettie was fickle. By the spring of 1859 she had cooled toward her persistent suitor. In a letter dated June 21, 1859, from Howard's Neck (her cousin's place in Goochland County), the blow fell. "What has changed me," she wrote, "I cannot tell. . . . I was never worthy of your love, never! I only request that you will either return or burn my many miserable notes and pray that you may forgive me for writing them. . . . Believe me that I can never forget your kindnesses to me. . . . Ever your friend—Bettie."[15]

Relations were not entirely broken off but continued sporadically on a more or less formal basis. Bettie accepted flowers, they attended a concert or two together, and exchanged a few letters, but that was about as much as she was willing to do. In January 1861, after another rebuff, Walter wrote her, "I must love you without any return, yet I could not see you another's. Oh! Heaven grant that I may be removed when the day for this arrives. I could not, could not see it. Oh Bettie, I dread so much, very much that event."[16]

Then the war intervened. Taylor wrote her irregularly. His letters were guarded and he signed himself "Your sincere friend"; but his true feelings remained unchanged and he adamantly refused to abandon hope.[17]

On April 17, 1861, in response to President Lincoln's call for 75,000 volunteers to put down the rebellion in the states of the lower South that had already seceded, the Virginia Convention adopted an ordinance of secession withdrawing the state from the Union. An immediate need arose for men with military education and experience to serve at headquarters of the Army of Virginia then being organized in Richmond under the command of General Robert E. Lee.

Aside from his military education at Norfolk Military Academy and V.M.I., Taylor had served in the Norfolk volunteer militia organization known as "Company F" since its inception in December 1859. Beginning as orderly sergeant, he then became second lieutenant, receiving a commission in the Virginia Militia from Governor John Letcher, which was to date from December 1, 1860.[18] In April Taylor was elected first lieutenant of Company F, and on the last day of the month the unit was mustered into state service, becoming Company G of the Sixth Virginia Infantry;[19] but Taylor's service as an infantry officer was destined to end almost before it began.

Governor Letcher had directed two of his aides and advisors, Colonel Francis H. Smith and Commander Richard L. Page, to make selections for service at army headquarters. Smith, the superintendent of V.M.I., of course knew Taylor intimately, and Page, a naval officer, was Taylor's uncle by marriage and a first cousin of Robert E. Lee. Under the circumstances it is not surprising that Taylor was chosen for such duty. There was, however, little hint of nepotism, for "so vast are the interweavings of such Virginia families that Taylor had never before seen Lee and the General had never heard of the dark, quiet young man, then attired in the uniform of [his] Norfolk militia company."[20] A dashing figure he must have made in his dress uniform of blue frock coat, blue trousers, black cap, epaulettes, sash and sword (see fig. 3).[21]

On May 2 a telegram from Richmond addressed to Lieut. W. H. Taylor was received at Norfolk at 12:30 via the Norfolk and Petersburg Railroad telegraph line. "Repair to headquarters at once," it read, "and report for duty to Col. F. H. Smith—by command R. L. Page Naval Aid D Camp to the Governor."[22] Early the next day he took a train to the capital and on arrival went to the Spotswood Hotel. He was there having breakfast, when Robert E. Lee, who was to have such a profound influence on his life, entered the room. "I was at once," Taylor recounted years later, "attracted and greatly impressed by his appearance. He was then at the zenith of his physical beauty. Admirably proportioned, of graceful and dignified carriage, with strikingly handsome features, bright and penetrating eyes, his iron-gray hair closely cut, his face cleanly shaved except a moustache, he appeared every inch a soldier and a man born to command."[23]

Commissioned a first lieutenant in the Provisional Army of Virginia, Taylor was assigned to Lee's headquarters.[24] There he came in close contact with Colonel Robert S. Garnett, adjutant general of the state forces, a man whom Taylor described as the best informed and most capable in military detail he ever met and to whom he was greatly indebted for the experience and knowledge gained while serving under him.[25] Personable, able, and devoted, Taylor grew rapidly in his job and soon made himself indispensable.[26]

To Eli Barrot, a fellow employee at the Bank of Virginia, he wrote on May 13: "There is a great difference between my present work & what I was required to do at the Bank. I now begin in the morning after breakfast & am kept constantly at it until 10 or 11 (at night), only allowing myself intermission for meals. . . . I do not object to the hard work for many reasons, not the least of which is that the Genl does the same. Oh! Mr. Barrot he's a trump, a soldier, gentleman & above all a Christian."[27]

In the ensuing weeks Lee's headquarters was engaged in the monumental task of creating an army from the ground up. At this early stage the availability of manpower was not a matter of concern, for such was the rush of volunteers to enlist that many, for the time being at least, had to be turned away. The pressing problem was one of providing arms, ammunition, equipment, transport, food, and training for those willing to fight.[28] That Taylor's performance of his duties met with Lee's approbation is indicated by his promotion to assistant adjutant general with the rank of captain as of May 31.[29]

On May 23, by a vote of 125,950 to 20,373, the people of Virginia had ratified the ordinance of secession previously adopted by the Virginia Convention, and on June 8 the Virginia armed forces were transferred to the Confederacy.[30] Thus Taylor's commission as adjutant general of the state troops ceased to be effective, and for a time his status was in limbo. General Lee, notwithstanding, continued him on duty with his headquarters and a month or so later obtained for him a commission as first lieutenant of infantry in the Regular Army of the Confederate States,[31] with orders to report to him for duty as aide-de-camp. Lee had been authorized by the War Department to assume control of the forces of the Confederate States in Virginia and on May 14 had been made a brigadier general in the Regular Army of the Confederacy, the highest rank then existing.[32]

Late in May the Confederate capital was transferred from Montgomery, Alabama, to Richmond. On his arrival there President Jefferson Davis made Lee his chief military advisor, since Lee had his "unqualified confidence, both as a man and a patriot, and had the special knowledge of conditions in Virginia that was most useful."[33] Rather than assign Lee to command in the field, however, Davis decided to keep him nearby in Richmond available for consultation. Consequently Taylor and the other members of the headquarters staff remained on duty in the capital until after the first great clash of arms at Manassas or Bull Run on July 21.

Meanwhile the military situation in western Virginia had been deteriorating steadily, and now that the threat of a Federal invasion from Washington had been postponed indefinitely by the decisive Confederate triumph at Manassas, Davis sent Lee west in an effort to straighten out the chaos existing in that region. Not only had the Confederates under General Garnett been defeated by the Federals led by General McClellan, the future commander of the Army of the Potomac, and Garnett himself killed, but the Southern forces were split into three small, semi-independent commands, the leaders of which were not only uncooperative but on occasion outwardly antagonistic.

On July 28, 1861, Lee set forth from Richmond, with, to say the least, a modest entourage consisting of his cook, a body servant, and two military companions, Colonel John A. Washington and Lieutenant Taylor.[34] On the Virginia Central Railroad they journeyed via Hanover Junction, Gordonsville, and Charlottesville to Staunton in the Shenandoah Valley and thence on horseback to Monterey in the Allegheny Mountains, where the remnants of Garnett's defeated army lay encamped. Taylor thoroughly enjoyed the ride into the mountains and recounted that the "air was most invigorating and a delightful change from the heated atmosphere of the crowded city."[35] Sharing these feelings, Lee wrote his wife: "I enjoyed the mountains, as I rode along. The views were magnificent. The valleys so peaceful, the scenery so beautiful."[36]

Yet, when the mountains themselves were reached, Taylor found a "most impracticable, inhospitable, and dismal country. . . . For weeks it rained daily and in torrents; the condition of the roads was frightful; they were barely passable. . . . The troops were sorely afflicted with measles and a malignant type of fever, which prostrated hundreds of each command. Rations were short and clothing insufficient."[37]

Despite such trials and privations, Taylor would look back longingly on his intimate association with General Lee and Colonel Washington, and to the time "when that little military family of three, with one wagon for our equipage and provisions, and two servants, constituted the headquarters of the general-in-chief." Colonel Washington conducted morning and evening prayer and, in Taylor's words, "a spirit of devotion to the Giver of all good and of love for all His works pervaded that camp in the mountains that was in striking contrast to the spirit of passion and hate that animated the men who had precipitated trouble and arrayed in hostile ranks the two sections of our country."[38]

Colonel Washington, described by Freeman as "a gentleman of the highest type and a true aristocrat,"[39] was killed while reconnoitering with a cavalry patrol on September 13, a crushing blow to Taylor. The body was returned the next day under a flag of truce, and the impressionable young lieutenant later wrote:

> I was greatly shocked in the contemplation of my noble companion and friend cold in death, . . . and I began to realize something of the horrors of war. And then I asked myself why it was so,—why were these people, so lately friends, arrayed in hostile ranks with such deadly purpose? And as I reasoned, it seemed to me that one side was acting clearly on the defensive; its country was being invaded, its homes and its firesides threatened; all that it asked was to be let alone and to be permitted to enjoy the fruit of victory it had won jointly with the other from England, in the establishment and maintenance of the principle that all governments derived their just powers from the consent of the governed. But what motive impelled the other side? Was it the lust of power? Was it the distorted view of the idealist of his duty to force his theories upon his neighbor? Or was it the development into action of the implacable hatred that had long slumbered in the heart of the abolitionist against the so-called aristocracy of the South? As these questions forced themselves upon me, I became embittered; resentment took possession of my heart, and the man on the other side became my enemy. A fratricidal war! How sad it was![40]

Now the tiny headquarters group was reduced to the general and his young aide, housed in a solitary tent. When on occasion a visitor was entertained, Lee shared his blankets with Taylor, turning over those of the latter to his guest.[41] One very cold night by their campfire Lee suggested that they put their blankets together for warmth, and "so it happened," Taylor recalled, "that it was vouchsafed to me to occupy very close relations with my old commander, and to be able to testify to his self-denial and his simplicity of life in those days of trial for all."[42] At the end of October, Lee, accompanied by Taylor, returned to Richmond, and the dreary and abortive campaign in western Virginia came to a close.

Taylor paid a visit to Norfolk and, in stark contrast to conditions in the mountains, found the troops there well dressed, fed and supplied, with little to do. "Guard duty and company and battalion drill," he commented with a touch of sarcasm, "seemed to constitute the only demands made upon the time and patriotism of the men." He watched "a number of volunteers passing through the streets of the city in handsome uniforms, with nicely starched collars and cuffs, in all respects appearing as if 'on parade' in time of peace; and it looked to me as if the soldiers were enjoying a holiday, so striking was the contrast between these men and the poor ill-fed, shivering fellows I had served with in western Virginia."[43]

In November he accompanied Lee, when the latter was sent south to supervise the establishment of a line of defense along the coasts of South Carolina, Georgia, and east Florida. On their arrival in Charleston, South Carolina, a special train was waiting to carry the general and his staff on the Charleston and Savannah Railroad to Coosawhatchie, the station nearest Port Royal Sound, where headquarters was established.[44] During the following four months Lee devoted his efforts to improving the defenses of Charleston, Fort Pulaski, and Savannah; to obstructing the waterways up which the Federals might send their ships; and to posting Confederate forces to protect the railroad.

On assumption of the command of the Department of South Carolina, Georgia, and East Florida, Lee issued General Orders No. 1, dated Coosawhatchie, November 8, 1861, in which Captain Walter H. Taylor, Provisional Army, was announced as assistant adjutant general. At the time Taylor was in fact a first lieutenant, infantry, in the Regular Army of the Confederate States, but Lee was in the habit of referring to him as captain, for that had been his rank in the Provisional Army of Virginia. This somewhat nebulous situation was clarified at year's end by his appointment as captain in the Adjutant General's Department of the Provisional Army of the Confederate States to rank from December 10, 1861.[45]

To Taylor duty in the deep South was a welcome respite from the cold, the rain, and the privations of western Virginia. "We had excellent quarters," he wrote, "a genial climate, the greatest profusion of lovely flowers, roses of many varieties and camellias blooming in the open air and gently swayed by the softest Southern breezes."[46]

From time to time Lee and his aides journeyed to Charleston to enjoy the social life of that fascinating city. On one such occasion they approached the city as the great fire of December 11, 1861, was getting under way. The newly completed railroad abruptly ended on the south bank of the Ashley opposite Charleston,[47] and they were crossing the river in an open rowboat, when Taylor observed a glow in the northeastern sky. At the time he thought little of it, and the party proceeded to the dining room of the Mills House on the southeast corner of Meeting and Queen Streets.[48] As the evening wore on, however, the rapidly spreading flames grew in intensity, advancing nearer and nearer to the hotel. Shortly after eleven o'clock Lee, Taylor, and a few others climbed to the roof to get an unobstructed view of what Taylor was later to describe as "the grand and awfully sublime spectacle of a city in flames."[49] The scene that met their eyes was described by Major A. L. Long, who had that night reported for duty on Lee's staff: "More than one-third of the city appeared a sea of fire, shooting up columns of flame that seemed to mingle with the stars. From King Street eastward to the [Cooper] river, extending back more than a mile, stores and dwellings, churches and public buildings, were enveloped in one common blaze, which was marching steadily and rapidly across the city."[50]

By midnight the flames were lapping at the buildings across Meeting Street. To have remained longer would have been foolhardy, though as matters transpired the Mills House was eventually saved by placing water-soaked blankets around the window casings and any exposed wood. Escape was made by a back staircase through the cellar, with Lee reportedly carrying a baby in his arms and Taylor and another aide bringing up the rear. They commandeered a nearby omnibus and spent the remainder of the night in the home of Charles Alston on the Battery, far from the path of the flames.[51]

Often duty was less than onerous, depending on the activity of the enemy, and Captain Taylor occasionally visited Savannah as well as Charleston. He was there enjoying himself early in March, putting up at the Pulaski House, where he boarded for almost a week at a cost of $1.43 (Confederate!) per diem and entertained friends at dinner followed by cigars.[52]

This pleasant interlude, however, soon drew to a close. Lee was ordered to return to Richmond and on March 13 was assigned to the somewhat anomalous post of military advisor to the president, who under the terms of the Constitution was commander-in-chief of all Confederate armed forces. In this capacity Lee was provided a personal staff consisting of a military secretary, a colonel, and four aides-de-camp with the rank of major. As the only member of the staff in the Southern Department who had accompanied Lee back to Richmond, Taylor was given the choice by the General of remaining in the Adjutant General's Department or being appointed one of Lee's aides. Predictably he chose the latter, later giving as his principal reason that he would thus "be spared much confinement about headquarters and the annoyance and trouble of attending to papers and routine work, and be more on the field."[53] Vain hope, indeed!

Following the wounding of General Joseph E. Johnston at Seven Pines, the president directed Lee to take command of the forces in the field opposing McClellan's Army of the Potomac, which was then closing in on Richmond. Special Orders No. 22, dated June 1, 1862, announced the appointment to the troops and for the first time officially referred to the Army of Northern Virginia, a name destined to go down in history. The order was signed with the words that were to become so familiar in the months and years ahead: "By order of General Lee, W. H. Taylor, Assistant Adjutant-General."[54]

Lee soon found himself overwhelmed by the volume of official papers that inundated headquarters whenever a halt occurred in active operations. Petitions and grievances added their weight to the inevitable flood of orders and correspondence involved in the administration of an army of over 80,000 men. This was a side of military life that Lee detested. Initially, when a large batch of papers was submitted to him every morning, it was his practice to arrange his aides around him in a semicircle and pass each paper to one of his staff with instructions as to its disposition. Shortly, however, he found this was taking up too much of his time, and he put Taylor in charge of the Adjutant General's Department at army headquarters.[55]

Thus, on this young officer barely twenty-four years of age was placed the heavy burden and responsibility of acting as Lee's alter ego in matters of administration—a task he was to perform with tact, efficiency, and good judgment to the very end at Appomattox. Whenever possible he shielded the commanding general from the annoyance of detail and routine, and in his own words, "It was truly a knotty and difficult case that reached him after that, unless it involved an officer of very high rank."[56]

In various ways Lee showed his confidence in his adjutant general. Not only did he on occasion authorize Taylor to sign documents in his name,[57] but more importantly at times of crisis on the battlefield he entrusted him with the delivery of crucial orders to his division and corps commanders. The first opportunity arose during the bitter fighting of the Seven Days battles outside Richmond in late June and early July, 1862, as Lee strove to drive McClellan from the outskirts of the Confederate capital. The outcome of the campaign and the fate of Richmond itself depended on Stonewall Jackson turning the Federal right at Gaines Mill. When that redoubtable officer was uncharacteristically slow in getting into position, it was Taylor whom Lee dispatched to find Jackson and hurry him forward.[58] Two days later he was sent to Magruder at Savage Station to urge that commander, with his three divisions, to press on the rear of the retreating Northern army "rapidly and steadily."[59] And at Malvern Hill on July 1, he was assigned the responsibility of conducting Huger's division to the front.[60]

But Taylor was not to be denied a taste of action on the battlefield. When Pickett's brigade of Longstreet's division assailed the Union position at Boatswain's Swamp at Gaines Mill, he impetuously led a charge of the Eighteenth Virginia Infantry. A member of the color guard of the regiment remembered that "just as we had fixed bayonets and started down the long open incline at double quick an officer appeared on horse back in our front, leading and encouraging us to certain death rather than fail. I enquired, I think, of my Captain, Randolph Harrison, Co. E. 18th, of blessed memory. He told me it was Col. Taylor of Lee's staff."[61] Shortly thereafter Hood's Texans, men whom Lee was to say never failed him, spearheaded the final assault all along the line that led to victory. The struggle was bitter indeed. The First Texas lost almost three-quarters of its 800 men and the Fourth, its field officers all killed or wounded, ended the battle under the command of a captain. The following day, as he rode over the battlefield, Taylor found the ground so thickly strewn with bodies clad in blue that he had difficulty keeping his mount from trampling the Federal dead and wounded.[62] Typically, in his later writings he made no mention of his part in leading the charge of the Eighteenth Virginia, nor did he dwell on the fact that Lee had entrusted to his care vital orders to his division commanders.

With McClellan's army bottled up at Harrison's Landing on the James River and the immediate threat to Richmond lifted, the scene of active operations shifted northward. At the end of August, in a stunning triumph at Second Manassas, Lee "suppressed," in his words, the "miscreant" Pope. The next day Walter wrote to his sister about how his duties carried him from one portion of the field to another, enabling him to observe the whole affair from the highest hills. The sight of Longstreet's men driving the enemy before them he described as sublime.[63]

As the Army of Northern Virginia crossed the Potomac into Maryland on its first invasion of the North, President Davis announced his intention of joining Lee, who had issued a proclamation urging the people of that state to cast aside their Northern shackles and take their rightful place alongside their Southern brethren. With his customary tact, Lee wrote the chief executive that, while he would be glad to consult with him at any time, he could not recommend that Davis undertake such a journey and that he was sending Major Taylor to explain the difficulties and dangers involved. Thus to his young adjutant he entrusted the delicate task of dissuading the president. As events transpired, Taylor learned at Warrenton on his way south that Davis had abandoned his plan to join the army and had returned to Richmond. After reporting by telegraph to the president there, he proceeded through the mountains into the Shenandoah Valley directly to Winchester. There he fell in with his friends, Captain Frank Huger and Major John S. Saunders, the latter his future brother-in-law.[64]

On the way back to the army the three companions reached Hagerstown, Maryland, and put up for the night at the Hamilton Hotel. At one or two in the morning they were awakened by a commotion caused by a rumor that a Northern force was marching on the town. Saddling their horses, they beat a hasty retreat and spent what was left of the night in a hayrick some distance away. When daylight came, they learned that a large body of Federal cavalry escaping from Harper's Ferry had passed along the road near their hiding place and they had indeed had a close brush with capture.[65]

Having rejoined Lee in time for the desperately fought but inconclusive battle of Sharpsburg or Antietam on September 17, 1862, the bloodiest single day of the war, Taylor accompanied the battered Army of Northern Virginia in its retreat south across the Potomac. He felt the army had given a good account of itself against overwhelming odds.[66]

There followed several months during which the army rested and was recruited and re-equipped. In December Lee moved to the south bank of the Rappahannock near Fredericksburg to intercept the Army of the Potomac. McClellan having been relieved of command, the hapless Burnside, in a vain effort to break through on the direct road to Richmond, hurled his three grand divisions, totaling more than 100,000 men, against the Army of Northern Virginia posted on the rolling hills in back of and to the south of the town.

Taylor later wrote that he had never witnessed such a battle as Fredericksburg. In the morning, "when the curtain of fog was lifted and the sun lit up the scene, . . . as if by magic the hosts of the grand Federal army were disclosed in martial array extending from the city down the river as far as the eye could reach. The bright muskets of the men glistened in the sunlight and countless flags with the stars and stripes floated with the breeze and marked the direction as the troops were manoeuvered into line-of-battle formation to the sound of soul-stirring music." He witnessed, too, from an adjoining hill on which Lee had established his headquarters, the suicidal attacks of Burnside's right wing against the sunken road on Marye's Hill, where 9,000 Northern soldiers fell.[67]

At the end of January, 1863, the Army of Northern Virginia went into winter quarters nearby. Taylor noted that Lee's headquarters near Hamilton's Crossing were simplicity itself, consisting of five or six army tents, one or two wagons for transporting equipage and personal effects, and a few orderlies. "There was no pomp or circumstance about his headquarters," wrote another observer, "and no sign of rank of the occupant, other than the Confederate flag displayed in front of the tent of Colonel Taylor, the Adjutant-General."[68]

The mass of correspondence facing him Taylor described as "simply appalling." At all hours of the day and night packages of official papers arrived from every corps and independent command, involving matters great and small: furloughs, reports of enemy activity, intricate questions of the relative rights of officers of the line and staff, innumerable requests for details for a multitude of purposes. Disposition of all such dispatches and documents fell on Taylor's shoulders, and in those days there were no typewriters or other laborsaving devices to lighten the burden. He became adept at separating the wheat from the chaff and made it a point to submit to Lee only such matters as demanded the consideration and decision of the commander in chief.[69]

It was at this time there occurred the oft-related incident involving Taylor that illustrated Lee's occasional outbursts of irascibility, the alacrity with which he regained his self-control, and his ever readiness to make the *amende honorable*. It had been a difficult day. Taylor had found it necessary to submit some vexatious matters requiring resolution, and, as he did so, he observed that the general was in an irritable mood, indicated by a nervous twist or jerk of the head and neck peculiar to him when annoyed. Matters did not go smoothly, and the younger man, concluding his efforts were not appreciated, petulantly threw down at his side the paper under consideration. Calmly Lee turned to him and in a gentle voice said, "Major Taylor, when I lose my temper, don't let it make you angry."[70]

Such contretemps, however, were the exception, and the atmosphere at headquarters was for the most part relaxed and informal. "There was between General Lee and his military family," Taylor recalled, "a degree of camaraderie that was perfectly delightful. Our conversation, especially at table, was free from restraint, unreserved as between equals, and often of a bright and jocular vein."[71] The general, he added, was fond of a joke and not above teasing the younger members of his staff.

With the coming of spring a welcome change came over Taylor's life. As the skies brightened and the muddy roads dried out, the armies were once again on the move. Now he could get out in the field and, when the shooting started, experience on occasion the excitement and the danger of battle.

Early in May was fought the battle of Chancellorsville, generally regarded as Lee's tactical masterpiece. Taylor witnessed the final assault that drove the Northern army from its fortified position. "I can never forget," he wrote, "the scene as the victorious, yelling Confederates pressed forward and passed General Lee near the Chancellor house, which was on fire and burning fiercely. As they caught sight of their general the men rent the air with their cheers of victory, and pushed forward, waving their hats on high and calling his name."[72]

At Gettysburg on the first day, after the Union First and Eleventh Corps had been defeated and driven through the town, Lee entrusted to Taylor the crucial verbal order directing Ewell—now in command of Stonewall Jackson's old Second Corps of the Army of Northern Virginia—to seize the high ground of Cemetery Hill. Had this been done, Confederate artillery would have commanded, and in all probability rendered untenable, Cemetery Ridge on which the Federal line was subsequently established, against which Pickett's men charged in vain on the third day, July 3. But Lee, in accordance with his custom of giving tactical discretion to his corps commanders on the spot, qualified his directive to Ewell with the fateful words "if practicable."[73]

Brave and devoted as he was, "Fighting Dick" Ewell was no Stonewall Jackson. New to the responsibility of corps command, he hesitated and in the end did nothing. The opportunity was lost, and in a mismanaged battle, over which controversy still rages more than a century later, Lee suffered defeat.

Four days after the fighting ended Taylor wrote his sister that they had been unable to drive the Yankees from their "Gibraltar," a term he employed, with pardonable exaggeration, to describe the rocky eminences of the Round Tops, the Devil's Den, and Culp's Hill. Yet, with his irrepressible optimism, he assured her they hoped to get up another fight soon.[74]

Taylor's thirst for action notwithstanding, no fighting of consequence occurred for more than three months after Gettysburg, as the two armies took up position confronting each other along the headwaters of the Rapidan River in north central Virginia. During the lull he took a leave in Richmond to court Bettie Saunders, at last successfully: he returned to headquarters with her promise to marry him. His letters to her thereafter were frequent and long.

In mid-October Lee turned Meade's right, compelling the latter to withdraw across the Rappahannock, and retreat northeastward along the line of the Orange and Alexandria Railroad. At Bristoe Station Hill's corps struck the Northern forces in a costly, bungled attack. Walter wrote Bettie, "I have felt humiliated ever since. There was no earthly excuse for it." The next day Lee went over the ground with A. P. Hill, whose corps had been so badly handled. Dismayed by the useless sacrifice of life and observing the dead bodies still lying on the field of battle, he came as close as he ever did to openly rebuking one of his corps commanders. "Well, well, General," he said to the crestfallen Hill, "bury these poor men and let us say no more about it."[75]

When an isolated *tête-de-pont* at Rappahannock Station on the north bank of the river was overrun and its garrison captured in November, Walter lamented to Bettie, with more emotion than historical perspective, that it was "the saddest chapter in the history of this army."[76]

In December the Army of Northern Virginia went into winter quarters in the vicinity of Orange Court House, and Taylor settled down to the arduous duties of assistant adjutant general of the army. Promoted lieutenant colonel in January,[77] he assumed ever increasing responsibilities at headquarters and, in effect, served as chief of staff, especially on those occasions when Lee was called to Richmond for consultation and was absent from the army.

With the coming of spring Taylor's thoughts turned to the prospect of another "on to Richmond" campaign by the heavily reinforced Army of the Potomac, now under the overall command of General Grant, which lay menacingly along the north bank of the Rapidan. On May 4 Grant's army of over 100,000 crossed the Rapidan and plunged into a desolate, virtually uninhabited expanse aptly named The Wilderness. Formerly covered by a virgin forest of hardwood, the countryside for miles around had been stripped of its trees to fuel the iron furnaces that dotted the area. In their place had grown up a vast thicket of scrub oak and chinquapin, interlaced with matted vines, where visibility, save for an occasional clearing and the narrow dirt roads that crisscrossed it, was limited to a few yards. Ever the aggressor, Lee determined to contest Grant's passage through The Wilderness and ordered his three corps to attack the right flank of the Union army as it marched southward.

In the ensuing struggle Taylor witnessed the first of the "Lee to the rear" incidents. On May 5, Heth's and Wilcox's divisions of Hill's Third Corps had been heavily engaged in throwing back repeated Northern counterattacks. When darkness finally put an end to the fighting, the men were exhausted, their line of battle in disarray. Nevertheless, on the assurance that Longstreet's troops of the First Corps would be up to relieve them before dawn, little preparation was made for the morrow. When Longstreet was delayed and the Federals renewed their assaults at sunup, Wilcox's troops were forced to give way, streaming to the rear in disorder. A crisis was at hand.

Lee, who had passed the night on the farm of the Widow Tapp in a clearing hard by the Orange Plank Road, caught sight of the leading elements of Hood's Texans of Longstreet's corps coming up at the double-quick. "Hurrah for Texas," he shouted and spurred his horse Traveler to lead them in a countercharge. Taylor, who had been in the thick of the turmoil bearing orders for the army commander, recalled "a stalwart fellow, of swarthy complexion and earnest expression, who passed by the general's horse, as the troops were advancing in line of battle, and cried out, 'Go back General Lee, this is no place for you—go back and we'll settle this!' "[78] And settle it they did.

Correctly anticipating that Grant, having been checked in The Wilderness, would move by his left flank to Spotsylvania Court House, in the evening of May 7 Lee sent Taylor and his fellow staff officer,

Charles Venable, to tell Jeb Stuart, who was holding that point with his cavalry, that Confederate infantry of the First Corps was on the way to support him and to hang on. Riding through the darkness of the silent forest, the two young men talked of their commander's uncanny ability to divine the intentions of his opponents.[79]

Having won the race for Spotsylvania by the narrowest of margins, Lee disposed his army in an irregular triangle, the rounded northern apex of which was dubbed the "Mule Shoe" by the men because of its shape. Late on May 10, Federal troops broke through the line on the western flank of the salient in an attack that threatened the whole Confederate position. Lee spurred forward to personally rally the troops where the break had occurred, but his staff urged him not to expose himself. "Then," he replied, "you must see to it that the ground is recovered." Instantly Taylor galloped to the front into what he described as a "pandemonium of excitement and confusion." His horse shot from under him, he mounted another, seized a flag, and led a charge that restored the broken line. Writing years later, with characteristic self-effacement he dismissed the affair in these matter-of-fact, somewhat stilted words: "After earnest endeavor, the officers leading, our troops finally went forward with a rush and recaptured the works driving the enemy back with great loss."[80]

But at the time, he revealed his true feelings to Bettie. After assuring her it was not rashness but the necessity of encouraging and rallying the troops that carried him into a position of such extreme danger, he confessed he was lucky to be alive. "God has indeed been merciful to me thus far," he wrote. "My preservation really appears miraculous. Poor Bella [his horse] is doing tolerably well. The only wonder is that she and I were not completely riddled—so close were we to the Yankees, & that too between their line of fire & ours."[81] The soldier whose mount Taylor had commandeered when his own was shot down wrote to him: "I am certain that was the hottest place I was in during the war, and I was in it from the first battle of Manassas to the surrender at Appomattox Courthouse. . . . I have nothing to show I was ever in a battle but the five scars I have on my body and would like to get a certificate from you that I followed you that day to pass down to my children in after years."[82]

Despite the tenacity of the Confederate resistance, Grant kept on hammering. Early in June he suffered a bloody repulse at Cold Harbor, losing in a matter of minutes more than 7000 men in a battle aptly described by Taylor's friend, Venable, as "perhaps the easiest victory ever

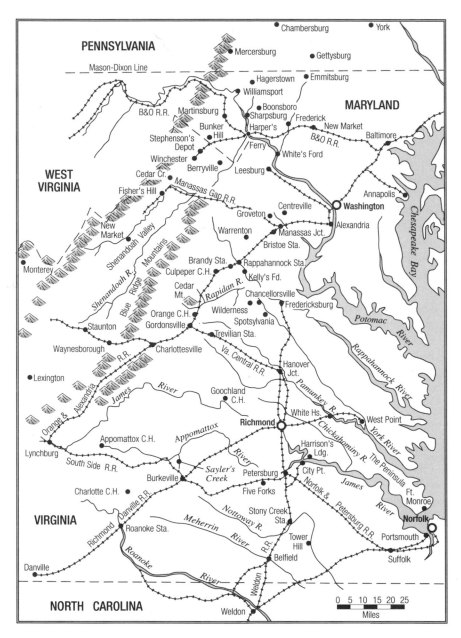

Map 1. Virginia at the time of the Civil War.

granted to the Confederate arms by the folly of the Federal commanders."[83] Then, abandoning direct assaults on entrenched positions, he
moved his army south of the James River, and the siege of Petersburg,
that was to drag on for the better part of ten weary months, began.

Taylor selected for army headquarters a spot known by the eupho-
nious, though somewhat unlikely, name of "Violet Bank," where Lee
and his staff were to remain for three months. Overworked and op-
pressed by the heat of midsummer in the Virginia low country, he at
times found his patience tried to the breaking point.

As the weary months of the siege dragged on, attrition took its toll
of the Southern forces, while Grant, with the almost limitless human
and material resources of the North behind him, could replace his
losses at will. Confederate successes at the Crater and Reams Station
only postponed the inevitable, as Grant kept extending his left, forcing
Lee to stretch his lines thinner and thinner.

The coming of winter brought intense suffering to the ragged soldiers in the trenches, and the specter of starvation reared its ugly head.
Ample supplies of foodstuffs existed in the lower South, but transportation was a problem. Southern railroads were in a shambles as track
and equipment wore out and could not be replaced. The army ration
had to be cut to the bone. And yet, with the optimism of youth and
wholly convinced of the righteousness of the Southern cause, Taylor
refused to despair.

By spring Grant was on the move, extending his left ever farther
westward toward the Southside Railroad, one of Lee's last two essential lines of communication with the shrinking remnant of Confederate
territory to the south. To counter this thrust Lee stripped his already
thinly held lines, scraped together a mobile force of cavalry and infantry,
and, with McGowan's South Carolinians in the lead, attacked the exposed left flank of the advancing Federals at Dinwiddie Court House.

Taylor was in the thick of the fighting. Described by one observer
as "a fine looking young man distinguished for his superb gal-
lantry,"[84] he attempted to seize the flag of Orr's South Carolina Rifles
and lead a charge, but the color sergeant refused to give it up. Not to be
denied, Taylor galloped forward between the lines, waving his hat and
shouting, "Come on boys!"[85] With a cheer the Confederates surged
forward crushing everything in their path. "The frenzy of battle seemed
to have taken possession of the Southerners," Taylor later wrote, "and I
never took part in or witnessed a more spirited and successful assault."[86]
But, alas, it was all in vain. The odds were too great, and the ground

had to be given up. The next day Pickett was overwhelmed at Five Forks and Richmond's fate sealed.

Late in the afternoon of April 2, as the evacuation of Petersburg was about to begin, Taylor approached General Lee and, in the words of Freeman, "preferred as strange a request as ever adjutant general put forward on the day of a general troop movement."[87] He wanted, he said, to go to Richmond to marry Bettie Saunders. Would the commanding general let him go? If so, he promised to rejoin the army on the retreat early the following morning.

The day had been a shattering one for Lee, quite possibly the worst of his military career. True, Gettysburg had been a bitter disappointment; yet, save in retrospect, only that. Now ruin, stark ruin, stared him in the face. Morning had brought word of the magnitude of Pickett's disaster at Five Forks the day before. Worse yet, the whole attenuated line on the Confederate right was crumbling. Hurriedly Lee dictated the dread message that was handed to Jefferson Davis in St. Paul's Church: Richmond must be evacuated that night. Under heavy artillery fire, Lee abandoned his headquarters and withdrew to an interior line to arrange the details of the evacuation of Petersburg. To Taylor fell the responsibility for the drafting and delivery by courier and telegraph of the necessary orders and dispatches.

When the day's work was done, he presented his petition to the general. Contrary to the too prevalent impression that he lacked emotion—a later writer would call him "a marble man"[88]—Lee had a soft spot in his heart for the young, especially young ladies, and he was well aware of the ardent love affair between his adjutant and his sweetheart, who was working in a government bureau in Richmond. Was he swayed by sentiment or did he desire, in a delicate way, to show his appreciation of Taylor's long, faithful services on his staff? Both may have played a part. At all events, despite the crushing burden of responsibility resting on his shoulders at this critical hour, he listened sympathetically and, though expressing surprise at its timing, granted Taylor's request.

In high spirits Walter, accompanied by a courier, galloped to the railroad station at Dunlop on the north side of the Appomattox River. There he found an ambulance train, consisting of a locomotive and several cars, waiting to carry to Richmond the last of the wounded requiring hospital treatment. When asked if he had another locomotive available, the railway agent pointed down the track to one receding in the distance northward, saying, "Yonder goes the only locomotive we have, besides the one attached to this train." Undaunted, Walter turned his horse over to his courier, with instructions to rejoin him in the capital as soon as possible, jumped on the hospital train locomotive, and ordered the engineer to uncouple it and give chase. The pursuit was a long one, continuing to Falling Creek, almost three-quarters of the way to Richmond. There success crowned their efforts. Walter transferred to the locomotive they had overtaken, dispatched the other one back to Petersburg, and went on to the city without further incident.[89]

A week before, when the desperate Confederate attack at Fort Stedman failed to break the Union line encircling Petersburg, Walter had written Bettie in his last letter from the field that he could see no cause for hope and that he regarded the fall of Richmond—"the contingency we have fearfully anticipated"—as a foregone conclusion. He pointed out it might well be impossible to remove the Surgeon-General's Office—where Bettie was employed—from the capital in time. In that event they would be separated by the Union lines, as he accompanied the army in its retreat westward. To his pleading that "if we must be separated, in God's sight let us first be united," Bettie gave her assent.[90]

On Sunday, April 2, a telegram came to Walter's brother Rob in Richmond. It read, "I will be over some time today. See Bettie and have her explain. Make all needed preparations."[91] At the time Bettie was staying at the home of Lewis D. Crenshaw on West Main Street, where, as the day passed and the evening wore on, all hands were busy preparing food for the soldiers from north of the James who would pass through Richmond on the retreat—tea, coffee, bread and biscuits with ham, hoecakes, whatever could be scraped up at the last moment.

Still no word from Walter. After dark, Bettie remembered, "They dressed me in a new black mousseline, lined with grey linen that shone through, and some one laughingly remarked, 'Anyhow, her body is grey.'" For the bride Mrs. Crenshaw produced a pair of white kid gloves, and, at last, shortly after midnight, the groom arrived with his family and Dr. Minnegerode, the rector of St. Paul's church. The wedding took place in the invalid Mrs. Crenshaw's upstairs sitting room. "Tears and sobs were the only music," the bride recalled, "and when dear old Dr. Minnegerode, who had known us both from childhood, threw his arms around our heads as we kneeled for his blessing, he too, wept."[92]

The ceremony and wedding breakfast over, Walter and Bettie's brother, Colonel John Saunders, mounted their horses in the predawn darkness, and in the lurid glare of the fires raging in the lower part of the city, crossed the James on Mayo's bridge, just before it was put to the torch, on their way back to the army. "No one who was in Richmond on Monday, the 3rd of April, 1865," Bettie wrote, "can ever forget the terrors that beset us. Shells were exploding everywhere, mothers were weeping for their boys and absolute misery reigned."[93]

As the starving and dejected, but still defiant remnant of the once redoubtable Army of Northern Virginia wearily plodded westward along the line of the Southside Railroad, Taylor's every moment was occupied with the myriad of duties devolving on the staff of the commander in chief during the retreat that was to end at Appomattox. For him the night before the surrender was a sleepless one. Lee had sent him to take charge of the long wagon trains that so encumbered the army in its efforts to outdistance the pursuing enemy forces, to do what he could to expedite their movements and to see to it that they were parked safely for the night. The performance of this task made him realize that if the effort to save the wagons was persisted in, the end was very near.

When he reported the next morning, the general said to him, "Well, Colonel, what are we to do?" Taylor replied he was afraid the trains would have to be abandoned, but hopefully this would enable the army to make good its escape. Lee acknowledged this might be so but reminded his young adjutant that a number of his senior officers had agreed the time had come to capitulate. "Well, sir," Taylor answered, "I can only speak for myself; to me any other fate is preferable." Personally, Lee said, he felt the same way, but that to fight on and spill more blood would serve no useful purpose, and that he had arranged to meet General Grant with a view to surrender and wished Taylor to accompany him.[94] The latter, however, shrank from the prospect of witnessing the humiliation of his idol and begged off with the excuse that he had already ridden twice through the lines that morning—conduct he later confessed "I could not then, and cannot now, justify."[95]

In accordance with the terms of the surrender, Lee and his staff gave their parole that they would not take up arms against the government of the United States until properly exchanged. For his protection from arrest or annoyance each officer and soldier was provided with a paper containing his parole, signed by his commander and countersigned by an officer of the Federal army. Taylor signed in Lee's name for members of the staff, but when it came to his own case, he asked

Lee if he would personally sign this evidence of his parole. The document, countersigned by George H. Sharpe, Asst. Provost Marshal General, U.S.A., read:

Appomattox Court House, Va.

April 10, 1865

THE BEARER, Lieut.-col. W. H. Taylor, A.A. General A. N. Va., a paroled prisoner of war of the Army of Northern Virginia, has permission to go to his home, and there remain undisturbed.

R. E. Lee

General[96]

When the heart-rending, symbolic act of surrender—the stacking of arms, the laying down of the tattered battle flags—was over, Lee, in the company of four of his staff officers including Charles Marshall and Taylor, whom an observer along the road described as "gaunt and pallid in ragged uniforms,"[97] began the sad, weary journey back to Richmond. His sword sheathed forever, now only a paroled prisoner of war, he was yet, in Taylor's words, "a monarch still in the hearts of his countrymen,"[98] and such he would ever remain in the affection of the people of the South.

A few days after his return to the devastated capital of the now-dying Confederacy, Lee yielded to the urging of photographers and permitted Brady to make a portrait of him. To accompany him on the back porch of the house at 707 East Franklin Street, still clad in the Confederate grey he wore himself, he chose his eldest son, George Washington Custis Lee, and Walter Taylor (see fig. 13).

Though their paths were now to separate, Lee's affection for his young adjutant remained undimmed during the five and a half years of life that lay ahead of him. It was to Taylor that he addressed the letter urging his former soldiers to accept the outcome of the war and go back to work. "Virginia," he wrote, "wants all their aid, all their support, and the presence of all her sons to sustain and recuperate her."[99]

After a fortnight in Richmond assisting Lee in the transition from military to civilian life, Taylor borrowed the general's rickety old ambulance that had accompanied them from Appomattox and set forth with his bride on a delayed wedding tour to Goochland County. The second day out, as they were crossing the James, the mules became un-

24

manageable and plunged into the river, dragging Walter along with them. There was a good deal of joshing at the bridegroom's expense, but the contretemps passed off without serious consequence, and the young couple spent a happy month in the country visiting relatives. In June they went to Norfolk, where, in Bettie's words, they "started life anew, poor but proud."[100]

Taking Lee's admonition to heart, Taylor lost little time in repining. The first order of business was to find gainful employment—easier said than done in the chaotic and depressed conditions that followed the collapse of the Confederacy. Stymied for the time being at home, he journeyed to Baltimore. There he contacted a friend named Wood, who optimistically talked of establishing a line of steamers to link that city with Norfolk. Walter, however, dismissed the idea as visionary and its proponent uninformed, giving it as his opinion that it would be many years before "Poor old Norfolk" could support such an under-taking.[101]

"I very much fear," he wrote to Bettie, "that the public institutions in Baltimore as in Norfolk stand too much in dread of the Federal au-thorities. I begin to discover that I am too well known as a rebel and fear that I will be forced after all to migrate to New York City, where I am told a man's Southern proclivities are rather in his favor."[102]

The next day, assuring Bettie he was "anxious to secure a position in the world which will enable me to shower all manner of pleasant things on your dear head," he warned her not to expect much of any-thing from his visit, adding that while he found many kind friends willing to interest themselves on his behalf, "the Banks are afraid to offend our gallant conquerors by placing in position so deeply dyed a rebel as your old man. . . . I will try to find you a ginger cake."[103]

Back in Norfolk empty-handed, he entered into partnership with Andrew S. Martin and engaged in the hardware business for a number of years, the firm eventually operating as W. H. Taylor and Co.; bank-ing, however, was his true interest. Returning to that profession, in 1877 he became president of the Marine Bank, a post he held with dis-tinction until his death in 1916.

His outside interests were legion, and for over fifty years after the war he was recognized as one of Virginia's most respected and influ-ential citizens. At various times he served as president of the Seaboard Insurance Company, a director of the Mutual Fire Insurance Company of Virginia, president of the Perpetual Building and Loan Association of Norfolk, associate member of the Norfolk and Petersburg Cotton Exchange, and president of the Commonwealth Club.

In the development of Virginia's railroads he played a prominent role. While a member of the state Senate, he was instrumental in securing the passage of legislation authorizing the consolidation of other lines with the Norfolk and Petersburg to form what eventually would become the Norfolk and Western Railway. Of this extremely profitable coal carrier, one of the nation's great railroads, he served as a director until he died in 1916. When, a year before his death, failing health prompted him to offer his resignation, the president of the road urgently requested him to withdraw it. "You have the high esteem and personal friendship," he wrote, "of every member of the Board of Directors of the Norfolk & Western Railway. . . . It is the sincere wish of the President of this Company and the Board of Directors that we may have the pleasure of your presence at the meetings and for a long time to come the benefit of your wise judgment on matters on which you are so thoroughly informed."[104] The resignation was withdrawn. Taylor's railroad interests included the presidency of the company that projected and built the original line between Norfolk and Ocean View (a bayside suburb) in 1879, and he continued to head this enterprise until the road was sold in 1895.

For all his prominence in business affairs and public service, the guiding light of his life was devotion to his family and his church. As was not uncommon at the time, Bettie and he raised a large family. Eight children were born to them, suitably divided: four girls, then four boys. There must have been few dull moments in the Taylor household, for, in addition to her own ample brood, Bettie's sister and her son lived there. "Uncle Gus," a deaf-mute, helped out with the washing, cleaning and cooking, a not inconsiderable task, when one considers that the table was set for a dozen family members at each meal, and frequently there were guests to add to the number. Predictably the children played tricks on Uncle Gus, but they all shared in the chores and lightened his burden somewhat. They were devoted to their mother and she to them. By all accounts it was a happy home and a center of hospitality.[105]

In common with and no doubt influenced by such Southern heroes as Lee, Jackson, and Stuart, Taylor had unquestioned faith in the efficacy of prayer and shared with them a recognition of man's dependence on his Maker and the promises of his Redeemer. For years he was a member of the vestry and a trustee of Christ Church in Norfolk and, quite appropriately, was the owner of Pew No. 1 adjacent to the altar. To the very end he remained an active supporter of the church and all good works connected therewith, giving generously not only of his time but of his means as well. When, in 1908, a new edifice was planned, he pledged $1,000 toward its completion.[106]

Complementing his work with the church, he was prominent in the founding and support of a number of Norfolk's leading eleemosynary institutions. He was a charter member of United Charities and served for a time as president of the Eastern State Asylum. His generosity was not limited to public benefactions, for he often unobtrusively lent a helping hand to individuals in need, especially old Confederate soldiers who were down on their luck.

His loyalty to the cause of the South and to the memory of Robert E. Lee never faltered, and in postbellum years as the events of the war were endlessly debated, he became, in the words of Freeman, "a court of last resort" in all matters having to do with the military fortunes of the Confederacy.[107]

Not surprisingly, Taylor was a Democrat in politics. As such he represented Norfolk in the Virginia State Senate for four years from 1869 to 1873. In the protracted and bitter debate over the readjustment of Virginia's prewar public debt he took the high moral ground that it should be paid to the last penny, writing to his friend and former companion in arms, Ham Chamberlayne, that the people must be educated to "a manly discharge of their duty as Virginians and honest men."[108]

When the Populists began clamoring for cheap money in the 1890s as an antidote for the ills of the state's farmers, Joseph Bryan, famed editor of the *Richmond Times-Dispatch,* appealed to Taylor to give him examples of the prosperity of the truck gardeners in the Norfolk area in order to demonstrate to the wheat growers that the latter were suffering, not due to any lack of currency, but because they were unable to compete with the large and highly productive farms in the West. Referring to "the wild fancies with which our agricultural classes are now being stuffed by artful and unscrupulous demagogues and office seekers," Bryan assured Taylor that "one plain statement of indisputable fact is worth the whole whirlwind of this bombast."[109] He added that he knew Taylor would oblige, as he had always shown a spirit of self-sacrifice when public interests were at stake. The latter's reply was evidently persuasive, for in thanking him for it Bryan wrote, "You make out a better case than I had hoped for."[110]

From 1870 to 1873 and again from 1875 to 1879 Taylor served on the Board of Visitors of his old alma mater, the Virginia Military Institute, the treasurership of which he had turned down just after the war, no doubt due to the meager stipend the position offered. In 1889 Taylor was appointed to represent the Commonwealth of Virginia at the centennial celebration of the inauguration of George Washington as the nation's first president, a signal honor for one no longer active in government affairs. (One of his fellow delegates at these ceremonies was Col. William A. Tower, the editor's grandfather, who represented the Commonwealth of Massachusetts.) A lesser compliment, but one that touched him, came in his last years, when he was invited to speak at the ceremonies marking the seventy-fifth anniversary of the founding of V.M.I. To his regret he was unable to accept.[111]

Taylor's conviction of the righteousness of the Southern cause never wavered, and in the postwar years he devoted himself to making certain that history would recognize the overwhelming odds against which Robert E. Lee and the Army of Northern Virginia contended. It had been Lee's hope, never to be realized, to write a history of his campaigns, so that the bravery and devotion of the officers and soldiers he led should be transmitted to posterity. For help in establishing the strength of the army at various periods, most of the official returns having been lost or destroyed, he turned to his former adjutant. The best Taylor could do at the time was to provide Lee with estimates based on the memory of the chief clerk in the Office of the Adjutant General of the Army of Northern Virginia, whose duty it was, under the supervision of the adjutant, to compile the field returns of the army from those of the several corps.[112]

Some ten years later, having ascertained that many of those returns had found their way to the archives of the United States War Department in Washington, Taylor sought permission to examine them. Though others with similar requests had been turned down, he met with success, having based his plea on the fact that he himself had supervised the preparation of many of the documents. He journeyed to Washington, where he met a cordial reception, and made extracts of the returns. These he subsequently incorporated in *Four Years with General Lee*, published in 1878 by Appleton in New York, thus making available for the first time authoritative figures on the much debated question of the comparative strength of the contending armies. The startling disparity of numbers "makes pardonable," he wrote, "the emotions of pride with which the soldier of the Army of Northern Virginia points to the achievements of that incomparable body of soldiery, under its peerless and immortal leader."[113]

In 1906 he completed a second book entitled *General Lee, 1861–1865*, a somewhat more formal study of the campaigns of the Army of Northern Virginia. By then, however, interest in the war had waned, and Appleton in New York, as well as Doubleday, Page, declined to publish it unless changes were made to increase its popular appeal. This Taylor refused to do, and the book was eventually published by the Nusbaum Book and News Company of Norfolk. To his friend Lord Wolseley in England he presented a copy, which elicited from the retired field marshal a long and cordial letter of thanks, written from Hampton Court Palace, in which he invited Taylor to visit him and his wife there in the house presented to her by "our late Queen of blessed memory." Wolseley recalled with pleasure the kindness shown him by Taylor and the other officers at headquarters, when, as a young man over forty years before, he had paid a hurried visit to the Army of Northern Virginia. Of Robert E. Lee he wrote that he was "one of the very few truly great men I was ever privileged to be personally acquainted with."[114]

A sometime contributor to the *Southern Historical Society Papers*, Taylor often dealt with the strength of the Army of Northern Virginia in decisive battles. His article on Gettysburg, which gave his assessment of the causes of the lack of Southern success, met with the approbation of Lee's second son, "Rooney," one of Jeb Stuart's brigadiers, who wrote him, "I was very much impressed by your article. . . . I cannot sympathize with you in your, gentle it is true, strictures upon Gen Stuart, but on the whole yours is, as it ought to be, the clearest and fairest account of that great battle I have read."[115]

Not surprisingly, in view of his close relations with Lee, Taylor was continually appealed to in the postbellum years to settle controversial points in connection with the conduct of the war. "His conclusions," Freeman wrote, "seldom were the subject of dispute, because he possessed a memory that was both tenacious and accurate. His word usually was final with Confederates."[116] Yet not always. Colonel Mosby, the intrepid partisan leader who went over to the other side after the war, became a Republican, and fed at the Federal trough for years by accepting employment from the United States government, wrote a friend in 1909 that he had a war on his hands with Taylor, "a staff officer of Genl Lee whom I flayed in my book. I shall prove that the aforesaid Col. Walter Taylor has deliberately and wilfully falsified history."[117] But this was the exception, and by then Mosby had lost face with most Southerners and few would accept his word against Taylor's.

Among the latter's correspondents were men from all walks of life, Northerners as well as Southerners. From Boston came letters from such distinguished Brahmins as Charles Francis Adams, enclosing an advance copy of the address he was to deliver at the Lee Centennial Celebration at Washington and Lee University, and the historian John Codman Ropes, inviting him to deliver a paper on Lee before the Military Historical Society of Massachusetts.[118]

Understandably, the bulk of his voluminous war-related correspondence was with former Confederates, including such prominent figures as Lee, Jefferson Davis, Longstreet, Early, Wade Hampton, John B. Gordon, and "Little Billy" Mahone. From a historian's point of view some of the most important communications were those exchanged with E. Porter Alexander, erstwhile commander of the artillery of the First Corps of the Army of Northern Virginia, and a lifelong intimate friend; and Colonel William H. Palmer, adjutant general of A. P. Hill's Third Corps.[119]

The "ifs" of Confederate history were, predictably, aired at length. *If* Stonewall Jackson had not been seized with the strange lethargy that possessed him at White Oak Swamp during the Seven Days, would McClellan's army have been destroyed? *If* Ewell had seized Cemetery Hill on the first day or Longstreet attacked earlier on the second, would Gettysburg have had a different ending? *If* Davis had not relieved Joe Johnston from command of the Army of Tennessee, would Atlanta have fallen to Sherman? *If* Petersburg had been abandoned before it was too late, would Lee have been able to unite with Johnston in the Carolinas and crush Sherman, or at least protract the war until the North tired of it?

On a more personal basis, Taylor kept in close touch with his old commander, who from time to time sent news of the Lee family and expressed an affectionate concern for the Taylors and their growing brood. "Remember me most kindly to your mother, brothers and sisters. Though you would never show me your wife," wrote Lee, tongue in cheek, "tell her I bear toward her the love I feel for you."[120] And again, "You will have to bring Mrs. Taylor and the babies to Lexington to see us. I fear I shall never be able to get to Norfolk to see you."[121]

Living on tidewater, Taylor was often importuned by his friends to send them some Hampton or York River oysters, considered a great delicacy. "The barrel of oysters you were so kind as to send me by Bryan [their old headquarters steward]," Lee wrote, "have converted our Easter celebration into a feast."[122] And on another occasion: "The oysters arrived in the packet-boat all right and in due time have been much enjoyed. They were finely flavored and as plump as eggs."[123] From Jefferson Davis, to whom Taylor sent messages of encouragement in the trying years immediately following the war, came a request, not only for the prized oysters, but a Smithfield ham as well.[124]

Taylor took a continuing interest in his former companions in arms, quietly lending a helping hand to those in need, and on occasion taking a prominent part in Confederate affairs. When the Lee Memorial Association was organized in 1870, he was appointed a vice president in company with fourteen generals, and at the unveiling of the statue of his old commander in Richmond in 1890 he rode in the procession in an open carriage and occupied a place of honor on the speaker's stand among the distinguished guests. Two years later at the dedication of a statue of A. P. Hill he was an aide to the Chief Marshal, General Harry Heth, and served in a similar capacity to Governor Fitzhugh Lee, when the Soldiers and Sailors' Monument was unveiled in 1894.[125]

When General Lee paid a farewell visit to Norfolk in 1870, the year of his death, Taylor met his old commander in Portsmouth, escorted him on the ferry across the Elizabeth River, and drove with him in his carriage through the streets of the city to the accompaniment of the welcoming shouts of the crowd, interspersed by the shrill rebel yell.[126] At Robert E. Lee's funeral in Lexington in 1870 he was a member of the Committee of the Virginia Legislature attending and was accorded the signal honor, along with his old friend Venable, of being seated with the family immediately in front of the pulpit.[127] He played a leading role in raising funds for a monument to the Confederate dead in Norfolk. The shaft was to be surmounted by an heroic figure of a color-bearer, and to make sure every detail was authentic, Taylor wrote to the current superintendent of V.M.I., General Scott Shipp, "I am anxious to obtain a rough sketch of the chevron of the color-sergeant as it was during our days at the V.M.I. Will you please help me?"[128]

As the years slipped by, the affection and esteem in which Walter was held grew apace. A cousin of Bettie's sent Christmas greetings from London in 1913: "May you both be long in the land, so that these younger generations may continue to see what inspiring examples of the truest manhood and womanhood the Old South could produce.

When I desire to illustrate personally its virtues and graces, I always point to you two."[129] Commented the *Ledger-Dispatch* at the time of his death, "The people of Norfolk, by reason of his gentle, courtly and generous manner, had come to love him, a man of the greatest nobility of character, an earnest Christian, a brave soldier and splendid citizen and one of the manliest of men."[130]

The cornerstone of Walter Taylor's business career was the presidency of the Marine Bank, a position he held for almost forty years. In addition he often served as executor or trustee of estates and as a director of various commercial enterprises. As a successful man of affairs he prospered in a modest and conservative way, quite in keeping with his character, for he would have shunned the pursuit of money for money's sake. In 1895 he recorded his net worth as $88,468, a respectable sum for those days. His business acumen, nevertheless, did not spare him an occasional bad investment. In 1908 he paid $300 for 20 shares of Radio Telephone stock, hoping to cash in on the wave of the future in the field of communications. But the venture hardly fulfilled his expectations, the company ending up as North American Wireless, totally worthless and its officers indicted for using the mails to defraud!

At all events he was in a position to provide his family with some of the newfangled domestic conveniences that proliferated in his later life. Witness, for example, the purchase in 1912 of a sporty, blue, twenty-horsepower Reo automobile, replete with nickel running gear, a far cry indeed from the battered, mule-drawn ambulance in which Bettie and he had set forth on their honeymoon half a century before.

By the time of his death in 1916, Taylor's net worth had increased substantially to $185,967. In his will he left the entire estate "to his cherished wife."[131]

If a long and active life is any indication of good health, it is safe to say that Taylor enjoyed it until the onset of his final illness. True, he suffered from "rheumatism," a malady that today would doubtless be referred to as arthritis, and in 1895 he checked in at Johns Hopkins Hospital in Baltimore for a consultation at $20 per diem. Otherwise, there is no evidence to belie the impression of robustness so clearly reflected in a photograph taken in his later years (fig. 16). As 1914 drew to a close, however, he was compelled to miss a meeting of the Board of Directors of the Norfolk and Western Railway for the first time in the memory of the president, who wrote to him, "Somehow or other I had felt as though sickness and pain should not come to you. I had looked upon you as a young man, but I guess both of us will have to admit the years are going by and we cannot stop them. . . . I beg you to take it quietly."[132]

But rest proved not enough. It was the beginning of a long illness that would drag on for over a year. After a meeting of the Mutual Assurance Society of Virginia in Richmond he told his old friend Colonel Palmer, as they walked to the train depot together, that he had gone several times to Johns Hopkins and that the doctors there held out no hope of recovery, having determined that he was suffering from cancer. Palmer's premonition that they were seeing each other for the last time proved all too accurate.[133]

A Northern journalist visiting in 1915 wrote a moving description of Walter and Bettie in these waning months of his life:

> Colonel Taylor's keen, dark, observant, yet kindly eyes, were perhaps his finest feature, though, indeed, all his features were fine, and his head, with its well-trimmed white hair and mustache, was one of great distinction. Mrs. Taylor (of whom we had previously been warned to beware, because she had not yet forgiven the "Yankees" for their sins) was also present: a beautiful old lady of unquenchable spirit, in whose manner, though she received us with politeness, we detected lurking danger.[134]

To the Marine Bank, whose destinies he had guided for so many years, he paid a final visit early in February 1916.[135] Steadily he grew weaker, and as the month drew to a close it was evident the end was near. Out-of-town family members were summoned, and just before the stroke of midnight, with Bettie and their children at his side, he died peacefully on March 1, 1916. While his last thoughts centered no doubt on his family, out of the mists of time must have come glimpses of the charge he led at Spotsylvania, the closing scenes at Appomattox, and, above all, his midnight wedding to Bettie half a century before, whence he had ridden off in the lurid glare of a Richmond in flames to rejoin Robert E. Lee on the final retreat.

Even when allowance is made for the fulsome obituaries that were de rigueur at the time, the tributes paid to Colonel Taylor's memory were such as come to few men regardless of station. Norfolk's leading journal spoke of his high and rigid sense of honor, his self-poise and courtly manner, his unswerving devotion to duty.[136] To others he was a man of the greatest nobility of character, a brave and valiant fighter

33

during the war, a kindhearted, genial, courteous Virginia gentleman. "Few men," wrote the *Richmond Times-Dispatch,* "have been more honored in life than was Col. Walter H. Taylor of Norfolk, and few are more honored in memory than he. To have lived so that all men gave him reverence to the day of his death is memory fine enough, but to have lived so that in his youth he was the trusted adjutant of Robert E. Lee sets his name apart."[137] Added the *Richmond News-Leader:* "Heaven smiled on Walter H. Taylor."[138] But perhaps his life was best summed up by this simple tribute from the *Norfolk Virginian-Pilot:* "For half a century the name of Walter H. Taylor was a synonym for all that was honorable and of good report."[139]

By resolution of both houses of the Virginia State Legislature, flags in Richmond were lowered to half-mast, as they were in Norfolk. The funeral services, marked by their simplicity, were conducted at the family home at 300 York Street by Bishop A. M. Randolph, assisted by Bishop Beverly D. Tucker, and Taylor's friend of many years and fellow officer on Lee's staff, Rev. Giles B. Cooke. Among the honorary pallbearers were Captain Robert E. Lee, sole surviving son of the general; Colonel Palmer; and Lewis Crenshaw, in whose house in Richmond Bettie and Walter had been married on that memorable night fifty years before. The active pallbearers were four sons, three sons-in-law, and three nephews.[140] Colonel Taylor was buried in Elmwood Cemetery, and in less than four months his beloved wife took her place at his side. "She and the Colonel had journeyed so long together," wrote a friend, "that the world was no longer a congenial place for her."[141]

Chapter 1

Lee Takes the Offensive
May 1862 to August 1863
(Letters 1–24)

This first series of letters begins May 15, 1862, immediately after the evacuation of Norfolk. These letters are mostly to members of Taylor's family and deal chiefly with Lee's early triumphs and his invasions of the North in 1862 and 1863.

While Taylor's devotion to Bettie Saunders never faltered, she did not encourage a correspondence until the summer of 1863. Thus it was that most of Walter's surviving early wartime letters were addressed to his sister or, on occasion, other members of his family. Despite coolness on Bettie's part, he nevertheless wrote her from time to time prior to Gettysburg. But, alas, and to her later regret, she burned most of those letters.

Ten days after Norfolk was surrendered to the Northern troops he addressed her from the Confederate capital.

I

Richmond, Va

15 May 1862

Dear Bettie

Confident that you will be interested to hear anything from Norfolk,[1] and not knowing the dates of last advices from there, I have taken the liberty to say that I have just received a letter from Julia written the day before the evacuation (last Friday) in which she says "Fannie and I are going down to Mrs. Huger's at her request to collect the books and ornaments.[2] I have promised to take Bettie's furniture & Fannie the piano." She also mentions John's having received a note from you, requesting that someone be placed in the house or the furniture distributed.[3] I heard indirectly from Norfolk yesterday. Report says that the Atlantic Hotel and Dr Cooke had raised the Yankee Flag.[4] I hope this may not be so but would not be surprised. Lincoln was at Old Point and is said to have gone to Norfolk on a gunboat but did not get off. Oh Bettie, our poor dear home! Isn't it sad? However though cast down, we will not be in despair. Though sore stricken, we are not foresaken!

Mahone's brigade is on the south side of James River about 8 miles from this city. It is there we have obstructed the river and placed our batteries. We had a fight this morning with the enemy's gunboats. They were beaten back. The "Galena" was set on fire. The "Naugatuck" much injured and all of them have for the present retired. I have just had a report to this effect from Genl Mahone.[5]

I have already gone further than I intended. Ah! Bettie, a short while back I would not have had to write you in an apologetic tone. The privilege was mine to write naturally and as often as I pleased. Do you suppose I will ever forget those happy years? Never. The truth is I try but cannot. My love to your Mother, Patty & Mary & may God bless you Bettie[6]

Prays Yours as ever,

Walter

2

[To Bettie]

Near Richmond

16 June 1862

Your letter to Julia was handed to me by your cousin John a few days since, to be sent by first opportunity. On Sunday Genl Cobb went over, in accordance with a previous agreement, to arrange with the enemy for an exchange of prisoners, and I forwarded the letter by him.[7] Having since heard nothing of it, & having sent several on a former occasion, when a "flag" went over, I presume Genl McClellan has permitted their transmittal to Norfolk.[8] We have had letters lately, but I deem it useless to give you the items of news as I suppose you are well advised of all that is known concerning our dear city and its people.

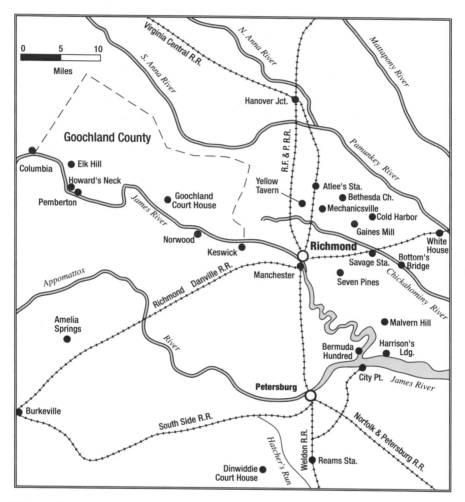

Map 2. Central Virginia, 1861–1865

If you see your Coz Jno [John] tell him I am ignorant as yet of the character of the arrangement for an exchange. Should it transpire that the exchange is to be <u>general</u> in the broad acception of the term, & not confined to the opposing armies along the Potomac, it will of course interest him, and I will advise him of the fact.

Say to your Coz Nannie,[9] if you meet her, that I have sent her letter. It did not go by the flag of truce but by the underground. I think the way by the "flag" the safer of the two. If she sends any more I will use my discretion & perhaps delay them for opportunities by flag instead of sending by persons who attempt the underground.

At this present all is quiet around Richmond. The fight, however, the grand battle must ere long come off.[10] It will be terrible, Bettie, the men will do their utmost on our side and the enemy will no doubt resist to the extent of his might. May God be with us. Give us your prayers dear Bettie. By His strength alone can we hope to succeed. Our cause is just and I am persuaded He will in His own good time bring us safely out of these troubles.

Give my love to your Mother, Pattie & Mary, my kindest regards to your sister, Mrs Hobson.[11] Tell Pattie I return her kisses with interest.

I cannot say when another flag will go over to the enemy. Of late the occasions have been quite frequent. If you have no better opportunity & desire it, I need not assure you it will give me great pleasure to send any letter you may entrust to me to take the chances by the first flag of truce. With the liveliest recollections of our past, I am as ever

Sincerely, your friend

Walter

McClellan having retreated to Harrison's Landing on the James after the bloody conflicts of the Seven Days, Lee began shifting his troops northward to meet the threat posed by the newly formed Federal Army of Virginia under Pope. On August 9 at Cedar Mountain Stonewall Jackson defeated Pope's leading corps. Taylor's next letter was dated shortly thereafter.

3

[To Mary Louisa Taylor]

Sunday 17 Aug '62

Dear Sister,[12]

We have reached a point some distance beyond Gordonsville and very near Orange Ct Ho. Our first night was spent on the very beautiful farm of Mr Burton Haxall; last night we made ourselves comfortable at this place owned by a Mr Taylor.[13] Such charming quarters cannot be long enjoyed however, as the troops are in motion. How far we go today I know not. Our march cannot be too rapid, as the great desideratum is to strike Pope before "little Mac" reaches this section.[14] The army is in fine spirits, and I pray I may not be disappointed in expecting much from it. The order was issued for the command to which the boys are attached to move on the night preceding my departure—so we will all be together again. You & Lydia had better remain where you are just yet unless you prefer to spend the balance of the hot weather in the country.[15] In that event select such place as pleases you and migrate. Since reaching this part of the world I find two blankets very comfortable. The change is indeed remarkable. But perhaps you experience the same in the east. I enjoy the scenery amazingly. Next to water, give me the mts, that is to say when I cannot have both. If you like, you might get quarters at or near Staunton or Charlottesville. But you must arrange just as suits your inclination or sentiment for all other things may be regarded as equal. I have just written to Custis Lee to get him to send my horse up with a wagon train that will leave Richmond next Thursday, but if the boys have not left before this reaches you & it is not inconvenient, let the mare accompany them provided she is apparently recovered from her lameness.[16] If she comes with them, one of them must see C. Lee & explain. If she is not well enough to travel, then let her remain. Love

Walter

4

Dr Wellford's House
near Rappahannock Riv

23 August 1862

My precious Sister,

I received yours of the 13th by Mr Jno. Taylor day before yesterday.[17] He met Dick who read it before forwarding.[18] Bro also enclosed dear Ma's letter.[19] I am truly glad she has two servants at least. I fear it would be expecting too much to hope that Moses will remain faithful. Rumor says we have Suffolk; I hope access to Norfolk will be easy hereafter, although we cannot expect to regain & hold possession of a town so completely at the mercy of their Navy. They cannot spare many troops however & their police duty will not be so thoroughly executed as to place any serious obstructions to underground communication. I expect many letters in future.

Genl Anderson's command reached us yesterday[20]—that is, it was for the first time encamped near our headquarters. This morning I met the boys & paid them a visit at their camp. Both are well—Dick's finger though a little troublesome, does not seem to pain him a great deal. Rob went almost immediately to look for the genl's supply train,[21] which I imagine contained the necessary ingredients for the "battercakes." I was glad to see all the Norfolk boys & that they were apparently well & cheerful. I cannot write about our movements. Too many letters have been captured lately (from the enemy) to warrant any one in putting in writing anything appertaining to our position or intentions. I trust however that all will work well. I wish we c^d strike such a blow as w^d end the wretched war. I <u>know</u> Lydia is bravely bearing up under her first trial since her married life began.[22] I suggested in my former letter that if we are likely to remain up here, which will no doubt be determined shortly, you might find comfortable quarters near Charlottesville or Staunton. But you must consult yr own convenience & inclination.

I am as well as ever except a cold in the head which is improving & will perhaps leave me today. At the end of the month get Mr Wilson to take my pay account to Major J. C. Hilter at the Q^r M^r buildings on Bank St near the War Dept & he will arrange it. Hoping that we will all through God's will be spared soon to reassemble as a family & enjoy the blessings of peace is the earnest prayer of your fond bro

Walter

Love to Lyd., Sally, Marcia & all.[23] I will write to Ma when I can & get you to forward.

5

30 August 1862

My dear Sister,

I have time but to let you know where and how I am. We have advanced to the old <u>Bull Run</u> lines and hope still to go onward. The fighting yesterday was pretty severe but successful with us.[24] Yet there is much to be done. The enemy know that the fate of their capital depends on the conduct of the army in front of us, and desperate indeed will be the struggle.

Anderson's division has not yet been engaged. I hope it will be up today. The boys were both well when I last saw them some two or three days ago.

I suppose the people of Richmond are utterly in the dark concerning our movement. It is not our capital that is now being defended. But the issue is not yet. God alone knows what is to be, but I trust we may continue to be blessed & aided by Him. Our advance to this place (near Bull Run) was one of the boldest moves of our so-called <u>timid?</u> General.[25]

I have not heard from you except by Mr Jno Taylor. Have written several times. I hope Lydia continues brave—my best love to her, Sally & Marcia & to all at home when you write.[26]

May God bless you begs yr devo bro

Walter

6

[To Mary Lou]

Near Groveton
(Bull Run Va)

31 Aug 1862

Knowing how anxious you will be after hearing of the battle, to know of our safety, I hasten to send you assurance of all three being unhurt.[27] We had on yesterday a terrific fight[28]—as severe as any of those around Richmond. The Yankees fought us as if in earnest, but they were not equal to our veterans & have fled to Centreville after being handsomely whipped. The slaughter was very heavy—their loss being greater than ours. On some parts of the field their dead lie in files thicker than they did on the Chickahominy. It was also a glorious fight to look at. In going from one portion of the field to another (and at this I was kept very busy) I had splendid opportunities of viewing the contest from the elevated points—it was sublime. From the highest hills, the whole affair could be observed. We have captured many prisoners, arms, cannons, wagons & personal baggage. The amount of commissary stores but trifling. A large part of McClellan's army was here. The balance I presume has by this time joined them & we have more work ahead. May God continue to bless us.

Genl Mahone was wounded soon after the brigade entered. His wound is reported not dangerous. Harry Wmson was just scratched. Young Voss killed—also Ripley. Dick Hopkins, D. Bell wounded. The former seriously in the arm. The latter I heard not dangerously.[29] These are all the casualties I have heard of amongst our acquaintants. Rob & Dick all safe. I had two or three very narrow escapes, but God was truly gracious. How very thankful <u>we</u> should feel.

I have no time to write more

May Heaven bless you dear Sister

Prays Yr devo bro

Walter

As Lee crossed into Maryland on his first invasion of the North, Taylor wrote from near Frederick.

7

[To Mary Lou]

Near Fredericktown Md

Sunday 7 Sept. '62

I wrote you, my dear sister, from Leesburg two days since. You will not be surprised therefore to hear of our being in Maryland. We crossed the river without opposition,[30] and now comes the "tug of war." The invasion policy is begun. May God continue to bless our arms and cause our general & these movements to be instruments in His hands for bringing about a speedy peace.

Your note announcing the accident that had befallen you was received on yesterday. I am so sorry to hear that you were hurt and quite sad at the thought of your helplessness & absence from all your brothers.[31] I hope though that it will not prove serious & that you will soon be free from all annoyance on account of the fall. Ma will have to go to you & Lydia. I think there will be no difficulty now in her doing so.

I suppose Dick is still with the general—where that is I cannot say. Rob I have not seen for several days, but he was well when last seen. The division is across the river & will be up with us today. This is a beautiful Sunday & I would like to go to Church, but hate the idea of being regarded as an interloper. About here I think the population about equally divided in sentiment. I can judge only from what demonstrations as I see. Some appear rejoiced at our advent amongst them; others manifest either indifference or a silence which bespeaks enmity. In eastern Maryland the Southern feeling is more decided. If we ever get there, no doubt many will join us. Now is the time for Maryland or never. After this if she does not rise, hush up "My Maryland."[32]

Our army is in fine trim and spirits. The men have supplied themselves with many needful articles from the towns, paying in Confed money wh appears to go very well. It is Hobson's choice however with the sellers. The Yankee papers of the 6th exhibit a gloomy picture for our enemy. Just now it does appear as if God was truly with us. All along our lines the movement is onward. Ohio, Maryland, they expect to see invaded. We are here & I trust Kirby Smith will ere long shell Cincinnati.[33] The army under Pope was badly whipped it is now acknowledged. Give my love to all. Take care of yourself & soon get well. Don't use the check for $100 now. I should like to settle with Stuart but am uncertain as to the fate of my letter wh you have not rec'd.

Affy Walter

8

[To Mary Lou]

Winchester Va.

12 Sept 1862

Since Dick & I telegraphed to you on yesterday from Winchester, you will not be surprised to hear from here. I was sent from Frederick City Maryland to meet his Ex. the President & Ex Govr Lowe.[34] Failing to meet them at Leesburg, I proceeded to Winchester & there learned that his Ex had returned to Richmond & the Govr had left for this place—so I was compelled to trudge along this way, since I could not return by the old route the army having moved & that being considered unsafe. Dick happened to go the same day to Warrenton on business for the General & of course we met with mutual surprise. How fortunate! Was it not? I earnestly trust that you are doing well & that the injury you sustained will not result seriously. I hear that Beauregard has been assigned to the Dept of SC & Ga.[35] If so Pemberton will I presume be sent here & John will accompany him.[36] If he does let him bring my horse along. I need her much. Destroy the check for $200 I have drawn I left with you. Love to all. Rob was OK Wednesday. Yr

W.

9

Don't let any of your friends sing "My Maryland," not "my Westn" Md anyhow.

Near Martinsburg Va

21st Sept 1862

I wrote you yesterday, my precious sister, but feeling that I cannot write too often in these exciting times, I will avail myself of the opportunity presented today, it having been determined to send a courier with official dispatches for Richmond.

I suppose it will be generally concluded that our march through—or rather into—Maryland & back was decidedly meteoric. It was however by no means without happy results. The capture of H[arpers] Ferry was sufficiently important to compensate for all the trouble experienced, and the fight of the 17th has taught us the value of our men, who can even when weary with constant marching & fighting & when on short rations, contend with and resist three times their own number.

The fight was certainly the longest & most severely contested of the war, beginning at dawn & ceasing only when light failed us.[37] We do not boast a victory—it was not sufficiently decisive for that. The Yankees would have claimed a glorious victory had they been on our side & they no doubt claim it anyhow. But if either had the advantage, it certainly was with us. They dared not resume the attack the next day & their left proposed a truce to bury the dead. Their prisoners (caught

44

yesterday) seem much disheartened & were evidently by no means persuaded that they had gained anything on Wednesday last.

After waiting one day for "Mac" to lay on & Mac declining to come to us, we quietly left him & came to Virginia, a more hospitable country, where the "Bushwackers" are on the <u>right</u> side & where the good people haven't the disreputable & unmannerly habit of shooting at Confed. soldiers from the windows, which habit the Marylanders practiced in Frederick & Boonesboro. So 'tis said by the cavalry.

We are today resting—a Sabbath indeed—for we needed rest. The army has had hard work I assure you & its condition demands a few days of exemption from battle. The Congress must provide for reinforcing us and then we will be enabled to realize their sanguine expectations. Give us the men & then talk about invading Penn. Our present army is not equal to the task in my opinion. You see the Feds get 3 or 4 thousand new troops a day & though we have done wonders, we can't perform miracles. My impression is that we are still to fight & that shortly & with God's help we will again be victorious.

I saw Rob yesterday. We are both well. Dick still with M.[38] I sent Mrs Saunders a short note, informing her of Capt John Taylor's death.[39] I wish I could write you the particulars but the courier starts now. Love to all.

Yr Aff

Walter

10

[To Mary Lou]

Between Martinsburg and
Winchester—Sunday morn'g

28 Sept 1862

We moved here yesterday, where we will probably remain some days. The object being to recruit and rest our army, collect the stragglers and endeavor to secure clothes and shoes for the many poorly clad, barefooted patriots who are suffering for the want of these necessary articles.

I believe my Chief was most anxious to recross into Maryland but was persuaded by his principal advisors that the condition of the army did not warrant such a move. This is conjecture on my part. I only know of his opinion & <u>guess</u> why he did not follow it. At this time it would have indeed been hazardous to reenter Maryland. With the men of the army that state now meets but little sympathy. One of the bands commenced the air "My Maryland" & was prevented from proceeding by the groans & hisses of the soldiers. This will convey to you some idea of the effect of the recent invasion upon the sentiments of the army concerning the people of that unfortunate state. I sent you a letter by Jno Page who started some days since for Richmond.[40] I saw Rob a day or two ago when he was well.

Dick I have not heard from since he went to look for his General, whom it is hoped may have escaped capture, since he took to the woods, promising to meet the others when the cavalry should have passed back. We are without anything positive since but I still hope they did not find Mahone & that Dick is now with him.[41] I suppose Lydia scarcely ever hears from D for his opportunities for sending letters must be rare—separated as he is from the army. Rob to whom I give all letters for D has now some five or six and I have one to console her for the absence of letters. She may be assured of his safety from hurt so long as he is away from the brigade. Maybe she would willingly resign all letters to have him absent from all battles.

I enclose a letter from Mr Rodman.[42] A Mr J. W. Griffin sent it to me. Forward it when you can. Clarence Garnett dined with us a few days ago.[43] He gave me your letter. He is well & wrote his uncle while at our Hd Qrs. I forward the letter.

Love to L, Sally, Marcia & all. Geo Peterkin was very well yesterday.[44] S can tell his mother. God bless you.

Walter

I I

[To Richard C. Taylor]

Camp near Winchester

15 Octo, 1862

My dear Brother,

Truly each day but adds to our already infinite indebtedness to our heavenly Father. To <u>us</u> he has indeed been merciful, allowing us even to see how everything is ordained for good. When I review the events of the past few years & dwell in thought upon the innumerable blessings bestowed upon our circle, I am overwhelmed with a sense of intense gratitude for His fatherly kindness & deplore more and more my own unworthiness. The workings of His hand can be traced in all that has befallen us. To Him I render all homage and praise as the author of all the good we have and hope for & thank Him especially for the last evidence of His protection in preserving your sweet wife in her hour of danger & bringing safely into the world your promising boy[45]—another link in our blessed family chain.

To you & Lydia I tender my hearty congratulations on the occasion of your happiness. May the youngster be a lifelong source of comfort to you & bear living testimony to the truth of the old adage "like father, like son." I fear his Grandmama will be even more restless than ever within her restricted limits, & put forth all efforts to escape from her Yankee imprisonment, in order to gladden her eyes with the sight of her new charge.[46] I bespeak for the young gentleman a great deal of petting & warn you to beware lest his numerous aunts and uncles spoil him in spite of his wise & prudent parents. These bachelor uncles are particularly to be dreaded, so for one I say look out.

I hope dear sister has by this time entirely recovered from the effects of her fall & is in every other way well & happy. I would regret exceedingly if the little commissions I sent in my last letter were to be troublesome to her. I thought the shirts could be ordered to be made, & trust that she did not undertake them. The pants I want especially—the material is a matter of but little consequence, so it is warm. I also want a cap or hat. It being unanimously conceded that the one I now wear is a disgrace to the staff. With these additions to my outfit, I will be ready for winter & the bad weather we must daily expect in this latitude.

I have been to see Rob several times of late. He has been a little under the weather, but insists upon it that he will not knock under. He is improving & will I think soon be himself again. It is needless to say how I am. As usual, in the enjoyment of the largest appetite that ever went unappeased. What would I not give for some of Sallie's Laplands,[47] served up in the style I used so much to enjoy in her room, instead of the beef, flour & water which now constitute my breakfast, lunch & dinner. However, poor as our fare is, I manage to fatten on it.

47

We are still quietly resting in camp near Winchester, our army much improved & largely increased since our battles in Maryland. But to be efficient this army must be clothed. A supply has reached us, but the quantity thus far received is wholly inadequate.

The only excitement we have had lately was consequent on Jeb Stuart's cavalry raid into Md and Pennsylvania.[48] It was an entirely successful expedition and executed in Jeb's usual & unequalled style. Look at your map. McClellan's army occupies the ground lying along the Potomac between Williamsport & opposite Leesburg, & extending back to Hagerstown. To circumvent such an army as his in this position was of course a hazardous undertaking. Our cavalry crossed just above Williamsport & made immediately for Mercersburg, thence to Chambersburg, Emmitsburg, New Market & recrossing the Potomac just where we first entered Maryd at White's Ford near Leesburg. At Mercersburg we captured many state prisoners—Mayor, Post Mr, Town Councilmen, etc., the object being to hold them as hostages or means of exchange for our political prisoners. In Chambersburg no man could be found who held an office, either state or Government, all having cleared out. But here they captured and destroyed a large quantity of arms, stores &c. In passing through Pennsylvania every horse was taken that was likely to be useful, these being considered legal captures, & Jeb returned with 7 or 8 hundred fine Penna horses. The citizens were perfectly dumb with astonishment & would hardly believe they were Rebels. Under the supposition that they were Feds the Dutch girls fed them with apple butter, etc., & when it was discovered who we were, whiskey was freely offered but in nearly all cases declined. At Emmitsburg the demonstration was indeed flattering, all residents there being Southern sympathizers. The women actually cheered—3 regular cheers. Time would fail to relate the many laughable incidents that occurred. Their passage back was disputed but in vain. All arrived safely and in fine spirits.

My love to Ma & all.

Yr devo bro Walter

For the next six months Taylor's letters were few and far between. In January '63 he wrote Bettie declaring undying devotion, despite rebuffs and two years of separation. At last she relented, at least to a degree, and late in February told him she did not love another. There followed expressions of sis-

terly affection and the assurance that he stood foremost among her friends. In ecstasy Walter replied with renewed hope and the conviction that this happy turn of events was, indeed, God's will.

12

[To Bettie Saunders]

In Camp [at Hamilton's Crossing]

26 Jany 1863

When in Richmond last it was my desire and firm intention, Bettie, to have had a few moments of unrestrained conversation with you. In this, as you are aware, I was disappointed. You will remember the evening when I met you; twice after this did I call with the hope of having my wishes gratified. You know the result; and now I find myself once more compelled to resort to a letter in order to say what I would so much prefer telling you in person. Do you wonder what all this prelude is to lead to? Or can you already guess my meaning?

My object is simply to assure you that my sentiments towards you are unchanged. Simply to tell you that still at this time, after hoping and fearing, after my many bitter disappointments, my attachment is ever the same and only altered in so far as its fervency has been increased. After two years separation, and more than that length of time without the shadow of a hope, I still entertain for you the same earnest unswerving devotion.

I need not here tell you how every act of your life but makes you more attractive in my eyes. Nor is it necessary for me to assure you how constantly I think of you. You know all, Bettie; and indeed if asked for my motive in writing this, it would be difficult for me to define it. I will be better satisfied however after it is done. I expect no response, least of all a favorable one—and yet I wish you to know, Bettie, how earnestly and deeply I have loved you. Mine was no evanescent affection, nor can I by any possible effort overcome it. Please don't censure me for this; but bear with my weakness. Perhaps I shall not trouble you any more. If this should be calculated to displease you I trust to your goodness of heart for pardon and beg you please let it make you none the less my friend. Remember this is my misfortune, tis not a fault.

Whatever our future relationship, that God may keep and bless you shall ever be the constant prayer of your sincerely attached friend

Walter

13

[To Bettie]

In Camp

4 March 1863

I fear that on sight of this, you will consider me the most importunate of men, and an incorrigible bore and conclude that I am determined to force myself upon you as a regular correspondent. But I cannot forego the pleasure of assuring you of my sincere gratitude for, and high appreciation of your kind and considerate letter, whilst I but perform a duty in acknowledging its receipt. As it was your avowed desire that it shd be more than kind, let me tell you it is the very essence of kindness, and every line is fraught with sentiments which evince a sweetness of disposition rarely equalled, and which well accord with the known excellence of the heart from which they emanate.

Indeed this sweet letter has made me really happy, & tonight I am unusually lighthearted. Though I had no reason to think the reverse the case, yet your own assurance that you <u>love</u> no one else has afforded me infinite relief; and that you should class me first & foremost amongst your friends, and feel for me the interest and affection of a sister, is well calculated to gratify me; and I must be careful lest my vanity is excited to an unreasonable extent. I esteem myself favored indeed since you have given me this assurance; there is but one thing that could cause me to rejoice more, and that would be the acme of all my earthly hopes and aspirations. But Bettie, I would be content to occupy the position you assign me forever and be very happy in so doing, provided no one should take that place in your affections which I am denied. Please pardon such egregious selfishness, but in this matter I really cannot be generous. I feel, Bettie, as if we now for the first time understand each other; and oh! this is so much more satisfactory to me than that terrible feeling produced by what I construed into a chilling, perfect indifference, which threw a restraint upon my every action, made you altogether unapproachable to me & from the effects of which

50

I have but just recovered. Now I hope I was in error. Now matters do not look so dark to me and I am more hopeful. Do not misunderstand me—your letter was as <u>plain</u> and <u>intelligible</u> as it was interesting—but still I may hope. Yes! I will hope and believe—not that all my wishes will be gratified; but that God will so ordain the course of our lives as shall be most conducive to the happiness of each and that I will be enabled to accept humbly, resignedly & with thankfulness whatever in His goodness He shall direct.

Had I any apprehensions about your spiritual welfare, your letter would have done much to dissipate my fears. For, even with those who are strangers to God, there is always greatest cause for hope when one is fully aroused to a sense of one's own wickedness; and it is not remarkable that a Christian fully alive to his danger and conscious of his own feebleness and insufficiency, shd be impressed with fear and awe in contemplating his condition. But fear not you, Bettie, God is your sure refuge, and you have only to cast all your hope on Him. I <u>too</u> wish that I could be again blessed with that peaceful, indescribable <u>spirit</u> which years ago I experienced & which seemed always to bring me into close proximity to my Saviour. But I am so hardened; ah! sad indeed have been the effects of this unhappy war—not the least of which has been the bitter spirit towards our enemies which it has engendered, but which is entirely at variance with the commands given for our guidance—and then there is such an utter absence in our army of any external evidence of piety. Would that I could more profitably employ this Lenten season. I never have an opportunity of attending Service, and am generally kept as constantly occupied on Sundays as on any day of the week.

Do you know the happiest days of my life, as I look back, were those when together we were accustomed to visit our pretty grave-yard? The morning walk and its associations so admirably prepared me for the duties of the day. Oh! I was very happy then! and were you not? Are such times never to return? Tis true we shall never be so free from care again. But are we not dear to each other, and by prayer and earnest endeavor may we not enjoy the same close communion with our God? Yes. Let us try! Let us mutually assist each other, and surely our efforts shall be blessed with success, and we shall again be as happy! You remember well, B, the night of your confirmation? Ah how full was my heart <u>that</u> night! But I must not, must not go on in this strain. With my new resolves it is dangerous for me to dwell upon these brightest, sweetest incidents of my life. I cannot refrain however from thinking of them; and many and many a time even with all the awful surrounding of battle and death I go back in memory to those glorious days and am lost to all else.

But I must not fatigue you. I have received two letters from Julia and one from Fannie and have answered none of the three. As yet I have been unable, for indeed I am worked very hard, and it is a complete mystery how I have managed to write this hurried letter, for which I crave your indulgence.

Interrupted as I have been and with two of our clerks crazy for me to clear out of the office, it must be very disconnected—but that matters not—writing is not my forte. I wish I could see and talk to you. I could do so now without reserve—and I am confident it would be of advantage to me.

Our friend Frank Huger is in a fair way of being promoted Major[49]—but as this is as yet a Headquarters secret, and something may intervene to prevent it, it would be well to keep it to ourselves for the present. He is a good fellow and deserves it.

Please present my kindest regards to Mrs. K. and to Patty and Miss Lizzie,[50] to your Mama and Mary and Mrs. H—when you write—my best love.

Excuse this horrid looking place just below, but it was the only sheet of paper available.

Mr. F. J. Hooker is quiet.[51] In a few weeks now we will be again active—and, though I dread the awful consequences of battle, I dare say it will be well for us when it comes.

Good bye—May God bless you prays yr attached friend

W.

Following the battle of Chancellorsville, he wrote Mary Lou.

14

8 May 1863

My dear Sister,

I sent you a telegram on the day before yesterday stating that Rob and I were unhurt. God has truly blessed us & we have special cause for thankfulness. The past week has been a most eventful one. The operations of this army under Genl Lee during that time will compare favorably with the most brilliant engagements ever recorded.[52] When I consider our numerical weakness, our limited resources and the great strength & equipments of the enemy, I am astonished at the result. Surely the hand of God was on our side. Never was it more plainly demonstrated that He can save by many or by few. Oh! how thankful should our people be that such an ally is ours. I hope and pray they will appreciate His many blessings & strive to be a righteous nation, a Godfearing and Godloving people.

The General's telegram, which you have undoubtedly seen in the papers, has already informed you of our movements and several battles. The crossing in our front near Fredericksburg was made as a feint with a hope of diverting us from the real attack on our left and rear. Hooker seems to have adopted the same plan which Genl Lee executed on the Chickahominy. The result however is not altogether similar.

It was soon discovered by our wise Chief that the main attack would be made above. Accordingly he left a small force to guard the heights in rear of the town and marched with the balance to meet Joseph. We drove him easily on the 1st inst (for some miles) until within a short distance of his fortified position near Chancellorsville. It wouldn't do to attack him in front, so Jack with his foot cavalry was put in motion to come in upon the right rear.[53] It is stated that the Yankees, who could see the direction our wagon trains were pursuing, questioned the citizens as to where the road would lead, and a shrewd one told them directly to Richmond, which made them believe we were retreating and caused them to be much elated.

On the 2d Jack's Corps rather surprised the enemy's outposts in their rear, went immediately to work, scattered the first corps which opposed them to the four winds of heaven and drove all that faced them to within a mile of their stronghold, Chancellorsville.[54] The fight was continued until a late hour at night and it was then and there brave, glorious old Jack received his wound. He was in advance of his men and it is believed was shot by them. But do not <u>give</u> me as your authority for saying so. Genl A P Hill was slightly wounded about half an hour after Jack.[55] The command of the 2d Corps then devolved on Stuart.

On the 3d <u>the fight</u> occurred. I wish you could see how strongly posted and thoroughly fortified the enemy was. While the 2d Corps

53

had been engaging the enemy's right, two divisions of the 1st Corps (Anderson's & McLaws') occupied him in his front.[56] On the morning of the 3d the left of the line of the 1st Corps was moving towards the right of the 2d Corps till a junction was formed, and then the whole line advanced and assaulted the enemy in his breastworks. We carried every point and soon victoriously held the whole field of Chancellorsville.

In the meanwhile the two Corps of the enemy near Fredericksburg had taken Marye's hill with but little opposition, the two regiments of our position there having been surprised. We here lost some artillery; this is the only flaw in last week's work. Having carried Marye's hill the enemy held the plank road which led to the rear of our forces above. They at once began to advance in that direction. On the afternoon of the 2d they were met at Salem Church by our troops sent to arrest their progress. Wilcox's, Semmes' & part of Mahone's brigade were here engaged & repulsed the enemy handsomely and killed & captured many.[57] Frank Mallory was killed.[58] Carter Williams, who acted very gallantly, is, I believe, mortally wounded.[59] Of this I am not positively informed, so say nothing about it. There are other losses amongst our acquaintances, but I cannot now recall them.

I have recd my pants. They are too full and too long. Can they be altered? I am caterer this month. Can Mr. Wilson get me anything to eat? Can a fish be had now & then? piece of fresh beef? butter? vegetables &c? If you see a chance of getting anything, buy it for me. Thomas can always bring it up. We have peas, rice & potatoes. Can we not get greens of some sort? I would like also to buy a jar or two of pickles, can they be had. Never mind the price. But take nothing from Sally [Tompkins]. We should not & cannot use what her patients require. Try & let Ma know we (Rob & I) are safe. I have one or two irons in the fire not yet heard from as regards board for our host. My dear it is impossible to keep together unless we keep house. Nobody will take out a number of boarders and I do not wonder at it. The shirt is very nice and just what I wanted. Four makes me feel comfortable. I can wear one a week—didn't remove a rag or a boot during the week's work—and get them washed once a month.

Did the cavalry frighten you all? I am rather inclined to laugh at their impudence & harmlessness. The good people in Richmond should have caught them. It was well they cut the telegraph wire or the authorities would have worried Gl Lee to death asking him what should be done.[60]

Give my love to all. We have disagreeable weather, hope it will clear up tomorrow. I forgot to say Hooker made a speech to his troops near Chancellorsville telling them he had the crack Rebel Genl just where he wanted him—communications with Richmond cut off, surrounded, &c., but it didn't work right it seems.

W.

After Stonewall Jackson's death from the wounds received at Chancellorsville, Lee reorganized the Army of Northern Virginia into three corps, giving command of the First to Longstreet, the Second to "Fighting Dick" Ewell and the Third to A. P. Hill. This accomplished, the decision was reached to invade the North a second time, but before the movement began the greatest cavalry battle of the war took place at Brandy Station, June 9, 1863. Walter described the fighting in a letter to Bettie written a few days later.

15

[To Bettie]

Culpeper CHo

11 June, 1863

Immediately on the receipt of your note of the 4th enclosing a letter to Lieut. Hobson, I forwarded the latter as addressed.[61] On the morning of the next day the fighting commenced, and its delivery was delayed until yesterday. You will see by the enclosed note that your sister's husband (it is fair to presume) is unhurt. We had a grand cavalry fight, the greatest of the war.[62] Such charging and yelling was never before witnessed and heard on this continent. We occupied a range of hills, with large tracts of cleared fields in every direction, and whichever way the eye turned you could see squadrons charging squadrons, and whole regiments rushing like a whirlwind towards the opposing force and meeting with a shock that fairly shook the earth. The Yankees were in large numbers and managed to throw a force to the rear as well as right and left of our line and but for Stuart's quick eye might have sorely troubled us—but as quickly as thought he would detach bodies to meet those of the enemy and in every case our charges were successful and the Yankees driven back. We lost some fine officers amongst them Col. Williams who but two weeks since was married to poor Maggie Pegram.[63] I saw him as borne from the field accompanied by his adjutant Jno Pegram.[64] I was in hopes he was only wounded, but the poor fellow was instantly killed. We captured between 350 and 400 prisoners and one battery of artillery. Altogether our cavalry is justifiable in claiming an advantage, though neither can be said to have made a great dent. It was nearly an even fight. No doubt both sides will claim to have been victorious. One thing however is certain, whatever was the intention of the Yankees, they failed in executing their design.

We have letters from Norfolk as late as the 28th May. Your coz Nannie was uneasy about Miles, having seen an announcement of his death in the papers.[65] How wrong is the edition thus to publish rumors as facts. Mr. Rodman wants Mrs R. to leave with Mother, when this will be, we know not, but hope to see her and the children every day.

Leila Kerr suffers from heart disease (supposed to be) and she, accompanied by Fannie, has gone to Hagerstown Maryland.[66] Mr R. says not a word of Julia.

I saw Maggie Nash on yesterday. She spoke often of her Norfolk friends very affectionately. She manages to keep near Joe, who is with the cavalry near here.[67]

I have written you quite a letter, but very much doubt whether you can read it. I am so hurried. Give my love to your sister, Mother, Patty, Mary, Miss Julia and Miss Lizzie S. I am glad you are in the country.[68] You must enjoy it after crowded dusty Richmond. We are on another tramp, where we are to go is known to but few. You and Mrs Hobson may experience difficulty in communicating with your friends in this area. I hope you will always enclose your letters to me when no better means of sending them is presented. I am always happy to serve you. We have hard work before us but if a just God continues to lend us His assistance, all will be well. We hold our lives by a most precarious tenure. I hope to be spared to see you again, Bettie, but if not, you must remember him who loved you <u>so</u> earnestly and constantly.

May God bless and keep you prays yr devo. friend

W.

16

[To Mary Lou]

Send me some postage stamps.

In Camp

12 June 1863

I could not write you on yesterday as my time was constantly occupied until the hour for the departure of the train. I received your note, enclosing Ma's letter & was glad to have such recent date. Ma made no allusion to the insurance policy and I did not exactly understand what you meant by the paper sent up from Norfolk &c &c. The time has passed for the regular payment—though the 30 days grace may not have expired and I hope the premium has been paid. Mr. Parker, the agent, being in Norfolk, and Moses R & Uncle Gus being there to advise her,[69] it would be remarkable if the whole should fall through because of delay in paying the premium. I trust it has been arranged. You need not send my new pants. I only wished to make the exchange because these I have are so much better than those in Richmond.

You will have heard of the cavalry fight. I need hardly say anything about it. 'Twas the largest Cav engagement of the war fought with varying success, the advantage finally being on our side. We captured a number of prisoners (350 or 400), four flags and a battery of artillery. Lost some prisoners (estimated at 150) and some gallant officers. Poor Mag Pegram has been sorely afflicted. Her husband was a gallant fellow and died bravely fighting. They had been married only a couple of weeks. It was splendid ground for cavalry fighting—very large tracts of cleared & slightly rolling ground, here & there a commanding hill and but few impediments in the way of fences. There was any amt of charging, counter-charging, yelling and dust. The Yankees manoeuvered well—at one time they charged in the rear of our line, as well as on its right & left—but Stuart was too quick for them & as rapidly as thought dispatched troops to meet them, so that at one time we were engaged in front, rear, on the right & left flanks. Our men drove them off however after an engagement that was very suggestive of "forward four," 1st couple forward and <u>back</u>, 2d couple forward &

back &c &c, finally the 1st couple forwarded without coming back, & the enemy was forced to his single line of attack from the front. Altogether we can claim an advantage, and perhaps a <u>victory</u> but not a decided one. Love to all,

Yr devo bro

Walter

Following the battle of Brandy Station, the Army of Northern Virginia began the long march northward to Gettysburg. From Pennsylvania Walter wrote to his sister a few days before the battle.

17

Chambersburg Penn

29 June 1863

My dear Sister,

I intend trying a mail this evening and will send you a line or two, tho the chances of your receiving them are doubtful.

We have progressed swimmingly thus far and find the country a pleasant one. As we have had no fighting, I need hardly say Rob & I are all right. I called on Mr Parks, Mrs Osborne, &c in Hagerstown.[70] They were all well and sent much love to you all. I hope Ma will soon be with you. Prudence forbids my saying anything of army matters.

With God's help we expect to take a step or two towards an honorable peace. I believe the people here are most anxious for it. Some are solemn, but most smiling and in good humor—take our presence very quietly. I am happy to say our men are behaving themselves admirably. With one or two exceptional cases, no depredations have been committed. I send you a copy of one of the Genl's orders.

May God bless & keep you & lend us His aid now when so much needed—prays yr devo bro

Walter

His next letter was penned during the retreat from Gettysburg.

18

7 July 1863

Dear Sister,

Rob and I are all right; so are all we care particularly for or are interested in. No Norfolk boy hurt—Mahone's brigade at no time heavily engaged.

We failed to drive the Yankees from their Gibraltar.[71] On the first day whipped them & occupied their lines; on the second day still drove them & gained ground. Their last position was impregnable to any such force as ours.

We are all right at Hagerstown & hope to get up another fight soon. The Yankees left Gettysburg the same time we did, were preparing for it the day previous. After they find out that we left, they will of course claim a victory. I will write in detail when I can.

Geo Peterkin is unhurt; so is Hunter Saunders, Aleck, Harry Wmson & indeed all our old acquaintances.[72] Tell Bettie Saunders to let Miss Starke know her brother is safe.[73] I promised to let her know. Yours aff,

Walter

I hope Ma is with you. Kisses all around

W

After the return of the army to Virginia, Walter wrote his brother Dick a long letter, touching first on the loss of Vicksburg and then giving, in some measure, a strangely inaccurate account of Gettysburg. Certainly the Federal troops did not flee before Pickett on the third day, nor did the Northern army retire from Gettysburg before Lee did.

19

[To brother Dick—in camp near Richmond]

Camp near Winchester

17 July 1863

Presuming that Mary Lou may have left Richmond before this I will address myself to you and get you to forward this letter after reading it to our people wherever they may be.

I have written twice and telegraphed once since the late battle in Pennsyl[a] giving assurance of the safety of Rob and myself and, as far as I know, of all our immediate friends. I hope these advices have been received & that all anxiety on our account has been allayed.

I was rejoiced to hear that John was unhurt up to the 24th of last month and trust that ere this you have received later tidings from him and that he is well.[74] But for the loss of prisoners & the morale effect I would not much regret the fall of Vicksburg. Our people make a sad mistake when they attempt to hold such isolated points & attach so much importance to their being held successfully. After the enemy had obtained possession of the reach between Vicksburg & Pt. Hudson and held the same with their gunboats, I regarded the two points as of no more importance than any other two points on the Miss river. We could have prevented the free navigation of the stream by means of light and moveable batteries, and by concentrating our forces been enabled perhaps to have successfully resisted Grant's advance into the interior. Even now it seems to me affairs are terribly deranged out west. If Genl Johnston feels too weak to attack Grant, or rather felt too weak to attempt to relieve Pemberton, why so weaken Bragg to such an extent to make him powerless to resist Rosecrans?[75] Division and not concentration seems to be the order of the day out there. But it is not proper to criticise yet, nor do I blame anyone particularly; only it looks to me as if there was some lack of judgment or some mismanagement.

As regards our own affairs, I wish I could write you an account in full of all that has transpired since we left the Rappahannock but I cannot now do this. Indeed you are already aware of all that happened up to our arrival at Gettysburg and engagements at that place. On the first day we were eminently successful. We fought two corps of their army with two divisions & a fraction of ours and drove them handsomely, capturing a number of prisoners & reducing the two corps to less than half their strength. The Northern papers admit a loss in one corps of 66 per cent.

On the second day we were also successful & drove them from a very strong position, capturing some cannons & many prisoners. But now we came to a position that was a sort of Gibraltar. Their two flanks were protected by two insurmountable, impracticable rocky mountains.[76] It was out of the question to turn them. We reached the very base of the stronghold only to find almost perpendicular walls of rock.

Besides the natural advantages of the place the enemy had strength-
ened themselves very much by artificial works. There was no opportunity whatever for a successful flank movement and on the third day
two divisions assaulted a position a little to the left of their centre. Pickett's division of Virginians here immortalized itself.[77] Its charge was
the handsomest of the war as far as my experience goes and though it
carried the works and captured a number of guns, it was not well supported by the division on its left, which failed to carry the works in its
front & retired without any sufficient cause, thereby exposing Pickett's
flank. The enemy then moved on Pickett's left & forced him to retire.
The loss I suppose in killed, wounded & missing was about half of his
command, which however was very small, consisting of only 3 reduced brigades.

Tho not much affected by this repulse, it was deemed inexpedient
to make any more attempts to carry this place by assault. It was beyond
our strength, simply this. If we had have had say 10,000 more men, we
would have forced them back. As it was they did not resist Pickett but
fled before him & had the supporting or second division performed its
part as well, the result would have been different. On the next day we
waited patiently for the enemy to attack us. This they did not do nor
have they at any time since either attacked or manifested any desire to
attack us. They retired from Gettysburg before we did and only
claimed a victory after they had discovered our departure.

They only followed us with a little cavalry & horse artillery & their
attempts to annoy our rear were ridiculous and insignificant. We took
our time to Hagerstown, though to tell the truth we could not have
moved rapidly had we desired it, for it rained in torrents incessantly, as
indeed it did the whole month we were north of the Potomac. We arrived at Hagerstown & did not even hear of the enemy in our vicinity.
Why he did not attempt to intercept us must appear remarkable to
those who believe his lies about his grand victory. After four or five
days he made his appearance. This time we had selected the ground
and were most anxious for an attack. Our ordnance wagons had been
replenished, we had enough to eat & the high waters of the Potomac
gave no concern, if the enemy would only attack us.

We could not wait there for weeks & do nothing, nor could we afford to attack him in position, but if he would attack us, we would rejoice exceedingly. This the rascals dared not do, and their army, as they
say, anxious to meet us again & flushed (as they say) with victory, did
meet us & what next? They went to work fortifying as hard as they

could and as I have discovered from their papers since, anticipated an attack from us. As they manifested no intention of fighting us, it was necessary or at least proper for us to leave our position and go where we could subsist. We threw a bridge over the Potomac & in face of this tremendous Yankee army flushed with victory (?) came into Virginia without the slightest annoyance from the enemy, but the elements were certainly against us. I never saw it rain so hard and our poor fellows had a hard time of it, I can tell you. The Yankees must organize a new army before they can again enjoy an "On to Richmond." We crippled them severely & they cannot now make any formidable aggressive movement. We are again restive & ready for work. I will not hide one truth—that our men are better satisfied on this side of the Potomac. They are not accustomed to operating in a country where the people are inimical to them & certainly every one of them is today worth twice as much as he was three days ago. I am persuaded that we cannot without heavy acquisitions to our strength invade successfully for any length of time. Indeed had we been eminently successful at Gettysburg, in all probability we would have been obliged to make the same movements we have. Posterity will be astonished when the facts of this war are made known to see against what odds this little army contended. Even you would be surprised if I were to give you the figures of the Yankee army and our own.

I have just received Sister's letter of the 13th and am grieved to see that she has not received my letter. I wrote immediately after the fight & hoped she certainly would have rec'd it as soon as the Dept did the Genl's dispatches, which it accompanied. I did not know before that Mother had returned to Norfolk, tho I had received a letter stating she was detained in Annapolis. I try to be resigned & imagine that tho it now seems hard to us, some good will result from their cruel treatment of our household. God ordains all things well & I am assured we have only to wait patiently to see the good in this instance. We must get her some money if possible, or else she must borrow from the banks on some of her stocks or her real estate. I will send a draft to you by first safe opportunity for her half year's interest on her Virginia stock.

I expect Mrs Parks will write to Norfolk & advise of the safety of all of us.

Unlike most people I think Peace is near at hand & more probable now than when we entered Pennsylvania, that is, provided Genls Grant & Rosecrans are not allowed to overrun the whole west & do as they please. If they are confined to the fall of Vicksburg & that of Pt

Hudson all will be well, but if allowed to go where & when they please without any genuine show of resistance, why then we can't say what the result will be.[78] What the North is to be taught in order to secure peace is that a few military successes do not at all affect the ultimate result. Let them know that a success here and one there only prolongs the war without rendering our conquest by any means probable & they will not be able to resist the propositions of the Peace party in the North. Europe too may now think that we are weak in the knees & about to collapse and as sure as they do for fear of a reunion they will certainly recognize the independence of the South. The last thing they desire is to see us restored to the Union & if they see any apparent probability of it, they will move Heaven & Earth to prevent it.

Give my love to all at home when you write to Sally or Marcia and to all in Richmond. Aff yr bro

Walter

20

HdQrs. Cav.Div. A.N.V.

July 18th 1863—

Major,

The letter you mention was yesterday forwarded to Lieut Hobson. Gen. Fitz-Lee informs me to say that the Lieut is O.K. on the G.Q.[79]

Respt.

H. B. McClellan.[80]

[To Bettie]

Camp near Bunker Hill

20 July 1863—

I send you the above note in order that you may know that I delivered your Sister's letter, and that her husband is unhurt. McClellan's language may not be perfectly intelligible to you, the "O.K. on the G.Q." means that Mr. Hobson is well and hearty. I presumed that Mrs.

H. might not possibly have as late dates, & it would be a comfort to her to know this much.

I must thank you, Bettie, for your nice letter, which I appreciate very highly. I shall do myself the pleasure, so soon as my duties will permit, to write you at some length, for I do not intend that you shall regard this little scrawl as an answer to your last. I did not know that Fanny K. had returned to Norfolk. Have you heard from her or Julia lately? Did not the Yankees treat Mother cruelly? May God forgive them & help her!

The assurance contained in the last clause of your letter is very dear to me, my precious friend, & I need hardly repeat what you already know, that an humble but earnest prayer for your welfare and happiness always constitutes a part of my devotional exercises.

Sincerely & ever yours—

Walter

As I don't know how to address you now I shall have to enclose this to Sister. Please present my regards to your Coz. Mary.

—W.

21

[To Mary Lou]

In Camp Culpepper C. Ho

1 August 1863

Your letter, my dear Sister, of the 27th & that of the 17th by Bryan were received on yesterday.[81] The latter gave me the only positive information we had of Ma's movements after the pass was taken from her. I was confident that a letter must have missed me. It is always better to send my letters to the Adjt Genl's office. My friends there look out for & forward them.

I hope you find your present quarters agreeable. Don't think of the board & don't feel bound to return to Richmond when a month has expired. I will send down $160 as soon as I can see a Pay master. I sent a draft for $180 interest on Ma's state stock to Sallie by Jno Dickson few days since.[82] I have an abundance of clothes & will need nothing for myself for months to come, so you must never feel obliged to keep anything in reserve for my individual use. I had much rather that you remain in the country than return to Richmond in the heat of the summer.

I feel much annoyance & embarrassment at our Mother's position—never felt so helpless when anxious to do something in my life. I presume all will be well however, and trustingly leave the matter in the hands of a Kind Providence.

Poor old Norfolk! but 'tis what I expected. I guess Ma thinks me quite prophetic. I wish it was in my power to remove every one from the place in whom I feel interested. Only think of negroes in uniform parading the streets &, what is soon to be, guards for the whites. What a pass! God help the unfortunate ones who have to submit to it & give them patience in this their hour of dark trial.[83]

I cannot but help expecting Ma's early arrival. Ultimately they must allow her to come. If not she must try the blockade at all risks. Now that so few troops are there, communication ought to be quite easy.

I saw Rob last night. He remained with me till 11 o'clock. His general has twice tendered his resignation & it has been as often declined.[84] He (Gl Mahone) must be very unhappy & uncertainly makes those so around him, but Rob has too much animal spirits to be much affected by such things. Dick Walke has left the mess in disgust.[85]

The enemy is moving. Whether we will meet him here or near Fredericksburg cannot yet be said. The General's "Major Taylor" has interrupted me sadly while writing. I am now much hurried.

Yrs aff'y

Walter

22

[To Bettie]

Camp near Orange CHo

8th August 1863
Saturday night

I received your note of the 5th and this afternoon forwarded your Coz. John's letter in a way which I hope will cause him to receive it. Surely and soon. You know Bettie I am always most happy to have it in my power to contribute to your pleasure. I must therefore protest against your apologizing for troubling me when you allow me to do you so simple a service as to forward a letter. Nor must you confine yourself to such trivial matters. I desire you to understand it to be my earnest wish that you shall call on me, in any matter and at any time when an earnest, and old and well tried friend can be useful. If more is denied me, I shall at least insist upon being your nearest friend.

I first learned of dear George's death through a note from your Mother received two days ago. Poor Mrs. Green has been visited with a heavy affliction.[86] But Bettie it must be all well. Oh how consoling it is to feel that a just and wise Providence ordains all things for our good! How happy are those who can trace in the deepest afflictions and the sorest trials, the workings of the Almighty's hand. Though apparently at times a heavy hand, an awful and powerful hand 'twill not unkindly crush us. No, no it is His hand, and strong arm that is to support us. It is His inscrutable will that orders all things for us, and does them well. Blessed faith! Oh for an implicit, an unquestioning faith! To accept all as a gift, a blessing, and to view in apparent deprivations and distresses but measures to secure our ultimate happiness. I desire to regard death as an era only in life, only as the transition from a life of mixed sorrow and earthly pleasure to a holier happier life in God's hands beyond the reach of the contaminating influences of sin. And Bettie every one of those dear to us who die the death of the righteous but constitutes another link in the chain binding us to Heaven. When we regard death as the means whereby we are to see our Savior, to rejoin the loved ones gone before us and to enter upon the enjoyment of those unknown, unalloyed heavenly pleasures, of how much of its terror it is robbed! Thank God Georgie died a Christian! Thank Him Mrs. Green mourns not as one without hope.

> "One tie less below the skies,
> Another safe in Paradise"

I am glad to hear that your Mama has my ring. I was not certain that Pattie had it, but thought so. You know I value highly that ring and the one that Julia Robertson now has. The one is the memento of a youthful but none the less sincere and earnest friendship, blessed with many happy reminiscences; the other is all that remains to me on earth of one of the best and truest friends I ever had. She who was to me more than an ordinary friend, ever a kind, forbearing and loving Sister. Julia Worrell had few equals.[87] Hers was a character almost without blemish and twas a happy lot to have such a one, a loving friend. But though 'tis a pleasure to me to dwell upon these things in memory, I must not compel you to share my thoughts. Yet Bettie, you with me mourn the separation from one, and can sympathize with me in the loss of the other. In your letter of the 7th July, which I was so thankful for, you express a regret that Fanny K had returned to Norfolk. It was indeed too bad that we could not meet when all was so propitious. Frank Huger and I were confident of finding her in Hagerstown, but were doomed to disappointment. I was cruelly deceived for after I had entered the town I met a friend, who told me that he had heard a lady on the street inquire for me and say that she knew me in Norfolk. Why, of course, I thought, it must be Fanny; but no—'twas not, and to this day I am ignorant as to who my fair friend was. I made all sorts of inquiries of all sorts of people to discover if Fan was there, and even went so far as to enter a house in my miserable, rainy day suit, all dripping with rain and spattered with mud only to ask the question, "is Fanny Kerr in town"—and when I entered, I found myself in the presence of several ladies, none of whom I knew, and one old gentleman whom I didn't know though I was seeking him to find his son whom I had once met, and this son I thought could tell me if F. was there. The son was absent and I must ask the father, but I dared not make my inquiries before the girls (you are aware I was always very bashful) and I called the old gent aside, in another room, to have a private word with him. He was a Secesh sympathizer and I had been introduced as a member of Genl. Lee's Staff, so of course he thought my business was all important and accordingly assumed a becoming consequential air. I had a great mind to tell him that we were going right to Washington and wished him to show us the road; or that we had a private plot to kidnap old Abe and needed his services to assure its successful execution; but I finally put the question plainly to him and with a look of disappointment and disgust, he informed me F was not there and then turned to his brandy and water as a more entertaining subject. . . .

I fear that you all in Richmond do not understand our campaign in Maryland. At some future time, if you will hear me, I can tell you of the advantages gained, of the heroic conduct of most of our troops; their splendid, glorious fighting, their patient endurance of hardships and trials, of how near we came to accomplishing what would have surprised the world for its brilliancy and of the shallowness of the Yankee claims to a victory. This is a good old army—no despondency here;

though we hear of it in Richmond. You women, Bettie, must shame the men out of this miserable faint-heartedness, 'tis but next to cowardice.

Then Walter unleashed one of his most bitter tirades against the North.

My contempt for the Yankees, so far as regards their fighting qualities, increases every day. They are a miserable, cowardly race, and would our men fear them! would our southern soldiers for a moment contemplate the bare possibility of our being conquered by such a people? God forbid. I hear of the confidence of some being impaired, but they must be exceptions. Let these fearful ones come up here and look at our brave, glorious old veterans, see their bronzed but determined countenances, their tattered old battle flags, their thinned but still firm unyielding ranks; look at these fellows I say and the faintest heart will gain courage and confidence. I wish to Heaven we could go forth and meet the enemy <u>now</u> and punish him, as I long to do for his impudence, his vain boasting and unblushing falsehoods, but I know my Chief is the wisest and I await his word confidently. If they don't attack us soon I trust the General will see fit to hunt them up. With the help of Heaven we can and will whip them on any battle field in Virginia, whether of their choosing or ours. Miserable things! because we couldn't <u>annihilate</u> them when protected by walls and mountains of rock do they think to frighten us? Nous verons!

I am writing at night, all my comrades are asleep and everything is as peaceful and quiet as if war did not reign in the land. I have not time to write during the day and tomorrow will be Sunday. I determined to write tonight with the hope that I <u>might</u> get to church service in the morning. This privilege I now rarely enjoy. A poor Adjutant General can claim no privileges. If anybody is to be waked at night, to receive the innumerable dispatches, to remain in camp when all else are away, it is the <u>A.A.G.</u> Yes Bettie you are right. I do have to work pretty hard, but for this I care not. I am only too happy to know and feel that I am of some use. I never worked so hard to please any one, and with so little effect as with General Lee. He is so <u>unappreciative.</u> Everybody else makes me flattering speeches, but I want to satisfy <u>him.</u> They all say he appreciates my efforts, but I don't believe it; you know how silly & sensitive I am? Mary Lou says I am too exacting of my superiors—may be so? Whereas Joe Johnston and Beauregard and others have ten, twenty, & thirty Ajt Generals, this army has only one and I assure you at times I can hardly stand up under the pressure of work. Now I don't care a great deal for rank, but I do want to hear that I please my general. When every body else on the staff goes on leave of absences and I cannot, I am not satisfied to have others say 'tis because my presence here is necessary. I want him to tell me, then I'll be satisfied. Bettie you will pardon my egotism, this is only what passes through this crazy mind of mine, & I don't talk to others so but I am without reserve with you, & know you will understand me. You of all others know me too well to misconstrue what I say. Can I not talk plainly to you my nearest & dearest friend? Yes I do work hard Bet, but 'tis in a glorious cause & none of us can do enough. . . .

I fear you must be tired and 'tis nearly Sunday morning. May God bless and keep you, Bettie. Your promise to remember me is ever present with me, particularly do I recall it when in danger.

Your sincere friend

Walter

23

[To Bettie]

[Undated, probably ca. Aug. 15, 1863]

I met an officer today just from Vicksburg, or Miss rather, and learned from him much in regard to our recent operations in that quarter, and how matters now stand. I trust that the Court of Enquiry which has been ordered will exonerate our friend General Pemberton, but certainly there was great mismanagement somewhere, and we lost ever so much simply for the reason that a good head to assume general direction of affairs in that section, was wanting.[88] With the combined forces of Pemberton and Johnston the Confederates could have met the enemy on nearer an equality, as regards numerical strength than was ever the case with this army in its engagements with the Federal army of the Potomac—28,000 in Vicksburg, Johnston a similar number, making a total of 56,000! Grant certainly hadn't over 100,000 at the time when we all expected Johnston would move. I don't think he had 75,000—But put it at 100 & they were less than two to one. At Chancellorsville, one of our most sanguinary engagements, the Yankees had

69

over three to our one, & indeed Posterity will be astounded when the real facts are made known and our comparative weakness in numbers is exposed to public view. Now our troops in the West are in every respect equals of those here in Virg[a]. Why is it then that we never succeed there? Simply because they need a leader. We must have another great Captain. This is the cause humanly speaking. God alone knows what other & greater reasons there may be.

I was rejoiced to hear from my western friend that your brother, John, had arrived in Richmond and as I this morning approved a furlough for Hunter, I hope you will all have a happy family gathering & that you will be able to pay your Mother & Sister a short visit with the boys.[89] I like to hear of your being in the country, for I am satisfied that you will then get plenty of fresh air and exercise. Is John pleased with his position in the West? I have often wished that he had not left this army. Our artillery is now organized on a splendid footing, and in every battle is remarkably efficient. The artillery officers also have a fine chance for distinction. The batteries Jno formerly had have been unfortunate, their commander does not appear to have realized the anticipations formed of his ability. The battalion of which they form a part is said to be in a worse condition than any other in the army.[90] I am glad, that our friend Major Frank is in a different command. I am trying my best to help him on with an additional star, and have good reason to think that he will receive it—but as it would be premature, please say nothing of it.[91] If Jno had remained he would have stood a fine chance for advancement. However he may have attained this with Pemberton, for I really am ignorant of his rank at present. I am very sorry I could not see our John but rejoice to hear that he is so well and hearty.[92] I would run to Richmond to see him, but fear that Ma may soon arrive and I could not get away twice even if I succeeded in one instance, which I regard as a matter of doubt. . . .

I heard of Mrs. Heth's arrival in Orange & determined I would go to the village once, at any rate, and pay her a visit. I found her very well & together with the general (her general) we took a most delightful ride.[93] She has paid Genl Lee one visit, and I was told this morning that she and Mrs. Walker (Miss Mercer) were coming here this evening but they did not. . . .[94]

As for Julia, in spite of the old age which, according to her own account is gradually coming on her, I am persuaded she will never, save for short periods, be otherwise than cheerful.[95] But, indeed they have much to bear, theirs is apparently a most unenviable lot just now.

How humiliating it must be to have such witches in power over one, to control, to order one's every act! God grant that my poor, persecuted Mother's next effort to escape from their tyranny may prove more successful. Certainly she has been sorely tried. . . . [End of letter not found]

24

Camp near Orange CHo.

21st Aug. 1863

You are a charming comforter, Bettie, and the dearest and best of women. I am better satisfied since the receipt of yr. letter with its assurances of sympathy and its words of encouragement than I could possibly have been at the reception of any promotion or other official manifestation of approbation from the War Department or my commanding General. What would poor man do, what would he be worth but for the softening, purifying, all powerful influence of his most precious gift, his highest treasure—woman!? Whenever I am harassed by an accumulation of miserable paper calling for my attention or annoyed by any imaginary unreasonableness or ill temper on the part of my Chief, how much it adds to my patience and stimulates me to greater efforts to perform my duty manfully with a single eye to the good of our cause, when I imagine your face looking over my shoulder with its encouraging smile and an approving look in those dark fathomless eyes, so pure, so irresistible in their expression? Ah! my good angel, it is a sweet and yet a sad reflection to me, to think of the unlimited control exercised over my whole life, my every act, by my intense desire to win and be worthy of you. Sweet, because it is very pleasant to have as an additional incentive to good deeds the desire to do that which will please one so dear to me, and because I am happy in the thought that you are my best earthly friend and are really interested in my welfare; and yet sad because when I contemplate the future and the probability of—But please forgive me. I did not desire to encroach upon the forbidden ground. I must not interrupt our present most agreeable relationship, only to cause you displeasure and sorrow, and me a still greater deprivation than that I have already sustained. Just look over these few lines, dear Bettie, (please let me say it in an innocent and friendly way) and pardon my weakness, my frequent

71

repetition of this weakness, but remember the cause of its manifestation & be lenient.

I could hardly realize as I read and re-read your letter,—your nice
comforting letter that it was really from you. It is the greatest treat that
I have enjoyed for many, many months. You know, Bettie, here-to-fore,
or <u>recently</u> rather, I have shared your enclosures with Hunter or Mr.
Hobson; but in this instance it was all mine, for my own special benefit
and from you. And it appeared so natural to me to receive letters from
you, and so recalled our earlier days of friendship, that I was almost
persuaded that the past two years of reserve and estrangement was but
a troublesome, bad dream; and I am so happy, Bettie, that you could
once more treat me in an unreserved manner and with the familiarity
proper between two old and very dear friends. How shall I account for
this? Are you just becoming my friend? Have you heretofore only
imagined that you were such, only endeavored to be such from motives based upon an imaginary debt of gratitude an expression of
which you have frequently given utterance? Or is it indeed explained
in that part of your letter wherein you tell me that you have to a great
extent conquered your regard for "what the world thinks"?[96] However I am too truly grateful for the pleasant change to care much for
discussing the causes which have influenced it. It is enough for me to
see and feel that it has occurred. If you know and choose to do so, you
can inform me on this point, and if you do not, I am satisfied to remain
in blissful ignorance.

I fear my letters will appear remarkable to you because of exces-
sive tautology and want of connection, but it is absolutely impossible
for me to write three consecutive sentences without being as many
times interrupted by some courier or soldier. I wish I could go out here
into the woods and devote an hour exclusively to communing with
you, free from intrusion and all annoyances, but I do not intend to offer
any apology, for you are not hypercritical and know full well how to
make allowance for the short comings of your friends. I commenced
this letter on yesterday and from present appearances and my past experience, I judge it will require a fortnight for its completion provided
I say all I wish to & the enemy keeps quiet.

I received a kind letter a few days since from, well—you couldn't
guess who in a year and you will be as much surprised as I was—from
Miss Ella Carrington.[97] She informs me that her father has purchased a
new place 2 1/2 miles from Richmond & gives me a most kind & cordial invitation to her "Sunnyside" home and begs that I will extend the

same in her name to all my Norfolk friends—that they will always regard the Norfolk people as relatives &c, &c. Better than this, she sent
me a lot of the nicest tomatoes and other vegetables & promised if I
will not take it amiss (no danger) to send us a box of nice things. Of
course these little attentions are all for General Lee but I will enjoy the
goodies nevertheless. . . . The news from the enemy in our front is that
they are sending some troops (one or two corps) down the Potomac,
their destination supposed to be Charleston.[98] Old Sumter seems to be
in jeopardy. They may succeed in battering it down but even when we
have to leave it, it will be untenable for the enemy and at this stage of
the proceedings this will be an anomalous position truly for the old
fort, the original bone of contention. Some houses in Charleston, even
the whole city, may be destroyed but I don't think Yankee troops will
ever occupy it.[99]

. . . I wish it was in my power to attend church service oftener than
I do, for I feel a great need of spiritual nourishment. Not once in 3
months do I get to church! Frequently, when I have endeavored to do
so without success I have been called upon during the hours I would
have been absent to attend to matters which could only be decided by
myself, so I have almost given up all expectation of getting to church
until I am relieved of my present duties or receive a leave of absence.

Even on the day of Fasting & Prayer I was occupied all day unable
to obey orders as to its observance or follow the bent of my inclination.

. . . May God bless & keep you. Yr friend

Walter

Chapter 2

Campaigning along the Rapidan
October to December 1863

(Letters 25–37)

---

*U*ntil after Gettysburg Bettie discouraged correspondence. Now begin Walter's virtually weekly letters to her that form the bulk of the correspondence henceforward. At first their focus is on the military, but he soon begins to confide his deepest romantic and religious sentiments to her.

There is an eight week gap in the letters here. During part of that time Walter was on leave in Richmond. He settled his mother, who had at last escaped Norfolk, and successfully courted Bettie. In September, during his leave, she evidently accepted his proposal of marriage, on the conditions that the engagement be secret, and that the wedding be postponed until after war's end. Note the possessive pronoun in the salutations.

For three months following Gettysburg the contending armies remained inactive, licking their wounds. However, Lee set out the middle of October in a limited offensive to turn the right flank of the Army of the Potomac, which then occupied a line north of the headwaters of the Rapidan river. The move, via Warrenton, compelled Meade to withdraw across the Rappahannock and retreat northeastward along the line of the Orange and Alexandria R.R. In a costly and mismanaged attack A. P. Hill's corps struck his rear guard at Bristoe Station.

25

Camp near Bristoe Station,
Orange & Alexa Rail Road

15 Octo 1863

I have been constantly on the move, my dear Bettie, since leaving Richmond, & we have now reached this point without bringing the enemy to a general engagement. They seem to be by no means anxious to gratify us in this particular, & manifest an earnest desire to reach their

74

stronghold near Alexandria. I am afraid that we will not be able to force them to a battle. We have had some few trifling affairs, but nothing worthy the name of a fight. Our men are in excellent spirits & condition and with God's help, if we do meet Meade's army, we will give a good account of ourselves.[1]

From time to time I have made inquiries after Mr. Jno Hobson & up to yesterday he was unhurt. I tell you this that you may let your sister know as I'm sure he has not been able to write himself.

When we finish this little business now on hand, I will write you all the particulars of the movement, & merely send this to inform you where our army is & what 'tis doing, as Richmond is I presume filled with vague rumors. I do not think we will bring the Yankees to a fight today & after they get to Alexa hardly know what we will do. Cross into Maryland I <u>hope</u> but fear not. God bless you—Sincerely yours

Walter

26

Camp near Bristoe Station
Orange & Alexa Railroad

17 October, 1863

It is one week today, my dear Bettie, since I left Richmond to rejoin the army. Since that time we have been constantly on the march until yesterday, when we halted for rest and for the purpose of destroying the railroad and in other ways placing impediments in the way of any advance on the part of the enemy this Fall. On reaching the cars on Saturday morning, I for the first time received positive information from our special messenger of the army having commenced to move the day previous. This gave it nearly two days start of me, but I resolved to overtake it that night if possible. On arriving at Gordonsville we were all intensely disgusted to learn that positive orders had been left that no officers or soldiers should be allowed to proceed to Orange, or to start after the army until further orders. But by applying my all powerful "open cesame" I obtained horses for myself & messenger & in less than an hour after the arrival of the train was on the road to Madison CHo. at which point the army halted the night previous. The animal I rode was a poor one, but by the assistance of the courier, who applied a switch behind & my own switch & spurs, I managed to reach

HeadQrs by eight o'clock at night. It was a good ride of 32 miles as I started after half past one. I was determined however to catch up that night, if twas the last work performed by the old government beast I was using. I am glad to say he did not suffer & started on his return the next day quite gaily. On Sunday we continued our march for Culpeper CHo, where the enemy had been in position, with a view to reaching his flank or forcing him to retire. On reaching a point 5 miles from the Court House we learned that Meade had taken refuge on the farther side of the Rappahannock river & it was necessary to try another flank movement. On Monday therefore we started for Warrenton by way of Warrenton Springs. On reaching the river near this latter point our progress was opposed by the enemy who held the opposite side. We very soon succeeded in driving him away & forcing a passage at the ford. Had Pattie and Maria seen me there, they would undoubtedly have concluded that I was in search of that furlough wound about which we talked.[2] The General & the rest of us had taken positions on a high hill commanding a view of the river and the ground for which we contended. Between us & the river was a large plain or piece of low ground over which our skirmishers extended & I wandered to the foot of the hill just as the advance was sounded & the brave fellows moved forward with their usual shout or Confederate yell, as 'tis called. Without any reflection I was carried along with them until I neared the road leading to the ford, when I saw a squadron of Cavalry detached from one of our regiments and charge handsomely down to the river— through and over it—scattering the Yankees before them. It was a pretty sight & the desire to follow was irresistible & away I went just as the second squadron charged over. But the enemy made no stand and the infantry was soon streaming over the bridge which the enemy in his haste had been unable to destroy. We camped near the Springs that night & passed them the next day on our way to Warrenton. Of course they are torn to pieces & completely destroyed. One house alone is standing & all looks desolate. We reached Warrenton early on Tuesday & there remained til Wednesday. The citizens were rejoiced to see us & were exceedingly kind in extending to us their hospitality &c. I felt it due to one young lady with whom I was conversing to account for my exceeding stupidity by telling her that I was suffering very much from Neuralgia—this seemed to excite her sympathy & in a short while she had prepared for me the nicest cup of hot coffee that I have enjoyed for a long time. One lady insisted on my going to her house & taking a room, another sent me an ointment; indeed altogether I was quite overpowered by their kindness, but thank Heaven, I was soon relieved of all pain, and am now myself again. On Wednesday, we left Warrenton & reached this place the same day. Here Hill's advance met a corps of the enemy and at once engaged it. Our other corps came up in good time & we ought to have punished them severely but matters were not managed properly & they all escaped us & what is still worse they got the best of what little fighting there was. Our people were not put in battle correctly, too few of one corps being engaged and the other not having its line of battle in the proper direction. By an unpardonable mismanagement the Yankees were allowed to capture five pieces of our artillery and I have felt humiliated ever since. There was no earthly excuse for it, as all our troops were well in hand & much stronger than the enemy. It was a shameful affair and whilst I am unable to say who was responsible I regret that nearly every one who dares to speak openly blames our friend Genl. H—— (your cousin's husband).[3] However its all over now. The next morning it was discovered that the enemy had retreated towards Centreville and behind their fortifications to which place I presume we will not follow them. For the past two days we have been destroying this railroad which is highly essential to them in their "on to Richmond" and from present indication I think as heretofore that a general engagement is improbable & that the fighting in this state is pretty much over. The enemy will hardly make any serious advance this winter and next June you know we are to have Peace. See if I am a prophet!

As I passed along day before yesterday, I was sorry to see Duncan Robertson superintending the burial of some of his company, though unknown ones to me.[4] One named Cole was killed & one named Willie Robinson had both arms blown off & afterwards died. Besides these Alfred Simmons lost an arm & a soldier named Carr was also wounded. These are all from Company F.[5]

Poor Capt. Tom Barraud was mortally wounded & I fear is already dead.[6] His cousin May Baker told me on yesterday morning that he was then dying & unconscious. I feel so sorry for his poor wife.[7] May God help her.

I wrote you a day or two ago that Mr. Hobson was unhurt up to that time; as his regt. has not been reported in any engagement since then I presume he is still safe and sound.

We have taken about 1500 prisoners, forced the enemy back to Alexandria & Centreville without any general battle & gained from him for a time at least a large portion of our State. This, in a few words, sums up the results of the late move—and I cannot but think it well for us that it has been ordained that we should accomplish this without a battle and its terrible concomitants.

I anticipate but little active service now before we go into winter quarters.

I was surprised to see how very naturally I resumed my old position and duties. It is very different tho the life I now lead and that I have enjoyed during the past month. I could but contrast, as I meditated in my tent last evening, my position then with what it was a week previous. And I certainly rejoiced that I did not leave Richmond Thursday as I contemplated, for then I should have missed that pleasant walk to Hollywood yesterday week, which I delight so to look back upon.[8] Indeed <u>all</u> my reminiscences connected with my visit to R. as well as to "Howards Neck" are of the happiest character, as Starke forced me to tell him by some of his allusions & questions.[9]

I received a note from your brother John this morning, dated Richmond, so I presumed he has retd. from the Neck.[10] Tell him I will do all I can to advance his wishes and advise him of anything favorable that may occur. I hardly think Snowden Andrews will consent to leave the field, though it is possible he may do so to take Col. Rhett's place as 'tis both a pleasant and an important one. . . .[11]

My chances for visiting the Neck Christmas are pretty blue but I cannot tell yet, I may be able to go when the time comes. I would be very glad if I could meet you there at that time, but will not complain if this is denied me for really my precious, God has blessed me exceedingly and far above my deserts. Even now as I write to you, my own Bettie, my heart overflows with thankfulness for the many mercies & particularly the last & crowning one, bestowed upon me by a Kind Father.[12] May God teach me to be truly thankful, make me worthy of you & keep you safely prays your sincere W.

A few days later the Army of Northern Virginia returned to the south bank of the Rappahannock River, leaving at Rappahannock Station a fortified bridgehead on the north side. Over two weeks passed quietly, as Meade's army approached the river. On the night of November 7, however, the tête-de-pont, in a surprise attack, was overrun, and most of the men in the two brigades of Early's division manning it were captured. This unexpected turn of events rendered Lee's defensive position untenable, and he withdrew the army to the

south bank of the Rapidan, whence it had started out a month and a day before
for Bristoe Station.

27

Camp near Rappahannock

Sunday 25 Octo 1863

My last to you, my dear Bettie, was written yesterday a week from Bristoe Station. On the day following we took up our march in this direction, having accomplished the complete destruction of the Orange and Alexandria Railroad from Bristoe to the Rappahannock river, and there being no inducement to either man or beast longer to remain in that most barren section of country. Moreover—the enemy manifested no disposition whatever to meet us, and we would soon require a replenishing of our supply of provisions. Never have I witnessed so sad a picture as Prince William County now presents. Tis desolation made desolate indeed. As far as the eye can reach on every side, all is one vast barren wilderness—not a fence—not one acre cultivated—not a living object visible: and but for here and there a standing chimney, or the ruins of what was once a handsome and happy home; one would imagine that man was never here, and that the country was an entirely new one and without any virtue save its vast extent.[13]

Without any molestation whatever from the enemy, we reached the Rappahannock river by noon, and here, owing to the inefficiency, not to say imbecility, of our engineer corps, we were subjected to a tiresome & profitless delay of several hours, before the Ponton bridge was ready for the crossing of the troops. That evening, however, about one half the army with the General in Chief and Staff crossed to the south side of the river, and we pitched our tents in our present location, which by the way, being a bare eminence with a northern exposure is by no means a pleasant one whilst this cutting wind prevails; but tis one of my commander's idiosyncracies to suffer any amount of discomfort and inconvenience sooner than to change a camp once established. So the minor lights must submit, quietly, grin and endure. On Monday morning the balance of the army reached this side of the Rappahannock, and since then with the exception of one or two brilliant cavalry affairs, reflecting much credit upon our arms, we have had a period of quiet and inactivity, by no means unacceptable, after the exciting race of the previous week.

As soon as it was evident that Meade would not fight us, there was much talk amongst officers and men of a probable detachment of another large slice of our old army for duty in Tennessee.[14] But as the season for active operations was far advanced, I thought it extremely doubtful whether such a move would be determined on, or indeed whether it would promise any good results. This excitement seems to have subsided, and impelled no doubt by the very cold weather of the past few days, the men have turned their thought to the subject of winter quarters; and the all absorbing question at present is, "where will we winter!" Poor fellows! I wish we could provide comfortable houses & clothes for all of you, or even say where you will winter, that you might make such preparations for the cold as circumstances would admit. The last three days have been disagreeable, indeed as regards the weather dark and gloomy overhead with a pelting rain and a bleak northeasterly wind. . . .

Then at last, at the end of his third letter since his return from leave, Taylor permits himself to turn from military matters and express his joy at Bettie's capitulation.

What care I, personally, about these minor discomforts. I view the world and all around me through the medium of a pair of glasses as it were, which possess the happy faculty of magnifying all that is beautiful and virtuous and dissipating everything of an unpleasant nature which would force itself upon one. Indeed, Bettie, in the realization of my fondest hopes, I can scarcely persuade myself that tis not all a pleasant dream from which there must soon be a mournful recall. I am very happy. I wish I could make you know <u>how</u> happy! God bless you dear Bettie, my heart is filled to overflowing with love for you, and my soul expends its whole powers in its offering of thanks to Him who has so abundantly blessed me. . . .

I very often wish that I had a likeness of you, but I am aware of your aversion to having one taken, and for this reason I did not and will not request it. In its absence, however, I can find consolation in the thought that the original is mine, and indeed I always bear about with me, and have but to turn my eyes within to see, a most admirable picture of you, one far more faithful & beautiful than the photographist could make. Though not much given to building extravagant castles in the air, I delight, in thinking of the future, to place this picture and myself in a home of our own, and to dwell in anticipation upon the many ways and means I shall employ to make the original of the picture happy. Oh Bettie, you must! you will be happy for where there is such a will towards attaining an object as I possess in this, there must be a way & with God's help I'll secure it. . . .

I hope soon to hear from you. Yrs. sincerely

W.

[postscript omitted]

28

Camp near Brandy Station

31 Octo, 1863

My last, my dear Bettie, was written from this place, or rather from our old camp about a mile distant, on last Sunday, one week tomorrow. 'Tis now late Saturday night, and having finished my labors for the day—being in the enjoyment of a nice warm tent for I have had constructed a model chimney and fire place that work to a charm. I deem the time a most propitious one for a little confab with you, and to acknowledge the receipt of, and at the same time thank you for, your nice letter of Tuesday and Wednesday. . . .

Old Sandy is a dear fellow, and a sensible one, to take you to ride. I only wish I could return some of his many kindnesses and lend him Bella for your use.[15] The little nag is perfectly well and I know pining to have you ride her. Though she started from Richmond a day before I did she only reached me last Wednesday, and now I have no use for her, for Genl. Stuart when he was made aware that I had no horse sent me "Lilly Dandridge" a perfect little beauty, to use as long as I wanted her. She is a fine little thoroughbred, too small for Stuart, just the size for me, a pretty brown coat, full of life and elasticity and much admired by all who see her. Harry Wmson starts tomorrow or Monday for Elk Hill on foot.[16] I begged him to ride Bella & leave her at the Neck for Pattie's use but he will not ride. . . .

'Tis quite late, all are stored away for the night save me. My fire is out, the wind howls, and prudence tells me I must stop for the present, if I wish to meet the General at an early breakfast, and be fresh for tomorrow's work. As it will be Sunday, may the latter be very light. I will reread your precious letter, pray for you and then to sleep, I hope to dream of my nearest and dearest. Good night. . . .

Heaven's blessings be yours prays yr devoted

W.

29

Camp, near Brandy

7 November 1863

9 o'clock P.M.

This is my usual evening for writing, dear Bettie, and I had promised myself that pleasure but unfortunately we are all astir and I can only send a line or two to explain why I cannot write more. This morning about one or two o'clock the enemy advanced upon us at Kelly's ford on the Rappahannock river and at Rappahannock Station, effected a crossing at the former place and rushed upon our men (two brigades) who were at the latter place defending the bridge, overwhelmed & captured most of them.[17] Thus in a very few words I tell you the saddest chapter in the history of this army. There were captured about twelve or fifteen hundred men and a battery of artillery (4 pieces). Miserable, miserable, miserable management. But a bad beginning may make a good ending. We are all packed up and will move tonight. We are now on the outposts and this is not exactly the place for the Genl. Commdg. No sleep tonight and tomorrow an active, stirring Sunday. How singular it is that most of our battles & movements occur on that day when of all others we should most enjoy quiet and be most reminded of peace! But my precious, in the midst of all you see how constantly _you_ are in my thoughts. I could not allow our messenger to go to Richmond tomorrow without my letter, for I know not when another opportunity will be offered me. Genl. Meade means to fight, I think, and Genl. Lee will accommodate him but on ground of his own choosing. The issue with me is with God, but with His help I earnestly trust we'll be victorious.

I will tomorrow remember you are at Church and bear in mind that your prayers ascend in our behalf. May God listen to you and extend to us His assistance. I cannot tell you how much I want to see you, nor how very dear your letters are to me. I hoped this afternoon to receive a letter, not that I ought to have expected another so soon but I find myself anxiously watching every mail with the fond hope that it may contain one for me. Never mind, I know one will be here soon. Tell me, dear Bettie, that I am dear to you. Let me hear you say so. I anticipate a fight with feelings a little different from those experienced heretofore, for I flatter myself now that there is one who will be anxious about me, one solicitous for my safety and one who will earnestly pray for my preservation from harm. Tell me if this is not so with you, Bettie my dearest? God hear your prayers and protect me in the time of danger.

Though we have much to make us sad tonight, I am still buoyant with hope and am confident our men will acquit themselves handsomely. We have a brave lot and if we meet Meade tomorrow they will render a good account of themselves. May a kind Providence continue to protect us, may He guard, bless and keep you, my own Bettie, is the earnest prayer of your

Walter

30

Camp near Orange

14th Novem 1863

My dear Sister,

I only received yours of the 3d on yesterday. . . .

I hope you will carry out your intention of visiting the Lee family. Mrs Lee (the old lady) is very sweet and attractive.[18] I feel that I could love her. I <u>don't think</u> I could entertain the same for the Gen'l.[19] Go and see them by all means. I am glad Ma has been. The General has declined the house proffered him by the Council. <u>We</u> knew he would. I don't understand Mother's allusion to the loss of the General's horse—what horse? He has lost none—none that we know of here. And who in the world said his person was not well guarded? Is Mr Gatewood the person who has been entertaining you all?[20] Why I wonder if he knows

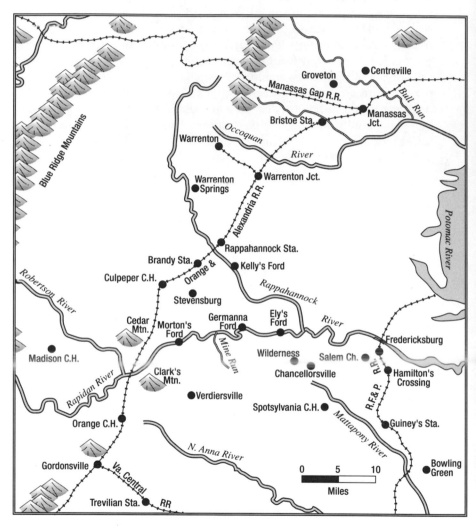

Map 3. Northern Virginia, 1862–1864

that the battalion of guides & couriers—Gnl Lee's Body Guard as they are pleased to call themselves—the "Guides, Scouts, Couriers, Detectives and Scamps" as we call them—always attend our Chief's person & never camp more than a mile from him. A good joke bro. G has played off on you all. Don't be alarmed. We aides will shield him from all danger. Ma appeals to me most pathetically to "see to this for the country's sake." I couldn't help reading this to my brother staff officers. We were considerably entertained because of her evident but unnecessary anxiety. Remember bro. G is very green—he's no soldier & wouldn't recognize danger in the field when he saw it. Rest easy ladies. I pledge you my word the Tycoon shall not be kidnapped. Whilst we were at breakfast this morning my tent took fire and my wardrobe & me were in great danger, but fortunately the boys extinguished it & save a yard or so of canvass destroyed, no harm was done.

Little May mustn't acquire the head ache habit that Nina and I had before her.[21] Let Nina study her own language as much as possible—also French—but protect her from Latin, Greek & too much algebra, sine cosine &c &c. Make her read good English! Love to all—yrs

Walter

Meade manifests no very determined disposition to catch up with us. Can't tell you what he intends doing. We are quietly awaiting events. Hold him in no fear whatever. The two brigades we'll say nothing about.[22] That was a sad accident—But not so bad save the disgrace. It does not weaken us much numerically and not at all morally. Let him come, & with God's help we'll maul him.

I must again caution you all against crediting the Richmond rumors, and earnestly hope you will deviate from the general custom in the Capital and always wear a smiling cheerful countenance. Remember as our trust is not in man, the loss of numbers of men will not affect the result. God is our sure help & upon our weakness will build up our strength.

Good bye again.

Yr devoted brother

Walter

31

[To Bettie]

Camp near Orange CHo

15 November 1863

For the first time I think since the commencement of the war Sunday has come upon me unawares. I had persuaded myself that it was to come on the 16th of the month and all day yesterday and this morning I have imagined that this was Saturday & contemplated writing you a letter tonight as usual. When George Peterkin came in just now and asked me if there was any objection to his going to attend service in Orange, I was highly entertained at his having, as I thought, gained a day. How I made such a mistake I cannot tell. As the roar of artillery is again heard this morning, I hasten whilst time is left me to acknowledge the receipt of yours of last Sunday and to thank you my dear Bettie, for all that it contains. I cannot tell you how anxiously I watch the mails when the time arrives when I think I may reasonably expect a letter. When there is none, I bear my disappointment like a Trojan and patiently await another day. And when the earnestly longed for favor makes its appearance I almost tremble with delight. Oh Bettie, my precious one, your letters are very dear to me. When I read them, I am almost transported with joy to see that you are my own truly my own. My happiness is almost too great when I perceive that you too look forward to our future with anticipations of a happy life together. When we shall be all in all to each other. When I shall study and labor, oh! so earnestly and faithfully to secure your comfort and happiness. Hitherto, dear Bettie, my devotion for you has struggled alone under most adverse circumstances, it could not develop itself because it was unrequited: 'twas not encouraged; but now that it meets with reciprocal sentiment on your part, now that I can properly remove the restraint which I always imposed upon it, it assumes mammoth proportions, it absorbs my whole being. Did I not feel very secure, yes, did I not recognize the kind hand of Providence in bringing us thus together finally after my many hopes, fears and prayers, I should tremble indeed when I realize how entirely dependent I am upon you; when I have to confess that you are all to me, light, life, everything. . . .

But little of importance has occurred in the army since my letter or note of last Saturday. From the papers, you have no doubt learned of our movement to the south side of the Rapidan. Contrary to my expectations the enemy was very tardy in pushing his advantage, after our misfortune at Rappanhannock Station. Soon after my note to you was dispatched, we struck tents, packed the wagons and sent them to the rear—only moving ourselves about twelve o'clock. Before leaving our camp we built the most immense fires in all our new chimneys, to show how nicely they would draw; and wrapped in my overcoat, I stretched out in front of mine upon a pile of straw and soon lost consciousness in a sweet sleep. I was presently awakened by an exclamation from the General addressed to those around to the effect that Major Taylor was a happy fellow, meaning that I could sleep, whether circumstances were propitious or the reverse, at any time. After the chimneys themselves, as well as the wood in the fire places, were consumed, for we were determined the Yankees should not reap the profits of our industry and skill, we commenced our march for the point where it had been arranged HdQtrs should be established for the anticipated engagement. So soon as we arrived there, it being yet some hours before day, the "happy fellow" again composed himself to sleep and awoke about day with a thought of his absent dear one and ready for Meade or "the newest fashions"—(Pray excuse the slang).

But the Yankees were apparently satisfied; at all events evinced no desire to bring on a general engagement and permitted us to remain in line of battle all day Sunday without any serious molestation. Sunday night, in pursuance of the original design of the General, we resumed our march for the Rapidan and encamped on the south side of that river that night. A day or two afterwards we changed camp to our present location—one much nearer Orange CHo. more central to the army and more convenient to all parties. It is a camp of my selection and I am pleased to see it gives general satisfaction. I hope we may have as nice a one for the winter, if we do not remain where we are.

When the thundering of the artillery commenced this morning, a message was received that the enemy was attempting a passage of the river at one of the lower fords; the whole army was at once signaled to be under arms and ready for battle and the General, with all the Staff save me, started for the front. I was left to attend to whatever should arrive in the General's absence, and was to follow when convinced there was really to be a battle and when there was no longer any necessity for my remaining at HeadQtrs. So I have had a nice quiet time to write and what is the best part of it, I have been relieved of all anxiety about the threatened battle, by the receipt of a signal message informing Genl. Lee that the movement was only a cavalry demonstration. So there will be no fight today. When it does come we have no fears as to the result. Don't you mind what you hear in Richmond, wait for my letters, I will always, when it is possible, keep you promptly advised of what is transpiring here. It is needless for me to admonish you as I did Mother yesterday, not to follow and put faith in Dame Rumor, and to deviate from the fashion in the capital, always wear a cheerful, hopeful countenance. Above all, don't wound our pride by feeling any apprehension on our account. Don't imagine that the enemy are to have it all their own way. Our confidence in God and our own strong arms is by no means impaired, and it is not flattering to see our good people doubtful of our ability to manage our old enemy, so often fairly beaten by this army. You ask if there is any prospect of our falling back to Richmond. I see none now. The enemy, I trust, will never force us back so far. I cannot say what we may be compelled to do through a want of forage for our animals; this depends on the departments in Richmond. Personally I would be gratified to be so near you; but with you I think of the country which would be laid open to the enemy and the people who would be exposed to their tyranny and I pray we may never relinquish again so much of the Old Commonwealth. I only wish the General had good Lieutenants. We miss Jackson & Longstreet terribly.[23] Poor Ewell[24]—a cripple—is now laid up and not able to be in the field. . . .

I was very sorry to hear of Mayhew Hobson's death.[25] Poor Mrs. H.—she looked so comfortable and happy when I saw her at home. When I thought how happily fixed the three brothers were, with their beautiful homes, I little dreamed how soon one would be taken away. I received a letter from [for] Mr. John H. a few days ago, enclosed to my care from Pemberton.[26] It was post marked 9th & reached here on the 12th. I presumed it was about his brother and sent it over by a special courier. Mr. Hobson had just been to Stuart's HdQ. to try and get a leave of absence and there learned of his brother's death. I am sorry that he cannot go home now, but Genl. Stuart tells me there is but one Lieut. with his Co. Apart from this, which would preclude any merriment at the Neck so soon as Christmas, I very much fear that my chances for a leave so recently after my last are quite poor. But I can ride to Goochland in a day and when you go there, I shall certainly do likewise if practicable, and if my stay must be limited to one day.[27] Our Staff is very small now and is growing smaller. Two of them, I know, will expect to visit their families next month. This leaves but one other besides me. I expect to lose my tent mate Venable.[28] He is the only congenial spirit I have here, and I shall miss him very much. He is a great friend of Col Preston's and the latter wished him to take a place with increased rank in the Conscription Bureau.[29] I think he will take it. He has a wife and two children & has seen 3 years field service. He consulted me and I advised him to go. The truth is Genl. Lee doesn't make our time pleasant here & when promotion is offered his staff elsewhere, it is not to be wondered at if they accept the offer. Don't say anything of this as Venable has told no one else. As for my promotion, please don't expect it; for I shall feel badly if you think I should advance and I do not. I only care for it on your account but Genl. Lee will not push us up tho every body else goes. I have given over all expectation of being more than a Major—certainly as long as his say governs the matter.[30]

I heard from Frank Huger a few days since. He had just received a letter from Fanny Kerr. Said she was well but not in good spirits. I don't wonder at it, she must have written about the time of Dr. Wright's execution.[31] He tells me Fanny wishes to know if certain rumors regarding you and me are true. He seconded her in her request for information. I think my reply should have satisfied you. Tell Mrs. Jack Preston (that is if you choose) that when her husband applies for leave of absence I will be faithful to my promise & help him.[32] His application the other day was to join Genl. Hampton under orders[33]—that is on duty, & as Genl. H. was then en route to the army, it was not proper that the Major should go. My love to all at the Neck; to Pattie & Maria & Mrs Petty.[34] Are my letters too long? Goodbye. God bless you. All is quiet now. Your W.

I am glad to say there has been a change of opinion, as regards the person most responsible for the Bristoe Station misfortune. Genl. Heth is not so much blamed. I intended mentioning this before.

Walter

32

[To Bettie]

Camp near Orange CHo

21 Novem 1863

Having a little quiet this morning and the time being most opportune, I have determined to take time by the forelock and not allow Saturday to slip away as was the case last week without a letter to my absent dear one. Before my work begins I will at least have time to start my letter and hope for time to night or tomorrow to complete it. After a week of the most beautiful and pleasant weather this morning opened with a mist & warm rain, and as His Excellency the President is expected to arrive today on a visit to our army, we are all lamenting the departure of the good weather of the past week. . . .

There is nothing of interest appertaining to the army that I can tell you. Since my last letter of the 15th, we have been perfectly quiet. Nor has the enemy displayed any activity whatever. They must now move very soon or settle down quietly for the winter. Though the week has been a quiet one in most respects, the monotony of camp life has been somewhat relieved by some little gayety and at our camp by visitors. Custis Lee came up some days since and as I was better acquainted with him than the balance of our party,[35] I have thought it a good time to carry out my intentions, formed sometime since, of taking more exercise and sticking less closely to my office papers. So I have been roaming about the country and enjoying myself generally, sometimes being absent whole mornings; but then at night I pay dearly for the pleasure & am so worried at the work which accumulated during my absence, that I determine to go out no more. But then again the mornings are so fine and the scenery so beautiful, that when next a ride is proposed, I cannot resist the great temptation. There is a prominent point about eight miles from our HdQrs, "Clarks Mountain"—from which we have the grandest view of the Blue Ridge and surrounding country for miles that I ever beheld. All the camps of the enemy too are exposed to our view— just below us as it were. I have often wished I had you with me to enjoy these rides & particularly this charming view from the mountain. . . .

Monday, Novm. 23rd.

I commenced my letter on Saturday, but did not enjoy that complete immunity from interruption which I hoped for and anticipated. On that day I was compelled to desist from writing and accompany the General to the cars to meet Mr. Davis, who arrived during a pelting rain, and immediately went to our camp. He spends the day with us and after dinner goes to a house in the neighborhood to sleep. Fortunately he finds our commissariat in excellent condition. We have recently had some nice presents—such as fresh butter, [I]rish and sweet potatoes, turnips, venison &c. So you see we poor soldiers sometimes enjoy very good fare. But you mustn't tell on us for it may put a stop to the contributions. Tomorrow we have a grand review of the 2nd army Corps, and on the day following one of the 3rd. Corps. Fortunately the weather yesterday and today has been propitious. Now it is fair, but there are some indications of snow. I think I shall avail myself of the opportunity afforded by His Excellency's presence and whisper a few private wants in the Executive ear. For example he must approve a "Staff bill" this Congress, & not pocket it as he did the last. This bill must give solid rank to the A.A.G. of a General commanding an army or a military department, and then Gen. Lee will be forced to advance me, and I shall be gratified because it will please a certain young lady, who shall be nameless but who, in the kindness of her heart, wishes the promotion and who is somewhat partial in her estimate of my claims and thinks I deserve it. I promise you, dear Bettie, I will advance if the war continues a few months longer. I cannot however, even to gratify my pride in this respect, wish for its continuance for the war cannot end too soon for me but, as I said, if it does continue, I will advance, if I leave my present position and enter the line again. You shall be gratified. . . .

With you to encourage me, I should feel equal to almost any task not beyond human powers. As far back as I can remember your smile has been all powerful with me—now more so than ever. It is everything to me and I could know no happiness without it. I feel far more equal to the battle of life now that I know that I shall have my own Bettie as my companion to encourage and cheer me. To have a home to return to lit up by your smile, Ah! Bettie, what happiness there is for me in the simple anticipation of such a blessing. When the reality shall come, my cup will really be filled to overflowing. Happy, happy, picture. When this is predicated on Peace, is it a wonder that I should long, oh so earnestly for that event? In that word now centres all my hopes of earthly happiness.

It is now Tuesday evening, for so constantly have I been occupied and interrupted that I have been forced several times to put my letter by. As it is already too long, I will proceed to finish it at once. The rain this morning prevented the review that was to have taken place and His Excellcy. seeing but little prospect of an opportunity to see and be seen by the army, returned to Richmond by today's train. Lee and Brown, his aides,[36] who tented with me accompanied him and, as Venable is absent seeing after the position offered him in the Bureau of Conscription, I am all alone and anticipated a quiet evening—but I was disappointed and for the past two hours I have been prevented from resuming my letter by the presence of a number of visitors. My tent is a comfortable one—rather I have two—and every night the Staff honor me with their company. 'Tis generally agreeable but tonight I was impatient because I desired to get this ready for tomorrow morning's mail. . . .

Give my love to Mrs Petty & to all at the "Neck" when you write. Heaven keep you prays yr

W.

At the end of November Meade crossed the Rapidan in an effort to turn Lee's right south of the stream. However, finding the latter's defenses at Mine Run too formidable, he called off the attack and make good his escape in the nick of time, for Lee had planned an assault on the Federal left that he hoped would result in a second Chancellorsville. Chagrined, Lee said sadly, "I am too old to command this army. We should have never permitted those people to get away."[37]

33

Camp near Orange

26 Nov. 1863

We are just on the eve of another move and although I sent you a long letter on yesterday, my precious Bettie, I cannot allow the mornings mail to depart without sending a few lines, giving you the latest news. This morning and afternoon all the indications favor the supposition that the enemy is moving down the river and we have been busy preparing for a counter move in the same direction. Matters seem to be drifting towards our old & renowned battle field, Chancellorsville and Fredericksburg. You are aware the enemy occupy the line of the Rapidan on the north side, we on the south side. They will in all probability move to Germanna ford near the confluence of the Rappahannock and Rapidan, where they will cross. Then as we will be advancing in that direction there will be a clash somewhere between that point & Fredericksburg. If God will be with us there shall be a 2nd Chancellorsville as there was a 2nd Manassas. We will make up for the late reverse in Tennessee.[38] I must confess that is a severe blow. But what else could have been expected from an army in which there is so much disaffection and growling amongst its leaders? Bad enough it is indeed and just where we needed a success too. But it cannot be remedied now and long faces won't improve it. Matters do not appear over bright for us, but you know "man's extremity is God's opportunity." Our cause being the just one, will in the end be espoused by Divine might and so be successful. We have all our arrangements made to move before dawn in the morning. I have just returned from the General's tent, where I have been assisting him in writing &c. and now must close and give all my attention to packing up my papers and office fixtures. Another <u>nice chimney</u> to go by the board! I really am glad the engagement is about to come off. We shall have it over and then subside into comfortable quarters for the winter. Your letter mailed on last Saturday only reached me this evening. I had not received a letter for a long time—none since yours written last Sunday, two weeks ago, but I was confident that either one was on the way to me, or that you had been prevented from writing by some good reason. As I told you last week, of course, I had given up all idea of any merriment at the Neck this Christmas. I have just forwarded a letter to Mr. Hobson from your sister. I trust she will soon recover from the effects of her confinement and fatigue in nursing Mr. Mahew.[39] Can it be possible that poor Mary Garnett is so sick as to cause apprehension that she may die soon?[40] Please give my love to her, Bettie, and tell her I often think of her. So young, so sweet, she is indeed a "shining mark." What a comfort to her friends it is to know that she has the Christian's hope of a blessed life hereafter. For three years I have carried the enclosed lines "There is no such thing as Death" in my testament, with some other little pieces. This is the Christian's view. To me it is a comforting one. I will endeavor to keep you informed of what occurs during the next few days. Keep a stout & hopeful heart—committing you to the keeping of a kind Providence & with many earnest prayers for yr happiness, I remain yr fond & devoted

Walter

Much love to Pattie, yr. Coz. Mary & all.

34

Camp near Orange

5 December 1863

It appears an age, my dear Bettie, since I have heard from you. . . .

I wrote you a short note on last Thursday week stating that we were on the eve of another movement. By the dawn of the next morning we were many miles from Orange on our way to meet Meade's army which had crossed to the south side of the Rapidan river. It was intensely cold that morning; we left camp at 3 o'clock, the moon was shining brightly, the ground frozen as hard as ice. It was so funny to notice the effects of the cold upon everybody's beard—all around one's mouth innumerable icicles hung appendant from moustache and whiskers, reminding one of the popular pictures of "Old winter." I tell you it was certainly cold. As usual the General was ahead of every one else and we arrived at Verdiersville without any army whatever, the troops not having yet gotten that far. During the morning the army caught up with us and we proceeded to advance towards Fredericksburg.[41]

In the afternoon we first met the enemy. On the right there was a little skirmishing—on the left Johnson's division met and severely chastised a Corps of the enemy[42]—at the same time our cavalry under Gen'l Rosser attacked and destroyed a large ordnance train in the enemy's rear.[43] With the exception of one other cavalry affair no more fighting of any consequence occurred. On Saturday we selected our position and proceeded to fortify it in the course of an incredibly short time (for our men work now like beavers); we were strongly entrenched and ready and anxious for an attack. The General gave his attention to the whole line, directing important changes here and there, endeavoring to impress the officers with the importance of success in the impending engagement and presenting a fine example of untiring energy and zest. He was busy the whole time.

On Sunday as we were riding down the lines attended by Gen'l Hill with his staff and others, we came upon a collection of men engaged in Divine worship. We had been riding at a pretty fair gait, but the Gen'l at once halted and listened to the singing of the men. He heard the whole sermon and then as the benediction was pronounced reverently raised his hat from his head—received the blessing and then continued his ride along the fortifications. It was a striking scene and one well calculated to impress solemnly all who witnessed it. The parapet was crowded with men—here and there at proper intervals waved the battle flag & from many dozen embrasures frowned the now silent artillery. This all looked exceedingly warlike and it was a cheering thing to see that whilst ready for action our men did not forget that to secure victory divine help should be implored and from that moment I felt even more hopeful than before.

On Monday we confidently looked for an attack—it passed without one. The enemy was in our immediate front and they too had entrenched themselves. This looked rather queer to see two large armies face to face each busily constructing works for defence. Tuesday came and went without any attack. Our Chief had now become impatient & seeing how reluctant the enemy was to bring on an engagement he determined to relieve them of further embarrassment by becoming the aggressor and forcing them into a fight. Consequently during the night two fine divisions were relieved from the trenches and concentrated on our right, ready to be thrown on the enemy's left flank, & all necessary arrangements for a grand battle were completed before morning.[44] I was constantly awakened this night by couriers who were bringing information of the enemy's movements & everything tended to produce the belief that the next day we would again meet our old foe: but behold when day broke it was found that the enemy had fled & was fast making his way back towards the river. Pursuit was immediately ordered & made, but Meade had too much the advance of us and reached the north side of the Rapidan before we could overtake him.

Both armies then retired to their original positions. Undoubtedly we were most benefitted by the movement. We captured about 700 prisoners, 400 mules & horses, destroyed & secured some 1200 or 1300 wagons. Their loss in killed & wounded will reach perhaps 1000. So all things considered we may be said to have canceled Bristoe Station. A certain home feeling possessed me as we reentered our old camp and I felt very thankful that we were all safely back.

It was a bloodless victory for we enjoy all the moral effects of a victory without its inevitable distressing losses. Meade expected to take us unawares, turn our flank or force us from behind the fortifications on the Rapidan; or else he concluded that as soon as he crossed Gen'l Lee would retire to Hanover Junction. But he reckoned without his host for our General is not so easily frightened into a retreat or very readily change his front. I do not think it probable that the enemy will attempt another advance this season. I cannot say whether our General will or not. It is now getting pretty late and I dare say there will be no more fighting here this winter. If others in authority think this, it is just possible that the Gen'l and his personal staff will be sent west. Certainly some one is needed there but I confess I personally have no desire to leave Virginia and this brave old army. They had better send Beauregard and some twenty thousand of his troops, who could render much more service in opposing Grant than in witnessing artillery duels in Charleston Harbour.

Now that we are once more quietly established in camp the all absorbing question is "how soon can I obtain a leave of absence?" Numerous have been the inquiries of this sort addressed to me since our return. . . .

In a letter dated the first of the month Sister tells me that you had that day entered upon your new duties at the Medicine Purveyors and that you had told Maggie that you were much pleased.[45] This is a change you have not mentioned. I am rejoiced to hear that the position & its duties are to your taste. . . .

I am glad you have been able to visit the Neck though your stay was a short one & I hope your new interest will not prevent your enjoying a nicer, longer holiday soon. In returning from such scenes as you there witnessed to Richmond, it is not wonderful that the contrast is distasteful to you. But I am sure that my beloved Bettie after having determined what is right, she'll be happy in pursuing the course her judgment approves. Confident of this, I commend you to the keeping of a kind Providence with the prayer that you may be abundantly blessed with all that you can desire.

Your

W.

35

Camp near Orange

13 Decem 1863

The night is already far advanced, my dear Bettie, but I will at least devote what remains of it to the letter which should have been written to you on yesterday. Since the General left,[46] my work seems to have increased and so constantly have I been occupied that I have more than once resolved to do what I never did before, call for assistance. To add to my embarrassment the enemy's troops in the Valley have, since General Lee's departure, become exceedingly active; and between the many reports from the scouts and the exaggerated & stampeding telegraphic dispatches I receive, I sometimes am in doubt whether I am on my head or heels. They are reported moving up the Valley, and from the Kanawha and from Beverly and every which way.[47] Of course every commander thinks they are making for him, with special design of giving him battle. All want assistance, indeed express the opinion that it is all important that aid be sent them. They remind me of the good citizens I was accustomed to meet in Western Virginia. Every one seemed firmly impressed with the idea that the General and the troops on the opposite side were in the field solely with the view to his capture and destruction and would have you believe for this alone the war was waged. All yesterday, last night and this morning, I have been harassed by these miserable telegrams. I don't believe half of their contents and yet it is a terrible responsibility to assume, to disregard them. I desire to keep Genl Lee fully informed of what really occurs and is important for him to know, and yet he so dislikes to be unnecessarily annoyed by false or exaggerated reports, that I hesitate to be the medium of conveying uncertain statements. Then, I must keep Generals Ewell and Stuart thoroughly posted & altogether it is such a trial "playing commanding general," that I have concluded never to accept that position, when the Government awakes to a sense of my merit to tender it beseechingly to me. All jesting aside, I only hope the General will get back before I forget some serious matter or make any unfortunate blunder.

Chilton is away on leave of absence and my chum and tent mate, Venable, is off again early in the morning to spend Christmas at his home.[48] This leaves but two of us here. I think seriously of ordering an advance on Meade, or rather Pleasanton, as by the latest accounts he has superseded Meade.[49] You know they say "when the cat's away, the mice will play," and in the General's absence it is quite ludicrous to see the airs we small fry assume. I claim to be in command of the army and we have many jokes amongst ourselves on that point. Of course, we never trifle on these serious subjects outside of our family gathering, but here we feel privileged to do whatever we choose. I shall have to work even more zealously still when Venable goes; I make him— good fellow that he is—help me. I shall miss him much and fear that he will never return to us as I am quite confident he will accept the position in the Bureau of Conscription. Chilton's return is also extremely doubtful but on this particular, I am indifferent. You know the President appointed him a Brigr General, but the Senate refused to confirm the appt. Since then he has been quite unsettled and evidently desirous of returning to his old position in Richmond. He now says he will leave us unless Congress does him justice. I don't know what his views of

97

justice are, but others think that justice is the last thing he should desire. But I must not deal in such scandal. He must not be spoken of unfavorably by me, for my relation with him is a rather delicate one, and though I would be safe in your hands by others my motives might be impugned. You see he has the rank and credit of A.A.G. and I have the unthankful and unremunerative part of the position, namely the labor and the responsibility. So I must be silent—only I shan't cry if he doesn't return.[50]

You have undoubtedly heard of the General's presence in the city and of the many rumors to which it has given rise. It would be improper for me to speak openly even to you my dearest on this subject; but I may with perfect propriety whisper to you, for your information solely, that what I anticipated in my last letter, really occurred, but as yet no definite decision has been reached. I don't want to go out of Virginia or to leave this army, but personal considerations must yield to that which is now paramount to all else—the success of the cause. I received a letter from my Chief this morning in which he says that the Yankee army of the Cumberland is certainly falling back behind the Tennessee river. By the way, speaking of the Genl's letter reminds me that you once expressed desire to have the autographs of any of our great men. Thinking of this the other day I retained for you the original manuscript copy of an order issued by Genl Lee, setting aside Thursday last as a day of Fasting, Humiliation & Prayer, in accordance with the suggestion of the Legislature of Georgia.[51] I have also accidentally found one of that old hero, Jackson's letters to me, with notes from others which I shall preserve for you. In the future they may be valuable as mementoes and thoughts addressed to me and it will be perfectly natural and proper for them to be in your possession. I so much wish I had kept a Journal during the whole war and wonder why I did not, for certainly it would in after days have proved a source of enjoyment to have reviewed it. What would have answered the same purpose, I wish I had all the while been privileged to be your correspondent, for then I would have attempted to describe all of interest that occurred.[52] Though I must be blamed alone for not keeping the Diary, I plead not guilty on the score of the missing correspondence. My memory is poor and I fear I will forget much of interest that has transpired under my observation, but I join you, my precious, in the wish that one of these days I may have the pleasure of visiting with you that portion of the state that has furnished us so many battlefields, and of describing to you, as well as I can remember, all that was remarkable or worthy of note. Oh if that time would only arrive! Bettie, dear Bettie, I do so earnestly <u>long</u> for it. If the war could only be terminated, what would I not give? To have you made my own, own Bettie, my dearest inseparable companion, the sharer of my joys for life and eternity! . . .

As regards <u>my</u> morning rides, bless you my dearie, I have not enjoyed one since the Presid^t was here and for a week have been deprived of my afternoon half hour's gallop. Yesterday morning however I went to Church, rather a rare thing for me, because not often in my power to do. . . .

I have just received a telegram from the General. It requires some attention and I reluctantly put aside my letter, to be finished tomorrow. I am sorry it will not go by tomorrow's mail.

Monday afternoon— Having now a little respite and the telegraph for the moment being quiet, I will resume my pleasant occupation and endeavor to have my letter ready for the next mail. I had occasion a few moments since to send some letters to Genls Meade & Halleck by flag of truce.[53] I didn't know when such another opportunity would occur and availed myself of the occasion to send a short note to Fanny Kerr. As I knew no other direction but Baltimore, I fear she will hardly receive it. . . .

I am glad you girls are forcing those Richmond gentlemen into the army by performing their accustomed duty and regard the innovation as a decided improvement. Only you must not make yourself sick by attempting too much work. I shall pay special attention to those you mention and see that they are placed in a good position to <u>realize</u> a battle. There is no difficulty about Hunter's furlough. I will write him tomorrow to put in his application and I will arrange it. I can do this <u>consistently</u> & feel that I am not partial simply to gratify you. The "interests of the service" will allow the indulgence. I hope you will have a happy family gathering, and that next Christmas <u>I too</u> may be one of the number included in that circle. God bless you—prays your

W.

36

Camp near Orange

20 December 1863

Since my return from church this morning, my dear Bettie, I have been constantly occupied with work and visitors. I have completed all of the former for the time and have just seen Master Robbie off,[54] and will now indulge myself and enjoy a chat with you; though I judge that it is highly probable that when what I am now writing reaches Richmond, you will have left it for "the Neck." ... Only think but one day's ride with Bella. I am confident she would accomplish it in that easily. One day's ride and I would be with you! Isn't it trying & too provoking to have this happiness so near me, and yet not to be able to experience it. I am signing leaves of absence all day long, right and left, and still the "interests of the service" will not allow me just this little favor.

Oh what a wicked thing is this war! But I <u>will</u> be jolly in spite of it. Like Mark Tapley, I'll make it a <u>habit</u> to be jolly, even under adverse circumstances.[55] I declare I sometimes reproach myself for being so very light hearted—but you know how great reason there is for my happiness; and can fully comprehend how I wear a smiling face in spite of the unhappy condition of the country. Now though I shall have but a very ordinary time next week,—won't I be content when I remember that you are enjoying a holiday in Goochland, surrounded by those who are dearest to you, and from some of whom you have been so long separated? This will be Christmas enough for me. But if Mr Surgeon General or any body else should dare to place any impediments in the way, to deny this, then I should get angry and wouldn't be charitable in my estimate of the official's character, be the disobliging individual who he may. I hope and believe however that you will be allowed to go—it would be downright cruelty if you were not. How I wish I could have your "Ledger" for a few days. You should then have no back work to annoy you at least. Are you pleased with the change? My only fear is that it may keep you too constantly occupied—but if you once get the work up to date—that scamp Thinier's delinquencies[56]—I am satisfied you will be able to accomplish all that is required of you—to get along smoothly with the <u>current work</u> in the same time as was required at the Treasury Department. It must be some consolation to you girls to think that each of you, by occupying your present positions, relieves an able-bodied, strong man and adds one soldier to the Army in the field. Upon my word if the war continues much longer I expect to see the women of our land relieve the men of all character of work except the actual fighting. It will be convincing evidence of the earnestness of the people. And then after the war the men will feel that they cannot do too much to show their appreciation of such conduct. If there is any virtue in <u>my</u> earnest resolution, <u>you</u> certainly shall have a nice time to make amends for all you now endure.

My Chief is still in Richmond. Christmas is near so it would be but natural for him to remain with his family during the week, but it will be more in accordance with his peculiar character, if he leaves for the Army just before the great anniversary to show how very self-denying he is.[57] You seem to be quite anxious on the subject of his probable removal from command of this army in Virginia. I view from what I hear that there has been much discussion as to who was the best man available to take charge of Bragg's army; but the General in a letter to me a few days since, says he thinks it has been finally determined not to remove him from the Army of Northern Va.[58] Are you not glad? I cannot tell you how rejoiced I am to hear this. I was very much troubled on this subject for apart from consideration of the public good, I should have regretted very much the necessity which removed me so far from those most dear to me. When thinking of it lately, I have been quite sad at the idea of leaving you so far behind me and with so little prospect of hearing from you with any regularity. But I wouldn't let you see this and now my doubts and fears are all scattered to the winds. I'm myself again. I shall constitute a part of this old army. We'll have a quiet time in winter quarters where I shall have the satisfaction of hearing from you every week. We'll do our utmost to raise the numerical strength of the army to bring it to its greatest state of efficiency and then in the spring with a little addition to our numbers, to come from some unimportant point where they have too many troops—Charleston for example—then I say we'll cross Mason and Dixon's line the third time, and trust me—we'll stay there. With God's help I believe this army can do it. The "Reports" of the battle of Gettysburg show how very near we came to conquering Peace there and the next time, God willing and helping, we'll not only come very near to, but we will have a glorious victory and perhaps peace. You will regard what I say about Genl Lee's movements and the intentions of the Department with respect to him as "state secrets" known only to the high officials, to the members of the staff and to you and me. This knowledge is too precious for the dear people. We mustn't tell it to the herd—though it is astonishing with what remarkable accuracy they divine what really transpires in Cabinet councils.

I have received information from Alexandria, this afternoon, up to the 17th inst. In Washington war has settled down into politics and the all absorbing excitement at this time is the Presidential campaign of '64. McClellan will be the "copperhead," peace, democratic nominee for the next Presidency, and the present administration will make ev-

101

ery exertion to secure the renomination by the Republicans of Abe Lincoln. There will be no more active operations—at least they will not take the aggressive—either here or in the army of the Cumberland during the winter. Convinced in their own minds of their ability to crush the rebellion at will, they will "revise the job" so as to avail themselves of the war influence in furtherance of Abe's renomination in the spring. I trust they will continue thus, confident of their ability to <u>crush</u> us, and will make no efforts to recruit their depleted ranks or add to their army, for all this will only serve to make our task the less difficult to perform.

I hoped to have it in my power to send a letter to Norfolk by the same medium through which I received the above information, but fear I cannot be ready in time. I wished to write Julia again as I am fearful the letters I have recently sent by the underground route will meet the same fatality as their predecessors. By the way, do tell me Bettie, is there any truth in these sad reports mentioned in the newspapers about Mrs Dr. Wright's death and the derangement of one of her daughters, Pennie I presume?[59] I do hope this is not so. Have you heard how they have served Mrs Wm E. Taylor and Miss Sallie?[60] Literally turned out of house and home! Oh what a reckoning there is against those people—Butler and his crew![61] Bob Taylor says his mother actually has been allowed to retain nothing and his father is compelled to resign his seat in the Senate to go to work to support them.[62] Bob expects <u>Mrs Taylor</u> to visit him here shortly.[63] He seems very happy and told me when he first returned from leave, that he hoped his marriage would make him a better man. He was once a regular communicant, indeed continued to be such up to the time of his visit to Europe—but now he appears utterly indifferent—it is fearful to hear the way in which he talks at times. It may be that this is the turning point in his life. What an influence Miss Lelia can exert now if she will! And truly I pray she may. If she does and my hopes for Bob are realized, all will be well & they'll be happy—but without <u>this,</u> there will be no real happiness.

Your cousin John Selden has his leave of absence and will start for Charlotte tomorrow so as to be at home xmas. . . .[64]

I saw Hunter a few days since. You may expect to meet him soon, if nothing happens to prevent. May you all have a very merry time. Especially, my precious, do I wish you a happy Christmas. I trust I may have the next one with you, that together we may be spared to enjoy many such, and that each in its turn may find us nearer <u>Him,</u> the anniversary of whose birth we shall on that day celebrate. My love to yr Mother, Sister, Pattie & all at the Neck; and to your Coz Mary in Richmond & to Maria & Miss Immie when you write.[65] God bless & keep you, dear Bettie. There was no letter for me tonight. I hope for tomorrow.

Yr. devo.

W.

37

[To Bettie]

Camp near Orange C. H.

27 Decem 1863

The weather was very unpromising this morning and we had already had one or two showers of rain before the hour for starting to Church had arrived. I had made up my mind not to leave my tent, when I perceived that the General's horse was being saddled and he was making his preparations to go to Church. I concluded if he could go, there was surely no reason why a strong young fellow like me should be deterred by bad weather. My horse was therefore ordered and he and I trotted off to Orange. We had scarcely left camp when the rain commenced in earnest, indeed one would have imagined that our movement was the signal for it. We proceeded at a pretty rapid gait so as to be exposed for as short a time as possible, but what was our dismay on reaching the church to find all the doors closed & locked and nobody visible! There was nothing left to do but return to camp and though we were a little damp, I do not regret having made the attempt to attend service. On my return I found a lot of papers awaiting me, after disposing of which I read our beautiful church service. I think in our liturgy we have a great advantage over all other denominations. If alone, we can still have its benefits and indeed I must confess that when separated from my home and people as now, I enjoy reading it alone more than I do going through it in a strange church with strangers. I intend now, my precious, devoting this portion of the day to communion with you notwithstanding the immense file of official nuisances (papers) which has just been brought in from one of the Corps. I intend to ignore them for the while, and let them wait 'till tomorrow for my action. I wish they would let me rest on Sunday at least, but though every one knows the General would desire no work performed on that day except what was actually necessary, they continue to send all sorts of papers, as if their object was to persecute me, for I cannot generally be satisfied to <u>postpone</u> acting on what is submitted even for one day, not knowing what the morrow may bring forth. . . .

As you correctly surmised it was determined not to send General Lee west; but though I thought the matter would be <u>discussed,</u> I never <u>concluded</u> that he would be taken from us. I dreaded it and hoped against it, yet always regarded the change as very doubtful. I mention this because you seem to think that I had made up my mind that he was to go, and that my predictions have not been verified. I am thus particular because you might conclude that as I was wrong in this case, so also was there little chance for a realization of my hopes concerning Peace in the coming summer. You know <u>I am bent</u> on having it then. Cant possibly allow the war to continue longer. I can wait <u>impatiently,</u> it is true, but if it <u>must be,</u> I can wait 'till then for a consummation of my happiness.

. . . Ran Talcott is to be married on the 7th of next month.[66] He has asked me to wait on him, began his letter thus: "Dear Taylor, If you don't expect to be married yourself before the 7th of January, I shall anticipate you &c" Now wasn't <u>that</u> cool? Of course I can't leave here now, though I should like much to be of service to him. How sorrow and pleasure are commingled in this world. Whilst I thus write of weddings & consequent happiness, my thoughts revert to poor Runy Lee whose wife has just died.[67] The General his father is much distressed. She was a great favorite of his.—I was here interrupted by one of my visitors, who has just bid me good night after a couple of hours chat. My tent is the popular place for the evening gathering; not that I take the credit of the attraction to myself, but 'tis a sort of semi-official establishment open to everybody. Usually I am rejoiced to see my friends, but I confess I wished to be alone tonight. I shall bear your wishes in mind relative to the procurement of a dispatch of General Lee's for Miss Ellen Beall.[68] It will be impossible to get one of Jackson's now, & indeed it will be difficult to procure a dispatch written by my chief, as he scarcely ever writes them himself. The only autograph letters I have of his are those written to me. Will she have one of these? In your letter of the 17th you assert that your letters are altogether about yourself & regret that you have nothing of interest to write about. Now, Bettie, don't you know 'tis just about your own precious self I wish to hear? There is nothing of <u>half</u> so much interest to me. I wish you to tell me all about yourself—your joys and your troubles. The longer the letter & the more it concerns you, the better pleased will I be. It is a subject of which I can never tire or hear too much. Though Bob Taylor told me of his mother's troubles and his father's resignation, I had never heard of Mr T's return to Norfolk. This surprises me, he cannot expect to go there with impunity? It is a sad state of affairs in our poor old town. Can it be that those gentlemen whose names were published have taken Butler's oath?[69] I fear the alternative presented is this or starvation.

. . . [Starke] was so anxious to get a majority before going to Richmond. I did all I could and the paper went on with Genl Lee's favorable endorsement but it cannot be arranged until after certain legislation by Congress. I think he will be promoted before winter is over. . . .[70]

My friends Chilton and Venable are still absent. The former has been renominated to the Senate for the position of Brigadier, and I think will succeed this time in having the nomination confirmed. I hope so at least, for it will be very mortifying to be twice rejected. The latter I fear will leave us on the first of the year.[71] I shall then be, as it were, all alone. He is a nice manly fellow, of great intellectual attainments and a most agreeable associate. I dread the new comer, for the staff must be increased. While Venable is away I have determined to have George & Wick up here.[72] The poor little fellows must have a dull time in Rich^d and I have thought the novelties here would entertain them. They will probably be here on Tuesday. I hope I shall be able to keep them quiet and orderly, otherwise the General would never forgive me for bringing them. I wish I could have been with you to have enjoyed Mr Crenshaw's <u>egg nog</u>.[73] I am so very fond of it and haven't had a single glass this xmas. I am invited out tomorrow specially to get some, & though I have declined several invitations to dinner lately on the General's account, he being almost alone, I have determined to accept the bid in this instance, for I cannot resist the temptation offered me. I presume you will return to the city Wednesday morning, and I intend sending this letter by tomorrow's mail so that it will reach Town Tuesday and await your arrival the next day. I would like to write more, but 'tis already late, for I have been much interrupted, and I have just a little headache, aggravated no doubt by the huge pile of papers staring me in the face & claiming my attention. Good bye, dearest—Yr own

W

Chapter 3

In Camp at Orange:
January to May 1864
(Letters 38–59)

The paucity of military news during the long winter and early spring of 1864 induces a shift of subject matter to social gossip and ever increasing religious and romantic confidences. Yet there are also valuable vignettes of camp life in the Army of Northern Virginia.

38

Richmond Va

6 Jany 64

I leave in the morning, my dear Bettie, for Roanoke Station on the Danville Railroad. I am here quite unexpectedly to myself for the purpose of waiting on Ran Talcott, who will be married tomorrow evening. I need not say I was sadly disappointed in not meeting you; & have been much grieved to hear of your indisposition, but hope you will soon entirely recover. I will send this to my bank with the request that it be mailed to you at Pemberton if you do not arrive tomorrow as expected. Should you remain in Goochland beyond <u>Saturday,</u> please inform me by the first boat after you receive this. John Saunders goes with us to Talcott's marriage. Please give my best love to your Mother, Pattie & yr sister should you receive this at the Neck. Hoping soon to see you, my own precious B—and to find you perfectly well again I am as ever

Your devoted

W

Address me Box No 723

39

Camp Orange Co

24 January 1864

I'm out of patience, worried and annoyed beyond measure. I can't say how provoked I am, dear Bettie, because I have been compelled by inopportune visits from friends (generally most welcome in my humble abode) and by an extraordinary pressure of business to defer the pleasure of writing you until now when all have retired and but little time is left me for this purpose. But I will not cherish this frame of mind and even now, as I compose myself to commune with you, these cross feelings are being rapidly dissipated and I am myself again. A week has rolled around since I left Richmond and as I resume my former Sunday night occupation, I can hardly realize that my recent happy visit was not a dream. . . .

Such a night as last Monday, or rather the recollection of it, is well calculated to cause me to pine to be away from this horrid desk and back again with the dearest to me of all on earth, but I still feel the spiritual influence of your presence, and am too recently from you, knowing how your views accord with mine as to the proper place for strong young men, to allow a single murmur at my lot, or for one moment to entertain a desire for a soft place in this, the moment of our country's greatest peril. But 'tis under these circumstances, my precious, when duty separates me from you that your letters become exceedingly dear and in this connection let me thank you a hundred times, my Bettie, for your sweet letter of last week which reached me this afternoon. How kind it was of you not to await my letter—and need I tell you how I found any quantity of work when I reached here, how I have been compelled to take upon my shoulders the work usually performed by two in my absence (for Venable feels bound to assist Chilton in my absence, though he allows me to go it alone when I return), need I mention any of these things to explain why you have not sooner heard from me? I think not, for my darling you <u>know</u> that 'tis my constant aim, not only to contribute all in my power to your happiness, (and I scarcely think I ought to be so vain as to assume that my letters add to your happiness, though I <u>hope</u> they do) but also to manifest in every possible way my highest appreciation of the great blessing

I have in possessing such a treasure as your dear self. Now as regards your letters, I will do anything to oblige you. If you desire it and will say the word, I will have all that are now at my home sent to you. They are in a certain box which I can indicate which contains some seven or eight commissions, some letters from Fannie Kerr & Julia, invitations and other private papers. You shall have them all to keep for me or what is better to look over them and destroy none of yr own but such of the other papers as are valueless. This is what I have marked to do, but whilst with you had not the time for it. And if you insist upon it, I will hereafter burn every one I receive from you, one week after it reaches me. It would grieve me to do this for any other cause than your decided and expressed wish. But if it will gratify you it shall be done. I must say however I think there is no danger of the Yankees obtaining them as you fear by a surprise or otherwise. . . .

When I am again with you, it will afford me pleasure to make my appearance with such a companion at the President's reception. When this will be however is most uncertain—assuredly not before the close of the next campaign, and then when we have <u>peace</u>, if God in His mercy shall have spared me. I promise myself <u>much</u> happiness—and would prefer instead of <u>assisting</u> at some "happy individual's" wedding as you intimate, to be one of the two individuals most interested in the occasion. I certainly hope for this in the Fall, <u>peace</u> or <u>war</u>. Please reconcile <u>yrself</u> to it. The General appeared to have no unusual need for my services before my return. <u>Modesty</u> forbids me to repeat what others have said relative to my absence & return. . . .

Don't believe all you hear about the deprivations to which our troops are subjected, they are getting on quite comfortably now. My love to Coz Mary and your sister Kittie, Mother, Pattie & all at the Neck. 'Tis <u>late</u>, so good night.—Your devoted

W

40

Camp Orange Co

28 January 1864

My thoughts are with you tonight, dear Bettie. Several days are yet to pass away before my usual time for writing, but so entirely is my mind filled with your image that I surrender myself to the delightful pleasure of communicating with you, banishing all else from my thoughts. I have had a trying day—an unusually large amount of business—from early after breakfast 'til this moment. I have not left my desk, save for dinner. I'm tired, so weary. What would I not give to have you with me one short hour—half hour. . . .

I am alone this evening. Marshall went off to Richmond today.[1] Venable and Chilton have gone to a neighboring camp to play chess. I am afraid I am sometimes envious or selfish when I see these good fellows without care and with not enough to do to annoy or hurt them, but I cannot grumble now, this being one of the bad effects of my promotion;[2] heretofore being a gentlemanly A.D.C. I could quarrel to my heart's content, as I was required to perform duties not legitimately mine—now I must grin & endure it. I wouldn't call for aid now for my right hand, however much I may need it. Truly there is much virtue in a soft word—it does more than turn away wrath, it comforts and encourages. The General has just looked in upon me and kindly enquired if I had sore throat (my neck tie was carelessly cast aside), remarking at the same time that I should take some exercise & must ride out every day. It is kind of him thus to think of me, but the Chief forgets that if I were to run off daily, I alone would suffer because of the necessary accumulation of work during my pleasure taking. When the afternoons get a little longer, I intend to enjoy a daily ride through the woods, not only for the pleasure of the ride and the benefit to be derived from the exercise, but because this is my favorite time for thinking of you, my dearest—as I gallop through the woods and delight in admiring the beauties of nature, when everything is suggestive of holiness and purity—when the mind is engaged not only in admiring the wisdom and infinite knowledge of the Creator as displayed in the works of His hand, but in contemplating His unspeakable mercy in so abundantly blessing His creatures—then it is I recall the crowning cause I have for thankfulness; and your image is so vividly present with me, that I can, dearest, imagine that we commune in spirit. I need not say how under such circumstances my happiness wd be enhanced by your actual presence.

Saturday night 30th Jany—Circumstances are propitious, my dear Bettie, and I will this evening add a line or two to my letter, though I will not close it till tomorrow night, my normal time for writing. . . .

Though I did not receive my letter of last week before Sunday, I allowed myself to hope for another this evening and was of course disappointed, as it did not make its appearance. May tomorrow's mail produce the treasure—"better day, better deed." The miserable old official that presides over the Post office of North^n Virg^a has been applying for a detail of soldiers to assist him in distributing his letters, and as I haven't altogether gratified him, I believe he keeps my letters a few days at his office, by way of convincing me of the reasonableness of his requests and of forcing me to adopt his terms & send him the desired aid. I receive very regularly the big envelopes with huge <u>O. B.</u> on them but the smaller white fellows are more dilatory. I was somewhat surprised last evening to hear my old chum read an article in the Dispatch in which some gentleman or reporter (for I don't know the terms are always synonymous) had seen proper to give mention to my name. We both agreed that my case was hopeless—I had gotten into the newspapers—but this evening the General told me they also had good Miss Lee there (allusion is made to her frequent presents of socks &c to the soldiers) and I feel more comfortable since I have been made aware of such pleasant company in my imaginary degradation.[3] It is about time for my tentmate to return from his nocturnal chess entertainment and as his advent is generally the signal for a little altercation between us (for I must bully <u>somebody</u>), I will bid you good night. I hope Miss Bettie Brander is still in Richmond.[4] Marshall (her specialty <u>next to me</u>) went down to the city a day or two since intending to return today. As he did not come, I presumed it was because Miss Bettie proved too attractive to allow him so soon to tear himself away. A thousand happy dreams to you. Good night.

Sunday night and still no letter for me. I am confident however that one is on the way and I shall appreciate all the more when it comes because of its delay. I received tonight one from Mother enclosing one sealed to "R. T." from Baynie and one not enveloped to "Alexina" which I interpret to mean Aleck Tunstall, as it is evidently Baynie's handwriting.[5] I believe Mary Lou has the privilege of opening Baynie's letters before sending them to Aleck—and as they pass thro my hands, I too take a benefit, as it appears to be a <u>family</u> concern. The date is 16th January. Nothing new or of special interest. They have to use great caution in writing. Barnes has been removed and on receiving orders for the field, is said to have resigned.[6] (What brave fellows are Butler and he). Baynie speaks of "their physician" (her father not being able to practice because he will not agree to comply with the Yankee terms) and says she and Aleck "have just cause to be proud of such a friend" (father). From this I still have hope that the Doctor has not taken the oath. I trust it will prove to be so and that he may continue firm and steadfast. Baynie speaks very feelingly of the condition of things in poor <u>N.</u>

We had some excitement this morning but it soon passed away. A body of Yankee cavalry crossed the Robinson River (one of the branches of the Rapidan) and Lomax went out to meet them.[7] Their sole object appeared to be to rescue and carry beyond our lines the family of a renegade Virginian whose name I forget. He lived near the ford. They merely rushed across in some force, capturing a picket or two—as usual our men are so careless—and then recrossed without any fighting. I did not go to Church partly owing to this, and partly to work which had to be performed. We were notified on yesterday that Genl Breckinridge (formerly Vice Presidt U.S.)[8] would today visit General Lee, but he did not arrive.—May perhaps come tomorrow. I hope he can be comfortable with little for we have not much to induce visiting to our Head Qrs camp. . . .

Did your Coz Jno get his extension in time to answer his purpose? I sent it promptly by <u>Miles</u>. No doubt Mrs Heth is very happy in having the General with her. Poor, sweet Mrs Rodman! How I wish she had the same reason for happiness. Has Miss Lizzie made her appearance in the city yet?[9] If so, my kindest regards to her. What course has Calvert Petty chosen?[10] Has he left his Mother yet? If he joins the company I alluded to (and by the way it is <u>doubtful</u> if he can join this command under existing orders), I thought perhaps I could make him useful in my office. Does he write a good hand? I now employ five soldiers as clerks and need another, but I will only take one from our own Cavalry. Please remember me kindly to Mrs Petty and to all at the Crenshaws—unless you object to doing so. I ordered an assessment a day or two since of the damages committed on Mr C's farm in the vicinity. Lt Col Garnett who commands the batteries of artillery formerly under John is to be tried before an Examining Board for incompetency.[11] It may result in opening the way for John. But don't speak of it yet as coming from me. It will not do for me to go beyond 4 sheets. I must stop.

41

[To Bettie]

Camp Orange County

2nd February 1864

Tuesday morning and still no letter for me. . . .

111

Nothing so encourages me at all times, as to fancy that your eye rests on me with an expression of interest and may I add affection! I am especially fond and proud of your eyes. Dark & fathomless, they have ever had for me a peculiar fascination—and wherever I have been able to detect in them a glance of interest I have been rendered happy indeed. But whilst I have been thus lost in your precious orbs, the Clerks have surrounded me literally with papers. I must bid you adieu & assume my task.

Wednesday night. . . .

Hunter has just left my tent. As he will go to Richmond tomorrow, you will have seen him before this reaches you. He appears quiet but I would not think him low spirited. Nor do I think he looks as badly as you all do. I saw John's orders to Savannah before I received your letter. I am truly glad his matters were satisfactorily arranged and hope this assignment will please him. It carries him some distance from your Mother but Savannah is a delightful post especially at this season of the year. My winter there passed very pleasantly. Just before Hunter came in I had a visit paid me by a poor old gentleman of this neighborhood (Mr. Perdone) who is in a peck of trouble. He is a nervous, excitable old man and having a little coin and Virg^a Bank money he buried it with all his silver and his daughters' jewelry. It appears he was not satisfied with the first burying place & selected a second, then a third, in an old wood house. Some time since he removed his silverware and jewelry—& a day or two ago he took up his bank notes. I extorted from him that he was in the habit of frequently going to the spot and looking in to see that all was safe. Of course his actions were noticed by the servants and after his removal of the bank bills I presume, seeing the fresh earth, they supposed more valuables might be there. At all events this morning his servants were missing and the specie gone! Poor gentleman! He came to me for advice, but of course I could do but little. No doubt the servants are now with the enemy. Many slaves, employed by officers, have recently taken French leave. Our mess, sometimes for a day or two, is without meat—at times from necessity, at times from choice & on principle. Recently our col. boys declared (so I heard) that they couldn't stay if such short rations were continued.

Thursday afternoon—After I ceased writing last evening I became quite unwell—had oh! such a headache! I feared I was to be seriously ill, but fortunately I procured a little sleep and this morning reported "for duty" as usual. My chum Venable contemplated a visit to the City

& on this account I was particularly desirous to keep my feet, as he would have been compelled to postpone his trip if I was <u>useless.</u> Only a day or two ago, in conversing with someone, I mentioned how remarkable I thought it that I shd keep so well and hearty without exercise, and now this indisposition is perhaps sent me to teach how wrong it is to boast, and to remind me <u>to Whom</u> I am indebted for the many and great blessings I receive. I fear I am not sufficiently earnest in my thanksgiving—and who has greater cause to render thanks? and do not make proper efforts to manifest my appreciation of God's goodness by an unceasing aim and effort to adhere to His will.

Sin is indeed a powerful enemy! I do try—it may be not so zealously as I should—but I do make an effort to order my conversation aright and to shun deeds palpably sinful—but how difficult it is to regulate one's thoughts. Do you never have thoughts thrust on you as it were—not of your own conception—but as if some evil one was putting them in your mind to allure you into entertaining them if possible? This is my most serious drawback, and I know that if I wish to resist the tempter in this form successfully, I must be most vigilant and prayerful. At such times (I can speak from my own limited experience) there is great efficacy in <u>oral</u> appeals to the Throne for help. Such seriously uttered in faith, invariably bring the aid invoked. So, though the tempter is strong, there is a Friend mightier than he, to whom we always have access.

Another cause for apprehension with me is the rapid and erratic manner in which, I am sorry to say, my devotions are now too frequently performed. Is this because my position and duties have compelled me to acquire the habit of doing everything hastily—not <u>precipitately</u> however, for that wd not become my office, but in a <u>rapid</u> manner? But even if this be the cause, does it constitute a valid excuse? I am certain it does not. I can recall the time when my feelings were far different, when I approached God in prayer or when I read His word, than now. Am I retrograding in a spiritual sense? Certainly my convictions of what I ought to do are none the less decided now than then. I believe I may say my desire to be a Christian is none the less. Assuredly He is none the less ready and able to assist me. Do the troublous times really explain the difficulty? May it not consist in the constantly recurring excitements that characterize the life of a soldier in the field. May it not be, because from the very nature of war, the mind is entirely absorbed in contemplating its terrors—its innumerable sad concomitants? No, no, I am sure 'tis not. These are flimsy sophistries, emanating from my evil genius; bitter as is the conclusion, the secret is to be found in the heart. I confess that this is sadly the case with me. Oh! for a closer walk with God! for that quiet contented spirit which I once enjoyed.

> Return, O Holy Dove, return
> Sweet Messenger of rest,
> I hate the sins that made thee mourn,
> And drove thee from my breast.

Join your prayers with mine, Bettie, that together we may pass thro life's scenes a mutual support & comfort.

Saturday night—From present indications, my dearest Bettie, tomorrow will probably be an active day with us and I have determined to anticipate matters a little & complete my letter tonight as I may be deprived of my usual Sunday evening chat.

The enemy crossed some five or six brigades at one of the lower fords on the river (Morton's) and at the same time made some demonstrations with his cavalry above. This occurred this morning. It is impossible yet to say what is intended. We have had reports for a week of an unusual activity in their camp. It may be that a general demonstration is contemplated or possibly they may retire across the river tonight.[12] However our orders are to be "off at sunrise." Again the excitement comes on Sunday. May you be far more happily employed. A very different night will tomorrow's be to me from that spent three weeks ago with you. I respond most heartily to your suggestion that it would be far more pleasanter to have a repetition of the walk we then took ('twas nothing like two hours and a half, I wish it had been) than to have to write, when one must always be under restraint to a certain extent. As you have concluded to wait till I go to Richmond, when I can hand you your letters for safe keeping, that question is settled satisfactorily. I cannot tell you how much gratified I am at your decision relative to my retaining those I now receive, and not destroying them as I expressed a willingness to do if you desired it. I understand your motive thoroughly, my dearie, never fear misconstruction from me of act or word of yours. I am too jealous of yr letters ever to allow the slightest chance of other eyes than mine resting upon them. Did I not guess nicely about the copal trifles? I never would have imagined that you still had them, indeed from the manner in which you put the question I was induced to mention what of all things was probably most unlikely to prove the true solution. But I never could have forgotten them

114

Bettie, and of course I remember most distinctly the evening on the balcony at the Old Powhatan. Indeed what incident of our acquaintanceship is it that I don't recollect? Even the most trivial is well remembered. Many reminiscences are treasured up in memory,—some, at one time, I would like to have forgotten; but <u>now</u> I believe I cherish them all, even the occurrences which were painful at the time, and which entailed upon me much sorrowful meditation—for the enjoyment of the present quite obliterates all of the past that was not agreeable. You shall not call yourself "wicked creature" or suggest such a disastrous proceeding as my shaking you soundly. About that "other wish" of mine—the termination of the war, trip to Europe, &c, &c. I must say that in my sober moments, when I reflect upon the matter seriously, that I concur with you entirely. It would be extremely selfish in me to desire it now. Apart from the solemn consideration of the very precarious tenure one in my position has upon <u>life</u>, there are other contingencies, scarcely less important & not to be forgotten in contemplating such a step in these troublous times. What would be my feelings to see my dear "sensitive plant" the bride of a cripple for life? How sad to have one so young, attractive and beloved attached to a pair of crutches and a helpless man, or even clinging for support & protection on an armless sleeve? . . .

I trust that you have heard from Palmer and that he is safe and has had an opportunity of displaying his worth.[13] The army success in No Caro was not as great as we hoped for.[14] How few know where such movements have their origin. But I mustn't claim too much for our Chief. I fear I am already too proud of him and this army. I am glad you can enjoy a ride when you wish it & hope you will frequently call Mont's services into requisition. I wish you had Bella so that you could keep up with Miss Nannie. Tell Pattie that when I visit The Neck she shall ride the little black to her heart's content. Hunter takes splendid care of her. She is better off than ever before. The poor little nag I have is actually suffering for the want of exercise. I presented her with plenty yesterday afternoon and no doubt 'twas beneficial to both of us. . . .

I understand <u>Theatricals</u> are the rage now. Indeed those from Richmond say that the city is upside down. Mary Lou & Lydia declined going to Ives',[15]—they shd have gone to see the President if not the play.

I shall not forget the promise your sister made and shall certainly claim my kiss when in next week.[16] As to your requests—say no more

115

about them. I'll cry lustily enough if they ever become unreasonable, but of this I have no fear whatever. As the weather is bad you may not go to Norwood this evening to spend Sunday.[17] Wherever you may be, I shall think of you often. May a kind Providence ever guard and keep you, my precious. Give my love to Coz. Mary and all at the Neck. Write me soon again and please continue your "mistakes".

Yr devoted

W.

42

[To Bettie]

Though written some weeks since, & two notes have intervened, I send this that you may see how constantly I think of you & because it begins where my former letter ceased.

Camp Orange County

8 February 1864

I informed you before mailing my letter yesterday morning that the enemy had retired to the north bank of the river. We had scarcely ridden more than three miles early yesterday morning on our way, as we supposed, to a scene of active operations, when we were met by a courier from Genl Ewell bringing information of their disappearance. I was immediately sent back to Headquarters to issue the orders which this rendered necessary and to send telegrams to Mr President, Mr Excitable Elzey, &c. Was not sorry to spend the day quietly in camp, as it was Sunday and I was not over well having lost rest the previous night.[18]

What the enemy meant by this demonstration I cannot say. If attempted with a view of assisting the Beast in his movements against Richmond, it was certainly very weak and failed to accomplish the desired result, as it did not deter us from re-enforcing General Elzey.[19] Really in my opinion the latter had no actual need for more troops, but he is very easily alarmed and floods us with anxious telegrams. I only wish he would not have them put in cypher, as I have the trouble of interpreting them.

116

I presume there has been considerable excitement produced in the city by the near approach of the enemy. I have had not the least apprehension and perhaps have treated the matter too lightly. I cannot resist laughing however when I see what a fuss is created by one or two regiments of infantry and a body of irregular cavalry. Elzey seems to have been driven to Bottom's Bridge by one regiment of white infantry and one of black, at least that is all he has reported thus far. His pickets driven to Bottom's Bridge! I wonder if the Yankees experienced much trouble in driving them. A great deal more difficult matter, I infer, is to overtake them! So long as Elzey remains in command and that miserable body of mounted alarmists (not cavalry) is kept on the Peninsula, so long may we expect to witness a repetition of these shameful stampedes.

The performance of the Yankee cavalry on yesterday was as good as a play. They would form for a charge, would come on regularly and in fine style, until they were in range of our artillery—that is until they emerged from behind a hill which protected them from the fire—and then without even waiting to be honored with a shot, away they would scamper like a herd of frightened sheep. Such really laughable antics will be eulogized by their newspaper correspondents as "brilliant charges," "gallant exhibitions," &c., &c. What a truth ignoring people they are.

After they had crossed the river below (the cavalry was above), some of our men went to the bank of the river on our side & commenced firing upon a battery of artillery in position just opposite. Whereupon, the cowards cut their horses loose, and men and horses incontinently fled, leaving their guns behind. The Rapidan was between us and of course our men could not reach and capture the guns. One of the enemy's infantry regiments was finally induced to redeem the bad conduct of the artillerists and marched up & removed the pieces under fire. The whole affair is not worth the time and paper I've spent on it. If we can't whip that army we don't deserve to be free.

There was of course a great exodus amongst the army wives. Ramseur was on picket when the excitement commenced.[20] He sent word to Mrs R to go to Richmond but countermanded it in the morning before she had started. I understand Lelia Taylor did not leave. I am glad neither went, as I may possibly save my character and get to see them. Thus far it has been simply impossible for me to do so, much as I desire it.

You remember the mistakes that have arisen because of the similarity of name and rank between Bob and myself, and how I thought I would be free from them since I was raised a peg![21] Well this morning an old gentleman asked if he might congratulate me—had heard I had been or was about to be married. I told him I was not so happy and was not soon to be, that I was aware of. Oh yes, he said, I understood you were to be married to Miss Willis. I readily saw then how the mistake had occurred, for George Tayloe—Lt Col Tayloe—is in a few days to lead this young lady to the altar.[22] You see they are determined to make me happy. I suppose my friends are so convinced of the propriety and advisability of my taking this step that they immediately conclude I'm to be the fortunate individual (or victim—which?) whenever the gentleman's name is at all similar to mine.

Ash Wednesday [Feb 10, 1864]

As I am denied the privilege of attending Church service this morning, I will do what I consider next best, my dear Bettie, and employ my leisure moments by adding to my letter. This will benefit me quite as much as a sermon—indeed at times I am ashamed to acknowledge how great an incentive to tread the path of rectitude your opinion and the desire to be worthy of you, is with me. So aside from all consideration of pleasure there are weighty motives which prompt me to commune with you frequently. The General went to Church today and has just returned to inform me that I would have met with some Norfolk ladies if I had accompanied him. They spoke to him but he hasn't the slightest idea who they are, nor can I solve the question. There are none here except Mrs R. Taylor that I am aware of. The weather is superb today and I was feeling particularly well and happy. I don't think I was well last week. I was somewhat under the weather and I fear my letters lately have indicated as much, but today and indeed yesterday I am conscious that I am more myself. On yesterday afternoon I enjoyed a gallop—my little horse spirited and gay because of the very idle time she has had—acted as if she was on wires and I was in as wild a humor as she was. I intend to start again presently and oh what would I not give to have your company this beautiful sunny afternoon? How pleasant it would be if I was in Richmond and we could together take the tow path of the canal, my favorite—indeed our favorite ride. But because I can't have all I wish is no reason I shouldn't enjoy what I have—so I'll be off and away directly and think of you my precious all the time. You remember I've told you before that 'tis my custom in riding thus for pleasure, to surrender myself to my imagination—to fancy myself with you in spirit and I always return in better spirits and am made as happy as a King for having dreamed I was with you. I'm off but will not say Good bye for I'll still be with you.

43

[To Bettie]

Camp Orange Co

10 Febry 1864

I have just received a letter from Mary Lou informing me about dear Palmer.[23] It was the first intimation I had had of the fate of your brave, noble brother. I was aware of the character and intention of the expedition under Col Wood, and felt anxious to hear from it ever since.[24] I learned from you that Palmer was one of his party, but after seeing Wood's published report, I felt satisfied that all was well. How bright and joyous the dear boy was when last I saw him! Truly the ways of Providence are inscrutable and past finding out. Oh, how terribly sad is this war, when thus brought so distressingly home to us! Dearly bought indeed will be our nationality & liberty, when purchased by the sacrifice of such true, gallant spirits as him we now mourn. I pray most earnestly, Bettie, that God may soften this blow to your dear, dear Mother. It would be presumptuous and a profanation on my part to approach her with words of consolation. She is so strong in faith and such a pure Christian, that we may at all times learn from her the lesson how blessed it is to be enabled to receive whatever God sends with submission and thankfulness. Your mother has always appeared to me a living illustration of the truth that trials do indeed bring us nearer to our Saviour's feet, lay us low and keep us there. She knows that God of His very faithfulness has caused her to be troubled, and that His hand alone can sustain her. But I would have her know, Bettie, that she has my earnest sympathy in this her hour of renewed distress. I grieve with her, Bettie, for are not her sorrows and your sorrows my sorrows? May a kind and merciful Father strengthen her. Would to God it was in my power to assuage her deep distress, for I know her heart is sadly wrung by this visitation—her children are so precious to her—wrapped up in them, she cares to live only on their account. May Christ be with her & bless her with an abundant outpouring of His Holy Spirit.

119

And you, my precious Bettie, need not be assured how sincerely I mourn with you in this affliction. My heart throbs in unison with yours, Bettie, whether in sorrow or in joy. 'Tis hard to give up such a noble, manly, generous hearted brother—but let us bear in mind that the separation is but temporary, that he is <u>not dead</u> but has just commenced <u>life</u>. The earth becomes less and less attractive to us as those who are dear to us leave it; and it becomes us not to indulge in mourning or regret, but with faith to look forward to the time when in God's wonderful kindness we shall witness reunion above.

> Where the saints of all ages in harmony meet,
> Their Saviour and brethren transported to greet,
> While the anthems of rapture unceasingly roll,
> And the smile of the Lord is the feast of the soul.[25]

God bless and keep you and yours, my dear Bettie. I am glad Hunter is with your Mother.

My best love to your Sister, to Pattie and all.—Yr devd

Walter

44

[Covering letter to Tom Selden]

15 Feb '64

Dear Tom[26]

Will you be kind enough to forward the enclosed to Bettie if she is still at Howard's Neck or if she has ret'd to R to deliver it to her? Isn't it too sad about Palmer? He was a grand fellow and could not have died in a more glorious cause.

My kind regards to Mrs Knox, & believe me your friend

Truly

Walter Taylor

Camp Orange County

15 Febry 1864

You have been constantly in my thoughts, my dear Bettie, since my note to you of last Wednesday. It pains me, my precious, to reflect how many bitter, sorrowful moments you have endured in that time, but I trust you have not been comfortless. Earnestly do I pray that you may be enabled to discern through the dark cloud that has overshadowed you the hand of a mysterious but a kind, an all wise Providence. Still, even when viewed in this light—even though we are strong in faith and thoroughly persuaded that God does not willingly afflict or grieve us—even though we strive earnestly to bring to our hearts the conviction that these apparent sorrows and deprivations will ultimately prove real blessings—nevertheless 'tis a sad, sad dispensation to have so suddenly taken from us those so near to us, so dearly beloved. You know I can sympathize with you, for have not I suffered? Many times have I been called upon to give up those who were very dear to me and I know full well, my dearest, the bitter anguish that fills the heart in the first moments of such afflictions. Oh how painfully does the soul long to be at rest, how cold and cheerless does the world appear. My experience has taught me also, my dear Bettie, that 'tis often a mistaken attempt at kindness on the part of friends to offer words of consolation to one thus weighed down by grief,—but I well remember how sweet it was to see that those whom I loved and were left to me sorrowed and sympathized with me—to see that they wept in pity over the wound, though powerless to heal. I am assured that with you too such evidence will be acceptable and to a certain extent soothing. Then, whilst I cannot forbear entreating you to look up and bear in mind that 'tis God's work & therefore ordained for good,—whilst I would have you know that I would give any price could I have the power of softening this blow to you,—my principal object is simply to reiterate that you have my heartfelt sympathy—to tell you that I know how you suffer and that my sighs and prayers are mingled with your own. My own dear Bettie, may our merciful Father be with you, comfort and strengthen you. May he give you courage and strength to enable you to be your dear Mother's blessed comforter in this her hour of deep sorrow. This I am certain you have been. I only pray that renewed aid may be sent to sustain you in your efforts, to cast aside your own trials, and to soothe the achings of her heart and soften the force of this blow upon her on whom it naturally falls with the most violence. Look up, dearest, God's hand will assist you. Though there is much in the time to sadden us, let us not forget we have very much to be thankful for. God bless you, my own Bettie,—to His protective care I commit you my precious treasure. Give my best love to your Mother, who is as dear to me as if my own.

Yr devoted

W.

45

Sunday morning

21 February 1864

It was a great relief to me, my dear Bettie, when your letter written some weeks since was handed to me last evening. . . .

I was prevented from going to Orange today; and being alone I enjoyed reading the service and trust I was thereby benefitted. How complete, how beautiful our Liturgy is! It seems to have been so composed and arranged as to have in some portion of it special application to every conceivable case of trouble or suffering, prosperity or happiness. I thought constantly of you, dearest, and I trust God has this day blessed you with inward strength and by the inspiration of His Holy Spirit drawn you more closely to Himself. I today experienced somewhat of that happy, indescribable feeling of security and rest which characterized the time when I first declared myself a Christian, and about which I quite recently wrote you. Oh that I could always realize that Christ is near me, ready and anxious to assist me in my struggle with sin and that He is moreover pained at every departure from the true and perfect way into which my evil passions lead me. Could I always have these truths present to my mind, I think I would more frequently experience the sweet consciousness of a soul at rest.

By accident this morning I picked out a sermon commemorative of a Christian soldier who was called upon to surrender. There was much in it that pleased me and I thought there was much in it to console those to whom it was addressed and who were interested in its subject. However eloquent man may be, however happy his comparisons and allusions, however earnest his efforts to console, he can only to a partial extent soothe those whose hearts have been thus suddenly and painfully torn. God alone can comfort them, and it is a blessed reflection that with the <u>power</u> He possesses the <u>will</u> to assuage their grief. What transcending goodness is this, that God can be touched with a

122

feeling for our infirmities and is ever ready to support us when our hearts fail us, to cheer and comfort us when we are in despair. What is man that Thou art mindful of him, the son of man that Thou visitest him?[27] May this Kind Benefactor be with you, my own Bettie; and as I can pray that His choicest blessings may be upon you, I do not feel that I am altogether powerless to comfort you in your moments of sorrow.

I have already censured myself considerably for that doleful letter I sent you some few weeks since[28]—though really I was not suffering from an attack of the "Blues," nor had the General been extra cross; indeed for the last six months he has been exceedingly gracious, and most kind in his manner towards me; nor had Col C rendered himself at all obnoxious to me;[29] his manner has also been exceedingly friendly, and he has more than once indulged in confidential chats with me— told me very plainly once that he would not undertake to perform the labours of the Adjutant General of this army; nor was I envious of Marshall's visit to Richmond so far as that concerned B. B. but I am not so positive that I did not envy him the opportunity of seeing Bettie Somebody else.[30] The true solution of my meanness is that I was for a day or so quite indisposed. It was only temporary and my only regret is that I should have allowed my feelings to manifest themselves in my letter. I promise you will not soon suffer from a like affliction. I was never more well and hearty than now, so I cannot plead sickness as an excuse for a leave, though you hold out a strong temptation. The General will start for Richmond in the morning. Why can't he take me with him? He must know how anxious I am to be there. I presume he will go alone as he has said nothing of taking anyone. He is called to the City by Mr. Davis and I presume for the purpose of consulting. Bragg is now there and perhaps they desire to get the views of the "Chief" as to the best disposition to be made of him.[31] The only part of the matter that I don't relish is that old Mr Ewell will be trotting around here and assuming the airs of General Commanding during the Tycoon's absence, and I can stand no uppishness on the part of Lieutenant Generals, though I accept gracefully anything that comes from Genl Lee—at least I make great efforts to do so.[32] I am glad you get on so well with your work.

Old Turner did not know what a trump he was receiving in his office when he welcomed you.[33] I expect you will work so efficiently that they will desire to get rid of you, as it is such a decided reflection on his men. As you have progressed so famously with your work, I hope you will have it in your power soon again to visit "the Neck," for I am well aware what comfort both you & your mother would derive from the visit; and I have a positively selfish reason besides for advocating your so doing, inasmuch as I fully intend when a good opportunity is offered, to accidentally be there simultaneously with yourself. I must thank you for the kind wish expressed that you could assist me in my labours during your leisure moments—don't imagine that I would laugh at you for entertaining such an idea, for I assure you you can be positively useful,—the only difficulty is that I don't see how you could well sign "W. H. Taylor" and this just now is a decided bore and most fatiguing task. The additional star has not entailed upon me any additional burden. Indeed 'tis somewhat consoling to think that whether they will add to my stars or not, they cannot increase my work or responsibility, for one more charge would certainly prove to be the straw on the camel's back. But I am fast forgetting my resolution not to harp upon my official labours and must desist. Mark me though, I was led into this by your suggestions, and my remarks are not indulged in any complaining spirit. Indeed I am doing finely now & actually <u>make time</u> to read a little every night. From constant and incessant habit I have acquired the faculty of looking through a paper when folded and divining its contents, & can now sign my name without pen, ink or paper.

Moreover I feel much encouraged by the kind expressions of approbation which occasionally reach me from my friends. I have just now received official notice of another "Camp Taylor," named after "the courteous & efficient adjutant Genl of our Commander in Chief." What do you think of that? I dare say I had better ask, what do you think of me? For like St Paul I feel that I speak as a fool.[34] But I am sure you will understand. I indulge in this strain from no egregious vanity, but only mention such things to you, with whom I act without reserve and from whom there is no danger of misconstruction, only that you may see how I appreciate such evidence of good will and how far a kind word goes to encourage one. We poor mortals are all more or less susceptible of having our vanity flattered and I suppose I have my share of this characteristic trait in this connection. . . .

Remember me kindly to your dear Mother & Sister K.—Good night

Your devo

W.

46

[To Bettie]

Camp Orange Co

23d Feb 1864

I have just approved several hundred furloughs and thereby gladdened the hearts of as many brave soldiers and whilst awaiting the
preparation of more work for me by the clerks, I will devote such time
as they will allow me to a commencement of my letter. There is much
in this part of my occupation which reminds me of the numbering and
signing of Confederate notes and in the time I was appending my signature to the furloughs this morning, my mind reverted to the old
times in the Treasury Building. I recalled my first visit to the "Angels
retreat" and remembered so distinctly my every emotion whilst I occupied the seat near you in that dilapidated old room—may the Angels
forgive me!—in the building on Broad Street on the occasion aforesaid.
I was not so happy and contented as now, dear Bettie; on the contrary
I was in a state of hopeless uncertainty, or rather I should say, I was in
a <u>certain</u> state of hopelessness, but never before realized how very dear
you were to me and how positively unhappy I was at the knowledge
that you regarded me with indifference. You had a high color that day
and to my eyes appeared, if possible, more attractive than ever and
truly irresistible. All this by no means enhanced my happiness then,
but it added intensely to my anxiety; and whilst I could assign no good
reason for so doing, I still hoped as it were without hope. Then in
thought I was translated to the brighter and more cheerful room—to
which the term "retreat" was more applicable—on Grace St and I rec-
ollected the summons I received to appear before the Angels, for the
purpose of arranging for that memorable ride to Drewry's Bluff. Then
all the incidents of that ride were vividly recalled—and this carried me
on to the still pleasanter ride, enjoyed a little later in the season.[35] All
this occurred to me whilst I sat here signing those good fellows' furloughs. And some times as I put my signature to the paper thought of
the pleasure its receipt would afford to the gallant young patriot or glorious old veteran, for whose benefit it was intended. I pictured to myself the happy smiling countenances that would welcome him at home
and it really made me happy to contemplate the joy I was sure his re-

turn would carry to the hearts of those who loved him, and whose prayers for his protection and safe return had been so often offered. So, far from being burdensome this morning, my daily employment has been to me the source of much quiet enjoyment and pleasant meditation. I wonder if the brightness of the sun has not to a great degree caused me to take the philosophic view of a matter generally distasteful and tedious? All nature smiles today and it is as balmy and spring like as possible. A few steps from my tent and my eyes are feasted on as lovely and picturesque exhibition of the beauties of nature as can be found in a day's ride. How contented, how thankful and happy does the influence of the beautiful day make me! I wish you were here with me to experience the exhilarating effects of this fine country air. Surrounded with such striking evidences of God's power and wisdom and witnessing such numberless illustrations of his infinite goodness, we are induced to reflect on the just cause we have for thankfulness and to take a most cheerful and cheering view of our present condition. We lose sight of our sorrows and our murmurings are hushed, when we at such a time realize how abundantly we are blessed here, and in the rapturous emotions which fire the soul enjoy a foretaste of that ineffable bliss which we hope for when our time of probation shall have ceased. May your feelings at this time, my precious Bettie, be consonant with mine! May the sorrow which rests upon your heart be somewhat lessened of its weight by the soothing influences of His Holy Spirit is my earnest, heartfelt prayer.

I received a letter from your brother John last night which answers the question contained in my letter of yesterday concerning his desire to be in this army. He still wishes this and I hope he may soon be gratified in this particular. As my intimacy with him is well known here, I have to be guarded in what I say & do towards advancing his interests, less my motive should be misunderstood. John's chances I trust are good however, should an opening occur; & such an opening will occur shortly I think, though I would not have him to expect to be brought here, because of what I say. I shall be mindful of his wishes and do all I can to further them.

Thursday morning—25 Feb. I have just completed a letter to Julia, which I hope will reach Norfolk safely as I sent it north by a trusty agent (one of our scouts) who is to mail it in a Northern Post office. It is very little satisfaction though now to write letters, as one has to be so very guarded and I expect the epistles are not much valued when received, for the same reason. . . .

As I recently approved a leave for Bob T. I presume he and his wife have left these parts for Fluvanna.[36] She came and departed without my having called on her, much to my regret. Ramseur informs me that Frank Huger is soon to visit him up here. It will be nice now if I postpone visiting Mrs R. until Frank arrives, will it not? After a month's silence I on yesterday wrote Frank and presume he and my letter will pass each other on the road. Jack Preston applied for 5 days recently and to make amends for my former conduct I approved it for <u>seven,</u> so Miss Cillie must restore me to her good graces. The truth is I thought Jack might be well spared the two additional days (or weeks indeed) without any detriment to the public service.[37]

The reports received from the enemy's lines indicate an unusual activity as prevailing in their camps. It looks as if they were preparing some movement; and this coupled with the mild weather we now have warns us to be on the alert. Winter has nearly gone and the time rapidly approaches when active operations must be resumed. I am very hopeful about the coming campaign. Our army was never in better spirits and in discipline and efficiency is equal to any that ever existed. <u>Sunday night 11 P.M.</u> Under all circumstances and at all times my stock of patience is, I regret to say, exceedingly limited; tonight, my dear Bet, it is utterly exhausted. I contemplated having a quiet time to myself this evening in which to complete my usual letter. Good old Genl Early and other friends have sadly interfered with my intentions.[38] Soon after dinner the whole establishment, home folks and visitors, came into my tent and one incessant chit chat has been going on ever since. They have just left me and I must hurriedly close my letter.

It really seems impossible for the General to enjoy a short visit to Richmond that the enemy doesn't at that very time begin some demonstration. On yesterday morning a body commenced a movement on our left; they have gone on steadily towards Madison C. H. and though the reports are very conflicting, some indicating a general advance and others representing that Meade is rather expecting an attack; and although their intentions are not yet fully developed, yet from the unusual stir in their camps and other circumstance it is evident something exciting is on the tapis.[39]

President Lincoln reviewed their whole army a day or two since; their ladies have been riding along the banks of the river in front of our pickets, apparently sight seeing—their papers contain some notice of a ball etc. Some of the facts would imply a probable movement, others the reverse. Of course I must keep the General advised of all that oc-

curs And in my great care and anxiety to avoid appearing unnecessarily excited or laying myself liable to the charge of being a
"stampeder," I sometimes fear I may make my dispatches too moderate and sanguine.

Gen'l Ewell who is supposed to be in command doesn't relieve me
at all, nor does my friend Chilton who terms himself "Chief of Staff."
Neither has volunteered one single suggestion or in any way divided
the responsibility. As for Genl Ewell he is 15 miles away and though I
have kept him regularly & constantly informed of the enemy's movements yesterday and today I am yet to hear the first word from him.

The Genl (Lee) telegraphed me last evening that he would be up
today. I was so unwilling to cause him to travel on Sunday, that on last
night I sent him a quietly worded telegram putting the whole matter in
as unexciting an aspect as the facts would allow; and the result was he
remained in R^d. Tonight he informs me he will be here tomorrow and I
shall assuredly be easier in mind and better satisfied whatever may be
the result of the present movement. We cannot much longer expect to
remain quietly in camp.

The weather is uncommonly fine and the good condition of the
roads is really remarkable. I would rather that we take the initiative but
if it must be the other way, well and good. Our army is in excellent
condition in every way. Its morale is not to be surpassed—its sanitary
condition was never so good—it is now well fed—and strange to relate
is well and entirely shod. More could not be said in favor of any army
that ever took the field. It is somewhat disagreeable to reflect upon the
comforts we are to relinquish when the campaign opens, but I believe
the "whole concern" is anxious for the commencement. The common
talk amongst the men is their coming expedition to Pennsylvania and
what they intend doing there. The rascals declare they will have no
Genl Orders this time protecting the property of the enemy. They say
they abstained from touching anything last year out of respect for their
beloved Chief, but that this year he must give them no such order, indeed they are bent on supplying their wants and I fear we will experience much difficulty in restraining them within proper bounds.

I have recently had my tent floored, and am as comfortable as one
could reasonably desire to be. I wish you could look in upon me and
see how very cozily I am arranged. I cling tenaciously to such a comfortable camp & regret that I am soon to leave it. And then too my letters will be by no means so regular after we commence moving, and
this will be the greatest deprivation and trial of all. Oh how I wish I

could be with you just one little while again before we resume active operations. I would not ask a long time, but it would be <u>such</u> a comfort to see you, be present with you once more before we start for the summer. I don't see how my wishes can be gratified, but if the present little affair blows over, I shall assuredly make that effort. I do want to see you my precious, as the children say "more than tongue can tell." May a kind and merciful Father guide, comfort, bless you. My love to Pattie & Coz Mary. The last "special dispatch" for the night (I hope) is just received and I'll bid you good night dearest.

W

47

Camp Orange County

4 March 1864

Since my last, dear Bettie, we have had quite an exciting time here and no doubt you all in the city have been considerably agitated by the raiders.[40] I am glad to have a little quiet this morning, which I will improve by a chat with you. As you have had the war approach so near you this time and have no doubt heard all the particulars from Tom and the other heroes of the local forces,[41] I hesitate to recount our doings in this memorable occasion. My letters to you are the only "Diary" I keep, and I contemplate having them after the war to refresh my memory concerning the campaigns and operations of the army.

As I told you, the General was influenced by my temperate telegram to postpone his return to the army until Monday, thereby running great risk of capture, as the train upon which he travelled was the very last one that made the through trip, the enemy reaching the railroad but a few hours after the train had passed.

On Monday morning the reports I received clearly indicated some movement by the enemy, but I confidently relied upon the cavalry to keep me accurately & promptly informed and so kept cool, knowing moreover that the General would come to my relief in the afternoon. The party on our left (in Madison County) was the first of whose advance I received any information, and this was very late in reaching me. Before I was apprized of their advance at all, they were well on their way to Charlottesville, at which point we had not a single man. The country through which the enemy would pass was filled

129

with our artillery camps and wagon trains. Fortunately I had diverted the previous evening all trains moving from the Valley in this direction, but the artillery and wagons that were in camp were in great danger.

Genl Ewell, who was supposed to be in command of the army during Gen Lee's absence, was fifteen miles away from our Headquarters. Immediate steps had to be taken to prepare to check the enemy or he would have everything his own way. I was very much perplexed to know what to do. I essayed one effort to procure assistance from our "Chief of Staff,"[42] but his reply to the first question I put to him was so very muddy and exhibited such ignorance of the situation that I was convinced I was to receive no help from this quarter. I plucked up the necessary courage and on my own responsibility issued the orders for such movements as in my opinion the emergency required. Indeed for a short while I scattered things with a surprising looseness. When the General arrived I was all anxiety, as you may well imagine, for I knew that however well arranged matters had appeared when the orders were given, if further developments were not met by them, I alone would receive the blame. In a few words I related what the enemy had done so far as was known to me and what steps had been taken on my part to thwart his designs. To my infinite gratification and comfort, he had no fault to find.

The enemy was met near Charlottesville and repulsed, as you have already heard. Matters did not turn out so well on our right. It is with regret that I am compelled to say anything disparaging of our cavalry, but sad to relate the entire picket at Ely's ford on the Rapidan river were captured by the enemy. No one was left to give intelligence of their having crossed. In this direction the cavalry was our sole reliance, so the enemy actually reached the Central railroad before we were aware of their having crossed to this side of the river. The party, after cutting the road, proceeded to Richmd. You are better informed of what transpired there than I am.

On Tuesday we started for Madison to catch the Yankee cavalry and to chastise a corps of infantry which had moved to that point, apparently to protect or secure the return of the raiders on this flank. It was a most disagreeable day, cold with a promise of rain. We went bravely on, however, to within a couple of miles of the main body of the enemy. Here there followed one of those distressingly long conferences between those high in authority which too often result in the utter discomfiture of all of our plans, because they but consume time and give the enemy an opportunity to get out of the way. I don't like to witness these long talks. It was not so in Jackson's time.

After the consultation was ended, dispositions were made for an attack. Our advance had been deployed and was moving forward, when a courier dashed up to say the enemy's cavalry was moving toward a point in our rear. I thought this by no means serious as by placing a brigade of infantry to the rear of our column, we could bid defiance to their small body of horse and feel perfectly secure as to the few wagons we had with us. I am afraid I indulged a bitter spirit that evening, for I wished to give the Yankees a good thrashing for having put us to so much trouble. Thoroughly soaked by the rain and benumbed by the cold I was quite spiteful and anxious for the entertainment to begin. I was confident that we would have but little trouble in achieving a victory over the force in our front, for, from the reports we received, I was sure we certainly had as many men as they, if we didn't outnumber them. To my chagrin the order to "bout face" was given and we commenced to retrace our steps. All my feathers were drooping then, but imagine my disgust when I afterwards learned that the report about the cavalry was unfounded & when I moreover learned that the number of the enemy was not one half what they had been reported! It was really too bad. We could have utterly dispersed the whole concern had we <u>gone ahead.</u> Oh, for a Jackson!

I declare it was indeed piteous to see the heaviness, the indecision of our generals that afternoon. My chief is first rate in his sphere— that of a commanding general. He has what few others possess, a head capable of planning a campaign and the ability to arrange for a battle, but he is not quick enough for such little affairs as the one I have described. He is too undecided, takes too long to form his conclusions. He must have good lieutenants, men to move quickly, men of nerve such as Jackson. With such to execute and the Genl to plan, we could accomplish anything within the scope of human powers.

Well, we moved back as night approached and a cold snow storm set in. Our poor fellows had an uncomfortable night before them. We were 15 miles from our camp and halted for the night. I wish they all could have been as comfortable as I was. The Genl went to a house where the good people were very kind & furnished us with an excellent supper and a nice bed for the night. Next morning we returned to camp, made some ineffectual efforts to trap the party which were in Richmond, all of which failed as they didn't return this way.[43] Now they have all escaped, though I am glad to say after having accomplished very little. All things considered it is hard to say which was injured the most in the operation.

During the excitement we have of course been cut off from all mail communication with Richmond. The route will certainly be reopened tomorrow, at least it ought to be and will, I trust. . . .

I must see you before we begin to move. When this will be I cannot say, but if we are quiet a month longer, I shall certainly indulge the hope of meeting you. Chilton is to leave us. His rank doesn't suit him. The Senate would not give him his old date & he has declined the Brigadiership and requested to be relieved. I trust his successor will prove an agreeable associate as well as a competent officer. As he may regard himself as my <u>Boss</u>, I am particularly anxious.[44] C & I have gotten along quite well because he never molested me or interfered with my labours.

I must hurriedly close my letter.

48

Sunday evening   6 March 1864

My disappointment was great, my dear Bettie, when on yesterday I received dozens of letters both official and private, which had accumulated since the interruption of our communication with Richmond and could recognize among them none from you. . . .

By a letter recently received from Norfolk I am informed that Mr Rodman's course is approved by all his friends except the Sharps and their clique.[45] No doubt though our people have been misguided, their hearts are altogether with us. When I hear you sigh for your old room "at home," I find that I cannot entirely give up poor old Norfolk. Your likes are my likes, yr sorrows my sorrows. May our <u>home</u> soon be restored to us & may we at an early day secure one equally as happy as the old one was. May God bless & keep you, relieve & comfort my smiling one is the prayer of your own

W

49

Camp Orange County

8 March 1864

I was so glad, my dear Bettie, to receive on yesterday afternoon your letter of last Saturday. It was indeed a great relief to me. . . .

We have on duty at our Headquarters an old gray-haired Quarter-master,[46] who besides being the most efficient of his class I ever met, possesses peculiar attraction for me, because of his childlike simplicity and gentleness of disposition. The devotion between this amiable old gentleman and his wife is as fresh apparently as it was in their honeymoon. Every day he sends her a letter & she writes to him with equal regularity. It is truly refreshing to witness such unwavering affection. A few days since I was dining with him when his letters were handed in. With my accustomed impudence I laughingly commenced teasing him about his letters to and from his beloved spouse, and was cruel enough to take delight in seeing good old Harmon's (that's his name) face diffused with blushes, when I expressed my astonishment at his possessing so much sentiment, "Just wait," said he, "until you get a wife yourself and I'll bet you'll write her every day if not two or three times a day. You will send her a note at ten or eleven o'clock and you'll send her one at three o'clock." How I laughed at the idea. I wonder if I would. Do you think I would? And if I did, wouldn't the madam (whoever that unfortunate individual might be) become exceptionally tired of me? All joking aside, my affection & admiration of this honest Quartermaster was much enhanced by my discovery of this commendable trait in his character. It is a lovely sight, I think, to witness such undiminished, constant love between those who have grown grey in each other's companionship. . . .

I was aware that Theodoric Williams was to have been married.[47] You see all these young gentlemen are compelled to disclose their intentions to me that they may procure the necessary leave of absence. I declare you would laugh if you could see some of the applications which are presented for furloughs on matrimonial grounds. It frequently happens that the young lady writes a letter for the occasion, which the soldier encloses in his application to be perused by his commanding officers & considered in the light of argument in favor of his request. I had the pleasure this morning of reading quite a lengthy, loving epistle from Miss Sally Mitchell to one of our brave fellows, which really reflected great credit on Miss Sally because of the patriotic self denying sentiments it contained.[48] And would you believe it, I had the cruelty to deny the request? I was sorry I had to do it, but it is necessary in military affairs to keep down all sentiment & not give way to one's sympathy or predilections towards those so interestingly situated, but to bring everything to the hard, rigid test of the "interests of the public service." Sometimes the lady adopts the plan of endorsing her tender application thus—"forwarded & approved. I am willing" &c. I think I shall have to call on somebody one of these days to endorse a paper for me. Ho! but I forgot my time of probation is as indefinite as the continuance of the war. The General said jokingly in my tent a few evenings since that he could give no leaves after last week for the purpose of being married. Ah! Said I, I think I'll put my application in at once. But the cruel old Chief only laughed at me and replied that I had had my chance & if I didn't improve it, 'twas my own fault. I told him such matters could not be speedily arranged—or at least it took time with me—but I fear he is incurable, and I shall receive no more indulgences this winter, except the few days I must and will have just before we move, to enable me to spend a few happy hours with my precious old "captain." He cannot, must not deny me this. It will impair my usefulness if he does, for I have so set my heart on it, that it will not do to disappoint me. The recollection of that last evening with you, my dearest, is perfectly fresh and I take delight in recalling your words when you expressed the hope that I would be able to "run down again soon." You cant imagine how those few words cheered me—with what a happy, light heart I that evening wended my way homewards. Ah Bettie! how dearly I do love you and how earnestly do I appreciate even this slightest manifestation of a reciprocation of this sentiment on yr part!

Saturday night (12th.) Memory is busy with me tonight, my precious, reminiscences of the past crowd themselves upon me. Looking into my cheerful fire I live over again some of the happiest periods of my life. It is singular however, how at certain times one set of light impressions will be more vividly recalled than others, without any apparent connection between the time to which they relate and the present. Do you remember the entertainment given by the young gentlemen of our vicinity at the National Hotel? Well, I see you now as you then appeared just as plainly as if all the scenes of that night were being reenacted before me. Poor Capt Bowden compared you to a fresh <u>rose bud</u>.[49] I agreed with him fully, recognized the appropriateness of the comparison and deemed myself an object of envy to all the young beaux there gathered together, because I had the honor on that memorable occasion to be the escort of one so universally admired. Can you recall the japonica and the little ornament which I removed from one of the pyramids & adjusted in the centre of the bouquet? The curls, the pink dress—all this is so vividly recalled tonight. . . .

How very happy I was! How pleasant it was to linger at your back porch—how loth I was to leave—when your home was reached when we returned from those little gatherings, my habit was then to wander down to the river—that beautiful river of ours that you so long once more to see. I have been with you there tonight. Your letter of Wednesday, in which you refer to it, reached me just now and when I witness your attachment to our home and its lovely surroundings, my old attachment to it is rekindled & again I pray we may soon have it restored to us—not <u>Yankeeized</u> but the same dear old place we left it—but instead of wandering to the river I have strayed off altogether from my subject. Well as I was saying I would stroll down to the end of the street to enjoy that charming view from "the point," unsurpassed in its quiet beauty by any I have ever beheld—& then with my heart filled with thoughts of you, my Bettie, impressed with a sense of my great indebtedness for the many blessings bestowed upon me, I would pray earnestly for your happiness and mine, that I might be worthy of you, and that our whole lives might be as calm and sunlit as were the emotions engendered by the placid scene before me, where the smooth quiet water so exactly reflected the beauties of the glorious heavens that in the distance it was difficult to distinguish the one from the other, to decide where earth ceased & where the heavens began. So may it be with your life & mine, my precious & may we daily become nearer and nearer to our Saviour, so that when the end comes it shall be but a translation so gradual, so peaceful, that it shall be difficult to realize when existence here ceases and life there begins. . . .

There are so many hallowed reminiscences and associations connected with old Norfolk, that in view of your unchanged attachment to the place, I find it impossible not to cherish my former love for it or to look down upon it as something so sadly polluted as to be no longer worthy of our affection.

[The] Bishop is to preach at Orange C H tomorrow.[50] I am very desirous to go and hear him and hope to be able to do so, but the General has gone to Richmond again, and I cannot tell now how matters will be in the morning. Mightn't the General have taken me with him this time at least? How very mean & disagreeable he is always to leave me here when he knows how much I would like to accompany him. My dear, I pray don't use such expressions as calling me "for a time Commander of the army of No Virg[a]." You frighten me. It makes me fear something I may have said put the idea into your head. You are a dear little pet to promise not to destroy my fine letters again, but I couldn't easily forgive you for even <u>hinting</u> at the possibility of your "changing your mind and returning them to me," if it were not for the wish you express that you could recover some of them which were committed to the flames a couple of years ago. . . .

Love to Coz Mary. God bless you dearest. Your own

W

50

[To Bettie]

Camp Orange Courthouse

15 March 1864

The General did not return this evening as was expected, and so long as his absence is prolonged may we expect some movement of the enemy or other excitement, as some disturbance must of course occur as has invariably been the case heretofore, if for no other purpose than to annoy & embarrass those who usually look up to him. As I am constantly anticipating some such stir, I have determined to commence my letter now whilst I am in the enjoyment of a little leisure and quiet. We hear that besides our Chief there are in Richmond at this time Johnston, Beauregard & other prominent Generals.[51] What does it all mean? I presume they are arranging some terrible work for us. I would make but two requests of the council—one that they would insist upon the President's removing the present Commissary General and the other that they would return Longstreet's Corps to us.[52] With these changes I would hope for a decisive and beneficial result, and wouldn't care a penny whether the Emperor Napoleon recognized our Confederacy or not.[53] Our people are once again considerably agitated on this foreign recognition question. There may be some foundation for the rumor, but

I fear that it had its origin in the brain of some stock speculator who started the report to influence the market and thus enable him to advance his own personal aggrandizement. But though I relate to you all that actually occurs of an exciting nature in our army, it is not my intention to pervert my letters to you to essays on the present state and future prospects of the country. I see enough and hear enough of the war and its concomitants in the performance of my official duties and my letters are the only recreation and source of enjoyment which are vouchsafed to me at this time. I desire in mine to you to ignore all that appertains to the miserable bore, which the present struggle has become, except what might prove of interest to you. Before I dismiss the subject however, I will answer the question you put to me in your last, relative to the light in which we as Christians are to regard our enemies. I agree with you fully, my dear Bettie, that when we are told to "love our enemies" and apply the injunction to ourselves as regards our present enemies, the Yankees, it is not expected that we shall attach the equal significance to the word "love." It cannot be that it is meant that it should be received in its common acceptation. It is not to be expected of human nature that we shall entertain towards our bitter enemies the sentiment of affection which the word, literally construed would imply. But I do think it is intended that we should not cultivate hateful and revengeful thoughts—that we shd not exercise a bitter, unrelenting spirit towards them, but on the contrary return good for evil. Indeed it strikes me that the lesson is presented in its simplest form in the Lord's Prayer, wherein we are taught to say "Forgive us our trespasses as we forgive those who trespass against us," or as it is put in the Exhortation which the minister is required to make to the people (in our service) when warning them as to the manner in which the Lord's supper should be commemorated,—"and being likewise ready to forgive others who have offended you, as ye would have forgiveness of yr offences at God's hand." That is, we must forgive, if we expect or hope for forgiveness. Now, however much we may be wronged by our enemies, however great grievance may be committed against us, we never can be called upon to forgive as much as that for which God has promised to forgive us. Remember how heinous Sin is in His sight. It was for us that His son suffered death. We break His law every day and yet when we ask it, we receive a full pardon.

As we expect forgiveness then, we must forgive those who wish to do us evil. 'Tis out of the question, I admit, to feel any affection for our present enemies—'tis a hard matter to forgive them the great wrong done us. Bitter thoughts will arise, a desire for <u>revenge</u> will possess our minds, but 'tis against these we must struggle. In the Litany we every Sunday beseech God to "forgive our enemies, persecutors & slanderers," to "turn their hearts." I trust that with the whole Church this is no mockery but an earnest beautiful prayer. We don't pray for their success, we only ask that the offences they commit against God and ourselves may not be treasured up against them in the final reckoning. I don't hesitate to say that if I had the power and the opportunity I would utterly destroy their whole army, & yet I would not wish them any suffering in the future. I would do this not in a spirit of <u>revenge,</u> but as the surest way to put an end to the present unhappy, sinful war. Heaven knows I have no <u>love</u> for them and I can only pray that if it is my duty to love them, that I may be taught the lesson by the Holy Spirit. Otherwise I cannot consent to love <u>that</u> people collectively or individually, but still I try constantly not to cherish any sinfully revengeful thoughts towards them. When I reflect upon the suffering they have caused you, my precious, I feel these thoughts rising within my mind; for the moment I feel a desire to crush, to annihilate them. You whose happiness controls my every action, to be worthy of whom is my constant aim, whose affection is dearer to me than all else on earth, that these miserable creatures should inflict upon you the exquisite pain you have endured these past two months, why I would go to any extent to punish them—there is no torture to which I wd not subject them. Then dear Bettie, comes the second sober thought, & I am convinced that that which prompts these desires is not right in the eye of God. Did not I help crucify my Saviour? And has not His merciful Father forgiven me this unparalleled offence? Whilst we cannot love them, let us try earnestly to forgive them.

The Bishop has just paid us a visit. I was privileged to hear him twice—on Sunday & on yesterday, when we had Confirmation and Communion. The services were very pleasant indeed and the Bishop's sermons & remarks interesting, instructive and appropriate. It was today seven years ago that I was confirmed. I fear that I have not improved those seven years. So much has occurred in that time which I wish had never been. Seven years seems a long way back, and yet I can recall so many incidents of that occasion. On yesterday I took delight in allowing my thoughts to revert back, my own precious one, to the night of your confirmation. Oh, how inexpressibly happy I was that night! My Bettie, I wonder if I do now or ever can love you more earnestly, more entirely than I did that night? Perhaps my devotion for you now is more stable, more deeply fixed, because I am older and it has since been subjected to a rigid test, but certainly it cannot be more genuine or purer. . . .

Sunday night   20 March 1864

After a social chat of some hours the General and several other visitors have just left my tent, and I will devote what remains of the evening to a completion of my letter. I regret that I have nothing of interest to tell you. We are as quiet and comfortable as any army could desire to be at this season. Strange to relate our Chief went to Richmond and returned without our experiencing in the interval any excitement or commotion for which I feel very grateful, as I have been thereby spared the mental anxiety which any attention from the enemy under such circumstances usually entails upon me. We have commenced preparatory steps to place the army in condition for active operations, a resumption of which we must look for ere long. As far as I can judge from the latest papers we have from the North, it appears to be their intention to place Sherman where Grant now is and either to have the latter on duty as Commandr in Chief at Washington with Halleck as Chief of Staff, or to place him at the head of the army of the Potomac.[54] In either position I do not think he is to be feared. He has been much overrated and in my opinion, I am sorry to say, owes more of his reputation to Genl Pemberton's bad management than to his own sagacity & ability. He will find, I trust, that General Lee is a very different man to deal with & if I mistake not will shortly come to grief if he attempts to repeat the tactics in Virginia which proved so successful in Mississippi. Genl Chilton is no longer "one of us." He took his departure for Richmond a day or two since where he will remain permanently. This step will be fraught with one of two results for me. Either it will add to the nominal importance of the position or else the General will secure the services of some wise and more experienced man for his Chief Staff officer. Then, if the latter course is pursued, I must expect one of two things. Either I will continue the performance of my usual duties or, if the new comer has the spirit and pride that a man in his position should have, he will relieve me of that portion of my duties which should properly devolve upon the General's chief representative. Of course this would detract much from my importance, but at the same time it would materially lessen my labors. If I was older and so had more experience, I might expect to fill the position, but it would never do to have such a young man recognized in

139

such a position no matter how far capable he might be of filling its requirements nor how efficiently he might have performed its duties. I shall of course try to be reconciled to whatever arrangement is made, and this will not be very difficult as I can see some way in which I will be benefitted in either event. Do you remember how David Copperfield always imagined that Littimer looked at him in a manner expressively considerate and some times with contempt for his youth, as much as to say "Oh! but he is so very young"?[55] Well, that is the way I feel in my present position! I mean my old place. All my companions on the staff are my seniors, the youngest of them leading me by some ten years and we constantly joke about my tender years & diminutive size. So never mind how much of the duties I may perform, some older head must bear the name & in all amiability I must say that it is right that it be so. We are thus reduced at Head Qrs to the General, two aides and your humble servant. . . .[56]

Amongst other subjects we have discussed tonight was the sad state of our poor city & the tyranny of the Beast. Just think of the cowardly course he has pursued towards poor Mr Wingfield & Dr Armstrong.[57] When our enemies are guilty of such conduct, it is exceedingly difficult to acquire the lesson to which the first part of this letter relates. But nevertheless we must not forget our bounden duty &, hard as it appears, must endeavor to practice forbearance towards those who offend us. On Sundays I always think most of our dear old home. This morning I rode to Orange with the view of attending service, but found the Church so crowded that it was impossible to secure a seat; indeed persons were standing in the aisles nearly half way up, so I quietly came home. What would I not give if I could spend my Sundays in Richmond and what a greater happiness still it would be, if we were privileged to worship as of old at our own altar, so surrounded with sacred and happy memories. Poor little Sistress, though she can visit her Church, I fear she is as unhappy in the possession of this privilege (?) as we are in being debarred it. But let us hope—let us pray that the time is not far distant when our home is to be restored to us. Until then I shall try not to allow what I have lost to affect me by dwelling in thought on the many blessings and privileges which yet remain. I was so glad to hear from Mother that our Page is to be confirmed next Wednesday.[58] By the way, I omitted to mention that Bob Baylor was confirmed and communed last Monday. . . .[59]

I rec'd a letter from yr bro John on yesterday. He is still anxious to get here. Candidly Bettie, would you rather he remain where he is or come here? I sometimes think it wd be advisable to stay in Savannah. My love to your mother & Pattie and Sister and to Mrs Knox. My regards to Mrs Petty. May God bless you. Good night. Your devoted

W.

51

Camp 23d March 1864

My dearest Mother,

Since my last I have rec'd Sister's letter of the 15th enclosing one from Aunt Alex[60]—and on yesterday Bryan brought me yours of the day before with a note to Rob from John. My hat, shirts and socks all received safely. The former pleases me very much, only I think it is a little smaller than it was, but this can be easily remedied by use and moderate stretching. Sister tells me that you and Hunter repudiate the idea of Refugees paying taxes. I don't exactly understand how you will reconcile your consciences to this when the Collector visits you. I thought the tax law a great institution & the people generally seem to regard it as a wise enactment—but in order that good may result from it, everybody must try to ascertain how it affects them and how much they can contribute towards defraying the expenses of the Govt under its provisions, not how little they can get off with. Poney up! then, I say. Bryan tells me you are all very comfortable and from his expression "I tell you they live well at your house in Richmond" I infer you are doing things in style.

I would like very much to run down for a day or two before the campaign opens—it would be a great comfort to me to be with you a little while again—but I see no hope for it now. As you are perhaps aware Gl Chilton has left us & gone to Richmond. He will remain there. Heretofor I have not hesitated when I desired to be absent to let the whole burden down on his devoted shoulders, because it was his work not mine. Two others besides myself constitute all the immediate Head Qr staff. I do not know whether the General will have any one else or not. We are a very few for active operations and will have to work very hard. If no one comes who is my superior in rank it will perhaps add somewhat to my nominal importance—though not much to my labours except in this, as I said before, it will prevent absenting myself on leave. If some one does come and some older man of experience ought to come—then I shall expect one of two things. Either he will allow me to continue the performance of my present duties and look on complacently, as did my friend Chilton—or if he has any pride he will himself assume that portion of the labour which should devolve upon the General's Chief Staff Officer. So you see it matters very little to me personally how 'tis arranged—except the being deprived of all indulgence in the way of leaves of absence. Ask John how G.O. No 27 A &IGO will affect his general.[61] I think it <u>possible</u> he may be retired or reduced upon it. If there is danger of this Jno had better accept Uncle Page's offer.[62] There might be some chance of promotion down South. All things considered I am of the opinion he had better go with Uncle P. You who know all the facts can judge best.

52

[To Bettie]

Camp Orange County

25 March 1864

The first part of the week passed without my having <u>commenced</u> my letter as usual and I had determined to defer writing until Sunday, but circumstances are so propitious this evening that I must avail myself of the occasion to commune with my good angel.

. . . Bettie, I was not before aware how nearly similar are our experiences in spiritual matters. There is not a wish or sentiment contained in your letter which does not accord entirely with my own feelings. That yearning after that peace within which characterized my first days in the Church, is it not always present with me? Then again your wish that you were one of the happy band receiving the Bishop's prayer and blessing whenever you witness that rite of confirmation; even in this we agree, for I experienced the same desire on the occasion of the Bishop's last visit here, and never attend a confirmation that I do not feel an honest longing to have the good Bishop lay his hands on my poor sinful head and beseech God to defend me and cause me to continue His, to increase more and more daily in His Holy Spirit until I come to His everlasting Kingdom. . . .

I went to Orange hoping we might have services there, but I was disappointed. There is no regular minister here and we depend entirely on the visiting clergy.

I trust you have not suffered from a recurrence of that terrible neuralgic attack. Is it not an excruciating, noncontrollable pain? I have tried so many remedies, that I hardly know which to recommend and indeed I think there is very little efficacy in any of them. My experience convinces me it will always have its way, then finally cure itself. It must have been a great comfort indeed for your sister to have Mr Hobson so near her all the winter, but I don't know who deserves a good husband and to have him always with her, more than she does. Perhaps you will be tempted to return to the Neck with her—or will you wait till a little later in the season? It must be beautiful there in May or June. Will Miss Mollie go there?[63] I think I will resign my present position—retire to my 1st Lieutcy and apply for the position of enrolling officer for Goochland county to pick up conscripts, arrest deserters & ride horseback with Pattie[64]—we'll let you ride a little bit when you honor us with a visit. Don't you think it is a good idea? You see it will be such a safe style of warfare, (I mean as regards "blood and thunder" and do not allude to affairs of the heart) and maybe the good people will pet any exhero of the army of Nn Va. By the way, speaking of deserters &c, we have one of the finest & most striking illustrations of the patriotism of the Southern women presented here today that I have ever heard of. A soldier deserted some five months ago, and this morning his wife brought him back like a true woman, pleading that his offence might be forgiven and he restored to duty. She knew too that he would be liable to a trial by court martial and severe punishment; and yet she persuaded him to rejoin his comrades in the ranks. Too good a woman indeed for such a man.

Sunday Night—27th. I have just dismissed my usual Sunday evening visitors—it is a little later than normal. I have not very much time to complete my letter as I would desire. I managed to go to Church this morning & succeeded in securing a seat, though the house was filled to its utmost capacity. It seemed to me there are more ladies here than heretofore & I never saw so many brides at one time. . . .

The General met with three ladies on our return who were on horseback, and as they had to pass near our camp he invited them in to eat a slice of cake. You may not be aware that we do have cake here— and that too of the nicest kind—jelly and pound cake. We have been very fortunate during the past two months. Box after box has been sent to the General containing all sorts of nice things, and indeed but for these presents we would indeed be in a fair way to starve on the one ration order. Gov Vance of No Caro is here on a visit to his troops.[65]

Speech making, tournaments and reviews are the order of the day. There will be a review tomorrow and if the weather is favorable no doubt there will be as many ladies present as soldiers. Of course I never am privileged to attend these entertainments. Indeed I am rather glad to be excused, only I would like to hear some of the music; some of the bands perform remarkably well. Early this morning one within hearing distance of our camp played some very sweet sacred airs. It is no rare thing to hear them play hymns on Sunday. Indeed that which encourages me most now when the campaign is about to open is the decided interest that men and officers throughout the army appear to take in spiritual matters.[66] In this respect our Chief sets a noble example. He attends the meetings of the chaplains and in many ways tries by example and orders to inculcate lessons of morality and piety among the troops. How important it is at this time for every man in this army to pause and consider well his relation to his Maker. How many and who are to survive the bloody scenes soon to be enacted in poor old Virginia? Oh! would it not be comforting if we were assured that all who are to lay down their life this summer were ready and prepared for the final struggle? God grant that only such may be taken. Poor Lydia, as you have perhaps heard, has lost her favorite brother. His was a sad death, not like being killed in the heat of battle, but shot down by a miserable renegade or "buffalo," as they call them. . . .[67]

I didn't intend to fill two sheets of paper, but I find I am at the end of the second & haven't yet begun to say half I wish to. I guess however you have read about twice as much as was desirable and so, my dear pet, I will, after wishing you happy dreams, bid you "Good night." Your

W.

The following letter is not Taylor's, but from Julia Robertson to her brother Duncan—smuggled from Norfolk. It is a good example of the sort of "code" letter that Taylor found so difficult to understand.

53

Norfolk March 27, 1864

My dear "Isaac,"

It has been such a very long time since I have heard of an opportunity to write, that I am afraid you have imagined yourself forgotten by all at home,—far from it I assure you. We have patiently watched and waited for many, many weeks hoping to hear some tidings of you—unfortunately none as yet have reached us and we are forced to possess our souls in patience and take for granted that no news is good news. If this state of affairs continues much longer, I shall be most reluctantly compelled to patronize the Yankee route, as it seems to be the only way now of hearing from our friends. The underground system is becoming gradually extinct—frequently mails are brought in town and, just as we have them almost within our grasp, they are compelled to be destroyed. You cannot imagine the manner in which we are suspected and watched. We live literally in fear and trembling and as to our dear, noble, loyal men their lives are indeed a burden. I have never had it in my power to write since that wretched oath was administered in our town. I cannot describe one half of the misery we endured on account of it or how completely crushed and distressed we have felt ever since. You must never infer by word or deed censure of our people, for the course they took was the only one to be adopted under the circumstances. It stings me to the very quick to hear us sometimes doubted for an instant. I mean the sentiments of our citizens. I, of course, did not take it and I am sure if the happy people in "Dixie" experienced for an instant the miseries we have endured for very nearly two long years, they would appreciate, instead of blaming us. We have literally (excuse the expression) seen the devil, and not only this but we are compelled to get on our knees and hear him prayed for every Sunday save one (communion) of our lives.[68] Every one of us "secesh," as the Yanks term us, pray for our own dear rulers and I doubt if there are any more sincere and heartfelt prayers really prayed for Pres Davis than these offered up for him by his people frequently seated almost side by side with their bitterest foes. Absolve our ministers from all blame. It was either to make this sacrifice or lose our churches and then the pulpits would have been filled by ranting abolitionists. This of course would have banished us forever, and bitter as the pill is I, for one, prefer swallowing it to abandoning our church and having it prostituted by the hateful northern service, and besides I do not consider that we are called upon to make a sacrifice of our sole remaining stay and comfort. Some people think it outrageous to countenance this prayer and pretend to question other's sentiments. I consider mine and those of my acquaintances above suspicion and consequently turn a deaf ear to all such comtemptible insinuation.[69]

145

But away with the wretches and now, if I can, let me forget them for an instant and tell you of your friends. First let me again ask you if you have received any of the articles sent. I will give you a list—2 woolen calico shirts, 2 pr drawers, 2 pr socks, 2 silk handkys, and some soap and a tooth brush in the first bundle, hat and spectacles by another route, boots, pantaloons, cravats and collars in the last. These things should have reached you long ago, and I have been terribly disturbed for fear you have not had the benefit of them during all the cold weather. Take care how you acknowledge the receipt of them. You must write me a very mild, prudent letter; send it to Richmond and get some of your friends to forward it to me by "Flag of Truce" and be sure and mention the acceptable gifts (exasperating term) you have received from your kind friends and relations in "Dixie." This method will answer the double purpose of enlightening me and blinding the yanks. This tried arrangement would not be allowed for an instant if they ever imagined we derived the slightest satisfaction in writing letters for their inspection. I believe they are gotten up to make us feel still more our dependence on them and for the sake of the information they pick up in regard to the Rebs. I do not mean to patronize them if I can possibly manage to slip a letter through in any other way, if I can not, of course, I shall not hesitate to make them subservient to my convenience. I see your family very often. Your mother was confined to her room twice last week but is up and about as usual. Your father and the children are well and all so anxious to see you.[70] That pleasure being denied them, you must try and let them hear from you when you can. The children are most anxious to avail themselves of this opportunity but as I have only the privilege of sending one letter, I must try and write one to each of my three friends and compress them all in one envelope. The friends and relations of my friend and neighbor are so kind in mentioning you in their letters. I am so much indebted to them for their kind consideration. Your old friend Willoughby has been in so much trouble the guards have been stationed in the house and they have been subjected to all sorts of inconvenience and annoyance.[71] Mary Newton was married last Wednesday to "White" Jones[72]—a most unsuitable and unfortunate match. I should say a French ship has been lying off the Point for some time and the officers have been flying around quite extensively. I like one or two I know quite well, the others are a little too frenchy in their deportment to suit my ideas of decorum. It is well however to have foreign acquaintances. They have in many instances proved to be friends in need. We are just getting over the

worst snow storm I have seen since '56—the streets have been impass-
able since Wednesday. Tomorrow will be Easter Sunday and it looks
and feels much more like Christmas. I never hear either of or from our
friend [Bettie]. I suppose she is still in the country—her happy home
has passed into the hands of the enemy and been confiscated. Do you
ever see L? [Lelia Taylor] I think of both these dear girls so often and
long to see and be with them. Ask B [Bob Taylor] to tell his wife she
must write me by "Flag" and remember me to him most kindly. To my
precious E. H. [Ellie Henderson] you must certainly write and always
give my warmest love. I always send him a letter when I write you and
trust they sometimes reach him. To dear W [Walter] ever give my love,
tell him our mutual friend [Fannie Kerr] is well and has written him
frequently.[73] We confidently look for peace with the termination of this
year and are promising ourselves so much happiness in having our
dear ones home. As I must write to our friend, I must say farewell to
you. With ever so much to all my friends and much to yourself I remain as ever yours devotedly

[no signature]

54

[To Bettie]

Camp Orange County

3d April 1864

My evening visitors were a long time with me tonight and 'tis now
at least eleven o'clock and I have just begun my usual letter. The day, I
regret to say, has not been a satisfactory one to me, and not as profitably spent as I would have wished it. I could not attend Church service
and what is still more to be deplored I have not been able to read the
service as is my custom when compelled to remain at home on Sunday.
I often try to devise some way in which I can avoid work on this day
and wish particularly that I could so manage as not to keep my clerks
busy but I cannot so arrange it, really I cannot. It is truly a work of
necessity. If I were to postpone what accumulates during the day for
attention on Monday, apart from the inconvenience to the army, I
would find myself swamped when Monday came, because every day
brings just what I can accomplish and if the task were to be increased,

I am afraid that I shd prove unequal to it. Yesterday and today have been fraught with reports from the enemy in our front. They are said to be receiving reinforcements, sending back their sick and in every way preparing for the final great "on to Richmond." Two Corps are said to have joined Grant from the west.[74] No doubt he will call to his assistance every available man. But if we can only get old Longstreet with that portion of our <u>family</u> now under him, we will be able to meet successfully all that Grant can collect. The General called me into his tent this afternoon to talk over some matters, and after discussing several things all relating to Grant's movements & probable intentions he said "but Colo we have got to whip them, we must whip them and it has already made me better to think of it." He had been complaining somewhat and it really seemed to do him good to look forward to the trial of strength soon to ensue between himself & the present idol of the North. Our army increases daily. In morale & discipline its condition is excellent. We are taking the necessary steps to put the "concern" in fighting trim—reducing baggage—getting up horses—&c. Have entirely suspended leaves to officers and all begins to look like work. I am very hopeful, feeling confident that with God's help, we will defeat their last great effort & make this the last year of <u>serious</u> fighting. I have reluctantly given up all hope of getting to Richmond before we begin. Indeed I do not now feel that I would be justified in asking to be indulged. There is no one here who could relieve me of my duties & whilst no leaves are being allowed, for consistency sake the same rule should apply to army Headquarters. Aside from my desire to see and be with those who are near to me for a little while before the tempest is upon us, I have other good reasons for wishing to be in Richmond for a few days, but I must make up my mind to it, and try to be reconciled to what is demanded "by the interests of the service." I was and am very anxious, Bettie, to see you once more before the opening of the campaign. It would be such a comfort to me. Do you not wish it could be so? . . .

I was surprised to see in a letter from Duncan to Ellie Henderson that he was at Howard's Neck. In his application for leave of absence he stated that he wished to visit Charleston, has he been there? By the way, when you write to Julia, do tell her that I have heard from E. H. twice recently & that he is well and always speaks of his Norfolk relatives. Frank Huger came and spent the evening with me a few nights since, and I was certainly glad to see him and enjoyed our talk over dear old friends and affairs in our poor city, as they <u>used</u> to be. I wonder if I will ever meet those I knew and loved so well, & with a heart filled with gratitude look back upon these troublous times as past trials! Oh how happy we will all be if spared to see that day! Three long years have elapsed since I left home and yet this memory of those true friends and the happy time spent with them is so fresh with me that I can hardly realize how many & great changes have occurred in that time. Theod Williams paid me a visit day before yesterday, his special object being to procure a pass for Mrs W. & some of her family & friends to pass beyond our lines.[75] She is to return to her home. If she is to run away from him so soon, I don't see why they were married. Theod had her picture—two indeed—& seemed to take great delight in exhibiting them to me. One represented her as being quite pretty—the other less so. My chum Venable and I were very much amused to hear him talk of "my wife this" and "my wife did that." It sounded like a small boy's talk about a new toy. He is evidently infatuated & quite beside himself because of the novel joy of being a husband to the angel of his choice. . . .

I find that I have not said half I wanted—but will defer the balance till next week. I won't ask you to write for I know you will do so when you can.

W.

55

[To Bettie]

Camp Orange County

10 April 1864

I wrote you a long letter last night, Bettie, much more closely written than mine usually are, but on glancing over it, I had determined not to send it, as it doesn't at all suit me. In the first place it contains a great deal of trash in direct opposition to what you have advised me to do; and secondly I indulged some reflections in connection with the approaching battle which are rather too solemn. They do well enough when confined to my own mind, but no good would result from communicating them to you. [The letter referred to has not survived.]

. . . Well, Grant is receiving reinforcements as I have told you before; indeed I believe I've told you all about him that is worth knowing. The heavy rains will keep him quiet for a few days at least. It is very evident that the good people of Richmond expect us to allow them to have the pleasure of a siege & I presume from what I hear that they daily expect to see us come tumbling down towards and into the "defences,"—but indeed we can't gratify them so far, we prefer waiting here to do the handsome by Mr Grant and after that we contemplate a little pleasure trip. Don't you fear about Longstreet, he will be in the right place at the right time perhaps. The Northern papers state that Col Ould and Col Mulford have arranged for a resumption of the exchange under the cartel[76]—not General Butler—so I hope that may be communicated to the croakers. I wish some power would arrest those gentlemen in Richmond who wear lugubrious countenances & send them up here in irons that they might be made cheerful. Matters never looked so bright to me as now. I think we can now see daylight. Gold goes steadily up in New York—170 was the last quotation. If by Divine assistance we succeed in defeating Grant, it will leap at once to 200. And what is more, if God does add another to our list of victories, we may confidently look for peace soon thereafter. This army is determined, always presupposing Heaven's help, to accomplish this. It will be a terrible fight, but I believe our men will acquit themselves well. Many of us, who can say which? will be called upon to pay the purchase with our lives, but the issue will be glorious. How can those chicken hearted people in Richmond take such a gloomy view of things! Tell them to look at the wall of strong arms and brave hearts that defines our front, especially this firm old stonewall in Virginia. Can they not, after invoking the aid of a righteous & allpowerful God, confide in His protecting power? Shame on them thus to reflect on our scarred & well tried veterans! Put them to bed and administer the oath—they are fit for nothing else. As to the currency—in good time it will right itself—and even if it does not, what then? We have very little intercourse with the outside world and in our transactions among ourselves, what matters the currency? Let those at home raise corn and bacon and give it for the sustenance of the army. Let every man cease his growling and take hold, lend a hand in earnest. I really believe there are few who would desire and expect to receive their independence without raising a finger in defence of their liberties or surrendering an accustomed luxury for the maintenance of those who go forth to protect their rights. I hope these exceptions are few, for if we were all so, we would not deserve to be free, but be fit subjects even for the Yankees. The women, Heaven bless them, in their spirit and earnest works set these apologies for men an example worthy of emulation. . . .

I did not get to Church today nor on Friday. Would you believe it, although a tremendous congregation assembled on Fast day, there was no one to read the services or preach! Was it not too bad? The General said he would have written to the Bishop and requested him to send some one up here, had he known how matters were.[77] Miss M. Gay is visiting near us.[78] I would like to call on her but cannot properly get away. I am afraid she has had a very dull time, for it has rained incessantly for the past week. Tomorrow there was to be a great tournament, but I presume it will be postponed, as the ground is not in suitable condition for riding. Starke I understand is a leading spirit in such matters.[79] I suppose Robbie is generally on hand also. I heard that he was at Church on Friday with four young ladies on horseback. Miss Baynie is beyond the lines, but the merry fellow does the sensible thing, keeps a light heart and makes himself useful. We are to have a new chief engineer—no less a personage than Major General M. L. Smith.[80] He has tremendous rank for the position; it has heretofore been filled by a Lieut Colonel. We imagined at first that he might come as Chief A.A.G. but it seems the engineer department is to be his specialty. So I am still in the dark as to who is to come to my relief. I fear the time will have passed when I might be benefitted, before he arrives. We received intelligence this evening of a success on a small scale at Winchester. A party of our men attacked & whipped a body of the enemy's cavalry, capturing a number of prisoners, horses &c. It was a small affair but still gratifying.[81] All such encourage our men. . . .

God bless you, my precious Bettie. Good night. Your

W.

56

Camp Orange County

18 April 1864

I have had a most fatiguing day, Bettie, but as I am already one day behind hand I will not longer defer writing my usual letter. For a long while I have debated with my conscience whether it was positively necessary for me to work on Sunday. I had convinced myself that it was really necessary. Latterly I have thought much on the question & have been impressed with the importance of the decision and the responsibility resting upon me in asking it, for five others, my clerks, were also concerned & when I decided for myself I also decided for them. I determined to begin on yesterday a new plan to allow the work to accumulate until Monday and then see if I could not on that day accomplish all that was presented. It quite frightened me to contemplate the large pile of paper that on last evening awaited my attention. I enjoyed the quiet day except the consciousness of the work undone which was ever present with me. Other reasons prevented my going to Church in the morning, which I regretted only the more when I learned that Mr Peterkin had preached.[82] Understanding that he would hold service at night, I determined to avail myself of the opportunity of hearing him—so I went to Orange by a beautiful bright moon, heard a nice sermon and returned, I trust, somewhat benefitted. To make up for the quietude and rest of yesterday, I was up and at work some two hours before breakfast this morning and am so exhausted now that I expect the only result of this attempt at a letter will be that you will vote me a decided bore.

Nothing of interest with the army has occurred since my last. All accounts from the enemy indicate earnest preparations on their part for an early resumption of active operations. Their force in our immediate front has not been materially increased—all the troops that have come from the west have been concentrated at Annapolis[83]—the destination of this column is involved in doubt, but I hope all will be known in good time. If any change has taken place with us, we are in better condition and more hopeful than ever. Gold steadily advances in New York and I trust we shall ere long accelerate its upward tendency by administering a crushing blow upon their boasted commander in chief & his invincible (?) army. The General was directed some days since to inquire of General Meade if he or his Government sanctioned what Dahlgren had proposed and ordered in his address to his troops; this morning the answer came & it is to the effect that neither Gl Meade, Gl Kilpatrick nor the authorities at Washington ordered or approved the burning of Richmond, the killing of Mr Davis & his cabinet or anything else not rendered necessary by military causes.[84] That rascal Kilpatrick in his letter says that the copies (photographic) of the address which we sent were verbatim copies of an address which Col Dahlgren had submitted to him & which he had approved in red ink except that they lacked this approval and had that about burning the city & killing the high officials, thereby intimating that we had forged these copies & interpolated the objectionable exhortations. The low wretch—he approved the whole thing I am confident now. Gl Meade's disclaimer is much more decided and candid—that I had expected. Do not say anything of this unless you hear of it from another quarter. I have just received a report of their having moved the 5th Corps to the front, this looks like a preparatory step to a forward movement.[85] The issue of this approaching contest is fraught with vast consequences to our country and cause. I never felt more hopeful and am almost anxious for the fray. Many poor fellows are to fight their last fight on earth & many hearts made sad, but if God is with us and vouchsafes to bless us with victory how great a cause for rejoicing there will then be! Oh such a time as this, how anxiously should we, whose lives are suspended as it were on a thread, pray to be ready for whatever may be ordained. Oh God, how earnestly do I pray & hope that the light that is in me may not be darkness! Sometimes when I consider the mercy and goodness of my Saviour, his great love for his people & readiness to save them, I experience such a happy sense of security—and then again I tremble lest I should be deceiving myself with too much hope—lest I should be over confident,—ever sure of having obtained forgiveness. May God pity my great weakness and protect me. By the way whilst I think of it, let me tell you in case of any accident to my person or effects, that such of your letters as are not in Richmond have been destroyed. I never before burned any, but have none now with me save your last & that I will also destroy. So you need have no apprehension of the Yankees ever getting hold of any of them; & if accident befalls me you will get from my mother those that are in my trunk in Richmond. A few I preferred keeping & sent properly sealed in a package by the hands of my courier to be placed with the others in the receptacle set apart for my private papers. . . .

Oh I feel so light of heart when I can get away from my office, mount some eminence and take in the glorious prospect that is on every side presented to the eye in this pretty section of the country. There may be a great deal of wickedness in the world, there is unquestionably much sorrow, but for all that, it is a very pretty world and if we properly appreciate the blessings derived from our Maker whilst sojourning in it, it can be to a certain extent a happy world. . . .

Please say to Tom & Mr Adams I have investigated the matter of cartridges & find we are all right up here.[86] I presume you have heard that Longstreet is where I told you he wd be "in the right place."[87] Give my love to Coz Mary. Venable retd from a pleasure trip today. Marshall has been off recently. I wd make an effort to run down a day or two now—just a day or two before the battle, but it would be too great a <u>self</u> indulgence!—Sincerely

W.

57

[To Bettie]

The victory in the west occurred on <u>the last day of fasting & prayer.</u>[88] This shd encourage us.

Camp

24 April 1864

I have had a charmingly quiet day of rest. The weather is really spring-like; about twilight the air was resonant with the cries of the Whip-poor-Wills, which have a peculiar fascination to me, I presume because they announce the advent of my favorite season. I feel particularly calm & happy this evening. It is at such a time & with such feelings as the present that I long most earnestly for the presence & sympathy of—well, my dear Mother or any one else who loves me, or cares for & feels an interest in me. My new regulation, preventing work on Sunday, works admirably. It is true I have more to do on Monday in consequence, but consciousness of having been enabled by Divine assistance to forsake a sin, more than compensates for the extra labour of the latter day. I have never yet known anyone to be but benefitted by an earnest endeavour to do the right. We had Mr Minnegerode to preach for us this morning;[89] he gave a very fine sermon & I enjoyed the services very much if I except one or two unpleasant little incidents, for I had the misfortune to have a lady's dress catch my spur as she walked up the aisle, & strange to say, I was selfpossessed enough to relieve us both from embarrassment by a most dexterous & expeditious endeavour to induce the spur to let go; then the Church was crowded and I relinquished my seat for the ladies, succeeded in procuring another, I fear to the discomfort of my companions who were indiscreet enough to invite me in after the pew was filled to its capacity, & had scarcely taken my seat when a courier came up to me & delivered a dispatch relative to some movements of the enemy, which of course set every body around to cogitating what was in the wind. These little occurrences detracted somewhat from my enjoyment, but still it was a great treat to hear Mr Minnegerode. It is very kind of him & Mr Peterkin to come up here and officiate for us. . . .

We have Northern papers of the 20th. They candidly admit a severe Union defeat near Shreveport. Division after division was beaten, and finally their whole army was routed. With a heavy loss in men, artillery &c they have retreated to Great Ecore, a point some forty miles from the field of battle. It was really a grand success of our arms. Genl Forrest takes up the shout of victory at Fort Pillow and Genl Hoke on the extreme right sends back a glorious return from Plymouth.[90] We are very much cheered by these successes. A magnificent opening for the spring campaign. Truly God seems to be with us. We here are calmly awaiting the signal. From reports just received, it may be that the time is very near. During this winter I have made every exertion so far as I could with my humble capacity in my official position to raise this army to its highest state of efficiency. No effort has been spared to increase its numerical strength and to elevate its condition in every respect. Never was it in better trim than now. There is no overweening confidence, but a calm, firm & positive determination to be victorious, with God's help. I am proud of our army, and am almost anxious for the signal for the next & greatest struggle. A portion of our family has been returned to us. Old Pete Longstreet is with us and all seems propitious. Give us yr prayers you good people at home. If Divine aid is still vouchsafed us, all will be well, and peace— glorious, welcome peace will visit us before the end of the year. Then we will be reunited at our old home, (I must confess it is still dear to me) friends, dear & loving, will be restored to us and comparative happiness will once more fill our hearts. Did you read the trial by "the Beast" of Mr Armstrong?[91] Was it not enough to make one's blood boil? These are the enemies, Bettie, that we find it difficult to forgive. . . .

I have much to call me to Richmond, but the probability of an engagement here, in conjunction with arguments recently advanced from a source most powerful with me, deters me from asking an indulgence at this time. It may be better as it is. If I am spared, well & good, if not, still, no doubt, well & good. . . .

As ever Yr

W

It is well for you this sheet is so small for I have scarcely made a beginning of what I wd like to say.

———————

Julia's "Dear Isaac" letter of March 27, 1864 (Letter 53) has gone the rounds and, after a month, reached Taylor. The following two letters contain his response to it.

———————————————

58

Camp

27th April 1864

My dear Bettie,

Duncan was so kind as to send me his letters to read, and directed me, after perusing them, to send them to you & request you after reading to send them to your Mother. I send them at once instead of waiting for my next letter. D. also says he will be obliged if you will retain his specs for the present, as he has a good pair with him. I am very sorry that Mr Rodman has had so much trouble, but don't exactly understand the difficulty. Why did the Congregation wish him to resign? Was it because of the oath?[92] Is it Margaret Newton who is said to have married, and please tell me what Jones is it that has thus been made happy.[93] Our good Norfolk people are compelled to write so carefully that their letters are enigmas to me. Robbie received two today from Miss Baynie—have not yet heard of their contents. Your nice letter mailed on Monday reached me last night—quick time. Many thanks, my pet; it came sooner than I even dared to hope. I am very tired tonight & will defer my letter until the usual time. Oh! Bet you will be ashamed of me, when you know what a terribly cross, unstable fellow I am becoming. I get so impatient sometimes & allow myself to be so annoyed by these miserable papers, that I fear ill temper will become chronic with me. Though it is very trying to be constantly, unceasingly up to one's eyes in business and papers, I cannot excuse myself. I will try to do better. If I get <u>cross,</u> you must cure me. Do you really wish me to come to Richmond? I don't believe you. If I thought so, I might <u>possibly</u> make the attempt, but you can't induce me to think that you care a fig either way. You & Coz Mary "<u>saw enough of me</u> last winter." Aren't you both ashamed to wound me so?

W.

59

Camp Orange County

1 May 1864

Having dismissed my visitors, my dear B, I will devote the balance of the evening to you. I have enjoyed a peaceful, pleasant day. Old Mr Wilmer preached for us and gave us a most excellent service. . . .[94] After service I rode to the camp of Genl Mahone, the second visit I have paid his headquarters in six or seven months. I am indebted to you for this visit—which, by the way, I exceedingly enjoyed. Duncan had hardly left my tent on yesterday when I received the letters you enclosed from Norfolk. I immediately sent after him but the courier was unsuccessful, so today I determined to take them myself, and at the same time hear the news. I enclose you Julia's letter at Duncan's request. I feared that whilst Julia had not forgotten me, that she perhaps considered herself aggrieved because of my apparent silence, inasmuch as she never receives the letters I send her. But the message through you & the allusion & message to "dear W" in the enclosed, I am vain enough to take all to myself & so my doubts have been dissipated. I also presume that "our mutual friend" she mentions as having written to me is Fan K. . . .

Dear Julia argues strongly for those who have taken the oath; whilst I will not condemn or judge them, I still hold to my former opinion that had our people maintained a firm, unyielding position, the Yankees would have been nonplussed & would have been no more tyrannical, no more unreasonable than they were under existing circumstances. The motives of our friends were unquestionably good. The wisdom of the course pursued, I deem as questionable. Mr Rodman has my most earnest sympathy. The good man no doubt was prompted in all that he did by a sense of duty. Why the congregation should take exception to his conduct, I cannot understand. I really loved Mr Rodman, and shall feel very sad to know that he is altogether separated from us. I dont think the congregation should have taken any action in the matter in the absence of so many of its members in "Dixie." We certainly should have been allowed a vote. . . . Duncan, Robbie & Gl Mahone gave me many new points of interest concerning the doings of Norfolk people. I am entirely isolated from all my old friends & rarely learn anything from our old city. I expect that I am not aware of one half of the changes that have occurred there during the past three years but never mind, we will have a happy reunion there in less than a year, and <u>then</u> I shall find no difficulty in informing myself accurately.

Burnside has joined Grant.[95] It will take them perhaps three or four days to get matters into shape for an attack. At any day after that period, we will not be surprised to hear that the last "onward" has commenced. Grant may perhaps manage to get together seventy or eighty thousand men—the latter figure will, I think, cover every man he has or will have for this battle. If all our army is placed under Gl Lee's control, I have no fear of the result.[96] Even as matters now stand, with the help of God, we will render the usual good account of victory. I am deeply impressed with the vast importance of success in this campaign. If Grant's army is demolished, I don't think there is a doubt but that peace will be declared before the end of the year. If we are defeated, which may a Kind Providence prevent, then the war must drag on a year or so longer. Oh how earnestly should our people pray for God's help in this emergency. I fervently hope we may be succoured by His timely aid. Our cause appears to me <u>so</u> just and the designs of the enemy <u>so</u> unreasonable and wicked that I can but expect that God will be on our side. Our people should pray not only for victory and peace, but for the brave fellows whose lives are to pay the price of these blessings. The thought occurred to me in Church this morning, as my eyes rested upon several general officers and then upon the officers of lower rank & upon the men, "how many of these are here perhaps for the last time?" Pray for them, my dear good angel, and always include in your petitions an appeal for mercy towards your own but weak & erring Walter. I have frequently thought today of the communion you were enjoying and longed to be with you. My thoughts have been serious, but not sad. It becomes us all & particularly those of this army at this time, to look well to our spiritual condition, to be sure to secure a reasonable hope that we may be prepared for whatever may be ordained. May God be with us individually & collectively. The beginning of the end is, I believe, at hand. Oh, how joyful to both nations will be the tidings of Peace! Only think, dear Bettie, how happy we shall be at peace, at rest once more—to return to our homes and old associations! I pray God to spare me, if it is His will, to enjoy these great blessings with you my precious one. Oh, Bet, I shall feel that my cup of happiness is full when that time comes. This view of life certainly makes it more attractive to my eyes, and yet 'tis a glorious thing to die in defence of one's country and loved ones. This is the first battle I have regarded in anticipation since <u>last September</u>. Previous to that time I was accustomed to look forward to a fight with far less anxiety than I now do. Then, outside of my own family, I knew of no one who took any special interest in my fate, or who would be personally interested in it. Now my mind is constantly filled with thoughts of my little "sensitive plant" and I can't help being a little anxious.[97] But we will place the result in God's hands my dearest, fully assured that all will be well. Day by day our army advances in numbers and efficiency—all are buoyant with hope. Reports from the enemy represent their men as by no means anxious to encounter us—many say they will not cross the river. We attach no consequence to their idle speeches, but they do not indicate an enviable state of feeling on the part of the soldiers of Grant's army. Never did matters look so bright for us. I hope soon to be able to announce a great victory to you. The time has passed when I might <u>possibly</u> have visited Richmond. My dearest, if I could be with you but one hour, it wd be such a comfort! But 'tis all well. Let us ever hope and pray. Give my love to Cousin Mary and to all at "The Neck" when you write. Has Coz M left the Treasury Dept? You only spoke of her sister leaving for Columbia.[98] Bet, you have never explained to me about the blanks from the Conscript Bureau I constantly see filled out in yr handwriting. Please don't attempt too much.[99] May God bless & keep you always Yr devoted

W.

Figure 1. Walter Taylor as a cadet at the Virginia Military Institute, ca. 1855. (WHT Papers.)

Figure 2. Bettie Saunders, ca. 1860. (WHT Papers.)

Figure 3. Taylor as First Lieutenant, Company F, Sixth Virginia, April 1861, in the uniform of the Southern Guard, Virginia Militia. (Eleanor S. Brockenbrough Library, Museum of the Confederacy, Richmond, Va.)

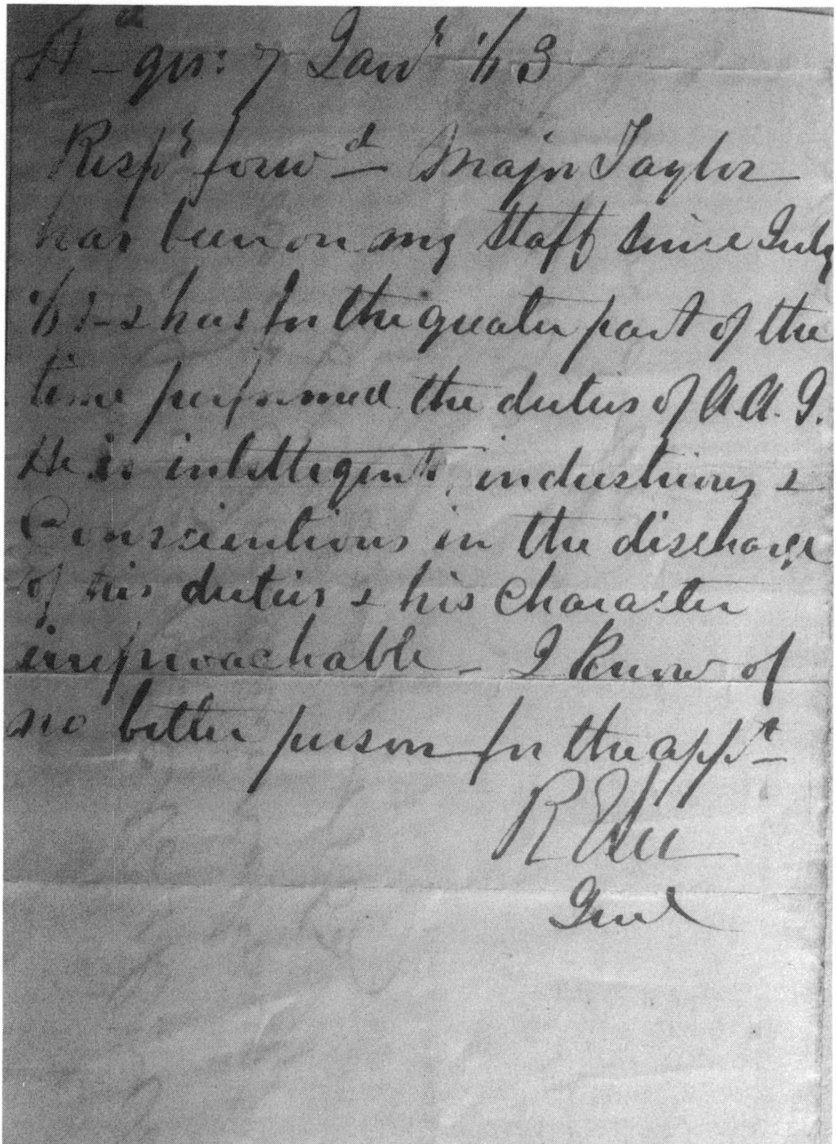

Hd-qrs: 7 Jan^{y} '63

Resp^{y} forw^{d} — Major Taylor has been on my staff since July '61 & has for the greater part of the time performed the duties of A.A.G. He is intelligent, industrious & Conscientious in the discharge of his duties & his Character irreproachable — I know of no better person for the app^{t} —

R E Lee

Genl

Figure 4. Lee's endorsement of the recommendation for Taylor's promotion to major, January 7, 1863. The text reads: "Resp^{y} forw^{d}—Major Taylor has been on my staff since July '61 & has for the greater part of the time performed the duties of A.A.G. He is intelligent, industrious & Conscientious in the discharge of his duties & his Character irreproachable—I know of no better person for the app^{t}." (Courtesy of Stuart Symington Taylor.)

Figure 5. Carte de visite of Walter Taylor as Major, C.S. Army, 1863. (Eleanor S. Brockenbrough Library, Museum of the Confederacy, Richmond, Va.)

Figure 6. Howard's Neck, near Pemberton, Goochland County, the home during the War of John D. Hobson and Martha B. S. Hobson, Bettie Saunders's first cousin. Frequently mentioned in the letters as "the Neck," Bettie's country retreat. (Wight, *Story of Goochland*.)

Figure 7. Elk Hill, home of Colonel Randolph Harrison and Elizabeth Williamson Harrison, four miles above Howard's Neck, in Goochland County. Resort of Taylor's friends on leave during the War. (Wight, *Story of Goochland*.)

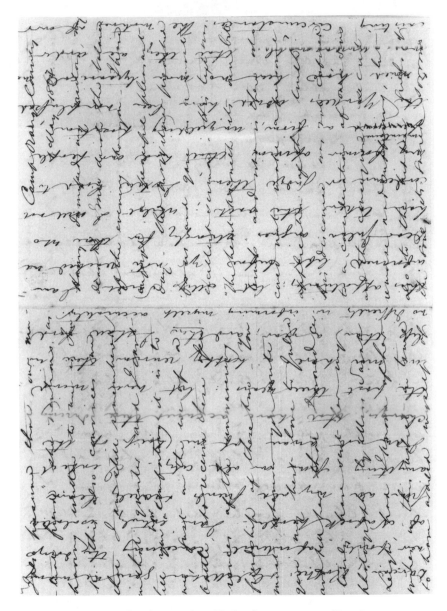

Figure 8. An example of a wartime Taylor letter, cross-written to conserve paper. (WHT Papers.)

Figure 9. Medallion of General Lee and his staff, taken at Petersburg, September 1864. Taylor is directly to the left of Lee. (Eleanor S. Brockenbrough Library, Museum of the Confederacy, Richmond, Va.)

Figure 10. Walter Taylor as lieutenant colonel and AAG on Lee's staff. Detail of medallion. (Eleanor S. Brockenbrough Library, Museum of the Confederacy, Richmond, Va.)

Figure 11. Norwood, the wartime home of Nancy R. K. Selden and Miles C. Selden, Sr., Bettie Saunders's uncle, in Powhatan County, across the James and downstream from Howard's Neck. (Christian and Massie, eds., *Homes and Gardens in Old Virginia*.)

Figure 12. Keswick, the home during the war of Bettie's uncle, Dr. William A. Selden, and his wife Jane D. Selden, in Powhatan County downstream from Norwood. (Christian and Massie, eds., *Homes and Gardens in Old Virginia*.)

Figure 13. Brady photograph of Taylor (on the right) accompanying General Lee, and G. W. C. Lee, on the porch of Lee's house on Franklin Street, Richmond, April 1865, shortly after Appomattox. (Library of Congress.)

Figure 14. Taylor as a civilian, age twenty-seven, 1865 or 1866. (*C.V.*, 24: 234.)

Figure 15. Bettie Saunders Taylor shortly after the war. (WHT Papers.)

Figure 16. Taylor in later life, photographed in uniform by B. S. Campbell, Norfolk. (*Norfolk Virginian-Pilot*, March 2, 1916, WHT Papers.)

Chapter 4

The Wilderness to the Crater:
May to August 1864
(Letters 60–76)

During the bloody campaign from the Rapidan to Petersburg the letters become briefer. Though military news predominates, several important engagements, notably Cold Harbor, are unfortunately passed over in silence.

On May 4, Grant's army of more than 100,000 effectives crossed the Rapidan and entered the Wilderness, where, on the next two days, a bloody but indecisive struggle occurred. The two armies clashed again at Spotsylvania Court House, May 10–12.

60

Near Spottsylvania C.H.

15 May 1864

A courier will start for Richmond in the morning, my dear Bettie, and though it is now quite late, I will send you a line or two to inform you of our good condition, prospects &c. We have had some very severe fighting & a <u>great deal</u> of one kind & another. With one single exception, our encounters with the enemy have been continuously & eminently successful.[1] In the Wilderness we enjoyed several victories over vastly superior numbers—on arriving here we were blessed with another signal success. After we were established here, the enemy attacked every portion of our lines at different times, and with the one exception mentioned, were invariably handsomely repulsed & severely punished. The 12th was an unfortunate day for us—we recovered most of the ground lost but cd not regain our <u>guns.</u> This hurts our pride—but we are determined to make our next success all the greater to make amends for this disaster. Our men are in good heart & condition—our confidence, certainly mine, unimpaired. Grant is beating his head against a wall. His own people confess a loss of 50,000 thus far. He is moving tonight—we expect a renewal of the battle to-morrow. God has been good & kind, & has miraculously preserved me. Asking a continuance of his blessings & mercy & committing you, my precious one, to His Protective care, I remain yours as ever

Walter

61

Telegraph road [between Spotsylvania and Hanover Junction]

22 May 1864

Yours of Wednesday last, my dearest, has just reached me. I have not yet had time to finish reading it. Many, many thanks dear Bettie. I wish you to write regularly—a courier comes up from the Adjt Gnl's office & can always deliver my letters safely. If you knew my precious how I prize your letters, I am confident you wd gratify me in this respect. God has indeed been merciful to me thus far. My preservation really appears miraculous. Poor Bella is doing tolerably well. The only wonder is that she & I were not completely riddled—so close were we to the Yankees, & that too between their line of fire & ours. It was not rashness, dearest, that carried me in such a position, but necessity. Our troops required encouragement & some one to rally them.[2] May God bless you. I must be off again. Pray for our cause & remember always your own & devoted

W.

62

Camp Hanover Junction

23 May 1864

It is early morning and before the duties of the day begin, my dear Bettie, I will add something to the two or three lines sent you on yesterday. For the first time since the 4th of this month, I on yesterday was spared the sight of the miserable Yankees. On the day before it was discovered that the enemy was leaving our front & making towards Bowling Green. He dared not, as we prayed he wd, attack us again at Spottsylvania. With several rivers between us he could move to Bowling Green and below without any danger of our intercepting him. He wd thus get some miles nearer Richmond in a geographical sense, but in reality be as far from it as ever, because this army will still confront him, let him change his base as often as he pleases. To counteract his new design, our army was put in motion for this place. The enemy had the start of us, but by excellent marching we have again placed him in our front. I think it probable he will make still another move to the right & land somewhere near West Point.[3] This would of course necessitate our moving between that point & Richmond. You see we are gradually coming towards you. Why Grant did not carry his army to his new base without incurring the heavy losses he has sustained in battle, I can not say. If Fredericksburg was his destination he cd have obtained possession of it without the loss of 100 men. The same can be said of West Point. After his whipping in the Wilderness, he started for Spottsylvania C.H. hoping to reach there before Genl Lee. There were but few indications of his departure from our front at that time, but Gl Lee seemed to divine his intention & sent a corps to Spottsylvania just in time to meet the enemy at that place. We engaged & beat them back thereby securing Spots. C.H. As the result of this, the Northern papers say we retreated & Grant pursued us, whereas he was totally outgeneraled. No doubt the whole Yankee nation is this day glorying over our retreat to this place. Yet the battlefield was left in our possession & we marched here without any molestation whatever. This does not look like a retreat. Our army is in excellent condition—as good as it was when we met Grant, two weeks since for the first time. He will feel us again before he reaches his prize. His losses have been already fearfully large. Our list of casualties is a sad one to contemplate, but does not compare with his terrible record of killed & wounded; and the man is such a brute, he does not pretend to bury his dead, leaves his wounded without proper attendance, & seems entirely reckless as regards the lives of his men. This and his remarkable pertinacity are the only qualifications he has exhibited, which differ in any way from those of his predecessors. He certainly holds on longer than any of them. He alone of all would have remained this side of the Rappahannock after the battle of the Wilderness. This may be attributable to his nature, or it may be because he knew full well that to relinquish his designs on Richmond, even temporarily, wd forever ruin him & bring about peace. This is, I think, surely the last campaign. God grant us his assistance to bring it to a speedy & successful issue. Of late He has certainly favored us most signally.

Your letter of last Wednesday has been truly a great comfort to me. Oh, my precious, it makes me very happy to see you daily growing in grace & becoming more & more like your Saviour and drawing still nearer to Him. You have a sure hope, Bettie, and the lessons administered by the hand of a kind but all-wise Providence are having the effect He intended. With a spirit of <u>faith</u> & <u>submission,</u> dearest, you will always be contented and peaceful. Continue to strive after such a spirit. God will surely lend you the assistance of His Spirit in attaining this end. It is comforting to us in the field to know that the dear ones at home are daily assembling together in prayer for the success of our efforts. May Heaven hear and answer them & soon relieve us from our great trial. Only think of it, I am now but twenty-seven miles from you—what I write will be in Richmond tonight. What a temptation to <u>desert!</u> . . .

Thank God, with me, Bettie, that my life has been so kindly spared. The evidences of His protecting power have been more apparent during this campaign than ever before with me. I have been in many dangers, but He has covered me with the shelter of His wing. After my escape unhurt from the dangers, I have felt that I had, oh, such cause for thankfulness, and have mourned my great ingratitude towards the Giver of so many favors! When we visit I shall endeavor to give you some idea of our movements since Grant crossed the river, 'twould be useless to attempt it here. Ramseur is all right—slightly wounded & is again on duty. Huger all right. Hunter & Duncan well. Good bye for the present. God bless you prays

W.

63

Camp Atlee's Station

Early morning 30 May 1864

My thoughts are with you, my dear Bettie, this morning & whilst awaiting the General's pleasure, I will thank you for your letter of last Monday & Tuesday. For the third time I have just reread it, & as I finished my heart was filled with joy at the treasure I possess in my "sensitive plant." God bless you, Bettie, for the comfort and happiness you bring me. Though so near you, I find it difficult to send you even a short note, so constantly are my services required by the army, but despite all my engagements, Bet, my last and waking thoughts are of my nearest & dearest. Nine miles only separate us; what a temptation to absent myself if only for a few hours after the army is asleep. I might run into the city & return before day but then it wd not be exactly correct or in accordance with military rules—so I must control myself with the consciousness that I am near you. After the coming struggle is over, if God spares me, I hope then to pay a short visit to the city. Are you acquainted with the state of affairs with our army? It is all so familiar to me that I forget even to tell how matters stand. We are confronting Gl Grant & only waiting to have him located, to have his position &c well developed before the army is let loose at its old opponent. I trust our men will conduct themselves in a manner becoming soldiers in the army of North[n] Virg[a]. If so, & God still vouchsafes us his aid, then we shall have another victory to be thankful for. On yesterday afternoon the enemy appeared to be advancing towards us, and this morning I confidently expected to hear the firing of small arms before this hour. I wish I could have known it wd have remained quiet so long, for I should have made up with a morning's nap for all the rest lost last night. Waked out of sleep every half hour almost, by morning I am so stupid & heavy that it is difficult to make me recover my wits. After three weeks constant fighting, marching and watching I am happy to say however I am still able to keep up & perform my allotted task. The anxiety lest I shd overlook something or commit some serious blunder, tells upon me more than fatigue or loss of rest. The responsibility resting upon me frightens me at times, and each day I am so thankful if I can exhibit a clear and correct record of my acts. The Genl has been somewhat indisposed and cd attend to nothing except what was absolutely necessary for him to know & act upon & during the past week my cares have been thereby increased. He is now improving.[4] I had half a notion to get sick myself, but his attack frightened all sickness away from me. Now that he is himself again, I begin to feel worthless, but thank God I have a strong frame and my little weaknesses soon pass away. Every hour now I experience renewed strength at every breath of the invigorating air that prevails this glorious morning. May God keep you dearest, is the unceasing prayer of your attached

W.

Love to Coz Mary & all at the Neck.

64

Camp

1st June 64

After my return from Richmond, my dear Bettie, I could scarcely realize that I had seen and been with you, so hurried was my visit. Nevertheless it was a great comfort to me. How provoked I was with the miserable Penitent^y bell for striking twelve and then annoyed at my own selfishness in keeping my hardworking and brave little woman up till such a late hour. Can you forgive me? At daylight next morning I started to return & was soon at my customary place ready to do my best to practice humility and receive my clerks' snubbing with the best grace possible. Today we will probably have some excitement, but just now I am so far removed from the line of battle as to be almost ashamed of my position. Since the General's indisposition he has remained more quiet & directs movements from a distance. This is as it should be, & if we had capable lieutenants 'tis the course he might always pursue. All the rest of the Staff have been sent to the front with various messages—only I am tied to "mama's" apron string. But 'tis all well, every one has their appropriate duty & I must accept mine with cheerfulness. We are in good condition. By the way, think nothing about our numerical weakness when compared with Grant's army. Recently we have recd something less than several thousand reinforcements and have plenty of men to manage the enemy.[5] Indeed we begin to feel most comfortable. Our Hd Qrs are now near Mechanicsville, but although so near I will not expect to be blessed with another opportunity of seeing you, until the emergency shall have passed. Having been so far gratified as to be with you once, I must be contented but Oh Bet, how I long to be always with you! my own pet, you do not, cannot know how constantly your image is present with me. Amidst all my little troubles & annoyances, I ever see your face to comfort & encourage me. God bless you my good angel. Do you remember I spoke to you of a young friend—Ned Willis of Savannah who was formerly a staff officer & who had advanced so rapidly, since he changed into the line?[6] You know when I said how unfortunate it was for one to enter the staff & you laughed at me & imagined if I wd have been a Brigadier (you cruel girl). Well, the poor fellow was temporarily assigned to the command of a brigade & on day before yesterday recd a fatal wound. His body has gone to his family. Poor Willis—an only son. I feel so much for his family. Well, well, God's will be done. I commit you to His charge my dearest. Yr own

W.

65

[To Bettie]

7 June 64

Will be up presently—if agreeable to you, we will take a walk.

Yr W.

66

Camp [near Cold Harbor]

9 June 1864

I am still happy, my dear Bettie, in the recollections of my recent delightful, though brief, visit to Richmond. It is so strange to be suddenly translated from a scene like this where everything betokens strife & bloodshed, where war and its sad concomitants are ever present to the mind, to a state of exquisite quiet & happiness such as I enjoyed night before last. I can scarcely convince myself that my visit was a reality & not a happy dream. . . .

Affairs were tolerably quiet with us yesterday; but today this quiet has been complete & remarkable.[7] I have not heard a gun today, nor did I hear many during the night. I presume Grant is waiting for further developments in the Valley. Plague take that force at Staunton say I.[8] I fear it will be increased & prove troublesome to us. But though apparently about to be sorely pressed, I doubt not the good God who has always shielded us, will provide a way of defence and bring us safely through our trials. The pickets between the two armies are more amicably disposed towards each other than heretofore and have ceased the entertainment of sharp shooting. In consideration of the quiet which prevails, I have left the front & returned to camp to resume my old pastime of pouring [sic] over papers. The clerks inform me I have any

quantity on hand. I have disposed of one batch & still time enough before entering on another to send you this egotistical scrawl. I begin to
feel quite happy, I think it is owing to the fact that I am communing
with you, but I will not deny that the mint julep Bryan has just brought
me—so cool & refreshing—has some effect on my physical condition.
This extravagance is something unusual with me, but as I am an invalid I regard it as medical treatment rather than as the indulgence of a
fancy. I would gladly exchange it however for a nice glass of buttermilk
at "The Neck" if I could select my company. Oh Bet, isn't it mean that
we can't do as we please? Let's run away from the Confederate
authorities—bid defiance to the Surgeon General & those at conscript
law—and go to "Sister's." How sweetly Howard's Neck must look
now, & what would I not give for a stroll on the canal with somebody
about seven this evening! Never mind, I wont whine—this disagreeable affair must eventually have a termination & then we shall be all
the more happy, because the blessings we will then enjoy were for so
long a time denied us. Mr Hobson's command moved last evening.
Sheridan is about to enter upon another expedition[9]—in all probability
he will go to the Valley & our cavalry will follow & intercept him. God
grant that your cousin John may always be spared. Old U. S. Grant is
pretty tired of us—at least it appears so. We are in excellent trim—even
in fine spirits—and ready for a renewal of the fight whenever the signal is given. I fear our great danger is that we may become too self-
reliant and boastful. We are apt to take too much credit to ourselves &
to forget Him who is the Giver of all victory & who has so signally favored us.

. . . Write soon, dearest. Heaven's choicest blessings be yours—
prays yrs affectionately

W.

67

Camp 15 June 64 [near Malvern Hill]

Sundown

Dear Bettie

One of our staff and a friend of mine—Col Baldwin—chief of ordnance is quite sick.[10] He bitterly objects to going to a hospital, & is re-

ally endangering his life by remaining in camp. I regret I have no home of my own to which I can invite him; but remembering that Mr Crenshaw has set apart two rooms for wounded & sick officers, I have thought perhaps he wd accommodate Baldwin for a little while. I mentioned this probability to the poor fellow this morning & it seemed to charm him. Yet I hesitate to send him unless assured it wd be agreeable to Mr Crenshaw. Can you in a delicate way ascertain this & let me know by the messenger who bears this? He is a nice fellow & a thorough gentn. His home is in Staunton. I am quite well and most anxious for a letter, which wd entirely restore me. Nothing of importance today. Grant is at or below Westover.[11]

Yr own Walter

68

Petersburg Sunday

19 June 1864

The distance between us has been somewhat lengthened since my last note, my dear Bettie, and sad to say for the present I must relinquish all hope of a ride to the city. It was too provoking to be at Drewry's Bluff, so near, only an hours ride, and yet not be able to see you. Oh what a glorious life, who would not be a soldier? Everything at the Bluff suggested to my mind some incident connected with yourself. How I loved you that evening. How I wished to gallop ahead & join you & ride on & on faster to any place you might select away from the crowd & then enjoy your society all to myself. Well, may be after the railroad is completed & Grant again whipped & reduced to a state of acquiescence, I can make another flying trip to my nearest & dearest.[12] Let me thank you, Bettie, for your note of Friday. It was a great comfort to me last evening, to have it to enjoy after a tiresome day of dust, heat & noise. You cannot know my precious, how very valuable your letters are in my eyes. . . .

John will be with you tonight.[13] I was much surprised to see him last evening. Don't be uneasy about me, dear Bet, I am all right. When one is as determined as I am they must be O.K. God bless you. Yr own

W.

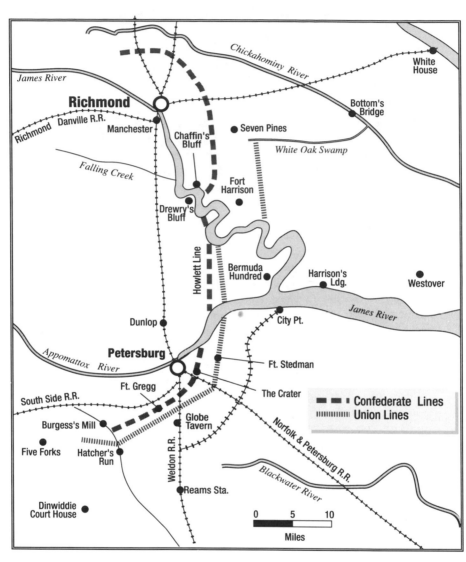

Map 4. Siege of Petersburg, 1864–1865

69

[To Bettie]

Camp at Violet Bank[14]

22 June 1864

Though it is quite late and everybody in camp has retired, I must send you a short note both that I may thank you for your nice letter of Sunday and that I may give you a bit of good news from the scene of war. For the past few days we have had only skirmishing along the lines, with artillery fire—but on yesterday the enemy manifested more activity, and commenced a movement to our right. The movement was continued today, so a part of Hill's Corps was sent out to check it. It so happened however that only 3 of Mahone's brigades (of Anderson's division) were actively engaged—of this number, his own brigade was one. This force attacked the enemy, drove them some distance, captured 4 pieces of artillery, 8 stands of colors and about 1800 prisoners.[15] The report is that the Yankees did not & will not fight with spirit—some of them are said to have laid down their arms & surrendered without discharging a gun. No doubt if our General could manage to attack Grant, & God vouchsafed us His aid, we could rout the enemy and perhaps bring about that much desired peace, which is to witness the crowning of my happiness. The Yankee pickets report that Lincoln is now on a visit to them. Their cavalry has started on a raid which probably aims for Burkeville (Mr Gordon had better look out) and may perhaps succeed in reaching the road, but this will not affect the final issue.[16] We are all in good heart, health & spirits. . . . Though the clock has struck eleven, the artillery continues to send forth its heavy roar & just this moment my ears were saluted with a volley of musketry. How natural and yet how unnatural all this appears! Did I ever tell you what Col Ives said of you? He told me some weeks since that he had heard news of me &c & went on to say how only a few days since in speaking of you he had expressed such admiration for you as to place you second only to his wife. He dwelt particularly on your expression, which so attracted him & oh! I can't tell you what he thought & said of you. The only difference in his opinion & mine was, he placed Mrs Ives first, wh. was natural, & I placed somebody else first—above all, wh. was not only natural but proper & just. God bless you, my good angel—Yr devo

W.

70

Camp at Violet Bank (Petg)

Sunday 3rd July 1864

What has become of my dear Pet that I should have been deprived of my usual letter this week. . . .

I would have made an effort to get to Richmond the past week but as there was a probability of your having left for the country I was afraid to risk it. The Yankees have been a little more quiet than usual and the time seemed opportune, but a visit without meeting you would have only served to make me cross. Please do let me know whenever you think of leaving so that I can regulate my movements accordingly. This is the first Sunday of the month. I have thought much of you and earnestly wished that I was privileged to partake of the Blessed Sacrament with you in St. Paul's. I had hoped at least to have received it here but the firing on this city has been so serious during parts of the week & the Church is in such an exposed position that Mr. Platt thought it advisable not to have service.[17] So I remained home— no, not <u>home</u> but in camp, and read our beautiful Liturgy. As if in deference to the sacredness of the day, the firing on the lines has slackened this morning & only an occasional discharge of cannon is heard as if to remind us that though allowed a respite, the trial is not yet over. What a blessed thing it will be when we can spend a day without hearing this perpetual annoying "pop-pop" of the sharp shooters, and the regular & incessant booming of the large guns! Is the day not near at hand when God shall send us the blessing—Can we not discern in the signs of the times some indications of an early Peace? I really think we can. Am I too sanguine? You will say I am too often so & will cite my predictions of last year to illustrate this better. Maybe it is so, but I would rather be over hopeful than desponding. It keeps me in good spirits at any rate and I have determined now that our good Norfolk people will take their Christmas dinner in the old town.[18] The coming December, our first duty will be to expel the wretched Northern interlopers that have ensconced themselves in our comfortable nests, restore matters as near as possible to their original status and then have a thankful, happy reunion. . . .

Some of my brother officers, who are far in the van of me as regards their pilgrimage on this earth of ours & who are therefore more proper & sedate in their deportment, often rebuke me for the frivolity and want of dignity, of which I am guilty, when treating with them on matters which <u>they</u> deem serious and whilst I confess they must be right—yet I must be allowed some escape for my exuberance of spirits, for in possessing you, my own sensitive plant, I have such cause for happiness that I cannot be otherwise than light of heart & sometimes ascend to the 7th Heaven and become unmanageable.

I fear Mrs. Crenshaw's patient is not likely to recover. Poor fellow, the case is a sad one. His brother was here yesterday & procured permission to visit Richmond to see him—at the same time he expressed a fear that he would not find him alive.[19] How thankful I am that Robbie is doing well[20]—Oh! you can't imagine what a relief it is to one to have those in whose fate you are particularly interested removed from the constantly recurring dangers of the battle field. It is not patriotic I know, but since Rob's wound, whenever his brigade goes into action I am so thankful to know that his life is not being placed in jeopardy. Still on Duncan's account I am always uneasy when those troops have been engaged until I hear of his safety. Genl. Alexander was wounded day before yesterday and our friend Frank Huger, though not the next in rank, has been placed temporarily on duty as Chief of Artillery for that corps.[21] This is a deserved compliment & I am glad old Frank is doing so well. He has many warm friends and admirers. . . .

God bless you dearest—Goodbye—Yr own

W.

71

Camp at Violet Bank

Sunday 10 July 1864

My last dear Bettie was written one week ago today. . . .

More than once I have been on the eve of proposing to the General that I should make a flying trip to Richmond and though I have as often deferred requesting the indulgence, I have by no means entirely forsaken my scheme for enjoyment. I shall urge it on him on motives of policy & for the good of the service; for I am willing to entrust it to any body who knows, if I am not always worth twice as much after my return from a visit to the city and you than I was before my departure. . . .

Nothing of interest has transpired here since I last wrote to you. Interest centers on these points. Even the Yankee nation seems to have forgotten Genl. Grant and the all absorbing topics now are "The Rebel raid"[22] and the "great naval fight." Our poor old "Alabama!" Isn't it too hard? Her antagonist was too strong for her and yet I glory in Semmes' pluck.[23] I only wish it had been the other that was struck. I am so rejoiced that Capt. Semmes made his escape. Oh! how mad the Yankees will be. No doubt they will demand his rendition; and an England might be bullied into compliance. I earnestly hope he will leave Great Britain and thus spare that nation as well as himself much mortification. I trust another Alabama will soon be afloat with Semmes in command and that her career may be as destructive to Northern commerce as was that of the former. We read a New York paper of the 7th with detailed accounts of the engagement & amongst the list of officers I find Midshipman W. H. Sinclair but see no mention of Arthur's name. Was he not on board and which Willie Sinclair—is it my little cousin or Mrs. Terry's son?[24] The surgeon who was drowned (it is feared) was pinned down as Dr. Galt from Norfolk.[25] Who is the mother of Tom Taylor's wife?[26] What a fright old Jubal has occasioned the Washington authorities. Oh! if Jackson was only where he is! He has had a splendid opportunity of accomplishing good, as yet we can not say what he has performed. Our last accounts of him came through the Yankee papers and of course have to be taken with much allowance. He was said to be in Hagerstown on the 6th. Troops have been sent from Grant's army; it is supposed to meet Early and defend Washington. It is impossible to ascertain how many have left but U.S.G. will attempt nothing of an aggressive character until their return so I expect a continuance of the present quiet and shall therefore, my "dear sensitive plant" hope soon to be with you.

Mr. Platt was on his way to town this morning to open his Church but when opposite our camp, the idea occurred to him that it wd. perhaps be found advisable to have service near us. Of course we advised the latter, for besides being far more pleasant in the shady woods than in a crowded building, it was safer, for shells frequently fall in the neighborhood of his Church and indeed since morning I have learned that on Friday one shell penetrated the basement of the building, where Mr. P. thought a congregation could assemble with safety. We had a respectable audience and he gave us a most earnest discourse; his text "How shall we escape if we neglect so great salvation." It was well selected and adds another to the many warnings we all have had

173

and which if not heeded will be bitterly recalled at the last day. I hoped that we might all take that appeal, the invitation he gave us, seriously to heart so that the day's services should be productive of naught but good. What would you not give Bettie for one quiet day in our old home Church. To be permitted once more to kneel & worship in Peace. I think I can enter into the spirit of our beautiful service there to a greater extent than any where else. Here for example we have all the concomitants of war; the boomings of cannon heard whilst the prayers of the congregation are ascending to the Throne of grace; and I cannot experience that calm happy feeling which I have so often enjoyed in dear old St. Paul's & more especially my own much loved Church.[27] Maybe this should not be so, for Christ is as near me here as there but happy associations certainly assist in making our devotions earnest, and I presume 'tis but in keeping with human nature that it should be so. . . .

The people here are very kind to us and send us many nice things, besides frequent invitations to dinner, supper &c. I have special reference to these near whose house we are camped, though all are very hospitable. One lady sent us a few days since some of the nicest ice cream & oh! how I wished you could enjoy some of it! Let me console you though, my precious, by telling you that in your absence I consumed your share as well as my own. You know how fond I am of it & it is now one of the greatest scarcities. . . .

Do tell Pattie that it is my real opinion that peace cannot be much longer deferred. Give my best love to her, your mother, Sister and all at the Neck. Also to Coz. Mary—to whom I always desire to send a return for her kind remembrances. Baldwin regretted his inability to pay his respects in person & tendered his thanks for your kindness to him. Good bye for a week. God bless you prays yr own

W.

72

[To Bettie]

Camp at Violet Bank

22 July, 1864

I had concluded that I would not write to you 'till next Sunday, just to punish you a little for telling me so cruelly that you didn't wish me to visit Richmond again soon, and the fact that I have received no letter this week rather encouraged my bad intentions. I find myself so constantly thinking of you however, that in self defense to say nothing of an uneasy conscience, I am constrained to put some of my thoughts on paper. . . . What do you suppose Lizzie asked Mag?[28] If "Walter had altered any because of his high position." Now wasn't that mean? I only wish for an occasion to lecture her quite seriously about so lightly estimating my head and heart. In the first place a Lieutenant Colonelcy is not such an exalted position, even if the individual is at the right hand of the "greatest man of the day" and privileged to receive his —— [letter damaged—word indecipherable]. . . .

Say to Coz. Mary that I will with pleasure forward as addressed the two letters I this morning received from her. Ask her why she didn't send me a little longer note. I might then have written one in reply and you know that would be second only to the "precious" one she wishes for from the Great Tycoon. She alluded to the good news we were to receive from the Yankee lines and reminded me of the fact that six instead of one or two days had elapsed since I asked if you would not like to hear it.[29] I declare we have had as many foolish rumors as generally prevail in Big Richmond; it has truly been amusing to observe how narrowly every one watches for incidents corroborative of the death of Ulysses. Indeed some are so unwilling to believe that he still lives, that even in the reports of this morning attention is called to the fact that the enemy's bands were on yesterday performing funeral dirges &c. But the last and crowning "grape vine telegram" is to the effect that Genl. Meade has secretly notified Genl. Wise (it is said, but with how much truth I cannot tell, that they married sisters) that he is tired of the U. States service & disgusted at Grant's treatment of him and that if our Government will give him a position, he will come over to our side and bring all his army with him.[30] Now what do you think of that? Didn't I tell you peace would soon be declared! This is the last excitement—if anything new & more refreshing should transpire, you shall surely be advised. These scamps in the trenches having become accustomed to the sharp shooting & mortar shelling, pass their time in circulating these preposterous stories & find some credulous enough to lend a listening ear. I should not omit to mention that Burnside has some thousands of negroes underground—not dead & buried— mining our works. Some of our fellows actually overheard them digging some fifteen feet deep & about as many yards in front of our lines of entrenchments. At least so they say.[31] No doubt these important facts will be announced to the public through the papers ere long, as was the death of Grant. Latterly our days have been exceedingly quiet & our nights disagreeably noisy. This incessant shelling is by no means conducive to peaceful slumbers. From present indications one would imagine we are to spend the summer and fall in our present position. Grant does not seem disposed to assault,—and if he was, I don't think his troops would be of like mind—and I fear we will never attack. We may be too late now but in my opinion it might have been successfully attempted when we first arrived; but this criticism doesn't become me.

I don't object to remaining here—the Yankees cannot do any more (nor as much) harm than in Northern Virginia & it is a proper relief to the poor people of that section to be rid of them for a while. . . .

You will see I am in a fly away humor today & must pardon my random way of talking. Much love to Coz. Mary. May Heaven bless & keep you Bet, Your own

W.

73

[To Bettie]

Camp "Violet Bank"

Monday, 25 July 1864

On yesterday Mr Platt again had service in our beautiful rural Church and in addition to the usual number of soldiers there were many ladies in attendance. All agree in the opinion that it is more delightful to have religious exercises thus under the shade of the trees than in a Church; yet I must confess I never can feel as devout out of a Church as when within its sacred walls. . . .

Lizzie had received your letter which you entrusted to my care. "Tower Hill" was visited by the Wilson raiders on their return and their conduct there was as it is reported to have been everywhere.[32] I presume however that you also have late dates from Lizzie so I will not bore you with a repetition of old items. . . . I have nothing of interest to report from the army. I told you we were expecting Meade to come over to our side & bring his whole army with him. All the houses in Petersburg are being prepared to receive them. Genl. Grant is also reported to have undermined Petersburg; his object is to come up in rear of the town & take us in reverse. He is said to have gotten as far as Sycamore St. and is believed to be running a train of cars under neath—as smoke is constantly seen to exude through the paving stones & a rumbling noise as of a railroad train—to say nothing of an un-earthly whistle—is frequently heard by gentlemen returning to camp after night, who have been entertained by kind people who treat them to ice water and <u>straws.</u> These with the secession of Illinois & the burial of Grant are the only items of news that have reached me up to this hour (3 P.M.) As Grant has been buried, I presume it is his ghost that is undermining Petersburg and this makes the matter only the more ter-rible.[33] We had a glorious rain last night. I may say <u>glorious</u> for I don't know who had better opportunities to judge than yr humble servant; inasmuch as the wind blew my tent entirely over (about 1 o'clock) & whilst I was left out in the cold with a bare face turned up to Heaven, receiving most amicably its copious & blessed shower of water, my companion was suddenly aroused by a thundering noise and felt something like an enormous snail (the wet tent) smack him in the face & thought Satan had finally gotten hold of him, until he overheard my frantic efforts to rescue myself from a premature death by drowning. Oh! a blessed thing it is, this living in tents in stormy weather. I have had strong apprehensions of a visitation by Fever & Ague since one o'clock exactly last night; and between that hour & morning I was compelled to sleep with one eye shut whilst with the other I watched the movements of my traitorous tent pole. Owing to this little incident I was not as much refreshed as usual by my slumbers, but the day has been so pleasant that but for the afore mentioned dread of an Ague, I would pronounce myself in a remarkably fine state of health. I omitted to tell you that some one had accounted for a small earthquake which we all experienced on yesterday by announcing that the whole of Genl. Grant's army was on the banks of the Appomattox shaking with Ague.—Are you all not rejoiced at Hood's success?[34] I will continue to hope for good news from that quarter, preferring this to anticipating evil as some do no matter what the results may be. Our friend Ramseur has not been so successful. It was a great pity he was sent off with a division when the whole corps was available.[35] Don't tell anyone I say so, but I have feared our friend Early wd not accomplish much because he is such a <u>Godless</u> man.[36] He is a man who utterly sets at defiance all moral laws & such a one Heaven will not favour. I hope to receive a letter tomorrow, if I don't, I shall continue merry & look for it next day.

I know how time flies & how difficult you find it to write but on this account I appreciate your letters all the more. Love to Coz. Mary & with ever so much to yourself. I am as ever yr own

W.

74

Camp at Violet Bank

1 August 1864

Many thanks dear Bettie, for your nice letter of the 24 ulto. . . .

We have a spirit medium near us who with remarkable accuracy foretold the fight of the 30th and its results, and who has proclaimed that Peace will be declared on the 3rd day of February next. Isn't this a charming spirit?

You have heard I presume, nearly as much as I can tell you of the last fights.[37] On yesterday General Meade requested a flag of truce to enable him to remove his wounded and bury his dead. It was granted and this morning we had a cessation of hostilities for four hours. I availed myself of the occasion to visit the lines and take a good view of the enemy & matters in general. At the point where the fight occurred our line of battle & that of the enemy are distant from each other only by about 75 yards & when sharp shooting is going on, it is certain death to show your head.

Here the Yankees drove their mine. We were countermining, but bless me the enemy were much deeper, and nearer the abode of darkness, and moreover were between our two mines, and early one morning our poor fellows were surprised by the explosion. The effects of this I cannot describe. The crater made by the springing of the mine is about 120 feet long & deep enough to put Mr. Mc's pretty house in bodily.[38] Great heavy guns were thrown a distance of 30 or 40 yards to the front, the whole face of the earth was upturned & many of our brave soldiers buried underneath. Those of the enemy who reached our trenches were nearly all either killed or wounded, guns, knapsacks, everything of this sort piled in one confused mass. It was well for us that the enemy asked the truce, for without it we could not have buried those of the enemy that were without our lines. I am glad to report that Mahone's brigade acted most gallantly, though it met with some loss. Kate Wilson's brother is amongst the killed. Harry Wmson wounded in the arm which rendered a resection necessary. Howard Wright very badly wounded. The two Hills also wounded. Duncan was on picket & not in the fight. Bob Taylor, A. Tunstall & Wood Williams were the only officers of the regt. that I saw all safe.[39]

It was a strange sight to witness Federals & Confederates commingling together between the lines; in some cases there was too much intimacy. I could not have approached the creatures whilst immediately before my eyes were hundreds of black soldiers, no doubt the majority of them having once owned masters in happy Virginia homes. There was but little mercy shown them in the engagement. They first cried "no quarter" and our men acted on this principle. What is the next play we know not, perhaps another mine. Of course everybody will hear mining now along the entire line—but our troops will become used to this mode of warfare as they have to all others. Grant has much yet to accomplish.

. . . I have been naughty today. My chum and I both lost our temper, became very angry & had an explanation. Consequently, I am not in a gale just now (I am writing on the 2nd now) & would like to have the company & sympathy of some one who knows me & can make allowance for my shortcomings. Are you such a one? Dearest, pray that I may be more gentle, more humble, not so dangerously proud. Heaven's choicest blessings be yours Yr

W

75

Camp at Violet Bank

Sunday night 7th Aug '64

The time is propitious Bettie and as the flies have retired for the night, I think I may attempt a letter to you without danger of losing my temper, though even now it is being subjected to a pretty severe trial by the numerous candle bugs and other plagues that are hovering around my light. We have here every variety of insect that ever was heard of, & these together with the scorching sun constitute a thorough destroyer of the last lingering spark of amiability that an Adjt General may have once possessed; still I am happy to be able to report myself jolly even under these adverse circumstances. . . .[40]

No doubt you have heard of the visit of my Chief to Richmond. I need hardly tell you that I declined to accompany him, which declination on my part was however perfectly unnecessary as he hadn't the faintest idea of taking me with him. . . .

A messenger has just reported here with two fine watermelons for "Col Taylor." I wish you could enjoy one of them. Only think what a mean trick one of my companions paid me the other day when a gentleman proposed that he should fill his pockets with plums for me, and he said that he didn't think it right that he should do it, as I was already too much petted. Wasn't that shabby?

But now do you know this trifling incident, in conjunction with my recent quarrel with the same companion, has occasioned me much serious reflection! Heretofore, indeed all my life, I have been blessed with a number of the most lenient, charitable and affectionate friends, between whom and myself there was no reserve & with whom I could take any liberty and this has spoiled me. I forget in my intercourse with my present associates that the same state of affairs does not exist. Ah! I cannot tell you, how much I miss the sympathy and affection of those <u>old</u> friends and how distant these new friends appear by comparison. But a good time is in store for me; I know I shall forget all that is now unpleasant so soon as our circle is reunited. . . .

<u>Monday morning.</u> . . . There has been very little firing on the city of late, so that really there is not much danger in the congregations assembling at the church. . . .

I saw by the orders from the War Dept that Johnnie (yr Jhn) had been placed on inspection duty under Col. Chilton. Why then has he gone south again? The news from Mobile this morning makes me somewhat anxious. I hope Uncle Richard Page & Jno are safe. . . .[41]

I received one of the kindest letters from Mr Crenshaw the other day that ever was written. He had heard of Harry Wmson's wound & offered him & any other sick or wounded friend of mine quarters & attention at his house. His letter was so creditable, that I have taken pride & pleasure in reading it to almost every soldier that I have met. I went to see Harry & found him doing well & comfortably fixed. After a while he will go to Chimborazo.[42] I am so glad that Robbie has gone to the country & hope he will now mend rapidly.

Ma informs me that Sallie Tompkins intends taking Sandy Starke's little sisters to live with her.[43] Isn't this like that good lady? I declare she is an angel on earth—or I should say she is a <u>true woman.</u> If every one strived to do good as she does how different matters would be—

and after all it is the true secret of happiness, to make others happy and be of service to our fellow men. I join in your wishes, my dearest, that you—that <u>we</u> had it in our power to care for all those who need attention & to reciprocate the kindnesses of those from whom we have received favours. And it is a pleasure to me to look forward to a life of usefulness with you. In my daily devotions I think of it and always embody therein a petition that "we may pass down life's tide a support & comfort one to the other—happy in our mutual love,—happy in doing good & contributing to the happiness of those around us and happy in the anticipation of that blessed time when we shall be taken to God's own glorious Kingdom there to praise Him, Father, Son & Holy Ghost, one God for ever." Yes, Bettie, we will find much happiness in contributing to the comfort of others, & I shall find a great incentive to efforts in this direction in as much as they will be shared by you, and even though we do not and may never own a "Westover" I trust that if God spares me health and strength, we will have a comfortable home and also be enabled to carry out our wishes of contributing to the comfort & happiness of others. To have you share a useful life with me, my precious, is my fondest earthly hope. God grant the time may not be far distant when we may enter upon that life. My love to Coz. Mary—to all at The Neck & my kind regards to Tom.[44] God bless & keep you, dear Bettie, is the constant prayer of yr devoted

W. . . .

76

Camp at Violet Bank

Monday morn 15 Aug '64

It is quite early my dear Bet. Main Street, Richmond is scarcely alive yet and I will devote myself for a short while to you before the work of the day seriously begins. Owing to the excitement now prevailing on the north side of the James, the General started off at an early hour this morning with all the staff save your humble servant, that is with his two aides, for we are a very small family, and I am left to hold up the establishment.[45] I cannot yet say what this movement on the north side of the river means, all night long I was annoyed by the wretched couriers, whose information after all was neither very important nor very satisfactory. . . .

I am sorry to say the cavalry corps has been reorganized, McClellan reverts to his former duties and the whole burden of my work again rests on my poor weak shoulders.[46] I can now see no hope whatever of my being able to leave camp, certainly none of a leave of absence unless I have a similar attack to that of last year; you may remember how <u>very sick</u> I was. It is too provoking, this being alone, why I cannot even go out to dine without being aroused from the table to return to camp as "General Lee wishes to see Col. Taylor." How unfortunate to be thus <u>important</u>. I wish the old chief had some older, wiser, more temperate head near him, for I daily become more and more convinced of my inability to fill the position I occupy: and then, I am so distressingly fiery, so lacking in humility. The General and I lost temper with each other yesterday, and of course, I was afterwards disgusted at my allowing myself to be placed in a position where I appear to such disadvantage. I couldn't help however; he is so unreasonable and provoking at times. I might serve under him for ten years to come and couldn't <u>love</u> him at the end of that period.[47] I don't intend though to take up my paper and your time with any account of my grievances concerning the "Greatest and best(?) man living." Suffice it to say we are on good terms now. When he left me this morning, he presented me with a peach, so I have been somewhat appeased. You know that is my favorite fruit. Ah! but he is a queer old genius. I suppose it is so with all great men.

I was compelled to desist from writing this morning because of my numerous visitors and the receipt of several packages of papers. I am still alone and it is getting towards evening. I presume the General will not return tonight. I must say that I have rather enjoyed my loneliness and would not object to their remaining away for several days. A telegram has just reached me reporting a very handsome affair on the part of Colo. Mosby.[48] He attacked the enemy's supply train near Berryville, captured about 75 loaded wagons, several hundred prisoners, five or six hundred horses & mules, two hundred head of cattle &c. I hope this is but the happy precursor of a complete victory by our forces in the Valley—and if we do meet with success there, I have but little doubt that Genl Grant will clear out.

Our poor friend Harry Williamson was compelled to have a secondary operation performed, and now is without his left arm. The amputation was rendered necessary by a profuse hemorrhage from the wound, but I received a message from him yesterday saying that he was doing remarkably well—fine appetite, sleeps sweetly &c. Dr Paige makes very favorable representations of his condition & so I trust all will be well. I think I told you of the kind letter I received from Mr Crenshaw, in which he invited Harry to his house. He would no doubt gladly have accepted but, his sister being at Chimborazo, he feels that he must go there, & I agree with him. . . .[49]

And then good Mr Cr. tells me to prevail on the Genl to bring this war to an end that we may have peace "and all the attendant ceremonies, enjoyments & hilarities." Oh! how I wish it could be tomorrow! But the sharpshooting that I now hear near me & the sounds of the heavy guns of James river that so distinctly reach my ear, proclaim Not yet—Not yet. . . .

My love to Coz Mary & believe me yr own

W.

Chapter 5

Stalemate at Petersburg:
August to December 1864
(Letters 77–95)

In late 1864 Walter is tied down at headquarters and frustrated at being unable to visit Bettie in Richmond. Long romantic passages predominate, interspersed with descriptions of social life in Petersburg. Though Grant's numbers were slowly wearing down Lee's beleaguered army, Taylor remains optimistic.

77

Camp at "Violet Bank"

24 August 1864

Four days have passed since my usual time for writing and still no letter has been mailed this week for my dear Bettie. Have you wondered what has become of me? . . .

I assure you, dear Bet, my time has not been idle since I last wrote you. In the first place I was ordered about midnight one day last week to move to the north side of James river, where I spent several days quite pleasantly, enjoying very much the companionship of my brother Dick, but oh! it was too hard to be so near my home & yet not be able to get there! Only think it was but one hour's ride on Bella to carry me to your presence, and indeed I wished so much to although you had not said "come." . . .

After a few days of comparative quiet and pleasure at Chaffins,[1] we started about 8 o'clock Saturday night, with every prospect of a hard rain, to ride horseback to Petersburg. Reached the site of our old camp about one o'clock; took a few hours rest in the porch of the house near us, and then went forth to the scene of battle. We had rather an unprofitable time of it on Sunday but were not much hurt; the only thing to be regretted is that we made nothing. This morning again the

184

General trotted me out and the day has not passed quite as agreeably as I would have wished. It was intensely warm and as I have been somewhat an invalid for the past few days, I suffered considerable discomfort. Of course on my return I found plenty of papers & it is only now after having disposed of them that I am able to devote a few moments to you. . . .

I suppose you have heard of Mr Rodman's having sailed for Europe. I presume we will soon have him coming in through Wilmington, that is if the Yankees don't attack the place, as stampeding Genl Whiting seems to think they contemplate doing.[2] The all absorbing topic at this time appears to be the armistice shadowed forth by Northern journals. Let them go on. If the fighting once ceases, there is but little danger that it will be resumed. By the way, how is this armistice to be considered by you and me? Is it not equivalent to an end of the war? Will not this cruel war then be over?[3] You know I only ask for information, being ready at all times to make yr convenience my pleasure. Of course I confess to a great deal of impatience but have every confidence in my Pet's cool & wise little head. I can't tell you how many complimentary things I hear said of you. I believe its all to comfort me however. I wish somebody was here to comfort me now. I am quite under the weather, old lady, having another visitation from my old plague neuralgia. But there's work to be done & I must grin & endure it. My love to Coz Mary & all that are with you.

Ever yr own

W.

78

Camp at Violet Bank

Sunday 28th August 1864

My last letter has scarcely had time to reach you, my dear Bettie, and perhaps you will not be glad to receive another so soon. . . .

I was today quite poorly. My good friends, the doctors, are physicking me often in admirable style, but they agree with me in thinking that change of air, relaxation from duty and plenty of exercise is the proper prescription for my case. I am determined however not to be really sick. If anyone was here to take my place, I shd. feel tempted to run off, but as matters now stand any absence is out of the question. Thinking a journey to Church might prove beneficial physically as well as morally, and confident that in any event I would feel no worse there than in camp, I started off this morning with the hope of having Mr. Platt to preach after hearing the service. In this I was disappointed as the sermon was from Genl Pendleton.[4] I am not so averse to hearing the General as others but am always sorry to see him officiate, because I know how the soldiers will talk about him. . . .

I sent Julia a note this morning (to go by flag of truce) begging her to let me know Fanny's address, it occurred to me that if she is in trouble it wd. be some consolation to know that she was remembered by her old friends and had their heartfelt sympathies. I could only assure Julia of Duncan's safety so far,—of Aleck's being unhurt, for the benefit of the Tunstalls, and of Uncle Harry's getting on very well since his arm was amputated. I went to see the latter on yesterday and found him very cheerful and comfortable. Says he has an enormous appetite. When the operation was performed he overheard the Doctors say that his life depended on his eating & this acted as a great appetizer, so that he eats all they offer him, devours a chicken & like "Oliver" calls for more.[5] We have had some desultory but quite severe fighting during the past two weeks and in summing up the results, there is a decided balance in our favor. Still the enemy retains possession of the Weldon Road. To do this however has cost General Grant about twelve thousand men, & really whilst we are inconvenienced by it, no material harm is done us.[6] From present prospects one may infer that we will be established somewhere in this vicinity during the winter. Tomorrow is the day for the Chicago convention;[7] perhaps it may lead to a temporary cessation of hostilities; but if we are to remain here during the winter, I see no objection except the scarcity of wood. Already it feels like the fall of the year. The afternoons & mornings are very pleasant now; I delight above all things to take a good canter on horseback when my duties will permit me, only regretting that I must go alone. . . .

Where is your John now? Has he not gone on duty under Col Chilton? I saw an order to this effect some time since.[8] Chilton is a very good fellow in his way, & certainly one would not be troubled much who served under him, if he knew how to manage his cards. Our Jno, poor fellow, has been really unfortunate. They say Fort Morgan is in the hands of the enemy;[9] this is all we know & therefore are not acquainted with the fate of the good fellows stationed there. The miserable Yankees are just now throwing shells into the town from their mortars; they make a great noise & come disagreeably near to our camp—but we are nicely hid from the Yankees & fear no harm. My love to Pattie & Mary.—also to Coz Mary & all. Ever yr devotd

W.

79

Camp at "Violet Bank"

Sunday 4th Sept 1864

It appears to have been but yesterday, my dear Bettie, that I last wrote to you & yet here again we are blessed with another Sunday. . . .

Everything is perfectly quiet on our lines but no doubt we will have some excitement ere long, for I am scarcely ever left alone at Head Qrs. that this does not occur. I had almost made up my mind to endeavor to spend today in Richmond, when Marshall informed me that he had special reasons for wishing to be in the city just at this time. And lo! Venable is possessed suddenly of a like desire to visit his home, and to cap the climax the General concludes to visit the President. They all left on yesterday and here am I alone. The General had not heard of the evacuation of Atlanta when he started; the President will be glad to consult with him as regards the best course to be pursued out there.[10] Perhaps it may result in General Lee's assignment to that army or at least he may be sent there to adjust matters. I can't say that I would be pleased at such an arrangement; it would take me too far away from home. Still I wd cheerfully acquiesce in anything that promised to advance our cause. I don't see how he can be spared from here, this is the most serious consideration. This, however, is all surmise on my part & nothing may be farther from the President's intention; and indeed I trust the latter may be the case. I suppose everybody in Richd. will be very blue over the fall of Atlanta. The question is what effect will it produce on the North? Some think it will impede the progress of the peace sentiment & injure the prospect of the McClellanites. It may however have the contrary effect. For as Lincoln & Fremont are both out & out war men, the other party must be unequivocally a peace party & have a decided peace man to secure the element in opposition to the administration & the war.[11] They must declare for peace to make a positive issue with the Republicans. Let them adhere firmly to their intention to propose an armistice & some good may result to us. My idea of the armistice is that the armies will remain as they now are. There will be no disbanding on either side; nor will they withdraw from our territory. We are a very proud & a very exacting people. I have heard many declare that we cd. consent to no armistice that did not require the withdrawal of the Yankee armies. This is unreasonable: it is not customary. Look for example at our armistice in the Mexican War, at that between the Allied Powers & the Russians in the Crimean War, & more recently to that in the case of Denmark & the German Powers. In no case were the armies withdrawn. I hope our people will be cool, dignified and brave, but not unreasonable, dictatorial or over exacting. Whilst I would not have them submit to any humiliation, or consent to any measure which would compromise our National pride & honour, still I think it wd. be equally as bad to have them ignore or treat with scorn any means which promise an honorable peace, because of some fancied wrong or some weak notion of our own great superiority and what is due our glorious, infallible (?) selves. We must not claim what it would be unreasonable to expect and we must also remember that we are not & never will be in a condition to dictate exactly what shall be. But pshaw! I don't intend to write an essay on the state of the country and will close with the hope that God will carry us safely through these troubles: that He will teach us <u>humility</u> & at the same time lend us strength to maintain our rights & to resist tyranny. Let it be remembered that we too have erred: we are very boastful, very proud, very sinful & need trials to bring us to a sense of our unworthiness and to greater efforts after holiness. My thoughts were troubled yesterday as I reflected upon our reverse at Atlanta & I was dreamily reading the psalter for the day when this verse recalled me "For Thou shalt save the people that are in adversity and shalt bring down the high looks of the proud."[12] The whole psalm is fraught with such comforting assurance.

I am rejoiced to hear that the girls are enjoying their visit to you. Ask Pattie if she can't pay me a visit. I will promise her any number of beaux and horses to her hearts content. You must be sure to manage matters so that you can return with them to the country. I really think you deserve & need it after your close application to duty. I am determined to rebel & have at least a months leave in October or Nov. I can hardly claim that my health requires relaxation from duty, for the Doctors say that although thin I am now perfectly well & in good condition yet I think I know better & that I will be worthless if allowed no rest this fall. All my pains have left me & I am once more my hearty self. The Doctors have prescribed Exercise, so Bella & I have a fine run every afternoon. When I go on leave I am going to ride from here to Norwood first with Miles, then I am going to Jn. Cocke's place and then I'll call on you at the Neck if you will allow me or I'll take a peep at Robbie at Elk Hill.[13] I will take horse, dog & gun & have a jolly time. Isn't that a pleasant programme for war times? Just as I write, as if in derision, a tremendous Yankee mortar is discharged & the continuous & constantly increasing whirring of the shell is heard until it explodes with a terrible noise on the roof of some house in the city not many hundred yards distant. The wretches made a systematic attempt to burn Peters'g not long since. The shelling from the mortars & the big guns is a grand pyrotechnic display & reminds me forcibly of the 4th of July in old times at Old Point. I think you will find it very convenient & very pleasant to have your room to yourself and will always have a nice place for your Mother or one of the girls, though you will unquestionably miss your Cousin Mary.[14] I shall, I know, when I am fortunate enough to get to the city, unless she will allow me to visit her in her new abiding place. I hold Coz Mary in high esteem, because she has always been so kind & considerate whenever we have met, and I like her, moreover, because I believe she is a true friend and seconds my claims to somebody's hand, wishing me success. Isn't it so? I am sober now and agree with you, again, as regards the armistice and our plans.[15] You are a wise little body and I really believe that I am another. On one point however I beg to differ. We are happy under existing circumstances, indeed I am very happy, and to be assured that you are, dear Bettie, is a proud reflection for me; but if Heaven spares me through this war with health and strength unimpaired, there shall come a day when you will confess that you are happier than you are now. To this end I intend to devote all my energy and such attainments as God has given me, and with such a motive I know I will succeed. And we will not only be happy ourselves but we will make others happy. How I long to be of some real use in the world. I wish to have some special aim different from that of overcoming Yankee tyranny. I wish to have the care of you, my precious, and with you as my helpmate to labour for the comfort & happiness of others. I pray God we may be happy and feel assured we will be even happier than we are now. . . .

Duncan is in hospital, at least I heard so on yesterday, he is not much sick, & his disease is apt to prove more annoying than dangerous. Those poor fellows in the trenches certainly do suffer many inconveniences and it fills me with dread to look forward to a winter in these fortifications. Indeed an armistice would come very opportunely just now. How will we have fires, where will we get wood? Our camp must be moved shortly for we are not much over a mile from the Yankee lines and when the leaves fall will be in plain view. I advocate taking a house in town and running the risk of a stray shell. By the way, there is a Photographist in town who has an excellent picture of Genl Lee & is anxious to have all the staff grouped around him. Qr Masters, Doctors & all have been taken but Marshall and me, and I have promised to go & sit tomorrow if practicable. Now his gallery has received one shell and is just in range of most of the guns & how can a body be expected to assume a pleasant expression under such circumstances. I am sure I shall look terribly frightened. As a reward for our trouble each one is to be presented with a copy of the whole, the Genl of course included. Would you care to possess such a famous group?[16] Please give my best love to Pattie and tell her I am most anxious to make Bella and myself serviceable to her and that I will be obliged if she will inform me where I can meet her late in October or early in November & whether at Norwood, The Neck, Richmond or where? I am determined to have a leave if I am spared, and to have a perfectly happy time out of sight of the army and removed from all the evidences of War. . . .

Good bye. Yr devoted

W.

80

Camp at "Violet Bank"

Sunday 11th Septem. 1864

    In due time, my dear Bettie, I received yours of Wednesday last for which I return my sincere thanks. . . .

    I have been forcibly reminded of Home today by the Chants in Church. The Genl proposed that we should go to Mr. Gibson's.[17] I had no choice, though I have generally attended St. Paul's, Mr. Platt's Church, but was so pleased that I have determined to attend Mr. Gibson's regularly hereafter, if we remain here. If the countenance can be taken as any idea of a person's character, he is certainly a pure, good man. I dislike to make any comparison, but he certainly impresses me more favorably than Mr. P. His Church is not completed & service is held in the basement, but whilst I cannot explain why it was, I certainly felt more devotional this morning than I usually did in St. Paul's. An atmosphere of deep earnestness pervaded the whole service. It is quite trying to accompany the General to Church or any public place. Everybody crowds the way and stops on the pavements to have a look. I get separated from him every opportunity that is offered. After service was over he carried me visiting. . . .

I have no army news of interest to communicate. The Yankees entertain themselves now and then by firing upon poor "little Petersburg." But beyond this everything is as quiet as possible. Our army is recruiting its numbers daily, and all the troops are in the best spirits and condition imaginable. Over four months have elapsed since this campaign opened and in my opinion Mr. Grant is as far as ever from taking Richmond.[18] The draft has been postponed in the North and this makes our security doubly sure. If our Government would only purge The Bureau of Conscription and bring into the field all the scamps that are skulking behind an agricultural detail or the certificate of an election to be a Justice of the Peace, we would soon have an army that would drive Grant howling to his gunboats. It is really disgusting to us in the field to see the manner in which men are allowed to evade service. I always considered Judge Meredith a man of intelligence, but he has lately made certain improper decisions & discharged soldiers from the army who had no legal right to such discharge.[19] I wd like to pull his Judgeship's nose well for him,—and the Court of appeals will surely upset his decisions, or else Congress will pass a law to put a quietus on his proceedings.

Monday morning—I was interrupted last evening and must now hastily close my letter. The General will go to Richmond this afternoon. He proposed that I shd go with him, but indeed I do not see how I can absent myself from my desk. It is a strong temptation & I may yet give in to it, but will nevertheless send off my usual scrawl. With ever so much love to Pattie, Mary & all. I am, dear Bettie, as ever Yr own

Walter.

81

Camp at "Violet Bank"
Sunday, 18th Sept 1864

I have been under very high pressure, my dear Bettie, ever since I left you and now for the first time since my return, I breathe freely, having once more obtained the upper hand of my papers. If I had staid away about three days more, I never should have caught up. Before I can take my much talked of leave of absence, it will be necessary to have my assistant determined on and put in traces. My brother officer who represented me during my absence worked nobly I am told, but not being accustomed to the duties of course, the work accumulated upon him. The General was very much entertained at my serious expression of countenance as I laboured to dispose of the papers requiring action, laughed heartily at me, facetiously tendered me some words of encouragement and altogether made fun of my situation. But I am once more myself "barring" a troublesome cold in my head, which I attribute to the sudden change from a tent to a house and then back again. This is but another evidence that life in a house during times of peace is more wholesome than existence in a tent (or tentfly) in times of war. I have just seen three men who were caught conveying a cargo of potatoes from Norfolk to City Point.[20] Our scouts sent the men here as prisoners. Of course they were trotted up to me that their cases might be disposed of. One of them will ever hereafter bless my name, if he discovers it, because I ordered that he should be placed in the ranks as he is of conscript age. The moment I hinted at such a course he was taken suddenly ill, but I trust will recover and in due time render his country efficient service; and when he becomes a famous warrior he will thank me. No doubt the prisoners were astonished at the interest I took in Norfolk & its people, and certainly appeared to be overwhelmed by the questions I showered upon them. However they were ignorant fishermen and though just from the city could give me but little information. . . .

I will bear in mind that my first duty to you is to contribute towards your defense, to labour here for your independence & mine, and to save our Home from subjugation. Work on, Bettie, it is better thus than an inglorious ease at such a time, and our rest will be sweet indeed when this tyranny shall be overpast, and we can smile as we take a retrospective view of our deprivations and annoyances. I wish you could have heard Mr. Gibson this morning. He encouraged us with the happy assurance that in the last day all will be made plain; we will then realize the wisdom and goodness of God even in those matters that now appear to us as troubles. We will then know that every trial sent us has accomplished some great good for which it was designed and happy will the man be to whom trials were not sent in vain. . . .

We have but little army news. I need not here recount to you the doings of Hampton's cavalry in its operations during the past week. You have no doubt heard all the particulars. I am particularly grateful for the 2500 head of cattle which were procured. Such captures make full amends for the loss of the Weldon railroad.[21] Genl. Beauregard has returned from Wilmington. I do not think that he will go West now. . . .

Meanwhile, you dear old tantalizer, I shall not cease to think of you & pray God send His choicest blessings on you. Love and a <u>kiss</u> to Pattie & Mary. Be sure to deliver the latter or I shall entrust no more to you. Yr devo

W

82

Camp at Violet Bank

Sunday 25th Septm, 1864

There is but little of the afternoon left me wherein to write my usual letter. . . .

Really Bettie you would have laughed, could you have heard some of the salutations of my friends this morning. It appears they all heard of your contemplated visit to <u>all</u> the army but me—indeed from Howlett's house on James river, where Frank Huger is stationed, down the entire line to the Weldon road, there has been a flutter of excitement in anticipation of your expected arrival.[22] Well some had learned of your not coming with Mrs. Heth and some imagined you had arrived and the consequence was that the former had for me a word or two of sympathy & the latter offered me their congratulations. As I was <u>of course</u> in the dark as to their meaning, you can readily understand my bewilderment. On yesterday Starke sent me a note urging me not to be selfish but to stay at my office during the next two days.[23] I replied that unfortunately I had no will in the matter, for a pile of papers and a sorrowful headache constituted an insuperable obstacle to my leaving camp & that if Petersburg had for me any unusual attraction I was not aware of it. He thought you would or <u>had</u> come. I doubted your coming & <u>felt</u> you had not come. After having occasioned so much excitement, can you not honor us with yr presence? I promise you a handsome welcome and an abundance of attention from every body worth seeing—which of course excludes me. I can rarely leave my attractive home & now that I have a new white tent and am all alone—I shall be a confirmed recluse. You will therefore be free from annoyance by yr "old plague."

I attended Mr. Platt's Church this morning where we had an interesting service in the baptism of General Stevens and his little infant.[24] After which Mr. Platt preached a very good sermon from the text "sufficient for the day is the evil thereof"—and although his discourse only embraced the evil of delay in professing Christianity, and the great importance of connecting ourselves at once with the Church, I thought a good application of the text might be made to the times, and an excellent lecture read to the croakers who imagine the Confederacy in a desperate strait and are ready to cry "enough" & take the oath. We are stirring matters up over here & propose to put the whole Bureau of Conscription in the army as a beginning of a great reform—after which we may get some soldiers in the ranks. Whereas now every body procures a detail or exemption. We also propose to make the negroes serviceable & some advocate placing them in the ranks—making soldiers of them—but for this I am not yet quite ready. . . .[25]

I find it difficult to confine myself to one sheet.

The Gen'l has sent for me. Goodbye.

W . . .

[postscript omitted]

83

Chaffin Farm

At night 6 Oct. 64

Though it is pretty late and I am to be off again in the morning, I cannot go to sleep, my own Bettie, before I write a line or two to let you know where I am and how matters are progressing with us. You will, I know, appreciate the causes which prevented my usual letter this week—and yet notwithstanding we are kept so constantly engaged, I have indulged the hope when looking at the church spires that I might get to see you for an hour or so. The General has only two of us with him, Venable and I, Marshall being sick. If matters quiet down I will certainly make the effort to meet you. Let me thank you, Bettie dear, for your letter of the 30th which reached me safely—and especially for the sympathy you expressed in regards our good old Dick. I can't tell you how anxious I was about him. At first all was uncertain—but I reconciled it to my conscience after a while to telegraph that he was captured. I wrote a note to Grant's adj. and he very promptly answered it, but though Col. Maury and Jack Ellerson were readily found, Dick was not among the prisoners though Col. Maury reported that when he was taken to the rear, he saw Dick who had a wound which wd require him to go to a hospital.[26] Next came a couple of telegrams from Doctors to this same aag of Grant's, stating Maj. Taylor could not be found at any hospital and my only hope was that he had been sent to Old Point, and yesterday I was relieved very much to hear positively of his being there and doing very well indeed. The boat came up today and I expect more definite information. His wound will be an advantage in one respect as it may serve to expedite his exchange.

. . . We are doing all we can to remedy matters here. (that is, Gl Lee is). It was unquestionably bad to lose Harrison, but with the enemy it is entirely a <u>negative</u> gain.[27] The place only benefits them inasmuch as it is thereby lost to us. Our effort to retake it was not an energetic nor systematic one. We could and should have retaken it, but matters were not executed as well as they were planned. We will try to be even yet, however. When you receive this, you may at the same time hear renewed firing. We will in all probability be at them again tomorrow, but unless you hear of an attack thro another source, say nothing of this. We had a visit from the President today. I hope he will get us some <u>men</u>. We want <u>men</u> badly. But there is life in the old army yet, and if properly supported, all is well. I have heard sad accounts of the croaking in the city—Fie on the weak kneed ones! Let every man be up and at work & not spend his time in idle laments over what may never occur. Oh! for a band of 20,000 determined patriots—only 20,000 would send Grant out of Virginia. But I fear most of us love life too dearly. We expect war without danger. The Yankee army here is a poor concern, save in its numerical strength & for its numbers it must be respected, but if every man we have would make up his mind to do it, we cd drive Grant from his works. Still, though our men have not altogether the old spirit, there are many here who will do anything to be expected of mortals; & if this faction is properly supported, all is well. Every where else in the Confed'cy all looks bright. Let us be firm here and the war must soon end.

I am afraid my furlough is pretty distant—I told Miles, the other day, we must have the fight first & then I would go with him; & so my predictions are verified as regards the fight. Will my hopes be realized as regards the visit to Norwood? My friend Jones tells me he met Mrs. Rodman & the Seldens at the Springs & had a charming time with them.[28] I hope all the party were as much benefitted as he appears to have been. Since I have commenced this I have been subjected to a constant run of interruptions. The troops are moving—telegrams arriving & going &c. &c. So pardon my wretched penmanship. I sincerely trust Mr. Hobson is well—indeed if it was otherwise, we wd surely have heard. Genl. Wickham intends resigning.[29] Poor Sandy Pendleton's wife has been visited with a sad affliction.[30] Only one year's married life! This is sad indeed, but would it have been better otherwise? Should they have waited? Isn't it selfish in men to marry at such a time? On the other hand, can she possibly regret the step now? Has she not much to console her she wd not otherwise have had? 'Tis a serious, doubtful question & each side has many advocates. I wish you could hear my good friend Sallie Tompkins—she could almost convince you it is better to ignore the war in such matters. By the way I never knew before how much good Sallie was interested in my "Sensitive Plant." There was no possible proposition which she did not make to secure your comfort & no argument she didn't advance to induce me to do what I told her was beyond my power & contrary to your fixed determination. She certainly set my <u>wishes</u> to work & her arguments, with those of others & the prospect of an indefinite protraction of the war, have unsettled my preconceived notions as to what is most advisable and proper. All is with you, Bettie dear, and your <u>wish</u> my <u>command.</u> I am ever ready when you beckon to me & if still to wait your pleasure, I am your most patient, humble servant!

I hope to whip the Yankees for you soon and then perchance I may get to Richmond. So soon as matters quiet down here, my Chief will have to fly to Petersburg, where his presence is much needed. Give my love to all at the Neck & at Norwood when you write—and accept a big share for yourself from your devoted

W.

84

Camp on Osborne Pike [near Chaffin's Bluff]

17 October 1864

To say that I experienced a sad disappointment, my dear Bettie, would convey no adequate conception of the emotions with which I left Richmond this morning without having realized the great happiness I anticipated in meeting you. During the whole of last week the wish was ever present with me that our headquarters might remain stationary until Sunday and that matters might continue quiet that I might once more enjoy a quiet evening with my nearest and dearest. I was not altogether selfish, however, and found consolation in the reflection that you, my precious, had enjoyed the pleasure of a visit to Norwood, the blessed realization of your ideal of a happy home; and my only regret is that your stay there was so limited. By the way, you may be there yet for aught I know, inasmuch as you did not arrive in Richmond by the Danville train, as I ascertained from my own observations at the depot about 8 1/2 this morning. I guess that you will return in a buggy with some of the boys, or some such conveyance far preferable to either railroad car or packet boat. I hope you found everybody at Norwood well and as happy as usual. Oh me! Will I ever get there? My chances for an immediate realization of this wish really appear pretty blue—but I will still hope on. Did Miles go up with Mrs. Heth?[31] I fear the old fellow will tire of waiting for me. I got into the City so late last night that I could see no one but my home people & Mrs. Petty, Miss Sue & the Crenshaws, whom I joined at Church (or rather at the Church door for I was too late for service) and accompanied home.[32] The General was absent until sometime after sundown and when he returned he brought His Execy the President with him. Mr. Davis heard me say I desired to visit Richmond and asked the pleasure of my company, which of course meant "Col T—you will ride with me to Richmond." Well, I had to wait until his confab with my chief was concluded—& this seemed an age—and then we started at a snail's dignified pace for the town. Mind you, all this time I was ignorant of your absence. The moon had risen, it was quite late and I was just the most anxious fellow in the universe to get ahead. Oh how I longed to spur His Excellency's quiet looking beast! But I was compelled to jog along slowly, quietly, after the manner of the royal family & take comfort in the great honor (?) conferred on me. If another opportunity is afforded me before we leave here, I'll manage better, that is, if you don't intend to run away regularly and if you do, you may just expect me to become desperate and follow you regardless of all consequences my absence might entail upon me and the country. Don't you tremble for the nation's safety after this terrible threat? When I am in Richmond I always make inquiries after the welfare of my lady

197

friends and their most humble servants & was glad to hear of Capt Thomas' rapid improvement and of Capt Iredell's anticipated happiness.[33] I am only afraid that I will be the recipient of a shower of maledictions in regard to the leave of absence to be sought for by the latter to enable him to consummate matters; for I have had numerous messages and commands that I must grant him the indulgence & find, by reference to my books that he not long since returned from a sick leave; & consistency will compel me, I fear, to disapprove. I have written to him however, to forward his application. I will do what I can for him. Your note of Friday morning has just this moment reached me. Though long on the way it is in time to dissipate the little remaining feeling of disappointment I cherished; for now that I know that you advised me of your movements, I am "all right" again. You are a charming little pet, the best girl in the Kingdom, my tantalizer and yet my good angel, a dear "sensitive plant" and the apple of my eye. May Heaven's choicest blessings be yours.

I hope the day is not far distant when I again may be blessed by the sight of you—until then goodbye—yr devoted W—

85

Camp

22 Oct—64

Your note of the 19th my dear Bettie, reached me on the evening of the 20th. No doubt thousands of anathemas and maledictions have been showered on my poor head because Capt Iredell's leave was not granted from Army Headquarters at the proper time. Miss Mattie, Miss Ellen, French, Dr. Williams and YOU have, I fear, formed a most unfavorable opinion of my sense of propriety, in my not doing everything in furtherance of the wishes of the attractive couple.[34] The truth is, I am really afraid to visit Richmond. And another truth is, I never made the same efforts to make it appear proper to grant leave, as I did in this case. The silly Captain (I mean Iredell & you see I'm spiteful) did not apply at all. I wrote him a note & advised him to do so. He took no notice of my note, nor of my advice. I then telegraphed Gen'l Hampton to know if he c'd be spared and until today heard nothing from that. That you may see how indisposed they were to recommend or approve his absence, I send you the paper alluded to, which please keep for me. Generally speaking when I telegraph the Corps Commander as in this case, all "approve" without remark. Iredell only returned from sick leave about 5 weeks ago. Dozens of poor fellows' applications on <u>same grounds</u> have been refused in the past month. So you see stern consistency required me to consider well before approving an application in which I was particularly interested. In such a case I am so fearful that my judgement may be biased by my desire to gratify, that for prudence sake I reluctantly, but invariably, either disapprove or refer to Gen'l Lee. As Iredell has not applied for an extension & for the reasons above stated I hesitate to extend his time. I hope to see you tomorrow evening. Till then Goodbye—yr own W.

24 Oct '64

If you will send me the bundle for Hunter by the courier who bears this, I can send it up by an officer tomorrow. Keep the courier as long as necessary. He has a note to the officer who is to carry the bundle. All that you must do is to address it to Hunter

Hunter Saunders
Care of Gregory's Ordnce train
Capt Mann Page
at Genl Early's HdQrs[35]
Valley of Va.

and the courier will take it at once to Maj. Wood's office where it is to be called for.[36]

Poor Ramseur is reported to have died of his wounds.[37] The report comes from the Yankees. God bless you my dearest. I hope the week may continue quiet—that I may see you next Sunday. These little flying visits to the city help me to work with cheerfulness. All my happiness, you see, takes its source from association with you.

Yr own

W.

Your letters will reach me much sooner if they are left at the <u>Adjt Genl's office</u> with Col. Withers or any of the officials there, than if put in the Post Office.[38] Just address

W. H. Taylor
A.A.G.
Head Qrs Genl R. E. Lee

86

[To Bettie]

Camp 27 Oct. 64

There are indications of a general movement. The enemy is in motion at all points. We may have to move any moment. Indeed it is what I have expected. The happiness of seeing you once a week was too great a blessing to last long; I could hardly expect another quiet week and a happy Sunday evening with you. Well, well, it is all for the best. It may be that after this we will enjoy a little rest and quiet. Genl. Hill at Petersburg reports the enemy making a general advance on his right. Gl Longstreet here reports a demonstration along his entire line and there is some activity on the river & between the James & Appomattox. So you see it looks like a sure enough advance.[39] May God be with us. I write you this hurried note amidst a shower of telegrams & dispatches, that you may know I cannot hope to meet you Sunday, & therefore if agreeable to my dear little "sensitive plant," I will expect a letter in lieu of the greatest happiness which could be afforded me. I shall think of you Sunday evening, indeed this I do always, but if you almost realize my presence at that particular time, you may know it is because thoughts of you fill my mind to the exclusion of all else. No doubt you can now hear the booming of the distant cannon as I do. The General has ridden away by himself. Venable is absent, Marshall unwell & though I ought to be here, I am not satisfied & will join my Chief & leave Marshall to manage Headquarters. I intended to ask you for a little piece of ribbon for a book mark to be used in my new "book of psalms" given me by an old soldier. I have no token from you at all. You know I cannot have your picture which I would so highly prize & I often feel a desire for some little memento received from your hands. Just a piece of ribbon, the veriest trifle will be of inestimable comfort to me. Oh Bettie; how cruel do I feel this continued separation to be! I so earnestly long always to be with you. To have it in my power always to secure a glance from those eyes that I am so proud of, and to be blessed with your continual presence to incite me to good works and enhance my happiness. Bet, did <u>any body</u> ever set so much store by another, as I do by you, my "precious pet"? I think not, because there is nobody else like you. Wouldn't it be nice to receive a telegram from Petersburg

stating that we had beaten the enemy & then we would not move perhaps. Ah! you see how I am catching at straws. Well, I'll make up my
mind to bear the disappointment & if I can't meet you Sunday, I hope
it may not be long before I do. Till then, dearest Bettie, Goodbye. May
God bless & keep you prays yr devoted

W.

87

[To Bettie]

Camp

30 Oct. 64

I am in the city & will be up presently. Hope you are not engaged
& I may have a quiet evening with you—

W

88

Camp 1 Nov. 1864

I must say good bye, my precious, but I earnestly hope that it is
only for a short while. You may remember I expressed a dread that we
would leave for Petersburg on today & so it is. The General informed
me last night that he wished to go over & as he might remain a <u>week</u> or
<u>more</u> we would have to take everything along with us.

Now I would feel perfectly reconciled to the change if I could think
that the "week or more" would cover our absence, but it may lengthen
into a month, unless we can get up some excitement on this side. But I
hope for the best & expect to see you again, dearest, before very long.
Meanwhile do write me when you can, always remembering however
that I would not half enjoy any letter the writing of which occasioned
you any discomfort or inconvenience. Can you not run up to
"Keswick" next Sunday?[40] Maybe I can get back by that day week. I
cannot tell, dear Bettie, how I will miss you next Sunday evening! Oh
what a comfort these visits have been to me. such a feeling of rest &
quiet happiness as I experienced in your presence night before last
sheds its influence over my every act & thought. After such a pleasure

201

I can return more cheerfully to my duties & bear any amount of annoyance with a quiet mind. See how much I am indebted to you, dear little sensitive plant. It sets my mind to work to penetrate the future & looking upon the three hours spent with you as but a foretaste of the happiness in store for me when the war shall have ended, it adds an earnestness that nothing else could to my prayer for the termination of hostilities. Then when you are my own sweet ---- & when we shall be no more separated here, Oh Bet how shall I measure my happiness?[41] God grant it may be measured by an estimate of your own; for I wish you to be just as happy as I shall be & I know you could not be more so.

I am so sorry that Sunday before last I should have appeared worried or distracted. It must have been only accidental—for I could not have carried any of my mental troubles with me into your presence. I invariably leave all these things behind me, & if I did not your dear presence would dispel them. It may have been the result of my little troubles, which had left their traces behind, though they had vanished. I was certainly too happy last Sunday even for the faintest shadow of such a thing, & this I trust you realized.

The General has gone ahead; he will take a ride along Pickett's line & I will go direct to Petersburg to select a camp &c. I fear we shall not secure so good a place as that we are about to leave. And now, my own Bettie, for a little while good bye. May a kind God bless you, comfort you & draw you daily nearer Himself is the constant prayer of your own

Walter

89

[To Bettie]

Petersburg, Va

7 Nov 1864

Though it is nearly ten & I have been hard at it ever since a little after day break, I cannot go to rest, dear Bettie, before I write a line or two to you. . . .

I very often question whether we are entirely right in postponing the time when I shall be your rightful protection. Why, officers of my rank in Richmond get a young fortune in pay for their services—a great deal more than you and I now get together & twice as much as you get. I often think, well, if I was there, with the kind offers made me, I could make Bettie as comfortable as possible & she could be mistress of her own time & actions. These considerations & the thought of your working day after day on those books and horrid accounts of eggs, milk &c stagger my conviction that we do right to wait for peaceful times. May God direct us both aright. I am sure we both desire to do what is proper, it is only a wonder to me that I do not advocate imme-diate action.

On leaving the north side the General left it to me to select an abid-ing place for our party here. I of course went where I thought he wd be comfortable, though I firmly believe he concluded I was thinking more of myself than him. I took possession of a fine house—had his room nicely cleaned out and arranged, with a cheerful fire &c, &c. It was en-tirely too pleasant for him, for he is never so uncomfortable as when comfortable, so a day or two after our arrival he informed me that he desired to visit the cavalry lines & thought it best to move our camp down; so to work I was compelled to go, packing up all my books & records & moving bag & baggage to the woods some 8 miles off. I pitched tents, confident we would remain at least several days, when lo! the next morning he informed me he thought we had better move back & so back I came to Petersburg & as I could find no better place, nor a worse one that was suitable, I took possession of the same house we had vacated, where I am now nicely fixed in a cozy little room & the General must be congratulating himself this rainy disagreeable night on not being exposed to the weather.[42] This is the first time I have been in a house, for on the north side I adhered to my tent. I had an invitation to dinner at Mrs Johnson's yesterday, but as I did not like the source from which I recd the "bid" or rather I shd. say the medium through wh. it was conveyed, I wd not have gone even had it not been Sunday and after communion.

I thought of you much yesterday, dearest, & communed with you in spirit as I imagined you too were partaking of the Sacrament in Rich-mond. I enclose for your inspection, that you may say which shall go to Mr. Rodman, two copies of my photograph. The artist sent them to me (not colored) with "his compliments"—a sort of remuneration, I sup-pose for having sat for his own gratification in the picture of the Genl. & Staff; & Mr. Bruce, who colored them, made me quite uncomfortable by insisting that his work shd. be gratuitous. One was for Sistress, but as she is so very loyal now, maybe it wd. be unsafe for me to send it as she might get in trouble.[43] What think you & which shall go to Mr. R? I have heard several remarks lately about going to the north side & therefore hope soon to see you. Wishing you happy dreams to-night, I am as ever Yr devoted

W.

90

[To Bettie]

Petersburg, Va

15 Nov 1864

I wonder if my pet is disappointed at not receiving my usual letter this evening? Here it is Tuesday night and not a line. When has such a thing occurred before? I have so often spoken to you, dear Bettie, about my official duties that I can not again enter upon a dissertation on the subject without subjecting myself to the charge of egotism. Suffice it to say that I feel that a straw placed upon my back in addition to what now devolves upon me would break me down. All day yesterday and again last evening I indulged the hope "well presently, I will be able to devote some time to Bettie's letter," but after nodding awhile at my papers—still unfinished—I was informed by my orderly that it was after twelve, and so reluctantly I was compelled to delay this pleasure another day. Now however I have such a favorable time, so quiet in my cozy little room with a cheerful, blazing fire that I have determined to ignore the horrid pile of official documents frowning upon me and claiming attention, and devote myself wholly to you. Just opposite our present abode there is a little nest, the exact counterpart almost of Mr. Mac's[44]—and if you were not constantly in my thoughts, I would be reminded of you every time I raised my head to look from my window. I can't say how often I have wished that I was as close to your little home that I might run away from my office and its petty annoyances and enjoy the pleasure of a quiet chat.

The prospects for our return to the north side are not so very promising just now. I cannot tell how it will be however, for the Chief may take the notion any day. I confidently hope every day for some indication on his part of an intention to visit the lines in that section—it would be like going back home, to get to Taylor's house again. Oh!

how I long for another such quiet Sunday evening as my last with you! But when thus separated, you cannot know how much pleasure it gives me to receive your letters. My heart was gladdened this morning by the receipt of yours written day before yesterday. It was such a comforting letter, my own precious, just like you, just what I wish you to be. Is there any body like you, sensitive plant, in the wide world? Would you not be a comfort to any boy (I intended to write <u>body</u>—but let it stand) and who has such a treasure as I possess in you? God bless you good angel, for the happy influence you now exert, and have ever exercised over my life. It is happiness indeed to contemplate a life with you here, my Bettie, but it fills my heart to overflowing to dwell in thought upon that blessed immortality to which, by the grace of God we can both look forward with a reasonable hope. Think of it, an eternity of joy; of quiet, heavenly joy! Can we ask more? And if God in his wisdom sends us trials to prepare us for this "eternal peace" let us remember that thus "the crown must be won" and how light—how insignificant will they appear! How you have encouraged me! Your letter reached me at an opportune time. I was well nigh faint—I was almost ready to cry out in despair—fancied my Chief had no sympathy for me and imagined my burden an unequal, unjust one and more than I could bear. But you have cheered me—wonderfully, my comforter, and with renewed energy and a much lighter heart I can apply myself to the accomplishment of my allotted task. When Mr. Minnegerode spoke of the influence over others for weal or woe, could you not recall an illustration of its truth in your own experience? Did you think of him into whose heart you have sent so many rays of sunshine, whose spirit you have so often cheered, whose actions, thought and words have so often been restrained within proper limits by a desire to be worthy of you? Yes, if you are ever at a loss for an illustration of your mission for good on earth, Bettie, think of me.

I also heard a good sermon on Sunday from Mr. Platt. His subject was the removal of the stone from Lazarus' grave, which Jesus required of those around him before he raised the dead. Not that he hadn't the power to move the stone, but this he required of those who were with him, because it was within the scope of their powers. And so in spiritual matters, He expects us to remove the stone from our hearts before He sheds upon us the light of everlasting life. We must do all that we can. He will do all that we cannot. We must exert ourselves, if we would secure the prize; or as the stamp on some of the fine foreign paper we are now receiving has it "aide toi, et Dieu t'aidera." I am glad you have Miss Lizzie with you and only regret that I cannot enjoy her visit also. 'Tis too bad that I should be away just now! But never mind, I will make up for it this Xmas. I am determined to have a good holiday then if I am spared. I hope Mr. Rodman will be successful in his efforts to reach our Confederacy. Miles is now at Norwood, he went up to bring Mrs. Heth down. I received another invitation to accompany him, but of course had to decline just now. Remember you are not to come over to see Mrs. H. whilst I am here. But on the other hand I should feel very badly if you were to come whilst I was on the north side. We have had several Richmond ladies over here recently. Of course I only had a glimpse of them. The street in front of my window is the favorite promenade—& now & then I see the ladies dash by on horses and wish Oh! if I cd only offer B a nice ride this evening!

I had a long talk with Eddie Galt on yesterday.[45] I learned more of Norfolk matters from him than anyone whom I have yet seen. Amongst other things he informed me that Fanny Kerr's mother had lost her mind. Did you know this? I had never heard it before; but Julia's language appears a little plainer to me now. Poor Fanny, what a hard life hers must be. I saw Joe Nash on yesterday—have not yet met Mag. Joe gets along famously—indeed was very slightly wounded. We expect to move our Headquarters to a point a very short distance from Mag when I shall perhaps see more of her. Her cousin, Mrs. Wells, is very kind to me and has promised me a dinner with dessert soon. The Petersburg people are very attentive to the General and the Staff reap some of the benefits—but for all this I long to be back on the north side.[46] I could cheerfully relinquish my comfortable room here to return to my tent there. Once or twice lately we have been on the lookout for the Yankees, but as yet no demonstration. I would not object to hear of a movement across James river because then we should have to go there to look after matters. All in good time though. I shall prize the sight of you, old lady, all the more for the delay in meeting. Give my best love to Mrs. Rodman, Coz. Mary & Miss Lizzie. Did you give Mrs. R. one of the photographs? Maybe she has forgotten she wanted it. By the way have you ever received Miss E. Beall's book.[47] Good night, dearest, sweet slumbers and happy dreams attend you. devotedly yrs.

W.

91

Edge Hill Virg'a

Sunday 27th Nov. 64

I was under the impression my dear Bettie, that it was quite late, but am agreeably surprised to find that I have ample time in which to write my usual letter before reason bids me retire.

. . . By way of inducement for you to come over and see Gen'l Heth's household (see how disinterested I can be), let me inform you that Miles is now at Wilmington—whither he went with Mr. Ficklin to bring back all manner of good things. He will return probably Wednesday or later, so you will be just in time on Sunday. Ficklin is a fine friend. He presented Gen'l Heth with a beautiful horse to say nothing of the fine cigars, nice white sugar, good whiskey (a secret), etc to all of which we this day did full justice.[48]

. . . Whilst Gen'l. Lee was in Richmond, I took it into my head to move, as a young married couple were waiting impatiently for us to vacate the house we then occupied & had given a gentle hint for us to depart by sending to inquire "when Gen'l. Lee would leave the house." The only house available was one some two miles from town which had been kindly offered some time previous. So bag and baggage we came to "Edge Hill" and here I am finely fixed in the parlour with piano, sofas, lounges, pictures, rocking chair, etc etc: everything as fine as possible for a winter campaign. After fixing the general and staff I concluded that I would have to occupy one of the miserable little back rooms of the house; but the gentleman in charge hinted that I might take the parlour and this decided me. I believe the General was pleased with his room and on entering mine remarked "Ah! You are finely fixed; couldn't you find any other room?—No—said I but this will do. I can make myself tolerably comfortable here." He was struck dumb with amazement at my impudence & soon vanished.

. . . I think I will have to seek duty in Richmond, particularly as it seems to meet with your approbation. What a gloriously easy time I will have whilst my old associates and companions in arms are enduring the hardships and privations incidental to a soldier's life in the field? What cause for congratulations I will have when I contrast my comfortable quarters out of harm's way with their slippery abode in the trenches and under fire!

Could any man be guilty of such thoughts, such a motive? I pity the unfortunate who is unwittingly placed in a position to appear as if he had entertained such. I was asked this week if I would accept a Colonelcy of a cavalry reg't. I replied yes,—of a Lieut. Colonelcy? still I replied yes, though conscious of my present unfitness for either, I would not hesitate to accept and try to fulfil the duties of even the higher of the two. What do you think of it? To be sure, infantry is more dangerous and it would be more manly to desire to be in a regiment of that branch of the service, but there is something dashing & very attractive about the cavalry when well managed. After all as we are told that we have to fight four years more, it matters very little where we render our individual services. . . .

Goodnight dearest—always nearest yr own

W—

[postscript omitted]

92

[To Bettie]

Sunday night 4 Dec 64

Edge Hill Va

"Then why art thou silent?" I believe that is the way the song has it. Why art thou silent? I have no doubt tis attributable to some good cause but, Bettie dear, I cannot tell you what a bitter disappointment each day of the past week has brought me; & still no letter. . . .

I saw Mrs. Heth and Miss Lizzie this morning.[49] They were at Church and the Genl and I had the pleasure and honor of a ride part of the way home with them. They patronized an ambulance and we were on horseback. . . .

We had delightful services at Church this morning, I don't know when I have enjoyed the communion so much, though my thoughts were at times sadly distracted. Mr. Patterson preached for us—his sermons are generally very good and always instructive in spite of his peculiar manner which is calculated to incite a smile even from the most serious and best.[50] Mr. Platt in appearance reminds me forcibly of Mr.

Rodman and yet they cannot be said to be alike. By the way, what of Mr. Rodman? A letter, sent me yesterday from home from Annie Robertson in Liverpool, says they hope that by this time Mr. R. is with us. Annie & Coz M seem to be nicely fixed; and although they cannot become thoroughly reconciled to English habits and notions are rejoiced to have such an asylum from Yankee rule.[51] I wish all our Norfolk people—that is those not capable of bearing arms—could be removed from the hated presence of the minions of the Beast. Poor little Sistress wd. be far happier in Liverpool than Norfolk.

Since the affair at Stony Creek we have had perfect quiet on our lines.[52] I think however we must expect some excitement soon; though unless Grant takes advantage of the present favorable spell of weather, it may be deferred until after Christmas. The Sixth Corps, which has been with Sheridan in Genl. Early's front, has started for City Point, so we are informed by telegram received not long since. If this be so, then in my opinion the time for another struggle draws near. I think we are ready and hope with God's help for success. It is sad to think that more of our brave fellows—the veterans of four years war are to fall without realizing peace. You remember Gracie about whose tact in getting Genl. Lee to descend from a dangerous position I told you when I was last in Richmond. You have no doubt heard of his death.[53] This excellent officer had passed through many hard fought battles, had escaped numberless dangers and finally was killed whilst quietly viewing the enemy, when no one dreamed of danger from the quarter which dealt the death blow. He too leaves a poor, distressed wife. A sad picture indeed! Certainly a soldier's life now is most precarious, but his death generally a noble one! In Gracie's case, thank heaven, we have every reason to hope that he has entered on those "endless, endless, endless ages" of happiness of which Mr. Platt spoke so eloquently last Sunday. He was to have brought his wife over here in a few days and I received his application to be allowed a short leave to go for her almost simultaneously with the announcement of his death. I hope she may find comfort in looking forward to the time when they may be happily reunited.

I hope it will not be very long before I am again blessed with the sight of you, though the prospect for a trip to the north side is quite blue just now in spite of the fact that the Genl. told me he was anxious to go over there. I shall instruct Grant to place the 6th Corps there when it arrives & that may move us. I am conscious that this is but an apology for a letter and fear that you will think me complaining. Please don't Bettie, I may be a little hurt, but 'tis just a little, & I am ashamed of that because I <u>know</u> good reasons have prevented my usual letter. God bless you, my own Bettie, and soon restore you to me with a lasting happy peace prays your

W.

12 o'clock I have just completed a note to Sister, and received a telegram from Ewell reporting considerable commotion of the enemy in his front this evening. Movements tend to Fort Harrison. I catch at straws & see in this some reason to hope for a trip to Chaffin's— Wishing you happy dreams—good night you dear old pet

W.

93

Edge Hill

Monday

12 Decem 1864

I have lost so much rest, dear Bettie, during the past week that I was compelled to seek repose last night at the time I usually employ in writing my letter to you. I always regret my inability to write on Sunday, because I cannot really find opportunity to write on any other day of the week. I am a little ahead of my work this morning however, & will at least let you hear why I do not write as usual. And did I <u>scold</u> in my last? Indeed I did not intend to be cross and disagreeable. Read the letter again, my pet, and I think you will find that my confidence was superior to the disappointment I naturally felt from not hearing from you. More than once I said I <u>knew</u> you had been prevented from writing from good causes. But we will not quarrel. I was too glad to hear from you.

We have had considerable excitement during the past week, nor has the end yet come. The wretched couriers were after me the whole night, and what a bitter cold night it was! As yet the enemy have accomplished but little. The whole movement seems to have been a grand raid on the Weldon railroad & though the bridge, which was the principal object of the expedition, was saved by the valor of our troops, they succeeded in destroying about 10 miles of the road.[54] There were other movements along the lines, but in results they were trifling. Last night another movement was reported but I think it was only reinforcements going to the first party. The weather is so intensely cold that doubtless both sides will be willing and anxious to return to their more comfortable winter quarters. If this passes away without a fight and quiet ensues I think it more than probable that we will move to the north side. . . .

Miles has returned from Wilmington and reports having had a glorious time. I sent the letter you enclosed to Miss Lizzie, she is but a short distance from us. I was never in such comfortable quarters as we now have since the war began. The only thing wanting is a fair lady to exercise over us rough men the influences which characterize your sex. I want somebody to <u>play on my piano</u>. Bettie Page promises to come and take care of me & supply me with good music.[55] After Church on yesterday I paid her and that family a nice long visit. They have moved to a very fine house & are as comfortable as could be. I was so much pleased, that, contrary to my expectations, I remained to dinner & almost till night. I am determined to cut out Starke, Buck Cooke, Jno Cocke & the rest of her admirers.[56] I have a nice long letter from Julia to Duncan. You know I am privileged to open and read all such. Julia writes in better spirits than I have ever known her to be since the evacuation. The letter is dated Nov. 30—quite recent. She mentions "The dear Captain!" most affectionately many times & begs for her photograph.[57] You know I never can understand these blockade letters but I translate one part of it to mean that Fannie K. will probably return to Norfolk & that her mother is improving. I am afraid the Yankees visited "Tower Hill," as they were all through that section. Poor Lizzie must have had a time of it.[58] I hope, my precious, you are refreshed & in fine spirits this beautiful morning. God bless my own Bettie prays

W.

94

Edge Hill, Sunday eve'g

18 Dec. 1864

For some time, my dear Bettie, I have been dreamily enjoying my cheerful fire, entertaining myself with thoughts of my absent one and wishing that I could spend these, my leisure moments, in your company and again realize the happy emotions which your presence always awakens. What would I not give for only five minutes, where in to amuse myself studying these deep brown eyes, that I might discover some story in which I was interested.

As this was but a vain regret however, and I was in a fair way of allowing my dreams to run away with the whole evening, I determined to give somebody else the benefit of my fancies, that my usual letter might not be missing whilst I indulge the pleasure second only to that I long for and cannot obtain. I have today listened to a good sermon from Mr. Platt; by invitation I spent a very pleasant time at Mrs. Wells' and partook of an excellent dinner;[59] had the cruelty to interfere with the happiness of two of my sweet cousin Bettie Page's admirers, returned home to be snubbed by the General for having dared to absent myself from my office, completed more work than I care to do on Sunday;[60] smoked the pipe of peace, concluded that I was on friendly terms with all the world, including the General, and settled down into a state of absolute quiet and contentment. . . .

I was at Gen'l Heth's a few evenings since. All were well. Miles & Miss Lizzie start for home on Friday next. I think the reason for putting it off thus late is that they may witness the tournament which is to be on the 21st I believe. The poor horses have enough to do and little enough to eat to render such an entertainment unadvisable for them, but I trust the spectators may enjoy it. It is a great disappointment to me to know that Miles & Miss Lizzie must go to Norwood without me. I hope to get off later in the season; but as one of my brother officers is exceedingly anxious to be at home on Christmas, and as he is a married man and has a dear little cherub at home that he has never seen, I of course gave way to him, for to press my claims under such circumstances would be most selfish. As he was recently at home, I hope he will not stay long and I am sure that my pleasure, though a little deferred will be none the less on that account. I would feel more at home at Norwood if Miles was with me; but as my principal object is to get away from the army and these plagued papers for a while, it matters little when I go, since by an edict some time issued, I was given to understand that my furlough could not be spent in your company. Mrs. Harrison of Elk Hill was so kind and thoughtful as to send me an invitation to visit her.[61] John Cocke also wishes me to go to his home. So the only trouble is to decide where to go and in all probability I will settle this question by remaining the whole of my short leave in Richmond. Bob Taylor has applied for leave. Duncan & Aleck Tunstall will do the same. I believe Robbie is also to go to Elk Hill. Altogether they have a reasonable prospect of a happy Christmas and I do hope they may enjoy it. When the excitement has passed, if I can only steal away to some quiet spot and take a good rest—for indeed I am very, very weary of this monotonous & exceedingly uninteresting employment, I shall be thankful. You have said nothing of your leave, Bettie. Of course you are to have some relaxation. It would be a great comfort to your mother to have you with her at this time. Are you not going to the Neck? I am so glad your Coz. John is at home. When you write or better still if you go there, do give my love to them all. I am so glad that Mr Rodman has arrived safely. No doubt his presence will enhance the happiness of the whole family these Christmas times. Did you see him? But of course you did, as he was in Richmond. . . .

We have had comparative quiet since the recent affair on the Weldon railroad. The Yankees fired a salute this morning. What induced it, is not known.[62] It is difficult to anticipate events now, but I think it more probable that Wilmington will be the scene of the next engagement than Petersburg or Richmond.[63] I did hope that we might move to the north side before Christmas—cannot say how it will be if we remain here. I shall not expect to experience much pleasure as usually attends the festival—but will strive "to be jolly" still. Invoking upon you Heaven's choicest blessings and with oceans of love I am yrs as ever

W.

95

Edge Hill

26 Decm. 1864

You were light hearted, dear Bettie, when you wrote yr letter of last Thursday, & certainly it made me most happy to read it, because of the assurance it brought that you were in good spirits. . . .

Don't you suppose I was sadly disappointed when I reached Richmond yesterday and learned you were not there. I did not even ask to go home to spend the day but much to my surprise my Chief proposed that I should spend Christmas with my mother and my sweetheart. Of course it required no persuasion to induce me to go. Though I had not received yr letter I felt almost certain that you had gone to the Neck; & though I wished to see you—oh! so much, old sensitive plant—I really was glad that your wishes were gratified, even whilst my hopes were disappointed. . . .

Of course you heard of Lizzie's having been chosen as the Queen of Love and Beauty. A Captain Atwell rode for her.[64] She seemed to enjoy the day very much—as disagreeable as it was—and the ball must have been a great affair, as it lasted till the morning of the following day. Mr. Rodman has been to see me once or twice. He is to enter the army as a Chaplain. He is to return home with Miss Lizzie but I suppose he will get tired of waiting soon and in despair take out by himself.[65] I wrote your cousin John last week about his leave. You see, Bettie, his command is now detailed in the Valley & Early acts finally on all applications for leave and all things considered it wouldn't be right to grant the leave from him. I sent him a pass which will allow him to remain at home until the first of the year and then if he returns to his regiment I could engineer him a leave, but I don't like to attempt it whilst he is absent.[66] It is all a mistake about Mrs Cullins having procured a leave for the Doctor.[67] I know all about that and he is indebted to me and not to his good lady. The General has just been in and says it is time for me to retire, so I must hurry up. I have been very happy the past few days and am so now—particularly this moment. I wonder if you can guess why? I received one or two, I might say several, presents lately which I call my Christmas gifts. I will show you some of them one of these days. Little sensitive plant I salute you! and another thing, little sensitive plant, I think you have the deepest, brownest, dearest "peepers" in the world. Can you guess why I'm happy, my precious dear little sensitive plant? Give my best love to your mother. I wish it my privilege to be one of your group this year and hope it may be the next. My love to "Sister" too. I hope she and the little stranger are very well.[68] Love to dear Pattie & Maria too if she is at the Neck—or has she returned to Charlotte?[69] May God bless and keep you, dear Bettie, and give you the comfort of His Holy Spirit at all times is the prayer of yr devoted

W.

Chapter 6

Edge Hill to Appomattox:
January to March 1865
(Letters 96–110)

Save for occasional denunciations of the inertia of the Confederate civil leaders, Taylor exhibits little anxiety of impending defeat. Indeed he insists that God will not abandon the South and that ultimate victory is sure. Now at last he proposes that they be married before they are separated by the fall of Richmond and Bettie gives her glad consent.

96

Norwood

18 Jany 1865

A week has passed, my dear Bettie, and I linger still at this happy home. Each day I find it more difficult to leave and every moment I regret that my leave of absence is so short. Truly, the more one has, the more one wants. I thought that I would be perfectly satisfied with two weeks holiday, and now that more than one half of that period has passed away it seems unreasonable that I should be required so soon to return. . . .[1]

I do not wonder, Bettie, at your attachment to Norwood. Beautiful indeed must the place be in the summer and the family must, I am sure, be always attractive. Charlie, he and Miles, are both at home invalid.[2] I am very much disposed to follow their example and cultivate some ailment just serious enough to require an extension of my leave. There is one thing I long for most earnestly, Bettie, and that is that you might be enjoying this visit with me. Because of your absence, I cannot help at times wishing I was in Richmond for an hour or so. Never mind. One of these days we will return here together, will we not! The wish has been very often expressed that Bettie could have come with me by several members of the household. I take pleasure in reflecting

215

that every spot that meets my eye is familiar to you and the rooms and walks possess an additional charm, when I reflect that they have been the scenes of many of your happy hours. Everyone is so kind that if Gen. Lee knew all he would pardon me, even if I overstayed my time a month. I wish to be with you two or three days before I return to the army. I cannot say when I will get away again and my precious I wish to see as much of you as I can before that dreadful spring campaign opens. That I hope is to be our last fiery ordeal. That we will come out of it with flying colors I doubt not, but that our success will be most dearly purchased is equally as certain. To be with you as much as possible before that time is my chief desire. Oh Bettie, I can't tell how fondly I cling to the recollection of the happy evenings I have spent with you during my occasional visits to Richmond the last six months! Those happy little spots in my monotonous existence give me but a faint idea of that happiness laid up for me in the future, when it will be as rare to be absent from you as it is now for me to be with you. Do you not also look forward to that time with anticipation of happiness? Please, dear sensitive plant, step out of your beautiful reserve for once and tell me—yes! God bless and keep you prays your

W

97

Monday 24 [23] Jany '65

Here I am, Bettie, regularly domesticated at "Howard's Neck." I was induced to prolong my stay at Norwood by the promise of Mrs. Rodman that if I deferred my visit she would accompany me. Although my furlough was fast drawing to a close, I could not resist the "please." She promised to say nothing of my ready mind to accept any excuse for prolonging my stay at her happy house. Are they not kind there, and was there ever a happier household? And what shall I say of the kindness of all the dear ones here? Oh, Bettie, I cannot tell you how I appreciate your Mother's affectionate reception and the considerate treatment she has extended to me, not only during this visit, but always! In every little act in all the managements for my comfort, I can detect her kind, considerate care. How can I ever repay her? Indeed I know of no way in which I can ever show my just appreciation of her unwavering kindness, but it shall be my steady aim to manifest this as far as practicable in my future life by an earnest, unfailing devotion to her and hers.

Mr. Hobson is very kind and I make myself as much at home with him as if I had some claims upon him. Your "sister" and little Mayhew (how is his name spelled?) are getting on finely. Of course the baby is a beauty indeed, "the prettiest child that ever lived." I never saw one that wasn't. Mrs. H. doesn't leave her room yet, but I am honored with an audience every day. Pattie is occupied with the children every morning but allows me the pleasure and privilege of an hour or two in her room in the afternoon. The children are beginning to know me and I beat Lillie and Cannon all to pieces playing checks though Mary is a little too much for me.[3]

On yesterday Mr. Hobson and I rode up to Elk Hill. It was a rainy day, but although I didn't mind that, I was afraid Mr. H. would find it very disagreeable; but he would go, though I begged he would not do so unless it was preferable to him on his own account. I had heard that all the company had left Elk Hill, but the house still appears to be pretty well filled. Lady after lady came into the parlor until Mr. H. and I with Robby found ourselves in a very decided minority. I did hope that Rob would be quiet when he came to the country, but they have been so gay at Mrs. Harrison's that I fear his wound instead of improving, has been worse. I begged the ladies to tie him, as that was the only way to keep him quiet in their presence.

When I left Norwood your Uncle William was considered very ill.[4] Since then we have no tidings from Norwood. God grant he may still be spared to his family! I came here determined to return immediately if your mother wished to go, but she concluded that she could not now leave your cousin Kittie and the children. I expect to take the boat this evening for Norwood, and on Thursday, if nothing prevents, shall ride down to Richmond. There I must spend two or three days. I wonder what my old chief will think of me? I hoped to receive a letter this morning telling me it was unnecessary to return before next Monday, but not a word have I heard from the army since my departure from Headquarters. Properly I should resume my duties tomorrow, but I cannot, will not deprive myself of a few days with you in Richmond. If I am dismissed for my independent or unauthorized conduct, I know you will find it in your heart to forgive me and care not for the rest.

If Misses Mollie and Maria are still with you, give my love to both.[5] I am so sorry I did not meet them at the "Neck." I received a note from Clarence asking me to wait on him.[6] It only reached me Saturday and

I fear my reply will not be received before the appointed time. I trust he will anticipate my absence and secure the services of someone else. I am sorry I cannot be present.

Hoping soon to see you. I remain your devoted

W.

(Your letter has not reached me. I hope to find it at Norwood)

98

[To Bettie]

Edge Hill

Sunday afternoon

5 Feby 65

Instead of a quiet comfortable Sunday, we have had one of considerable excitement, and even now the indications are that Grant is once more moving on us. I was late getting to Church, as we had Capt Semmes (Alabama) & Col Ives as morning visitors, and had scarcely become well engaged in the services when I received information that the Yankees were moving. I hurried home and was soon followed by the General who has now, with his two aides, gone towards the scene of action, whilst I have been left at Hd Qrs to attend to matters here.[7] What will my little pet, who thinks so much of those always at the front, say of this? Should not I also go where there is danger? A soldier, dear Bettie, must obey orders—though mine keep me here now, they have often heretofore carried & will frequently hereafter carry me into positions most uncomfortably hot. From the reports that have reached me, it appears the enemy are moving to attack us in force—whether he has been reinforced by Genl Thomas I cannot say but all things considered I wd rather that he should fight now than later.[8] We are in very good condition and by the help of God will render a good account of ourselves. . . .[9]

These plagued Yankees give me much trouble. I have been compelled to divide my time and attention this afternoon between you and them and fear they have rec'd the greatest portion. It seems now that they are on a raid towards our railroads—Southside & Danville. I have just recd orders from Genl Lee to direct certain movements. You see somebody has to be at Head Qrs. I declare I have just remarked to our host, I am the luckiest fellow in the world. Everything today (in my duties) has appeared to be arranged for my special convenience. It was necessary a few moments since for me to send certain orders to the Superintendent of the railroads, the Chief Qr Mr & the Inspector, each one difficult to find & I had to write a note to each, when lo! & behold! one after another all three walked into my room & saved much time & much trouble.[10] Am I not lucky? . . .

I cannot say now whether the enemy intends only a raid or at the same time will move against us here. I wonder what Genl Pegram will do with Mrs P?[11] She is near the scene of the excitement. Maybe Mrs Heth may have to go or may think it advisable. She will have an opportunity to return to Norwood, as Mr Rodman starts for that sweet place tomorrow. How I wish I could go with him! . . .

How sad it is about Capt Arthur Sinclair. I have just heard this evening that young Arthur was drowned also. Poor Miss Lelia![12] What a sad, sad blow. How she suffers God alone knows. May he support and comfort her.

I expect, Bettie dear, that we shall have a most trying spring. I do not yet know what will be the programme as regards the movements of Genl Lee. Tomorrow or next day I expect he will be announced as General in Chief.[13] I do not see how he can attend to all the administrative duties of this army & also direct military operations elsewhere. Then if he leaves, or rather if another immediate commander is appointed, what becomes of the staff? All my friends tell me I will accompany him. They intend a compliment. I thank them but how will I feel if he does not & I am left with his successor? Now I have no decided preference personally either way, but it would certainly cause me to feel unpleasantly to have this occur, knowing as I do what my friends expect. However I am ready for anything & will accept my fate with cheerfulness. But to what I was about to say: we will have a trying spring campaign. You know I am very sanguine always. I don't expect anything except success, but 'tis possible Sherman may trouble us here a great deal.[14] I have often spoken to you in a semi-serious way about what should be done if Richmond should be lost. I am now altogether serious. Don't you follow Ma's example & conclude that because I propose certain steps in event such a disaster should occur, therefore I look for the fall of the City. I dare not say a word to Mother now about it, because of her way of arriving at conclusions so rapidly. Understand me then. I hope & expect that we shall hold our own, but they may not be able to control Sherman and possibly we may have to make very important changes in the campaign and shift our position. I don't think this probable, only possible. In event of Richmond's falling, what would you wish to do? Of course you can now only speak in <u>general</u> terms, & say whether or not you would desire to move with the Confederacy. Would your mother's movements control yours & do you not agree with me in thinking that she & your Cousin Kittie would remain at the "Neck." From what transpired whilst I was at Mrs Hobson's I concluded that Mr H. advised that they remain in Goochland.[15] On the whole I dare say he is right. Now I could never be satisfied for you to be in the Yankee lines, & I would like to know seriously what your wishes would be. Please don't intimate that I have even suggested the possibility of our losing Richmond & don't believe that I think it at all probable, but I wish to be prepared for the emergency by being made aware of your wishes.[16] The <u>details</u> & <u>mode</u> of carrying out your wishes can be decided when the contingency appears less remote than I now conceive it to be.

I have caught up with my work. Whilst [I was] away the General had a taste of what I had to do & since my return has insisted on dividing the labour. He told me he had often thought I had too much to do and he did not wish me to do all the work. The difficulty heretofore has been that they would not allow me to decide how the work should be divided, but yesterday it was arranged as I desired it & although I have turned over but little to the others, still I will have at least two hours less hard work daily than formerly. Poor Venable is considerably disgruntled, but all will work out well shortly. Do give my best love to your Aunt Jane.[17] I shall do myself the honour to pay my respects to Mrs Hobson when occasion offers. Write your Coz John word not to start for Gordonsville—his command will probably return to the vicinity of Richmond and indeed is I expect now on its way there.[18] Give my best love to your Mother, Pattie & Sister & all the children when you write. My kindest regards to your Aunt Jane, Coz Mary & all yr household. God bless & keep you. Yr W.

99

[To Bettie]

Monday 6 Feby 65

After all, yesterday's excitement resulted in but little. The Yankees have not gone after our railroads—having been checked at Dinwiddie

C Ho.[19] They have extended their lines somewhat, but as yet show no disposition to attack in force. It may be the fight is still to be deferred. I had an opportunity to write by flag of truce through Genl Grant's Headqrs a day or two since. I wish very much that I could send Julia a letter but time only allowed me to write to Dick. . . .

I presume all Richmond is in a state of excitement about the return of the Peace Commissioners.[20] I hope all the croakers are satisfied and will hereafter keep silence. It will do us much good and I am really glad they went. Our people now know what they have to expect & unless we are a craven hearted spiritless people, the result will surely prove beneficial & cause every man & woman to be doubly determined to fight to the last. The impudence of those people! Oh, if I was only an army big enough to whip them all! The idea of submitting to them. I wouldn't be one of a people who would do such a thing. I wonder if you'll read this tiny scrawl. Good bye. Your own

W.

100

Edge Hill

14 Feb '65

I am behind hand this week, my dear Bettie, but am determined that you shall have my usual letter tonight even if other matters have to be neglected to enable me to write. I have been quite dissipated of late and this will account for my silence. I have been to the City more frequently during the past week than is my usual custom. I find that one has to do one of two things—either not go there at all or be constantly running in. The people are very hospitable & if you mingle with them, invitations to dinner, supper &c come thick & fast. On Sunday I dined by invitation at Mrs Johnson's where I met our sweet friend Jennie B. I declare I hope Capt Baird is worthy of Jennie,[21] but somehow I can't believe that he is. It would have gratified you, dear Bettie, could you have heard the earnest way in which the whole family expressed the wish that you would pay them another visit. I was asked if I could influence you to do so & when I gently intimated that it was not exactly my province to ask you to their house, Mrs J begged me then to give you a message from her. So in the name of the whole Johnson household, I tender you an earnest invitation to come to Petersburg. By the way, I have been informed that you, Mrs Petty and some of the Crenshaws were to come over after Calvert's return. Maybe you have been here and have gone back. Is it so?[22] Come, do come. I will promise to be the best boy you ever saw, indeed my duties compel me to be very moderate even if I wished to be otherwise. However apart from your enjoyment of the trip and the pleasure you would experience in visiting many of your old friends, I shall say I would much prefer meeting you in an unrestrained way in Richmond. The General went over yesterday. I think he might have taken me. I am determined to run over before very long. I desire very much to see Ma on certain matters relative to their movements and above all, my precious, I wish to come by to see you. Oh, Bettie, this is to me a most trying, cruel separation, and it does seem hard that although I am only two hours ride from you, yet I should be allowed to see you only once every two or three months. But the war must soon end and end successfully and then—then. Oh, my dear Bettie, if God spares me to see that time, my cup of happiness will indeed be full. This hope is now my greatest consolation; to reach that end, I will endure anything; & having realized the happiness I dream of, I will be able to look back on all past deprivations & trials with a calm and thankful heart, grateful to have attained so great a blessing at so small a cost. My own little ---- that is to be, how can I ever be sufficiently thankful to God for such a gift, such a treasure? Oh Bettie, how I wish I was less unworthy. God knows I desire to be less so and try and will strive to try to be less unworthy such a blessing.

You will have seen ere this that the General has assumed command of all the armed forces of the Confederate States. For the present he is to make his headquarters with the army, but a great many think it will be necessary for him to appoint some one in the immediate command of this army. Strange as it may appear, the next choice of the army is Genl Johnston.[23] Our forces in So Carolina have retreated from the Edisto to the Congaree, from Branchville to a point farther in the interior. Two Corps from Hood's army have been removed to Sherman's front and I do hope we will this time prove too much for that gentleman.[24] I would be much more hopeful if Genl Lee was there but nevertheless will hope for the best from Beauregard.[25] On our lines everything has been particularly quiet the last several days. . . .

God bless you prays Yr

W.

I O I

Edge Hill

16 Febry 1865

When my mind is as absolutely occupied with thoughts of you, my dearest Bettie, as is the case this morning, it is almost a necessity that I should write to you, that I may be to some extent consoled in being deprived of the greater comfort & pleasure of seeing you. I can't tell you, precious pet, how in these troublous times, these days of great danger and distress, of anxiety and care because of the uncertainty of the future, how my heart yearns towards you with the longing desire that I had the ability and the time to relieve you from all care and discomfort, to be able to say "Rest easy, Bettie, I can and will see that no annoyance, no danger, no anxiety shall come near you," but since God has, as you say, willed it otherwise, how thankful should I be, indeed how grateful I am, to know that my brave little girl has a courageous heart, a will and spirit which fits her for any emergency. Your letter of last Sunday reached me yesterday. I presume Calvert was not able to come to see me and so dropped it in the <u>Post</u> office as it was marked "Petersburg." I thank you earnestly for your letter. In all that you say I can see that the ruling motive is a consideration and thoughtfulness of me and an unwillingness to tax me with an additional burden, but whilst I recognize this and am not so infatuated as not to see the many impediments to what I would propose, still I cannot admit that that which will bring me such incomprehensible pleasure could in any way provide trouble or put upon my shoulders any burden for which strength wd not be supplied. I do not intend to enter into any argument about it however. I am acquainted with your wishes in the event of the contingency we mentioned and this suffices for the present. And here let me add that it was not my intention to alarm or excite you, for indeed I regard the contingency only as of the remotest possibility, and prudence requires that we should not be unprepared for it. My faith in the courage and endurance of this old army is unimpaired and with God's help we will always prove more than a match for Grant, and I really believe he can never take Richmond by force of arms. What do you think of the question of negro soldiers now? No doubt the experiment will be tried. My notions are still the same, but I cannot presume to place them in opposition to the well considered and matured views of so many of my wise superiors. It makes me sad however to reflect that the time honoured institution will be no more, that the whole social organization of the South is to be revolutionized.[26] But I suppose it is all right and we will have to be reconciled.

Our returned prisoners will help us much in the way of reinforcements, if a general exchange is really to be effected. I can scarcely believe that the Yankees will agree to anything so much to their disadvantage. I shall hope every day now to hear of the arrival of Dick or John or both within our lines.[27] Our poor fellows who have been so long confined and who have refused in the face of every temptation to take the hateful oath and blot their soul with the stain of perjury, which causes my dear sensitive plant to shudder, will make the best of soldiers. With what a vim will they attack their old persecutors! Oh, it is indeed almost pleasant to think how they will rejoice at being allowed once more to cut down their cruel adversaries. But I must strive against such feelings, for they are wicked. . . .

[No signature]

102

Edge Hill

20 Feb. '65

This has been a day of considerable bustle, my dear Bettie, and even now there are some incomplete matters claiming my attention. I will not longer defer my letter, however, for it is impossible to say what a day may bring forth in these uncertain times. Truly affairs are becoming quite exciting, are they not? If somebody doesn't arrest Sherman, where will he stop? Where are those who leave Richmond to go? I have taken the preliminary steps to provide a resting place for our flock in the neighborhood of Lincolnton, but the Yankees seem to be moving directly for Charlotte, which is in disagreeable proximity to that place.[28] It will be a sad alternative to have to remain in Richmond and be enveloped by the enemy; and yet I entertain very serious fears that with Ma and the children it will be a necessity, _if_ our army is compelled to move its position. No place promises security that I can see, except immediately with the army. I have always felt determined that my people should never be left in the Yankee lines, and it will be the saddest day of my life, if circumstances necessitate such a calamity. And what will the Surgeon General's office do? I am even more interested in that. You had better mount your horse and travel along with me until the uncertainty has passed and our affairs are once more straightened out. They are trying to corner this old army like a brave old lion brought to bay at last. It is determined to resist to the death and if die it must, to die game. But we have not yet quite made up our minds to die, and if God will help us, we will yet prove equal to the emergency. We are to have many hard knocks—we are to experience much that is dispiriting, but if our men are true, and I really believe most of them are, we will make our way safely, successfully through the dark clouds that now surround us. Our people must make up their minds to see Richmond go, to see all the cities go, but must not lose spirit, must not give up.[29] The battle has just begun, the man who bows the head or says surrender must not be tolerated. Oh for a man of iron nerve and will to lead us! We need a strong hand now. There can be no trifling, no halting or hesitation now without ruin. Our old Chief is too law abiding, too slow, too retiring for these times, that is to dare & do what I deem necessary, but nevertheless he is the best we have, certainly the greatest captain and in his own safe & sure way will yet, I trust, carry us through this the greatest trial yet.[30] I wish I could see you, Bettie, and have a good satisfactory talk: writing does very well in its way as a substitute, but 'tis a very "slow concern" when contrasted with a personal interview. I did hope that I could arrange matters so as to run to Richmond once more, but now I can see no reason for such a hope. The General left me but a few moments ago. My orders are to be in marching order, to lose no time, to begin my preparations tomorrow. These instructions apply to army Head Qrs only, which means, you will understand, that tho' the army will retain its position still a time longer, the General in Chief may soon bid a temporary adieu and repair to another scene of excitement. Of this, my dear, say nothing. Oh, Bettie, I must see you once more before the next act in this terrible drama! If we only had more staff I might hope for it, but Marshall is sick and Venable and I must manage between us, not only the Head Qrs of the Army of No Va but those of the armies of the C.S. . . . .

Then followed a bitter condemnation of the Northern troops closing in on Richmond.

Oh those wretched Yankees! How hard it is that they the miserable creatures should be the cause of our separation. Just think how happy this life might be but for their brutal persecution. Is it not humiliating to a proud spirit to be compelled to yield to brute force? If my strength was but equal to my will and wish, how grateful it would be to crush the contemptible things! That's a wicked thought, however, & I must struggle against it. But how can mortal cultivate humility, where the Yankees are concerned?

But ever the optimist, in spite of the gathering gloom, he added:

Here I have been rattling away, jotting down every thought that our unfortunate position suggested, without any regard whatever for your patience and the thousand and one things I really wish to talk to you about. It is very remarkable, but I certainly do feel a strange exhilaration when I contemplate our national prospects. My pulse is quickened as my thoughts in pleasing anticipation dwell upon the way we are going to throttle that upstart Sherman.

. . . Well, if the S.G.O. [Surgeon General's Office] is surrounded or surrenders, you know where to find your best friend. You have only to beckon to him and with heroic fortitude he will sacrifice himself without a murmur.

W.

103

[A note to Mrs. Knox ("Coz Mary") 21 Feb 65, not included.]

104

Edge Hill

24 Feby '65

Your letter of last Monday, brought by Jennie, reached me yesterday. I am so grieved, my precious Bettie, to hear that you were not feeling well and hope that violent headache has entirely left you. I value your letters, dearest, more than I can express; but I value your comfort more, and beg you will never write to me when so doing will cause you suffering. And how can I thank you for this last letter? Do you know, Bettie, that for the first time I now really begin to realize that my great love for you is reciprocated. The sensitiveness and careful refraining from any evidence of your attachment, which has always characterized yr treatment of me, but for which, however much I might suffer thereby, I could not blame you then, has prevented my entertaining the heart cheering, heart filling hope that your attachment for me fully equalled my earnest devotion for you. Now it is no longer a hope, but I accept the belief that this is a fact joyfully, thankfully. I feel, my darling, that I am no longer alone, that there is something in this world mine alone—wholly alone. Thank God for such a blessing. In His sight, my dear Bettie, I feel we are henceforth one.

I would have enjoyed above all these things a visit to Richmond last Sunday—especially as I knew that you were expecting me. Now that General Johnston has been placed in command by General Lee, I don't think that we will go to South Carolina—at any rate just now[31]—so that we can indulge the hope that ere long I may be permitted to enjoy a flying visit to the City. As you have confessed that you do really wish to see me, I'll make greater efforts to get off. I should like to spend a week in Richmond for a double purpose, first to see and be with you; second, to choke some of the wretched croakers that infest that place. Don't you lose heart, Bettie. I will not pretend that our condition at this hour is not a critical one. But though it is a crisis in our affairs—it is the same with the enemy. Suppose we concentrate on Sherman and crush him, would not the aspect of affairs be entirely changed? Well, that is not beyond the range of possibility—it may be done & I really hope for it. How much of South Carolina & Tennessee would the enemy then hold? What would resist our advance into Kentucky or Maryland?[32] You see much depends on the check given to Sherman's career and by proper management I believe he can be arrested. At the proper time I feel sure our Chief will exhibit himself in his full strength & prove equal to the emergency. Richmond may be lost—Sherman may be defeated, Richmond saved and our independence won. Let us take the bright side. Like prudent and wise ones, let us be prepared for the reverse, but beyond this let us not anticipate the evil. Our people must not despond. If they are worthy of liberty, they will not begrudge the price and will count all earthly things lost to win that & preserve our honor. It annoys me to hear the silly reports carried from mouth to mouth in Richmond. Don't you believe anything you hear of the army except what I tell you or what you get from some one else in whom you have equal confidence. Some of our weakest men have deserted their colors, but the desertion is not near so great as reported. We are getting something to eat & most of our brave fellows are in good heart, though grieved to hear of the despondency at home. Tell all yr friends to send words of cheer & encouragement to the army & themselves to keep a brave heart & determined spirit & to cease not in prayer. I have much to say but only intend this as a note of acknowledgement for your letter & as a word of encouragement in regard to our affairs. Time will allow no more now. May God bless you my own, own Bettie prays Yr

W.

105

Edge Hill

28 Feby '65

My letters follow each other so thick and fast, my dear Bettie, that I am afraid you will become tired of me. . . .

I had hoped that I would have enjoyed (shall I say you and I would have enjoyed?) the pleasure of a visit to Richmond on last Sunday. I had fully made up my mind to propose it to the General when to my dismay on Saturday night he was summoned to the city himself. Of course, this upset all my arrangements, but I do not yet despair and hope ere long to be with you. I have just received a telegram from the General informing me that he would return this evening. I earnestly hope that he has infused some spirit into the depressed Richmond functionaries. The Petersburg folks are becoming somewhat calmer; they have demonstrated one thing however, they are more interested in their pockets than in their country.

. . . Yes, I believe you are right, we have known and l---d each other long, precious Bettie, and don't fear that such a truth would make me vain or presumptuous—only truly thankful. What reconciles me to the necessary postponement of our m-----ge, dearest Bettie, is the fact that my vision of happiness is not limited to a few short years nor to this world. Oh God, how thankful I am for such a blessing for eternity. We must be separated for a while, darling, it must be sooner or later, but it will only be for a little while. 'Tis [it] not a necessary concomitant to our transition from this to a brighter and happier existence. But God is gracious and I hope for many happy years with you here, dear little sensitive plant, before that time comes. Don't dwell too much on the fighting. Pray for me and leave the future to our merciful Father. I shall make every effort to see you very soon. Heaven's choicest blessings be yours, dear Bettie, is the constant prayer of your

W.

106

Edge Hill

Sunday

5 March '65

Another week has passed away, my dear Bettie, and my hopes of seeing you are still unrealized. I might imagine that you were expecting me tonight, but presume you have before this learned of the General's presence in Richmond and my consequent retention here. At one time it occurred that it was his intention for once to offer to take me with him. Whilst we were discussing his contemplated trip, he remarked "I would like to have some one with me, I always require some assistance & since Custis has left I am much at a loss at times."[33] I regarded this as a gentle hint for me to offer my services & concluding that the time was opportune for me to put in my oar, I told him that I had been quite anxious to get to Richmond for a day but had deferred my visit because he had been so often absent. My effort failed— nothing more was said on this point and we exchanged views as to the best disposition to be made of one's family in these times of uncertainty. I was summoned to his room once or twice again and he finally told me that he always preferred that I shd remain here while he was absent, that he would feel better satisfied (or words to that effect). And so were my dreams dissipated, but I do not yet despair. I wd much prefer, however, that he would manifest his appreciation of my humble services in some other way. My anxiety to get to Richmond, my precious, has been very much increased since, like an honest little girl, you made those dear confessions that you were not altogether indifferent to

229

my coming. Don't be uneasy about your letters. I have become reconciled, since it is your expressed wish, to the burning of all of them. I do not commit them to the flames after the first perusal, but in a week after receipt. I will make it a habit to burn them. So now remove that embargo from your pen and express yourself naturally. . . .

You imagine, I really believe, that my last letter, or rather the last answered, was an attempt to humbug you into a sense of security. Indeed it was not.[34] I was then sanguine enough to indulge the hopes I expressed—but now—well I don't know that I will tell you what I think now, for you say that the state of affairs has made you very unhappy and I do not care to make you more so. But such a thought does you injustice—so would silence—and I am willing always to impart my views to my brave little ----. So, hold your ear and let me whisper.

You know I am blessed with a sanguine temperament. I do not, can not, will not yet despond, but I am annoyed, oh! so provoked, so thoroughly disgusted, to see the rapid, radical change in the tone of public sentiment in which (hold your ear close) our leaders participate.[35] Do you observe how openly people now talk of Terms—Peace—Reconstruction? I hear it, and you know the circle of my acquaintance over here is very limited. Oh this disposition or readiness to lick the hand that dealt the blow is revolting to me. Bettie, our eminent men—or what shall I call them? They are not Leaders, even those in high offices will tell us that the people are tired, that they are not supported by the people, that public sentiment has undergone a change &c, & hence their desire to avoid useless shedding of blood and secure peace. The idiots! The imbeciles! They forget that they are responsible for the tone of public sentiment to a far greater extent than are the people who look up to them. Oh! if Heaven would but vouchsafe to us a man fitted to relieve our poor country in this her hour of trial! One who cd produce system from the sad chaos that now reigns, organize determined resistance where now we have naught but confusion & an apparent absence of any decided plans; one of will and iron nerve who could guide the people and who would dare to fight the Yankees to the last. I do not think our military situation hopeless by any means, and am astonished at the sudden caving in of the majority of those in high positions. I cannot write fully on this subject for there is much that I might tell you, which I dare not put on paper; but one thing I confess, matters are far worse than I have ever known them or ever expected to see them. Unless this struggle is brought to a successful termination, how can a man be reconciled to accept the terms which would be forced upon us? Must we choose the life of a guerrilla or become an exile from home & country? But I will hope. As my trust is not in man but in God, I will not despair. We are sadly deficient, Bettie, in good, brave men capable of leading but I hope God will take care of us and provide a remedy in time. I cannot accept the belief that the cause is lost, that 4 precious years have been worse than wasted and that our whole future is blighted. You may wonder at the causes that have excited my fears; at some future time I will communicate them in person. . . .

We have drawn Pickett's division from its old lines, but I presume Capt. B. keeps Jennie fully advised of all his movements. I am very anxious to be present at J's marriage but fear that I cannot possibly so arrange it. Do give my best love to her and a kiss and tell her that I wish her every happiness. Such a dear little creature as our Jennie deserves the happiest lot.

Marshall accompanied the General to Richmond & as Venable was most anxious to go I induced him to trot off this morning and with the exception of our host, I am all alone at Head Qrs. The time was so propitious that I promised myself the pleasure of writing to you this morning, but visitors on official & unofficial business have kept me occupied all day and it is now about 10 P.M. I was very sorry that I could not get to Church today as it was communion Sunday. On last communion day I was called out of Church by the movements of the enemy. A Brigadier Genl informed me today that he was very desirous to have me made Colonel of one of his regiments of cavalry. I told him I would accept and he declared his intention of making the recommendation. What do you think of it? Would you recommend the change? I think it very desirable under existing circumstances. If I am to be a guerrilla & an outlaw, it will fit me for my future calling. Poor old Early, has he not had an unfortunate time of it? He finds himself at last without any army at all.[36] I am quite overwhelmed with the number of telegrams that I now receive at all hours of the day and night. They come now from all quarters of the Confederacy. You may expect to see me soon— certainly as soon as I can get away. God watch over & keep you, dearest, prays yr own

W.

107

Sunday afternoon

19 March 65

I have so much to say, my dear Bettie, that I scarcely know where to begin my letter. First of all, however, let me assure my little sensitive plant that from the depths of my heart I thank & bless her for her last letter. Dear Bettie, my heart is filled to overflowing when it accepts the grateful truths that you have presented. I am truly thankful, Bettie, that you have to some extent stepped out from the position of reserve you had assumed & allowed me to know and realize the extent of your interest in me. Nor do I think that there is any occasion whatever for your blushing at such a confession. . . .

Fear not as to your letters. I reluctantly, with a hesitating hand, burn every one. All that I had in Richmond have been destroyed. I am loth to part with them, but as 'tis your wish & the times are so uncertain, I think it best. . . .[37]

I can't say how grieved I was to learn of the proceedings of the Yankees at "The Neck."[38] But I suppose we can henceforward expect nothing better from them. Those who reside in the City are far less exposed to such annoyances than those in the country, because generally speaking when a town falls into their hands they establish some show of order—guards &c. I wish I could have another talk with you. You will have seen, if you read the President's message that the fact has been made public that Genl Lee proposed an interview with Gl Grant with a view, if possible, to take some measures which would lead to a cessation of hostilities.[39] It was this proposal, coupled with other facts known to me, that caused the apprehension I communicated to you. Since then matters have improved so far as our leaders are concerned. I think they are now determined to make the best fight possible. So you may reestablish your former good opinion of certain high military gentlemen of whom we conversed. Sherman moves on yet unchecked. However I should not say that exactly for Hardee fought a portion of his army several days ago. Hardee was attacked several times but repulsed the enemy with considerable loss.[40] There has been no general engagement. Tonight it is reported that the troops on our right are moving—it would seem in a southerly direction & prisoners say part of Grant's troops are going to N. Caro.[41] I will perhaps learn during the night. Some move is on hand. The trial of strength is approaching. With earnest prayers to God for his help, let us leave the issue with Him. The indications are that we will have a most trying spring and we must <u>expect</u> it and <u>nerve</u> ourselves for it. Still, with firm hearts and determined resolution we shall come off conquerors, no matter if we do experience a number of military reverses. I confess I cannot with any composure contemplate the prospect you foreshadow of our being separated by the Yankee lines. Is there no remedy for this? If I am called upon, Bettie, to leave you behind, circumstances must be very decidedly of a character to compel this course, to enable me to be reconciled to it. I cannot now say how matters will then be—something may occur, some change be developed which may justify a different arrangement. If the army should have to leave hurriedly without any definite understanding as to our future movements, I would of course recommend that you remain. Whether it is best for you to stay in Richmond or go to the country is a debatable question, & indeed this point also can be best determined on at the time. If on the other hand we are enabled to cripple the Yankees and then retire at our leisure to some other good position, maintaining intact our several organizations, the government &c, only surrendering Richmond and this section of Virginia, then I think matters would in all probability justify your keeping within the Confederate lines. In either event should you have to remain & should our affairs afterwards be reestablished on a good basis, I would then have you come through the lines & join me. I have one notion which urges itself strongly upon me, but I presume you would oppose it and as it might be regarded as a very selfish proposition, I will not press it. It has occurred to me that if <u>we are</u> to be separated by the lines of the enemy, for many reasons it would be far better & would much facilitate correspondence &c, if a certain short ceremony was first performed: and if at any subsequent time circumstances were such that you could join me, it would then be perfectly comme-il-faut. If you thought we were to meet tomorrow for the last time, would you desire or rather would you be willing to be married? I have allowed you to conceive what my <u>notion</u> is, whilst ashamed of its selfishness. I first announced an intention not to communicate it.[42] Come what will, Bettie, we will both be brave, remembering the cause in which we are called upon to make these sacrifices. Better this, better anything than submission to Northern rule! Oh if I could only secure you against any annoyance from those wretches! The separation, mental anxiety &c, are cruel as can be, but to know that the recent doings at Howard's Neck may be at any time repeated, this is still more distressing to me. In the City I do not think such outrages will occur. Aunt Alex is anxious for some of our household to go to her. Poor Sister is so distressed at the idea of remaining behind that I believe it would be better for her again to separate from Mother, but she is such a comfort to the latter that this would be equally cruel for her.[43] May God guide us all and enable us to be reconciled to His will. It is very comforting, my precious Bettie, at a time like this to receive a letter like the one before me, which I have just reread. Don't doubt for a moment that I will question one word of what you tell me. I am only too grateful and happy to have such assurances from your own lips, and yet as calmly, seriously happy as it makes me, Bettie, I cannot but smile—a very gladsome, bright smile though a mischievous one—when I reflect that for the first time you address me as dear W. You dear little pet, that one slip of the pen which you make has helped very materially to make me light at heart.[44] Can't you make some more such mistakes? It is very pleasant to see them. Never mind; when we are settled in that happy home that you sometimes dream of, and I fondly look forward to a realization of these pictures of the imagination, you can then pet me just as much as you please. . . .

When does Miss Maria expect to come over?[45] It will depend upon that & the movements of the enemy to be developed in the next 24 hours, whether you should come or not. If it appears I cannot again get to you, certainly I should advocate your coming here. If on the other hand I can see any prospect of my getting to Richmond again, I would prefer seeing you there. I will let you know what I think as soon as we discover what the enemy intends. . . .

The latest report we have from Norfolk is that Sallie Bloodgood has married Genl Shepley.[46] What do you think of that? The rumor says Genl S—another has it "a Yankee officer." . . .

The General has just informed me that I had better retire as we are to have an early breakfast. I agree with him and will bid you good night. Before I can write again we may be actively engaged, but rest assured I will always communicate when 'tis practicable. Keep a brave heart, Bettie dearest, hope for the best & always remember me in your prayers as I know you do, precious, without an injunction from me. I commit you to God's keeping, little pet, confident that in His wisdom He will guide all things for our greatest good. Love to Aunt Jane, Coz Mary & all at the Neck when you write. I shall fight the Yankees all the more earnestly since I have heard of their treatment of the dear ones there. Good night. Yr own

W.

20 March '65

There is no corroboration of the movement of the enemy reported last evening,[47] though it is still possible that it is being made. I am almost tempted to advise your coming over with Miss Maria, but matters are as yet a little too uncertain. The worst of it is that I fear I wd not be able to have you all to myself as I would wish. Army men are terrible visitors. You can never go into a house without meeting half a dozen or so. I should think the Pages were heartily tired of the whole sex. This is a lovely spring morning. What would I not give to spend it with my nearest & dearest? Write soon.

W.

108

Edge Hill

21 March '65

Late as it is, dear little sensitive, I cannot retire before I write a few lines in acknowledgment of yours of the 19th. . . .

I can't tell you how rejoiced I am at what Dr. Williams has said.[48] This or some other arrangement will, I earnestly pray, prevent our separation by the Yankee lines. I have not dared regard this as a certainty & indeed cannot, cannot. Bettie, what would I do—think of me dearest—how could I endure such a thing? No Bettie, no letters—what would become of me? Oh surely, such a fate is not in store for me. My life, my precious, is wrapped up in you. What would life be without you? I would still have duties to perform, but happiness would be an utter stranger to me. When the time arrives, some remedy for such a dread misfortune will be provided. We will not be thus separated, my dear Bettie, will we? Where are your new rooms? I hope you will find them comfortable and pleasant. If I can't see you at them, we will have to adjourn to kind Mrs Crenshaw's delightful sitting room when I again visit Richmond[49]—that is when you tell me I can come again without running the risk of making you tired of me.

I am quite perplexed tonight. Your coz John has applied for a leave of absence. None are now being granted & I dare not trust my judgement to make an exception at this time. I dislike so much the necessity for returning his application not approved, yet if I were to act myself, consistency would seem to require such a course. In the case of anyone else, I might possibly be more lenient, but with him if I were to approve, I would distrust my own judgement. There is but one course for me & that is to present it to the General, though I fear he will not grant the request. Fitz Lee's approval may possibly accomplish what I desire, as he, you know, is one of the royal family & of course his action should be sustained.[50] Do give my best love to your Mother, Sister & Pattie & a kiss to all the children. I hope the next fight we may be able to punish the Yankees for their insulting, cruel conduct. Kindest regards to all with you, to Mrs Petty & the C's. Calvert has not moved. I sent his letter by a courier as soon as recd. Good night, my dear Bettie. I wish you pleasant dreams of our happy home that is to be. Yr devotd

W.

109

Edge Hill

23 Mch '65

Accompanying this, little pet, is a letter from yr bro Jno, which he requested me to send to you. I did not expect to hear of his intended marriage at such an early day.[51] I wish so much that I could be with him, but just now I do not see how I can properly be absent any day. I am always hoping that I may spend a night in the City ere long, but wd not like to ask to be allowed to be absent during the day when there is so much to be done. Moreover at the special time he indicated, I fear I will have a great deal to occupy me. Let me whisper to you a little while. I think the dread contingency we have been recently discussing is approaching. I dare not say more even to you. Prudence dictates that your final plans be matured & that you keep "in light marching order" as we have it in military parlance. I cannot say what the next week will bring forth though the calamity may be deferred a month. But for John's approaching marriage, I would be strongly tempted to urge that you & Miss Maria pay a flying visit to Petersburg. I shall make one great effort to get to Richmond again. Indeed, Bettie, these are trying times, and now is the hour when we must show of what we are made.[52] It would be worse than useless to indulge in repinings & regrets to such an extent as will impair our efficiency or tend to dishearten those who look to us for protection. My mind is made up finally to leave Ma & the children, there is no alternative, they are so many. I am brave enough, my darling, till it comes to you. As I said in my last I hope that we will be kept on the same side of the lines. I feel that this will be so arranged, if not immediately, after a while. But if it is ordained otherwise, I will endeavor to accept my trial manfully. Nothing shall abate my determination to resist Yankee tyranny to the last extremity. Separation from you will be the most severe test to which I can be subjected, but with every principle of honor to support me, with pride & patriotism as my incentives I shall endeavor to live and if need be to die a good soldier & citizen. You shall never blush on my account. Even to one of my sanguine temperament, it is difficult to discern anything bright in our immediate future; but sooner or later the end with success must come.[53] Then, my precious Bettie, we shall be repaid for all these trials. We shall have a home, Bettie, and be spared the pain of cruel separation. I desire to look beyond the clouds that now envelope us, to that bright haven. What happiness it will be to have you with me always. So with submissive hearts but ever hopeful, we will each pursue the path of duty, confident of God's blessing in the end. It is my constant prayer to Him that He will guard and keep you. Your own

W.

110

Edge Hill

27 March 1865

This evening, my dear Bettie, my heart was gladdened by the receipt of your dearly prized letter of yesterday. I cannot describe to you the emotion to which it gave rise. You are the most unselfish, dearest little woman in the world. To have received so quietly and acquiesced so cheerfully to my very selfish proposition was indeed treating me with unprecedented kindness. I earnestly hope, my precious, that circumstances may be such as to obviate the necessity for our separation.[54] Matters have not improved since my last letter and I can see no cause for hope now which did not exist then. I regard the contingency we have fearfully anticipated as a foregone conclusion. What annoys me is the apathy, the listlessness which appears to have possessed those who control our affairs. Instead of facing the misfortune bravely and preparing for it in anticipation, with folded hands they lament our difficulties and danger and indulge a maudlin, complaining strain, whining & losing temper and doing all manner of things, save the right ones, whilst the whole country is ignorant of the impending calamity & blindly imposes implicit confidence in the sagacity and determination or <u>pluck</u> of him whom I am here rasping in such an unbecoming manner in the plural number.[55] But truly it is enough to make a body mad to see such imbecility—there is no other word for it. Well, as I was saying, the emergency must come. I now see no steps towards moving the several departments of the gov't; when the pressure is upon us, it may become impracticable. In other words, the Sgn Genl's office may not be removed and necessity may compel <u>our</u> temporary separation. Here, in my chair, I have for some time reflected upon this emergency. I have earnestly, prayerfully considered what course it is right for me to pursue. I have thought of my selfishness and of your sweet, ready acquiescence to my proposal—your utter forgetfulness of self and kind consideration for my happiness. I have thought of my position in the army, of my condition in life, of the dangers which attend the former and of the paucity of attractions of a worldly kind which attend the latter. I have looked to a prolongation of the war. I have looked to peace. In every aspect I believe I have considered the matter & to my sincere prayer that I might decide aright, the response seemed to come to me "trust in God." Trusting in His goodness and mercy, dear Bettie, I accept your terms. They are just what I would have proposed. Now remember I have not concluded that you are to be left; to the last I will hope against that, but should there be no help for it, if we must be separated, in God's sight let us first be united. I would be forced to admit that this is most definitely selfish in me, but for the blissful conviction which possesses me that your love is equal to my own, & that for <u>neither</u> of us is there <u>any</u> happiness not connected with the <u>other</u>. I cannot say how matters will be when the dreaded emergency is upon us, but I think I can arrange to visit Richmond at the proper time: My pet, don't be disturbed about a <u>leave.</u> I certainly will neither ask nor accept one. Genl Lee will settle that question.[56] But dear, dear Bettie, I cannot complacently contemplate our separation. Oh, I hope there will be something to prevent this. What a poor, powerless creature I am! Still if it comes, we must remember the cause & face it with unflinching determination to suffer this, even this, and all else, before I the stronger yield to our enemies. Of course as time wears on I will be able to discern more clearly what will occur, will keep you advised and we can be governed accordingly. But don't be startled to see me any day, relentlessly claiming that dearest little hand and all prepared (that means very dusty, with heavy top boots, spurs, armed to the teeth) to make you Mrs T, my own, own little w---.[57] I am going to be brave, Bettie, to turn over a new leaf and not dwell upon our separation in such a dreadfully low spirited way. I will look beyond the temporary evil to the happy haven which awaits us beyond in the world, and to that blissful immortality prepared for us in our Father's home. Our faith must not waver. We claim to trust in God, let us see to it that our acts attest the sincerity of the trust. If I have to leave you, darling, for a season, I will always bear it in mind that there is a merciful Friend and Father who is watching over you and keeping you for my happy return. I will remember that the pain I undergo is but the price of your independence and mine. Even if the worst should come and I be removed, still, dearest, you will have the happy consolation of knowing that but a very short while will intervene before we are again united to be parted no more. Yes, I will try to be reconciled to what God ordains. May both of us have strength to accept it submissively, cheerfully. I regret that I cannot be with you all tomorrow evening.[58] My best love to Pattie & your mother when you write. I wish Jno every happiness. I say nothing of our fight. 'Twas gallantly done as far as it went.[59] Between the battle field & the papers on my return, I was kept very busy. Heaven bless you prays yr devoted

W.

Thus ended the wartime letters of Colonel Taylor. Within the fortnight Richmond fell, Walter and Bettie were married, and the Army of Northern Virginia laid down its arms at Appomattox.

Appendix 1

My Wedding

This was written by Bettie Saunders Taylor in 1912 and published as a pamphlet for the benefit of the Norfolk Protestant Hospital. (Source: WHT Papers.)

Two weeks before General Lee's determination to leave Richmond to meet General Grant, I received a letter [let. 107] from Col. Taylor asking if in such an event I would consent to marry him at once. He had secured my mother's permission and thought that as his wife I could pass more safely through the Union lines. My heart was with the South and I wrote my glad assent. Two anxious weeks passed and one Sunday morning, the 2nd of April, just as I arose from my prayers, a servant announced, "Mr. Taylor wishes to see you." Thinking it was Walter, it did not take me long to get down where I found out my mistake, for it was his brother, Bob [Rob], who stood there with a telegram in his hand which read: "I will be over some time today. See Betty and have her explain. Make all needed preparations." "What does this mean?" he asked. I replied: "I have promised Walter to marry him if Richmond has to be left to the enemy. This means our capital is to be evacuated. Make all preparations at once." Imagine the dismay at my telling him and his family that Richmond was to be evacuated! I was living with my dear friend, Mr. Lewis D. Crenshaw, who had given me a home and a daughter's welcome; so I went at once to him and told him the sad news; and also that I was to marry Walter before he left. Such a dear, fatherly hug he gave me, and said: "Does your mother know? I would advise you to wait, my child." I said: "You have been a father to me and I need your blessing." "You may be assured of that, my dear," He replied. I then begged him to make preparations, but his reply was: "There must be some mistake. I was with the Secretary of War last night until midnight, and troops were then coming in from our lines." I assured him that Walter could not be mistaken; and he then went at once to see about his papers, etc. I went to old St. Paul's Church to service, leaving directions for Walter to join me there. My

241

pew was in the left hand gallery just where the beautiful memorial window to General Lee now is. When I saw my courier, the one who brought me my mail every day from headquarters, pass by me, he shook his head and passed out quickly. Just after the prayers, before the ante-communion service, I saw someone go up the aisle to President Davis' pew, and he immediately rose and went out. Then other officials were summoned and all left and the alarm bells began to toll. Old Dr. Minnegerode, the pastor, said: "My friends, our warning bell for all women to repair at once to their homes is tolling. There is some fearful trouble, I fear. All please leave who are going and those who remain come near to the chancel." I stayed, sending my two young friends May and Aline Petty (now Mrs. May Crenshaw and Mrs. Rufus Parks) home. After service I hurried back to Mr. Crenshaw to find every one feeding our poor, ragged, hungry soldiers as they passed. Tea, coffee, milk, bread and biscuits with ham and everything else that they had were given them. I remember twenty-eight hams had been cooked and sliced, but I cannot remember how many barrels of flour had been made into biscuits and hoe-cakes. We all worked until late at night and with sore hearts, bidding them do their duty and come home victorious. I think nearly every relative I ever had bade me good-bye that day and the tears fell like rain. I waited till after dark, but no news came from Walter, but the sweet love and cheer of the dear ones round me I can now feel. They dressed me in a new black mouselaine, lined with grey linen that shone through and someone laughingly remarked, "Any how, her body is grey." The material was so thin. Then I went to see dear Mrs. Crenshaw as she was ill in bed, and she said: "Go and get that pair of white kid gloves and adorn our bride." Soon after a telegram came saying that Walter was on his way, that I was to wait. He came on the last engine that left Petersburg that night and arrived with his family and Dr. Minnegerode at 12:30 A.M. We were then married in Mrs. Crenshaw's sitting room upstairs that she might be present. Tears and sobs were the only music, and when dear old Dr. Minnegerode, who had known us both from childhood, threw his arms around our heads as we kneeled for his blessing, he, too, wept. After a delicious repast, I went with Walter to his mother's where his brothers, Richard and John, were, having just been released from Northern prisons.

We returned to Mr. Crenshaw's where I bade Walter good-bye, and he and my brother, Col. John Saunders, were about the last persons to pass over the bridge to Manchester before it was set on fire. Very soon fearful explosions began at Drewry's Bluff and Chaffin's Bluff and then the arsenal was fired.

No one who was in Richmond on Monday, the 3rd of April, 1865, can ever forget the terrors that beset us. Shells were exploding everywhere, mothers were weeping for their boys and absolute misery reigned. One night about 9 P.M. on the 10th of April a gun was fired several times and servants ran in saying General Lee had surrendered. Words fail to depict the sorrow and woe that everyone felt.

Two weeks later General Lee returned to Richmond, and after serving the General for two weeks or more, Walter borrowed his ambulance and mules and we started on our wedding tour to Goochland.

The first day we lunched at Keswick with my uncle, Dr. William Selden; then we spent the night at Norwood with my uncle, Dr. Miles Cary Selden. Next day we started for Howard's Neck but in crossing the James River the mules became unmanageable, and Walter trying to quiet them, they all fell into the river, where, as he said, all three mules kicked to their heart's content, feeling that a Norfolk boy must be at home in the water. We all laughed to his extreme disgust, but he was soon out and reappeared quite fine in a new uniform. We spent a happy month in the country with dear relations and came to Norfolk in June, where we started life anew, poor but proud, for though our men had been paroled, our ladies owed no allegiance to the Federal Government. They fought with their tongues and will do until they die.

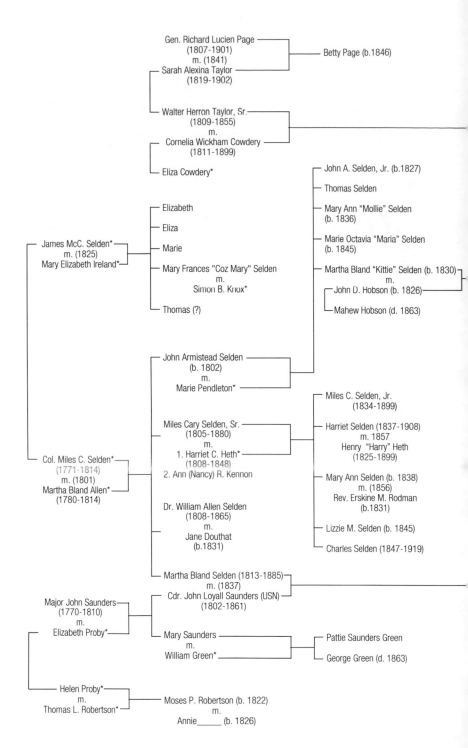

Gen. Richard Lucien Page
(1807-1901)
m. (1841)
Sarah Alexina Taylor
(1819-1902)
— Betty Page (b.1846)

Walter Herron Taylor, Sr.
(1809-1855)
m.
Cornelia Wickham Cowdery
(1811-1899)
Eliza Cowdery*

James McC. Selden*
m. (1825)
Mary Elizabeth Ireland*

Elizabeth
Eliza
Marie
Mary Frances "Coz Mary" Selden
m.
Simon B. Knox*
Thomas (?)

John A. Selden, Jr. (b.1827)
Thomas Selden
Mary Ann "Mollie" Selden (b. 1836)
Marie Octavia "Maria" Selden (b. 1845)
Martha Bland "Kittie" Selden (b. 1830)
m.
John D. Hobson (b. 1826)
Mahew Hobson (d. 1863)

Col. Miles C. Selden*
(1771-1814)
m. (1801)
Martha Bland Allen*
(1780-1814)

John Armistead Selden
(b. 1802)
m.
Marie Pendleton*

Miles Cary Selden, Sr.
(1805-1880)
m.
1. Harriet C. Heth*
(1808-1848)
2. Ann (Nancy) R. Kennon

Dr. William Allen Selden
(1808-1865)
m.
Jane Douthat
(b.1831)

Miles C. Selden, Jr.
(1834-1899)
Harriet Selden (1837-1908)
m. 1857
Henry "Harry" Heth
(1825-1899)
Mary Ann Selden (b. 1838)
m. (1856)
Rev. Erskine M. Rodman
(b.1831)
Lizzie M. Selden (b. 1845)
Charles Selden (1847-1919)

Major John Saunders
(1770-1810)
m.
Elizabeth Proby*

Martha Bland Selden (1813-1885)
m. (1837)
Cdr. John Loyall Saunders (USN)
(1802-1861)

Mary Saunders
m.
William Green*

Pattie Saunders Green
George Green (d. 1863)

Helen Proby*
m.
Thomas L. Robertson*

Moses P. Robertson (b. 1822)
m.
Annie_____ (b. 1826)

Appendix 2
Genealogies of Walter H. Taylor and Elizabeth S. Saunders

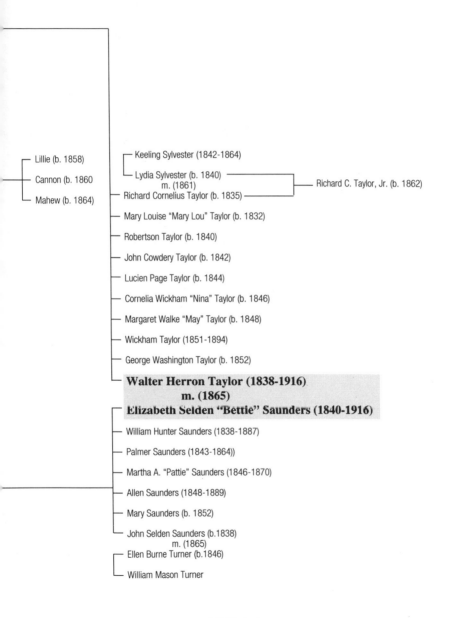

Lillie (b. 1858)

Cannon (b. 1860

Mahew (b. 1864)

Keeling Sylvester (1842-1864)

Lydia Sylvester (b. 1840)
m. (1861)
Richard Cornelius Taylor (b. 1835)

Richard C. Taylor, Jr. (b. 1862)

Mary Louise "Mary Lou" Taylor (b. 1832)

Robertson Taylor (b. 1840)

John Cowdery Taylor (b. 1842)

Lucien Page Taylor (b. 1844)

Cornelia Wickham "Nina" Taylor (b. 1846)

Margaret Walke "May" Taylor (b. 1848)

Wickham Taylor (1851-1894)

George Washington Taylor (b. 1852)

**Walter Herron Taylor (1838-1916)
m. (1865)
Elizabeth Selden "Bettie" Saunders (1840-1916)**

William Hunter Saunders (1838-1887)

Palmer Saunders (1843-1864))

Martha A. "Pattie" Saunders (1846-1870)

Allen Saunders (1848-1889)

Mary Saunders (b. 1852)

John Selden Saunders (b.1838)
m. (1865)
Ellen Burne Turner (b.1846)

William Mason Turner

* Not in text

245

Abbreviations

C.V.	*Confederate Veteran*
Journal	Confederate States of America. *Journal of the Congress of the Confederate States of America, 1861–1865.*
O.R.	U.S. War Department. *The War of the Rebellion: A Compilation of the Official Records of the Union and Confederate Armies.*
O.R. Atlas	U.S. War Department. *Atlas to Accompany the Official Records of the Union and Confederate Armies.*
O.R.N.	U.S. Department of the Navy. *Official Records of the Union and Confederate Navies in the War of the Rebellion.*
SF Files	Saunders Family Papers, Norfolk Public Library, Norfolk, Virginia
S.H.S.P.	*Southern Historical Society Papers*
V.M.H.B.	*Virginia Magazine of History and Biography*
WHT Papers	Walter Herron Taylor Papers, Norfolk Public Library, Norfolk, Virginia
WHT-SH	Walter H. Taylor Papers, Stratford Hall, Westmoreland County, Virginia

Notes

Apart from those for quotations, only the more rarely used sources are cited in the notes to the letters themselves. Most of the information was garnered from a small number of mainly standard sources. Rather than cite them repeatedly in note after note, we simply summarize them here.

The principal sources for biographical information and genealogical information were U.S. Census, 1850, 1860, 1870, Virginia (National Archives Branch Depository); Norfolk City Directories, 1851–52, 1859, 1860; Meredith, *Some Old Norfolk Families;* and Selden, *Samuel Selden.*

Military biographical sources were *O.R.; O.R.N.;* Bidgood, "General Officers and their Staffs"; Evans, *Confederate Military History,* vol. 4; Freeman, *R. E. Lee,* vol. 1, app. I-4; Krick, *Lee's Colonels;* Porter, *Record of Events in Norfolk County;* Sifakis, *Who Was Who in the Confederacy;* V.M.I. Alumni Association, *Register of Former Cadets;* Warner, *Generals in Gray* and *Generals in Blue;* and Wright, *Staff Officers.*

Sources for identification of military engagements were *O.R.;* Freeman, *R. E. Lee;* and E. B. Long, *The Civil War Day by Day.*

Information on churches and ministers is principally from Christ Church Papers (Norfolk Public Library); and Dashiell, *Digest of Proceedings in the Diocese of Virginia.*

Biblical quotations are from the Authorized (King James) Version of the Bible.

Preface

1. Freeman, *R. E. Lee,* vol. 4, 548.
2. Dowdey, *Lee,* 741.
3. Freeman, *R. E. Lee,* vol. 4, 548.
4. Ibid.
5. Taylor, *Four Years with General Lee,* 115.

Introduction

1. G. W. C. Lee to Taylor, May 4, 1905, WHT-SH.
2. Taylor, *Four Years,* 7.
3. Freeman, *Lee's Lieutenants,* vol. 2, 345.
4. Janet Fauntleroy Taylor (granddaughter of Walter H. Taylor), in a letter to the editor, December 1985, stated: "I have that medal which I wear attached to a bracelet."

5. Cooke, "Col. W. H. Taylor," 234. (For Cooke, see chap. 5, n. 56.)
6. Smith, *History of the Virginia Military Institute*, 19–22. Smith (1812–90; West Point 1833), a Norfolk native, taught at West Point and Hampden-Sydney College before coming to V.M.I. On April 17, 1861, he was called to Richmond to recruit, organize, and train Virginia State troops as colonel and aide to Governor John Letcher. V.M.I. was closed and the cadets were employed as drill masters. When Virginia joined the Confederacy he served briefly as colonel of the Ninth Virginia, then as commander of part of the artillery defenses of Norfolk. On January 1, 1862, V.M.I. was reopened and he returned to his duties there. Krick, *Lee's Colonels*, 325; Smith, *History*, 177–82.
7. V.M.I. Alumni Assoc., *Register of Former Cadets*, Class of 1857.
8. Robertson to Taylor, November 8, 1854, WHT Papers. (For Duncan Robertson, see chap. 2, n. 4; Liz Barron is unidentified.)
9. Report, Third Class, 1855, V.M.I. Archives.
10. W. H. Taylor, Sr., to Colonel Smith, May 29, 1855, V.M.I. Archives.
11. Report, Third Class, 1855, V.M.I. Archives.
12. W. H. Taylor, Sr., to Colonel Smith, July 25, 1855, V.M.I. Archives.
13. Norfolk *Ledger-Dispatch*, March 2, 1916, WHT Papers.
14. Taylor, memorandum, March 15, 1857, WHT Papers.
15. Bettie Saunders to Taylor, June 21, 1859, WHT Papers.
16. Taylor to Bettie Saunders, January 24, 1861, WHT Papers.
17. No letters to Bettie survive for the first year of the war, and only six from May 1862 to July 1863. Thereafter Walter writes weekly.
18. Walker, "Colonel Walter H. Taylor," 39–40; Commission, dated January 1, 1861, WHT-SH.
19. Walker, "Taylor," 40; Porter, *Record of Events in Norfolk County, Virginia*, 272, 309.
20. Dowdey, *Lee's Last Campaign*, 26; Taylor, *General Lee*, 21. (For Richard Page, see chap. 3, n. 62.)
21. Walker, "Taylor," 40.
22. Page to Taylor, telegram, May 2, 1861, WHT-SH.
23. Taylor, *General Lee*, 21–22.
24. Commission, May 3, 1861, WHT-SH; Special Orders No. 17, Virginia State Forces, Richmond, May 4, 1861, WHT-SH.
25. Taylor, *General Lee*, 22. Colonel Garnett (1819–61; West Point 1841), a major in the U.S. Army, resigned April 30, 1861, to become a colonel in the Confederate service, being promoted to brigadier June 6. He was thereupon assigned command of the troops in western Virginia, where he was killed while forming a skirmish line on July 13, 1861. Warner, *Generals in Gray*, 100.
26. Freeman, *R. E. Lee*, vol. 1, 189.
27. Taylor to Barrot, May 13, 1861, WHT Papers.

28. Freeman, *R. E. Lee*, vol. 1, 489–500.
29. Commission, May 31, 1861, WHT-SH.
30. Freeman, *R. E. Lee*, vol. 1, 508.
31. Commission, July 16, 1861, WHT-SH.
32. Freeman, *R. E. Lee*, vol. 1, 501; Wright, *General Officers of the Confederate Army*, 46–47.
33. Jefferson Davis, *Rise and Fall*, vol. 1, 340. Cf. Taylor, *Four Years*, 15: "[Lee] was retained in Richmond by the President to give the benefit of his counsel and advice in all important measures involved in the stupendous undertaking of suddenly transforming an agricultural people into a nation of soldiers, prepared for immediate war."
34. Freeman, *R. E. Lee*, vol. 1, 541. Colonel Washington joined Lee's staff along with Taylor in May 1861. Originally commissioned as aide-de-camp, he was soon performing the duties of AAG. He was a grandnephew of George Washington and a longtime friend of Lee's. When he was killed in western Virginia, Lee wrote, ". . . our greatest loss is the death of my dear friend, Colonel Washington." Freeman, *R. E. Lee*, vol. 1, 489, 574, 639.
35. Taylor, *General Lee*, 28.
36. Lee, Jr., *Recollections*, 39.
37. Taylor, *Four Years*, 16–17; *General Lee*, 35–36.
38. Taylor, *General Lee*, 29.
39. Freeman, *R. E. Lee*, vol. 1, 489.
40. Taylor, *General Lee*, 30–31. These words of Taylor's, penned over forty years later, are quoted at length, since they so clearly set forth his conviction of the justice of the Southern cause. It should be kept in mind that he regarded slavery as practiced in Virginia as a positive good.
41. Taylor, *Four Years*, 35.
42. Taylor, *General Lee*, 31–32.
43. Ibid., 35–36.
44. Freeman, *R. E. Lee*, vol. 1, 608.
45. *O.R.*, ser. 1, vol. 6, 312 (hereafter all citations will be to ser. 1, unless otherwise indicated); Lee, Jr., *Recollections*, 40; Commission, December 31, 1861, WHT-SH.
46. Taylor, *General Lee*, 36–37.
47. Black, *Railroads of the Confederacy*, 9.
48. The form of the original six-story shell of the Mills House still stands (in 1994) at the southeast corner of Meeting and Queen Streets in Charleston, swallowed up in a large modern edifice.
49. Taylor, *General Lee*, 40.
50. A. L. Long, *Memoirs of Robert E. Lee*, 135. Long (1825–91; West Point 1850) was an artillerist who served on Lee's staff from December 1861 to

September 1863, when he was promoted to brigadier general and made commander of the Second Corps artillery, in which capacity he served until Appomattox. Warner, *Generals in Gray,* 191–92.

51. Long, *Memoirs,* 134–36; Freeman, *R. E. Lee,* vol. 1, 616; Taylor, *General Lee,* 40–41.
52. Taylor, memorandum, March 1862, WHT Papers.
53. Taylor, *General Lee,* 42.
54. *O.R.,* vol. 11, pt. 3, 569; Freeman, *R. E. Lee,* vol. 2, 78–79.
55. Freeman, *R. E. Lee,* vol. 2, 234–35.
56. Taylor, *General Lee,* 56.
57. Dowdey and Manarin, eds., *War Time Papers of R. E. Lee,* 166.
58. *O.R.,* vol. 11, pt. 2, 605; Freeman, *R. E. Lee,* vol. 2, 136; Dowdey, *Lee,* 238; Burke Davis, *Gray Fox,* 90.
59. *O.R.,* vol. 11, pt. 2, 665, 687; Dowdey, *Lee,* 255; Freeman, *R. E. Lee,* vol. 2, 174; Rhoades, *Scapegoat General,* 84.
60. *O.R.,* vol. 11, pt. 2, 790; Rhoades, *Scapegoat General,* 98.
61. J. M. Spencer to Taylor, September 1, 1904, WHT-SH. This Randolph Harrison later became a lieutenant colonel in the artillery, but he is *not* the same Randolph Harrison (also a colonel of artillery) who was Taylor's acquaintance and the owner of Elk Hill. (See chap. 2, n. 16; Krick, *Lee's Colonels,* 168.)
62. Taylor, *General Lee,* 69; Freeman, *R. E. Lee,* vol. 2, 155–57.
63. Freeman, *R. E. Lee,* vol. 2, 264; Taylor to Mary Lou Taylor, August 31, 1862 (chap. 1, let. 6).
64. Taylor, *General Lee,* 119–21. (For Frank Huger, see chap. 1, n. 49; for John Saunders, chap. 1, n. 89.)
65. Ibid., 121–22.
66. Taylor to Mary Lou Taylor, September 21, 1862 (chap. 1, let. 9).
67. Taylor, *General Lee,* 147–51.
68. Ibid., 154; Dawson, *Reminiscences,* 88.
69. Taylor, *General Lee,* 154–56.
70. Freeman, *R. E. Lee,* vol. 2, 488; Taylor, *Four Years,* 77; Taylor, *General Lee,* 156. Although Taylor was first recommended for his majority on April 21, 1862, and was referred to by Lee as "Major" thenceforward, he was not confirmed as such until March 6, 1863, upon Lee's renewed recommendation. *Journal,* vol. 2, 223.
71. Taylor, *General Lee,* 157.
72. Ibid., 177.
73. Freeman, *R. E. Lee,* vol. 3, 148.
74. Taylor to Mary Lou Taylor, July 7, 1863 (chap. 1, let. 18).
75. Taylor to Bettie Saunders, October 17, 1863 (chap. 2, let. 26); Freeman, *R. E. Lee,* vol. 3, 183.
76. Taylor to Bettie Saunders, November 7, 1863 (chap. 2, let. 29).

77. Commission, January 15, 1864. Taylor's rank was to date from December 21, 1863, the day he was recommended for promotion. *Journal*, vol. 3, 490, 574.
78. Freeman, *R. E. Lee*, vol. 3, 287; Taylor, *General Lee*, 234.
79. Taylor, *General Lee*, 238. (For Venable, see chap. 2, n. 28.)
80. Ibid., 240.
81. Taylor to Bettie Saunders, May 22, 1864 (chap. 4, let. 61).
82. C. C. Taliaferro to Taylor, April 10, 1894, WHT-SH.
83. Venable, "Campaign from the Wilderness," 536.
84. Quoted in the Norfolk *Ledger-Dispatch*, March 2, 1916, WHT Papers.
85. Ibid. Cf. Hemphill, in *C.V.*, 464, who recalls Taylor as crying, improbably, "Come ahead, men! God bless you! I love every one of you!"
86. Taylor, *General Lee*, 270.
87. Freeman, *R. E. Lee*, vol. 4, 56.
88. Connelly, *Marble Man*.
89. Taylor, *General Lee*, 277.
90. Taylor to Bettie Saunders, March 27, 1865 (chap. 6, let. 110).
91. Bettie Saunders Taylor, "My Wedding," WHT Papers. (See appendix 1; for Rob Taylor, see chap. 1, n. 21).
92. Ibid. (For Lewis Crenshaw, see chap. 2, n. 73; for Rev. Minnegerode, chap. 3, n. 89.)
93. Ibid. Taylor's wedding earned a mention in a contemporary memoir: "At eleven o'clock on that night, Colonel ——, on General ——'s staff, came into the city and was married. In a few moments he left his bride, in the terrible uncertainty of ever again meeting." Putnam, *Richmond During the War*, 364.
94. Taylor, *General Lee*, 288.
95. Taylor, *Four Years*, 152.
96. Taylor, *General Lee*, 296.
97. Flood, *Lee, the Last Years*, 30. (For Marshall, see chap. 3, n. 1.)
98. Taylor, *Four Years*, 154.
99. Lee to Taylor, June 17, 1865, Brockenbrough Library, Museum of the Confederacy, Richmond, Virginia.
100. Bettie Saunders Taylor, "My Wedding."
101. Taylor to Bettie Saunders Taylor, July 21, 1865, WHT Papers.
102. Ibid.
103. Taylor to Bettie Saunders Taylor, July 22, 1865, WHT Papers.
104. L. E. Johnson to Taylor, February 28, 1914, WHT-SH.
105. Janet Fauntleroy Taylor, letter to the editor, December 1985.
106. Taylor, memorandum, April 19, 1908, WHT Papers.
107. Freeman, *R. E. Lee*, vol. 4, 548.

108. Taylor to Chamberlayne, July 17 (no year), Chamberlayne Family Papers, Virginia Historical Society. John Hamden Chamberlayne (1838–82) was an artillerist serving in a series of batteries. Captured on the Gettysburg campaign, he was exchanged and ended the war as a captain in Willie Pegram's battalion. His letters show that he shared Taylor's optimism of success up to the closing weeks of the war and had unbounded faith in the wisdom and practical ability of General Lee. Chamberlayne, ed., *Ham Chamberlayne—Virginian.*
109. Bryan to Taylor, September 19, 1893, Joseph S. Bryan Papers, Virginia Historical Society.
110. Bryan to Taylor, October 10, 1893, Joseph S. Bryan Papers, Virginia Historical Society.
111. Taylor to General E. W. Nichols, January 29, 1914, V.M.I. Archives.
112. Taylor, *Four Years,* 188.
113. Ibid.
114. Wolseley to Taylor, May 16, 1907, WHT-SH.
115. Taylor, "Causes of Lee's Defeat," 124–39; W. H. F. Lee to Taylor, October 6, 1877, WHT-SH.
116. Freeman, *South to Posterity,* 65.
117. Mosby to Arthur Clarke, December 11, 1909, John Singleton Mosby Papers, Virginia Historical Society. The book referred to was his *Stuart's Cavalry in the Gettysburg Campaign.*
118. Adams to Taylor, January 15, 1907, WHT-SH; Ropes to Taylor, September 3, 1896, WHT Papers.
119. Alexander to Taylor, September 4, 1871, August 20, 29, 1902, May 9, 25, and August 20, 1906; Taylor to Alexander, August 26, 1902, May 20 and August 24, 1906 (for Alexander, see chap. 4, n. 21); Palmer to Taylor, June 25 and July 24, 1905, June 24, 1911; Taylor to Palmer, 17 June 1911, WHT-SH. Colonel Palmer was present with Hill at the Wilderness, where he witnessed the first "Lee to the rear" incident, and continued with Hill through the battle of the Crater and the whole siege of Petersburg, until the day of the latter's death. After the war he was a bank president, sometime treasurer of the Southern Historical Society, and honorary pallbearer at Taylor's funeral. Freeman, *R. E. Lee,* vol. 3, 281, 289, 409; vol. 4, 47, 52; Norfolk *Ledger-Dispatch,* funeral notice, ca. March 6, 1916, WHT Papers.
120. Quoted in Taylor, *General Lee,* 310.
121. Lee to Taylor, April 13, 1868, WHT Papers.
122. Ibid. (For Bryan, see chap. 1, n. 81.)
123. Quoted in Taylor, *General Lee,* 314.
124. Davis to Taylor, March 4, 1877, WHT-SH.
125. "Association of the Army," 159; "Monument to General Lee," 190;

"Sketch of the Lee Memorial," 390; "Unveiling of the Monument," 342; "Unveiling of the Statue," 356. (For Harry Heth, see chap. 1, n. 93.)

126. Freeman, *R. E. Lee*, vol. 4, 457–58.
127. J. Jones, *Personal Reminiscences*, 457–58.
128. Taylor to Schipp, June 6, 1906, V.M.I. Archives.
129. Philip Alexander Bruce to Taylor, December 20, 1913, WHT Papers.
130. Norfolk *Ledger-Dispatch*, March 3, 1916, WHT Papers.
131. Meyer, "Walter Herron Taylor and His Era," 162.
132. L. E. Johnson to Taylor, January 16, 1915, WHT-SH.
133. Palmer to Walter H. Taylor [Taylor's son], March 2, 1916, WHT Papers.
134. Street, *American Adventures*, 260.
135. *Norfolk Virginian-Pilot*, March 2, 1916, WHT Papers.
136. Norfolk *Ledger-Dispatch*, March 3, 1916, WHT Papers.
137. Cooke, "Col. W. H. Taylor," 235; *Norfolk Virginian-Pilot*, March 3, 1916, WHT Papers.
138. "Col. Walter H. Taylor A.A.G.," 83.
139. *Norfolk Virginian-Pilot*, March 8, 1916, WHT Papers.
140. Norfolk *Ledger-Dispatch*, March 4, 1916, WHT Papers.
141. Carl E. Grammer to Elizabeth "Bessie" Taylor Baldwin [Taylor's eldest daughter], June 27, 1916, WHT Papers.

Chapter 1: Lee Takes the Offensive

1. Norfolk was evacuated on May 10, 1862, and the Union troops entered the same day. The city had been under blockade for a full year. Fortress Monroe and Old Point Comfort across Hampton Roads were in Union hands throughout.

   A vignette of the evacuation is found in a letter to Bettie Saunders's mother from a Norfolk friend: "I do not know that I ever mentioned to you that when we came away, our notice was so short of the intended evacuation that we left everything on earth we had behind, except part of our wearing apparel, a few bed clothes and table linen with our silver—and so crowded were the cars on that day with sick soldiers, their baggage, etc., that Pa had difficulty in getting our trunks taken." Emma Blacknall to Martha S. Saunders, January 8, 1864, WHT Papers.

2. Julia Robertson is referred to forty-seven times in the Taylor letters. All references to "Julia" (unless otherwise noted), and to "sistress," or "the little sistress" refer to her. Julia Robertson (1840–1927) was perhaps Taylor's closest female friend in Norfolk, just as her brother Duncan was his closest male friend. Her father, Duncan Robertson, Sr., (1800–1887), originally a Northerner, was a prosperous merchant and consul.

253

Fanny Kerr (b. 1838) was the close companion of Julia Robertson, and is usually referred to along with her. She had Northern connections, her mother being a New Yorker. She and Julia were the only close friends of Taylor who elected to stay behind in Norfolk at the evacuation.

Mrs. Huger is the mother of Taylor's friend Captain (later Colonel) Frank Huger, and the wife of General Benjamin Huger, commander of Norfolk and head of the Department of Petersburg, May 23, 1861, to July 1862.

3. John is Bettie's first cousin, Lieutenant John A. Selden, Jr. (b. 1827). This "Coz John" (or "Coz Jno") is not to be confused with Bettie's brother John Selden Saunders. (For the genealogical relationships of the Selden, Saunders, and Taylor families, see appendix 2.) Lieutenant Selden was ordnance officer of the First Virginia Artillery, and later of Cutshaw's battalion. He was the eldest son of John A. Selden of Westover.

4. A Dr. A. T. M. Cooke, president of the Gaslight Company, is listed in the directories. No other reference to this incident has been found.

5. Prior to his appointment as brigadier general in November, 1861, "Little Billy" Mahone had been colonel of the Sixth Virginia Infantry, a regiment raised in Norfolk in which two of Taylor's brothers and many of his friends served during the war. Promoted major general for his part in the Battle of the Crater in July, 1864, Mahone won a reputation as one of the ablest division commanders in the Army of Northern Virginia during the last year of fighting, distinguishing himself particularly at Reams Station.

6. "Your Mother" is Martha Bland Selden Saunders (1813–85), widow of Commander John L. Saunders, USN (b. 1802 in Norfolk), who died October 26, 1860. Bettie's Selden relatives are very numerous: Martha had six siblings and dozens of nieces and nephews on that side. After the evacuation she divided her time between Richmond and her niece's residence at Howard's Neck, Goochland County.

Patty (Martha A. Saunders) is Bettie's younger sister, about sixteen at the time of this letter. She spent much of the latter part of the war living with Bettie, and is greeted or referred to frequently in the letters.

Mary is Bettie's youngest sister, born about 1852. She visited Bettie only occasionally. Bettie also had a younger brother Allen still living at home; her other three brothers were in the war. *U.S. Navy Children's Claim*, (for children of John L. Saunders, 1888), WHT Papers; funeral notices, SF Files.

7. Howell Cobb was U.S. Speaker of the House and Secretary of the Treasury prior to the war and candidate for the presidency of the Confederacy. After service in the field, as a brigadier from 1862, he was promoted major general in September, 1863, and appointed commander

of the District of Georgia, where he devoted himself to improving the often contentious relations between Governor Brown and President Davis.

8. George B. McClellan commanded the Federal Army of the Potomac in the Peninsula campaign of 1862, during the Seven Days and again at Sharpsburg in September of that year. He was Lincoln's unsuccessful Democratic opponent in the presidential election of 1864.

9. Coz Nannie is most likely Mrs. Mary Anne Selden Rodman, born 1836 and in 1856 married to Rev. Erskine M. Rodman, rector of Taylor's church, Christ Church (Episcopal), Norfolk. Rodman stayed in Norfolk with his parish when she evacuated. She later returned to Norfolk, escaping again at her husband's urging about October 1863. She is Bettie's first cousin, a daughter of Miles Cary Selden, Sr.

10. The Seven Days' Battle around Richmond, June 26 to July 2, 1862.

11. Martha Bland Selden Hobson (b. 1830), wife of Lieutenant John D. Hobson and hostess of Howard's Neck, the country place in Goochland County to which Bettie and her family retired whenever possible. She is known as "Kittie"; and references in the letters to "Mrs. Hobson," "Mrs. H," "your sister Kittie," and "your sister" all refer to her unless otherwise noted. Kittie was actually Bettie's first cousin (a daughter of John A. Selden, Sr.). Walter became aware of this when he visited Howard's Neck in January, 1865, and calls her "your cousin Kittie" thereafter.

12. Mary Louisa Taylor (b. 1832) is Taylor's only older sister, and is referred to as "sister" or "Mary Lou." She is the addressee of most of the letters sent before August 1863, when Walter and Bettie became regular correspondents.

13. Haxall and Taylor are Orange County landowners, not otherwise identified.

14. John Pope was brought from the West and put in command of the newly formed Federal Army of Virginia in June 1862. He suffered a crushing defeat at the hands of Lee and Jackson at Second Manassas.

15. Lydia Sylvester Taylor (b. 1840) is the young wife of Taylor's older brother Dick. She is the daughter of Dr. Richard Sylvester of Norfolk, who lived two blocks east of the Taylors. Lydia and Dick married in 1861.

16. Custis Lee is General Lee's eldest son, George Washington Custis Lee. He graduated at the head of his class at West Point in 1854. During the war he served on the staff of President Davis and saw field service only at the end, when he was captured at Sayler's Creek on the retreat to Appomattox. On the death of his father, he succeeded him as president of Washington College, now Washington and Lee.

Taylor's horse, Bella, is mentioned frequently in the correspondence and is his sometime companion in the field.

17. Not Walter's brother John (now in South Carolina) but Major John Saunders Taylor (b. 1820) previously USN, then CSN, now in the artillery. He is not related to Walter, but most likely a Saunders cousin of Bettie's. He was a Norfolker, from Taylor's neighborhood. At this point he had only weeks to live.

18. Dick is Taylor's older brother Richard Cornelius Taylor (b. 1835), and since their father's death in 1855, titular head of the family. (Although Walter was looked on as the businessman among the brothers, it was Dick who inherited the family pew at Christ Church.) He began the war as a captain in Norfolk's Sixth Virginia Regiment, but from April 1862 he was an artillery major on General Mahone's staff. After the 1862 campaign he was stationed in the defenses of Richmond, until his capture at Fort Harrison. He never obtained his colonelcy.

19. "Ma" is of course Taylor's widowed mother, Cornelia Wickham Cowdery Taylor (1811–99). She stayed in Norfolk after the evacuation with her younger children, to guard her property. By 1863 she was trying every possible avenue of escape, finally making it to Richmond in the fall. At the end of the war she reclaimed her house in Norfolk.

20. Richard H. Anderson, division commander in Longstreet's corps. His division included Mahone's brigade, one of whose regiments was the Sixth Virginia. When Longstreet was severely wounded in the Wilderness in 1864, Anderson assumed command of the corps, with the rank of lieutenant general.

21. Rob or Robbie is Taylor's younger brother Robertson (b. 1840). He began the war as quartermaster, then adjutant of the Sixth Virginia, but in November 1861 was promoted first lieutenant and assistant adjutant general of Mahone's brigade. By 1863 he was a captain. He was wounded in the Wilderness and promoted to major, but never resumed active service. He convalesced mainly at Elk Hill, Goochland County, and with his family in Richmond.

22. Lydia was about seven months pregnant with her first child. Also her husband Dick was for the first time far from home on campaign, heading north toward Manassas and Sharpsburg.

23. Sally is Sally L. Tompkins, an old friend of Walter Taylor and his family. This public-spirited Richmond woman became an army nurse and earned the only commission (captain) given to a woman in the Confederacy. N. D. Taylor, "Florence Nightingale," 480–81; N. D. Taylor, "Worthy Honor," 358; K. Jones, *Ladies of Richmond*, 71–73.

Marcia is not identified. She is a Taylor relative or family friend staying with Mary Lou and Lydia in Richmond.

24. Taylor here refers to the action at Groveton in which Stonewall Jackson maintained his position in the face of heavy Northern attacks.
25. All references to "the General," "the chief," or even "the Great Tycoon" and other unspecified terms of authority refer of course to General R. E. Lee, unless otherwise noted.

    Prior to the Seven Days, detractors had dubbed Lee "the King of Spades," referring to his work in establishing coastal defenses in South Carolina and Georgia earlier in 1862.
26. "Home" in the letters always refers to Norfolk. Richmond and other temporary residences of his family were viewed by Taylor as places of exile.
27. I.e., Taylor and his two brothers Dick and Rob.
28. The second and decisive day of Lee's triumph over Pope at Second Manassas or Bull Run.
29. Henry ("Harry" or "Uncle Harry") Watson Williamson (b. 1823) graduated V.M.I. 1845, was appointed captain of Company G, Sixth Virginia in April, 1861, and in May, 1862, became lieutenant colonel of the regiment, a position he held until he was wounded at the Crater (July 30, 1864), where he lost an arm. He retired from the army in December, 1864. After the war he married Pattie Saunders Green, a first cousin of Bettie's, but at this time the "uncle" was honorific.

    The other names are of enlisted men in Company G, Sixth Virginia, whose first lieutenant was Duncan Robertson and which contained many friends of Walter and Bettie. The correct names of the casualties according to Porter's *Record* are Douglas Bell, Albert C. Voss, Richard Hopkins, and William G. Ridley. Porter, *Record,* 229, 269, 273–74, 279–80, 285, 310.
30. The Potomac.
31. Walter, Dick, and Rob were all in Maryland; John was in South Carolina. The three younger brothers (and two sisters) were in Norfolk with their mother, while Mary Lou was alone in Richmond.
32. A popular wartime song written by James Ryder Randall and sung to the tune of "Oh Christmas Tree." Its lyrics urge Maryland to "burst the tyrant's chains" and join her sister states of the South. Randall wrote in early 1861 when Federal troops entered Baltimore to forestall any movement for secession. "My Maryland" was declared the Maryland state song in 1939. Shearer and Shearer, *State Names,* 180.
33. E. Kirby Smith was present at First Manassas and took part in Bragg's invasion of Kentucky in 1862. Later that year he was given command of the Trans Mississippi Department, a post he held for the rest of the war. In February 1864 he was made the sole full general in the Provisional Army of the Confederate States. He surrendered May 26, 1865, almost six weeks after Lee had done so at Appomattox.

When this letter was written, General Kirby Smith was about to launch an invasion of eastern Kentucky from Knoxville, Tennessee. His cavalry raided as far north as the Ohio River across from Cincinnati, but the city itself was never seriously threatened.

34. "The President" in these letters always refers to President Jefferson Davis. Enoch L. Lowe was the governor of Maryland, 1850–53. As the Confederate troops entered Maryland, Lee hoped to hear from ex-Governor Lowe, an ardent Southern supporter. When Lowe made no effort to respond, however, and the state government failed to react to the presence of the Confederate army on its soil, Lee issued a proclamation urging the people to join their brethren of the South by their own free will. Murfin, *Gleam of Bayonets,* 105.

35. P. G. T. Beauregard succeeded Pemberton in the Department of South Carolina, Georgia, and Florida in September 1863. He was one of the six full generals in the Regular Army of the Confederate States; he was second in command to Joseph E. Johnston at First Manassas, commanded the Army of Tennessee for a time following the death of Albert Sydney Johnston at Shiloh, but is perhaps best known for his defense of Charleston, South Carolina, in 1863–1864, and Petersburg, Virginia, in June, 1864.

36. John C. Pemberton was born in Pennsylvania but married a young woman from Norfolk and cast his lot with the South. He spent a year in command of the Department of South Carolina and Georgia, then in October 1862 was sent to the West with the rank of lieutenant general. He is best known as the unsuccessful defender of Vicksburg. When he was forced to surrender that vital post on the Mississippi to U. S. Grant on July 4, 1863, he resigned his commission and served the remainder of the war as a lieutenant colonel of artillery in the trenches outside of Richmond.

"John" is here Walter's younger brother John Cowdery Taylor (b. 1842). He started the war as second lieutenant and aide to his uncle, Captain R. Page, CSN, but in May 1862, joined Pemberton as first lieutenant and ADC in South Carolina. That fall he followed him to Mississippi and was with him through the Vicksburg campaign to August 1863. When paroled he held a staff position in Richmond until March 1864, when, as a captain, he became aide to his uncle again, when Page was assigned to defend Mobile. John was taken prisoner after the fall of Fort Morgan, August 23, 1864, and remained in captivity until April 1865. In letters to Bettie he is called "our John" as opposed to "your John," Bettie's brother John Saunders, who, confusingly, was also a staffer of Pemberton. (Pemberton's in-laws, the Thompsons, were friends of the Saunderses as well as the Taylors.)

37. The Battle of Sharpsburg or Antietam.

38. I.e., General Mahone.
39. Captain (actually Major) John Saunders Taylor was killed at Sharpsburg September 17, 1862. Mrs. Saunders (Bettie's mother) was evidently a cousin of his.
40. Major John Page was quartermaster on the staff of General W. N. Pendleton, who in turn was Lee's chief of artillery.
41. Mahone, who had been seriously wounded at Second Manassas and was recuperating in the area, escaped capture and rejoined his command in time for the battle of Fredericksburg in December. Blake, *William Mahone of Virginia,* 45.
42. Rev. Erskine Mason Rodman was born in 1831 in New York state. Shortly after his ordination as an Episcopal minister he was given charge of St. Paul's parish, Goochland County. There he met and married Bettie's first cousin Nannie Selden in November 1856. In 1858 he was called to Christ Church, Walter and Bettie's church in Norfolk, where he served until April 1864. In October 1863 another Episcopal church in Norfolk, St. Paul's, was confiscated by the Union forces, and both congregations were combined at Christ Church. Because two ministers were superfluous and perhaps because of his Northern background, Rodman's pay was drastically cut and he was forced to resign. He eventually made his way out of Norfolk and by way of Europe and Wilmington, North Carolina, reached Richmond where he was reunited with his wife. The last we hear of him he was seeking a commission as chaplain in the Confederate Army, in the final months of the war. Altar Guild, *St. Paul's Church,* 31; Agee, *Facets of Goochland,* 121.
43. Clarence L. Garnett, M.D., (1841–89) was an army surgeon stationed at Richmond. In March 1865, he married Mary Garnett of Norfolk, a close friend of Taylor's, but he was not himself a Norfolk man, and his connection to Walter and Bettie at this time is unclear.
44. Lieutenant George W. Peterkin was born in Maryland in 1841. His father was Rev. George Peterkin, rector during the war of St. James Episcopal Church in Richmond, and a power in diocesan affairs.

    Enlisting as a private in April 1861, George rose through the ranks to lieutenant and regimental adjutant by May 1862. In June he was appointed ADC to General Pendleton of Lee's staff; by the end of the war he was promoted captain and AAG, still with Pendleton. He was ordained in 1869, and in 1878 was consecrated Episcopal bishop of West Virginia. Peterkin, *Handbook,* 255.
45. The newborn was Richard C. Taylor, Junior.
46. Taylor here refers to their mother, Cornelia Taylor, detained in Norfolk.
47. Sally Tompkins, with all her other accomplishments, appears to have been a good cook. A lapland is "a kind of muffin or gem—one egg, one

cup of milk, one cup of flour, pinch of salt, beat well." Craigie and Hulbert, eds., *Dictionary of American English*, 1399.

48. The very image of the dashing cavalry officer, with plumed hat and flowing cape, Jeb Stuart was in fact far more than that. An educated soldier, a brave and skillful fighter, he was second to none as a gatherer of intelligence that kept Lee informed of the intentions of the enemy. He took part in all the great cavalry actions of the Army of Northern Virginia, notably at Brandy Station in June 1863, and was celebrated for his bold raids into enemy territory. He met his end at Yellow Tavern on May 11, 1864, where he was mortally wounded while fighting to prevent Sheridan with his cavalry from reaching Richmond. He died there the next day, mourned as no Confederate hero had been since the death of Jackson.

    This marked the second occasion on which Stuart had ridden completely around the Army of the Potomac. With 1800 men and four guns he covered eighty miles in twenty-seven hours and brought off 1200 horses at a cost of one man wounded.

49. Frank Huger, born 1837 at Fortress Monroe, was the son of Benjamin Huger (later a general, C.S. Army). He graduated from West Point 1860, but resigned from the U.S. Army early in 1861 and by June was captain of his own battery in the C.S. Army. Soon after the writing of this letter Huger in fact attained his majority, to rank from March 2, 1863. His responsibilities as an artillery commander in the First Corps increased during the war, and he was made lieutenant colonel in May 1864 and full colonel in February 1865. He was captured at Sayler's Creek, just before the war's end.

50. This is the first of myriad greetings to "Mrs. K.," "Mrs. Knox," or "Coz. Mary," a woman who roomed with Bettie as a sort of chaperone from now until the end of the war, with a few interruptions. She was born Mary Frances Selden about 1829, and is Bettie's mother's first cousin.

    Of the numerous relatives named Elizabeth or Lizzie, this Miss Lizzie is most likely Bettie's first cousin, the unmarried younger sister of Mrs. Rodman and Mrs. Heth, Lizzie M. Selden. She was born 1845 and was thus Patty's age mate and companion.

51. Joseph "Fighting Joe" Hooker replaced Burnside as commander of the Army of the Potomac, but at Chancellorsville, generally regarded as Lee's tactical masterpiece, he suffered the same fate his predecessor had at Fredericksburg.

52. Reference here is to Lee's classic triumph over Hooker in the battle of Chancellorsville, May 2-3, 1863.

53. Thomas J. Jackson—the legendary "Stonewall." His Valley campaign of 1862 is often pointed to as a model of its kind. After an uncharacteristically lethargic performance during the Seven Days he

won back his reputation at Second Manassas, Sharpsburg, and Fredericksburg. At Chancellorsville, while leading the famous flank attack against Hooker's army, he fell mortally wounded. As an executive officer he had no equal, and many have believed that the hope of a Confederate military victory in the war died with him.

54. O. O. Howard commanded the Eleventh Federal Corps when it was routed in Stonewall Jackson's celebrated flank attack at Chancellorsville. Later he participated in Sherman's Atlanta campaign as commander of the Fourth Corps, and in the march through the Carolinas he commanded the right wing. A deeply religious man, he concerned himself with the plight of blacks after the war and headed the Freedman's Bureau.

55. Lee regarded A. P. Hill as the best division commander in the Army of Northern Virginia and, when the army was reorganized after Chancellorsville, gave him command of the newly formed Third Corps. He was killed outside of Petersburg on April 2, 1865.

56. Lafayette McLaws, a Georgian, was a capable division commander in Longstreet's First Corps of the Army of Northern Virginia. After Gettysburg he was sent West, quarreled with Longstreet, and returned to Georgia.

57. Colonel of the Ninth Alabama at First Manassas, Cadmus M. Wilcox served capably as brigadier or major general in all principal campaigns of the Army of Northern Virginia. After Gettysburg he took command of Pender's division and was a highly regarded officer, respected in both North and South. The day the Confederate line at Petersburg was broken, April 2, 1865, he conducted the Homeric defense of Fort Gregg.

General Paul Jones Semmes was born in Georgia, 1815. As colonel of a Georgia regiment he went to Virginia and was made brigadier in March 1862. He was with Magruder on the Peninsula, took part in the Seven Days, and fought at Sharpsburg, Fredericksburg, Salem Church, and Gettysburg, where he was mortally wounded, dying July 10, 1863.

58. Francis Mallory, born 1833 in Norfolk, was a slightly older contemporary of Walter's. Graduating from V.M.I. in 1853, he served in the U.S. Army until 1861. Starting as a lieutenant in the C.S. Army in March 1861, he was quickly promoted to colonel of the Fifty-fifth Virginia Infantry, serving in Heth's brigade of A. P. Hill's division until his death at Chancellorsville.

59. W. Carter Williams, a Norfolk native, began the war as an artillery lieutenant in Norfolk, but by July 1861 he was promoted to captain, Co. B, Sixth Virginia. He led three companies in a heroic attack at Chancellorsville and was mortally wounded May 2, dying the next day.

60. Units of Stoneman's cavalry under Colonels Judson Kilpatrick and Hasbrouck Davis reached the outskirts of the Confederate capital. "The

inhabitants of Richmond were astonished, but otherwise little was accomplished by Stoneman's bombshell." Ropes and Livermore, *Story of the Civil War*, vol. 3, 136–38.

61. John D. Hobson (b. ca. 1825), was the owner of Howard's Neck plantation in Goochland County, and the husband of "Kittie" Selden Hobson, Bettie's "sister." He was a lieutenant in the Fourth Virginia Cavalry, and saw action throughout the war, except for a four-month stint as a recruiting officer in Goochland in early 1864.

62. The Battle of Brandy Station.

63. In his report Jeb Stuart wrote, "Among our gallant dead I am grieved to record Colonel Solomon Williams, Second North Carolina Cavalry, as fearless as he was efficient." Williams was born 1835 in North Carolina, graduated West Point 1858, and served in the U.S. Cavalry till 1861. In the Confederate Army he rose to colonel of the Second North Carolina Cavalry in June 1862, serving in that capacity until his death. *O.R.*, vol. 27, pt. 2, 684.

64. Lieutenant John C. Pegram (b. 1837) and his sister Margaret (b. 1839) were natives of Norfolk. After Williams's death Pegram was promoted captain and made AAG to General M. W. Ransom; he was killed at Hatcher's Run, June 17, 1864. His father and younger brother served in the C.S. Navy.

   By an odd coincidence their cousin General John Pegram was also killed only weeks after his wedding in 1865. (See chap. 6, n. 11.)

65. "Coz Nannie" and "Mrs. R" are the same person. Lieutenant Miles Cary Selden (b. 1834) is her bachelor brother, and thus another of Bettie's Selden first cousins. Through most of the war he was aide to General Harry Heth, his brother-in-law.

66. Leila (or Eliza, according to the census) Kerr is Fanny Kerr's mother, originally from New York. She turns out to have been suffering from mental illness. The Kerrs' trip to Maryland was brief—by the time Taylor got to Hagerstown in the Gettysburg campaign, they had returned to Norfolk.

67. Margaret H. Bowden (b. 1839), was an old Norfolk friend of Walter's. Shortly before the war she married Joseph Van Holt Nash, a "dashing cavalry officer" (chap. 3, let. 49). At this time a lieutenant, in February 1864 he became a captain and AAG to General Chambliss, his position until war's end.

68. When Bettie is in "the country" or at "the Neck" she is staying with the Hobsons at Howard's Neck. This plantation is on a bend of the James River (north bank) in western Goochland County, immediately west of the postal village of Pemberton, Virginia. See map 2 and fig. 6; Wight, *Story of Goochland*, plate.

69. "Uncle Gus" has been identified by one of Taylor's grandchildren as a deaf-mute servant who did all the washing, cooking, cleaning, and lived and died in the Taylor household. "My father chuckled many times at the jokes the mischievous boys played on Unc. Gus." Janet Fauntleroy Taylor, letter to the editor, December 1985. Mr. Parker is not identified.

    Moses R is Moses Robertson, born 1822, a cousin of Bettie's on her father's side. He was a merchant and did no military service. Late in the war, according to the letters, he escaped to Liverpool, where he did well, perhaps dealing in cotton. McIntosh, "Proby Family," 217–20, 322–28.

70. Evidently the Parkses and Osbornes were acquaintances from before the war. Taylor was seeking information on Fanny Kerr, supposed to be in Hagerstown.

71. The Yankees' "Gibraltar" was Cemetery Ridge, particularly Culp's Hill and Little Round Top.

72. William Hunter Saunders (1839–87) is the younger of Bettie's two older brothers. He was enrolled as a private in the Third Richmond Howitzers throughout the war, though in 1863 he was detached to serve as an aide at the headquarters of General A. L. Long, commander of the Second Corps artillery.

    Aleck (or Alec) is Alexander Tunstall (1843–1905), son of Dr. Robert Tunstall and a young neighbor of the Taylors in Norfolk. He fled school in May 1861 to sign up in the Sixth Virginia, where he was sergeant major, and by January 1862 first lieutenant and adjutant, a post he retained until Appomattox. Morris, *First Tunstalls in Virginia,* 121–24, 179–81; White, "Diary of the War," 297, 302, 304.

73. Alexander "Sandy" Wallace Stark (as it is usually spelled), born 1839, had two younger sisters, Mary (1843) and Helen (1845), orphaned in the Norfolk yellow fever of 1855. The girls were boarded out with friends or relatives, while Sandy was given a commission as lieutenant in the U.S. Marine Corps. When the war began he was aboard ship in Asia and did not make his way back to Virginia, via San Francisco and New Orleans, until March 1862. He was promptly commissioned major of artillery and served mostly at Chaffin's Bluff in the defenses of Richmond. He was promoted lieutenant colonel December 1864, and ended the war at Appomattox. He remained a close friend of Taylor's until his death in 1898.

74. John here is Taylor's brother John C. Taylor, who was with Pemberton in the siege of Vicksburg.

75. Joseph E. Johnston, fourth ranking full general in the Confederate Army, commanded at First Manassas and opposed McClellan in the Peninsula campaign of 1862. Severely wounded at Seven Pines, he was succeeded by Robert E. Lee. Sent to the West the following year, he commanded

the Army of Tennessee in the Atlanta campaign until removed by Jefferson Davis, with whom he constantly quarreled. Placed in command of the troops in the Carolinas in February 1865, in the vain hope that he might be able to stop Sherman, he surrendered at Greensboro, North Carolina, on April 26, 1865. Symonds, *Joseph E. Johnston*, 356–57.

After his victories in the West at Shiloh, Vicksburg, and Chattanooga, U. S. Grant was brought east in the spring of 1864, promoted to the rank of lieutenant general and put in command of all the armies of the United States.

Braxton Bragg was the longtime controversial commander of the Army of Tennessee until his resignation following the disastrous Confederate defeat at Missionary Ridge in November 1863. A favorite of Jefferson Davis, he was recalled to Richmond to supervise the "conduct of military operations of the armies of the Confederacy" under the president. Jefferson Davis, *Rise and Fall*, vol. 1, 340.

William S. Rosecrans commanded the Union Army of the Cumberland at the drawn battle of Murfreesboro or Stone's River and suffered defeat at Chickamauga in September 1863, when he was superseded by Grant.

76. I.e., Culp's Hill and Little Round Top.

77. George E. Pickett, wounded at Gaines Mill, fought creditably at Fredericksburg, but his fame rests on the desperate assault of his division against the Union line on Cemetery Ridge on the third day at Gettysburg. "Pickett's Charge" has become a synonym for bravery in the face of overwhelming odds. His later career was less distinguished, and at the end his crushing defeat by Sheridan at Five Forks made the evacuation of Petersburg and the fall of Richmond inevitable, and led to his removal from command by Lee days before Appomattox. W. Harrison, *Pickett's Men*; Pickett, *Pickett and His Men*.

78. Port Hudson, Louisiana, the last Confederate position on the Mississippi, fell July 8, 1863, four days after Vicksburg.

79. Fitzhugh Lee, nephew of R. E. Lee and a favorite of Jeb Stuart, played a gallant role in the cavalry of the Army of Northern Virginia, especially at Spotsylvania Court House, where his division held off the enemy until the infantry of the First Corps arrived and secured the strategic crossroads. When Wade Hampton was ordered to North Carolina in January 1865, Fitzhugh Lee took command of the remnants of the cavalry corps of the Army of Northern Virginia and surrendered at Appomattox.

80. Major Henry B. McClellan, a cavalry staffer, was General Stuart's adjutant from May 1863. When Stuart was killed, McClellan was temporarily transferred to Lee's staff (May to August 1864); then he was

made AAG to General Wade Hampton, Stuart's successor as commander of the cavalry corps. McClellan, *Life and Campaigns*.

81. Bernard Lynch, universally known as "Bryan," was Lee's mess steward.

82. A John T. Dickson (b. 1840), son of a merchant, was a near neighbor and fellow parishioner of Taylor's in Norfolk. As his name does not appear in military records, he was evidently a civilian visiting army headquarters.

83. Taylor's lament refers to an incident of July 11, 1863, when the Federals staged a parade of black troops in Norfolk, and an irate citizen pulled out a gun and killed one of the white officers.

84. Mahone had been recommended for promotion to major general by his division commander, Richard H. Anderson, on March 30, 1863, but no action was taken on the matter until the following year. On June 7, 1864, Mahone declined an appointment to that rank, but at Lee's request he was made a major general to rank from July 30, 1864, the date of the battle of the Crater. Doubtless the long delay in his promotion (he had been a brigadier since November 16, 1861) contributed to Mahone's unhappiness noted by Taylor.

85. Richard Walke, Jr., of Norfolk, born 1840, began the war as a private in Co. G, Sixth Virginia, but by December 1862 had been promoted to first lieutenant and ordnance officer of Mahone's brigade. It is unclear whether he actually left Mahone in August 1863, as Taylor seems to say; in any case in May 1864 he was promoted captain and was made AAG to General R. L. Walker, commander of the Third Corps artillery.

86. The Greens were Bettie's first cousins on her father's side, Mrs. Green being Mary Saunders Green, of West Point, Virginia, at the head of the York River. George Green has not been found in the military records, so the manner of his death is unclear.

87. Julia Worrell (b. 1835) lived a few houses down from the Taylors in Norfolk and died sometime in the mid-1850s—most likely in the yellow fever of 1855.

88. After the surrender of Vicksburg, President Davis, at Pemberton's request, authorized a Court of Inquiry, originally scheduled to be held at Montgomery but subsequently postponed to Atlanta. The court, in fact, never convened, for a dispatch from Richmond stated that the exigencies of the service required all officers involved—including those summoned as witnesses—to report for duty in the field. As a result the court was broken up. Pemberton, *Pemberton, Defender of Vicksburg*, 208–9.

89. John Selden Saunders (b. 1838) was Bettie's eldest brother. At the war's beginning he was a second lieutenant in the U.S. Army, but by April 1861 he was captain of artillery, C.S. Army, attached to the Richmond Arsenal. By January 1862 he had his own artillery battalion, attached to

Anderson's division, and he shortly attained his majority. In October his battalion was disbanded and he was reassigned to the Richmond Arsenal as a lieutenant colonel. In early 1863 he went to the West to serve under Pemberton until the time of this letter, when he returned to Richmond. After that he was given few assignments and fruitlessly sought combat duty the remainder of the war.

90. The battalion referred to is that commanded by Lieutenant Colonel John Jameson Garnett, in Longstreet's corps. Garnett was finally suspended by Lee in February 1864 and relieved in April—but John Saunders never got the job.

91. Frank Huger did not obtain his second star (lieutenant colonelcy) until May 1864, ranking from February.

92. "Our John" is John C. Taylor, also recently returned from the surrender at Vicksburg.

93. This is General Henry ("Harry") Heth, Lee's first cousin and "the only officer in the Army of Northern Virginia whom Lee addressed by his given name," Warner, *Generals in Gray*, 133–34. He was born 1825, graduated West Point 1847, and served in the U.S. Army until 1861, including a three year stint pacifying the Mormons in Utah. In 1857 he married Harriet Selden (b. 1847), Bettie's first cousin. He started the war as Lee's quartermaster general in Richmond, then served as an infantry colonel in West Virginia before his promotion to brigadier in January 1862. After a period with Kirby Smith in the West, he joined the Army of Northern Virginia as a brigade and later division commander under A. P. Hill. He participated in all the major campaigns, was seriously wounded at Gettysburg, and ended the war at Appomattox.

94. Mrs. Walker (nee Mercer) is unidentified.

95. Julia Robertson at this point was pushing twenty-three.

96. Taylor dares not mention another possibility: that romantic feelings for him were awakening in her. This was indeed the case, as events were shortly to prove.

97. No Carringtons are found in the Norfolk records, so Ella is most likely a Richmond friend.

98. The rumor proved false.

99. Charleston did not fall until February 17, 1865, when Sherman's march northward from Savannah outflanked the city and rendered it untenable. The August 1863 bombardment of Charleston was part of a Union offensive which included the bloody and unsuccessful assault by black troops on Fort Wagner, Morris Island on August 19.

In the WHT Papers is a letter to Bettie from her younger brother Palmer Saunders, a midshipman in the CSN, who was an eyewitness to these events. The letter is dated August 24, 1863, from the CSS *Chicora*,

Charleston Harbor. Because of its intrinsic historic interest, I have elected to extract it extensively here:

> We came down here which is three miles below the city on the 10th of July & here we have remained except on several occasions when the monitors appeared to be coming in. But don't think we have nothing to do for we are constantly on the move transporting men, ammunition, & provisions to Morris Is. in small boats. We are in full view of the whole Is. & about three miles distant. And have seen all that has occurred since the taking of the southern end of the island to the almost total destruction of Fort Sumter. We witnessed both assaults on Wagner & you can well imagine what a fever of excitement we were in not being able to lend a hand. I visited Fort Wagner the next morning after the assault of the 19th & such a sight I never before, nor never wish to again behold. When I arrived they had buried some three hundred & there we[re] there upwards of five hundred men lying dead in a space not larger than our back yard at home. In some places they were piled 8 deep & mangled horribly. I thought prior to this that nothing could make me shudder, but I must acknowledge that it made me feel all the horrors of a battle. I walked over the whole field among the wounded most of whom were very badly wounded. Here & there you would come across a negro who was wounded with knots of our men around him frightening him to death with telling him he would be hung before sundown etc. It would be useless for me to try to picture to you the different scenes for it would take someone with a larger share of patience than myself. Our men were in fine spirits all engaged more or less gathering up the spoils. Since that day the Yanks have been constantly at work throwing up works & shelling the different batteries. On last Monday they commenced on Fort Sumter & today it is a perfect wreck hardly tenable & certainly not able to perform any large part in the defence of Charleston. I have just heard that we were to go down to take the place of Sumter, if so we will have our share of the shelling. Fort Wagner & Cummings Pt. are stronger today than ever, their terrific bombardments seem only to strengthen than demolish this almost shapeless heap of sand. We have thrown up powerful batteries all over the harbor & on James Is. to shell the enemy & it is one continual roar of artillery from morning until night. The Yankees opened on the city night before last from a small battery about 5 miles from the city throwing them this distance into the heart of the city. Everyone is leaving as fast as possible so I understand. We are all very anxious to have a fight but nothing seems to favor us.

Chapter 2: Campaigning along the Rapidan

1. George G. Meade replaced Hooker in command of the Army of the Potomac a few days before the battle of Gettysburg. When Grant was brought east in the spring of 1864 he retained Meade in that assignment.
2. Maria is Maria Octavia Selden (b. 1845), the youngest girl in the John A. Selden family, and, like Lizzie Selden of the Miles C. Selden family, an age mate to her first cousin Pattie Saunders (b. 1846).
3. This is General Heth; "your cousin" is his wife Harriet Selden Heth. Heth was blamed for the handling of his division in the bungled attack at Bristoe Station. Two of his brigades, those of Cooke and Kirkland, were shattered with a loss of 1361 casualties.
4. Duncan Robertson (1837–1915) is Julia Robertson's older brother and Taylor's closest boyhood friend—some prewar correspondence between them still exists (see intro.). Duncan was elected third lieutenant of Co. G, Sixth Virginia, the unit so dominated by Taylor's cronies. He was promoted second lieutenant in April 1862. He distinguished himself in heroic action at Sharpsburg, where he was wounded. By 1864 he was first lieutenant and in command of the company. He was captured at Burgess Mill, October 27, 1864, but paroled in time to surrender at Appomattox with the eleven remaining men of his company.
5. In Porter's *Record*, 273–74, these men are listed as: Cornelius M. Cole, William C. Robinson, Third Sergeant Albert B. Simmons (who died the next day), and Edward Kerr. The company is actually "G," though it was known as "F" in April 1861, when Taylor was briefly associated with it.
6. Thomas Lawton Barraud (misspelled Barrand in *O.R.*) was born 1828 in Norfolk. He was chosen third lieutenant of Co. C, Sixteenth Virginia, and by April 1862 was captain. In announcing his death, his commanding officer called him an "excellent officer." *O.R.*, vol. 29, pt. 1, 429.
7. Maria May Baker of Norfolk was not only Barraud's first cousin, but his sister-in-law, as he was married to her older sister, Mary Baker.
8. Hollywood is a famous parklike cemetery in Richmond.
9. This Starke is not Taylor's friend the artillerist A. W. "Sandy" Stark (see chap. 1, n. 73), but Captain W. Norbonne Starke from Louisiana (not Norfolk), and a rather obnoxious young man in Taylor's eyes. In early 1863 he was a staffer for General Winder in Richmond, but after Gettysburg he was AAG to A. P. Hill, a position he held until April 1865. He was promoted major in May 1864, to rank from February.
10. Bettie introduced Walter to her family's country place during his leave, and from now on he refers to it familiarly as "the Neck." Likewise their

hostess is no longer "Mrs. Hobson," but "your sister Kittie," or even "Kittie."

11. Richard Snowden Andrews was born 1830 in Washington, D.C. He began the war as a captain of light artillery; by late 1862, having been seriously wounded, he was posted as a major to the Bureau of Ordnance. In 1863 he was back in the field as a lieutenant colonel of artillery.

    Thomas Smith Rhett was a Carolinian and 1848 West Point graduate. From May 1862 to October 1863 he was colonel in charge of the artillery defending Richmond, but then he was sent to Europe to purchase arms. Taylor guessed right: Andrews did want the cushy European assignment and was detached in January 1864 to go there. But someone other than John Saunders replaced him in the field.

12. God's crowning mercy is of course Bettie Saunders's acceptance of his proposal of marriage. Not until the end of the next letter is Taylor able to pen a profession of his love for her—and even then it is hedged about with religious sentiments.

13. Northern Prince William County includes Bristoe Station and Manassas. Previous to the Bristoe Station campaign, it had already been devastated by the Manassas campaigns of July 1861 and August 1862, as well as by Union occupations in November 1862 and in the aftermath of Gettysburg.

14. Longstreet's First Corps of the Army of Northern Virginia had already been sent to the West in September. No further troops were sent.

15. Sandy is Alexander Stark, and Bella is Taylor's horse, which he had taken into the field with him when he returned from leave.

16. Elk Hill is an estate on the James in Goochland County only about four miles upriver from Howard's Neck. Randolph Harrison (a lieutenant colonel of artillery) was the owner and built the manor house in 1845. (See map 2 and fig. 7.) In 1853 he married Elizabeth Williamson, the niece of "Uncle" Harry Williamson. Elk Hill, "famous for its hospitality," became a resort for sick or furloughed officers, including Williamson and Taylor's brother Rob. Agee, *Facets of Goochland,* 104–7, map, 176; Wight, *Story of Goochland,* 68, plate; Harrison, "Sheridan's Raiders," 285–94.

17. A Confederate *tête-de-pont,* manned by two brigades of Jubal Early's division, had been established on the north bank of the river at Rappahannock Station.

18. This is Mary Anna Randolph Custis Lee, General Lee's wife.

19. Hardly a prescient remark, for Lee became the object of Taylor's undying affection after the war. Yet during the war Taylor felt strongly enough to reiterate this sentiment in a later letter (chap. 4, let. 76).

20. Rev. Robert Gatewood, born 1830 of an old Norfolk family, was an Episcopal minister and briefly pastor of St. John's Church in Norfolk,

before the evacuation. At present he was an army chaplain with the Richmond defense force.

21. "Little May" is Margaret Walke Taylor (b. 1848), and "Nina" is Cornelia Wickham Taylor (b. 1846), Taylor's two little sisters.

22. I.e., those lost at Rappahannock Station.

23. James Longstreet was the senior lieutenant general in the Confederate Army and commander of the First Corps of the Army of Northern Virginia. He was an indomitable fighter and a skillful tactician in battle, though charged with slowness at Gettysburg. Lee affectionately referred to him as "my Old War Horse." Critically wounded in the Wilderness, he returned to command of his troops in October and surrendered with Lee at Appomattox. At this writing Longstreet was in Tennessee with Bragg, not to return till April.

24. Richard S. Ewell, "Fighting Dick," took command of Jackson's old Second Corps of the Army of Northern Virginia on the latter's death at Chancellorsville. He lost a leg at Second Manassas and was criticized for his failure to seize Culp's Hill on the first day at Gettysburg. Loyal, dependable, and well-liked, he lacked Stonewall's dash and decisiveness.

25. Mahew Hobson was John Hobson's brother, and thus Kittie Hobson's brother-in-law.

26. Pemberton is the post office village about a mile east of Howard's Neck.

27. Goochland is the county on the north side of the James immediately west of Richmond's county, Henrico. In Taylor's usage "Goochland" refers specifically to the southwest part of the county along the river where a string of beautiful estate houses overlooked the James River Valley. (See map 2.)

    After listing the plantations here, including Howard's Neck, John Wise sums up the region in these words:

    > Scattered along the valley, owning respectively from seven hundred to two or three thousand acres, with slaves enough to cultivate twice the lands they owned, they were the happiest and most prosperous community in all America; not rolling in wealth, like the sugar cane and cotton planters of the South, yet with a thousand advantages over them, in the variety of their productions, in the beauty of their lands, in the salubrity of their climate, in the society about them, and in their access to the outer world. Wise, *End of an Era*, 139.

28. Major Charles S. Venable, after a start as an engineer and artillery officer, was on Lee's staff as ADC and AAG from March 1862 on, with brief interruptions. He did not take Taylor's advice and stayed on with Lee to the end, obtaining his lieutenant colonelcy in May 1864, to rank from February.

29. John Smith Preston was a Virginian who married Wade Hampton's daughter and moved to South Carolina before the war. Starting out as an aide to Beauregard and then an AAG of a brigade, he was put in command of a prison camp, and then was made commander of conscription in South Carolina. In July 1863, as a full colonel, he was placed in charge of the Bureau of Conscription in Richmond, being promoted to brigadier in June 1864. Wakelyn, *Biographical Dictionary of the Confederacy,* 353.

30. Taylor was promoted lieutenant colonel on January 15, 1864, two months after this letter. (See intro., n. 77.)

31. Dr. David M. Wright, a Norfolk physician, is the man who shot Lieutenant Sanborn, a Northern officer, during a parade of black troops in Norfolk, July 11, 1863 (see chap. 1, n. 83). Though he was summarily condemned to death, friends appealed the case all the way to President Lincoln, on the grounds of insanity. The appeal was rejected and he was executed October 23, 1863.

32. Major John Preston was AAG to Wade Hampton, then to M. C. Butler from late 1863 to the end of the war. As the letters reveal, Taylor was beleaguered by requests for leave by those who felt a claim on his friendship.

33. Wade Hampton, said to be the largest landowner in the South prior to the war, organized the Hampton Legion and commanded a brigade in Stuart's Cavalry Corps. When the latter was killed at Yellow Tavern in the summer of 1864, Hampton succeeded him in command of the cavalry of the Army of Northern Virginia. He was made a lieutenant general in 1865 and transferred back to the Carolinas. After the war he played a prominent part with his "Red Shirts" in restoring home rule to South Carolina and had a distinguished career in politics as governor of the state and as a member of the United States Senate.

34. Hannah Petty is listed in the 1860 Norfolk census as a widow with four children. After the evacuation she and her children boarded in Richmond at the house of Lewis Crenshaw, a friend of Bettie's.

35. Custis Lee was at this time serving as an aide-de-camp on President Davis's staff.

36. Lee is Custis Lee and Brown is Colonel William M. Browne, an aide to Davis since 1862.

37. Freeman, *R. E. Lee,* vol. 3, 202.

38. Taylor was wrong in his surmise, for Meade, after crossing the Rapidan, turned west rather than east toward Fredericksburg.

    The reverse in Tennessee was the Confederate rout at Missionary Ridge, November 25, 1863.

39. Likely a Hobson relative, Mahew being a given name in the Hobson clan.

40. Mary W. Garnett was born in Norfolk 1842, the daughter of a customs inspector. By the 1860 census, her family has disappeared, and at seventeen she was living with a druggist and his wife. This young, possibly orphaned, woman seems to have had a special place in Taylor's heart. She survived to marry Dr. Clarence Garnett at war's end and lived on to 1904, bearing five children.

41. On November 26, 1863, Meade crossed the Rapidan, attempting to turn Lee's right flank in what came to be known as the Mine Run campaign. Lee marched eastward to confront him. Failing to find a weak spot in Lee's defensive lines, Meade withdrew his forces on December 1 and went into winter quarters.

42. Edward Johnson, known as "Old Allegheny," served with distinction in Jackson's Valley campaign and led Stonewall's old division at Gettysburg and the Wilderness. Captured with the bulk of his division defending the Bloody Angle at Spotsylvania, he was later exchanged and led a division in S. D. Lee's corps in the Army of Tennessee during Hood's ill-fated Tennessee campaign.

43. Two weeks before he was scheduled to graduate from West Point in the spring of 1861, Thomas L. Rosser resigned and joined the Confederacy. He became colonel of the Fifth Virginia Cavalry, was wounded at Mechanicsville and later at Kelly's Ford, and as a brigadier commanded the Laurel Brigade. At Appomattox he refused to surrender and cut his way out, only to be taken prisoner early in May. After the war he served as chief engineer of the Northern Pacific and Canadian Pacific railroads. In the Spanish American War he served as a brigadier general of U.S. Volunteers.

44. Anderson's and Wilcox's divisions of A. P. Hill's Third Corps.

45. A letter in the WHT Papers to Bettie Saunders signed "J. Moore" and dated November 24, 1863, informs her of her appointment as a clerk in the Surgeon General's Office. She abruptly quit her previous job at the Treasury Department (which she had held since November 1862) and began her new job December 1. The "Medical Purveyor" is Dr. Samuel Preston Moore, Surgeon General of the Confederacy 1863–65. Dr. William J. Moore was from Norfolk and at this time was an army surgeon in charge of a Richmond hospital. He was no doubt the connection through whom Bettie got the job.

    Maggie, elsewhere called Maggie French, is evidently a coworker of Bettie's, whom Walter has met.

46. On December 9, Lee had been summoned to Richmond for consultation with President Davis.

47. Federal cavalry under Averell for two weeks raided railroads in southwestern Virginia, and there were also demonstrations up the Shenandoah Valley and from the Kanawha Valley, West Virginia.

48. Robert H. Chilton, after a stint as AAG in Richmond, was in May 1862 appointed colonel and aide to General Johnston. When Johnston was wounded and Lee took over his command in June, Chilton was one of the few staffers to stay on. He was Lee's chief of staff and Taylor's immediate superior until March 1864. Taylor liked him as a boss, since he was lax and left him to his own devices, but he had little respect for him.

49. On June 22, 1863, Alfred Pleasanton was promoted to major general in command of the cavalry of the Army of the Potomac. The rumor that he had replaced Meade was false. He disapproved of the Kilpatrick-Dahlgren raid on Richmond; in February 1864, he was relieved of command to make way for Sheridan and was banished to Missouri.

50. Chilton did return, but in March of the following year he asked to be relieved and was assigned to the Adjutant General's Department in Richmond. The Confederate Senate had approved his promotion to brigadier general on February 16, 1864, to rank from December 1863.

51. Though the other documents mentioned have not been found, a copy of Lee's General Order No. 103 exists in the WHT Papers. The text is as follows:

Hdqrs 7 Dec. '63

Gen'l Orders

No. 103.

In view of our national distress the legislature of Georgia, upon the recommendation of the Gov. of the State has set apart Thursday next the 10th inst, as a day of fasting humiliation & prayer and has invited the Congress, and people of the Confederate States, the army & navy to unite in its strict observance.

Accordingly all duties in this Army except such as are necessary will be suspended on that day, and the Chaplains of the several regiments, are desired to hold services appropriate to the occasion.

The mercies of God have been so signally & perfectly extended to this army that it cannot too humble itself in deep repentance for past sins, or too earnestly offer its sincere prayers for future guidance & protection. Let us therefore anew present our praise & thanksgiving, to our gracious Lord & Saviour for having relieved us in our many troubles, & humbly supplicate his deliverance from the dangers which threaten us: imploring him to strengthen our faith, confirm our trust in him, increase our repentance, and enable us to bow submissively to His holy will.

R. E. Lee
Gen'l

52. As previously noted, Walter's letters to Bettie did not begin in earnest until after Gettysburg—indeed permission to write her freely was evidently gained only upon their engagement during Walter's September to October 1863 leave. Before August 1863 he wrote her only in desperation, or in order to convey urgent family news—only six letters in fifteen months.

53. After Shiloh, despite his desultory pursuit of the retreating Confederates to Corinth, H. W. Halleck was called to Washington by Lincoln as general in chief. To make way for Grant in March 1864 he was demoted to chief of staff. A contentious, unpopular man, prone to blame others, he brought order and discipline to the army and was instrumental in raising men and material.

54. I.e., Robertson Taylor.

55. Mark Tapley is a character in Dickens' novel *Martin Chuzzlewit*, who repeatedly states that his goal is to be of cheerful service to others, and to be jolly in difficulties. Taylor refers to Tapley twice in the letters, and appears to take him as a model. Dickens, *Martin Chuzzlewit*, 61, 215, 445, 628.

56. Thinier is unidentified—perhaps he was Bettie Saunders's predecessor as Surgeon General's Office clerk.

57. Lee in fact did return December 21.

58. Braxton Bragg resigned as commander of the Army of Tennessee following the disaster at Missionary Ridge, and the question of his replacement was the subject of long conferences at this time between Lee and President Davis. While Lee was willing to undertake the task of assuming command in Georgia if the president so desired, he felt others could accomplish more with the Army of Tennessee than he could hope to do. His suggestion of Beauregard for the command failed to meet the president's approval. In the end the post was given to Joseph E. Johnston, and Lee remained with the Army of Northern Virginia.

59. Doctor Wright was executed October 23 (see chap. 2, n. 31). According to the 1860 census his wife was Penelope; their oldest daughter, Penelope N., was born 1840 and thus was a close contemporary of Bettie Saunders's.

60. William E. Taylor (b. 1809) was a member of Walter's church and lived in his neighborhood in Norfolk. He is called a grocer and a farmer in the records. He was major of a volunteer unit before the war, but when he failed to be appointed colonel in May 1861 he resigned and enlisted as a private in Co. F. of the Sixth Virginia. He fought in all the campaigns until friends obtained a discharge for him in 1863. Thereupon he was elected to the Virginia legislature. His wife was named Margaret, and their only daughter (b. 1835) was Sally.

61. Benjamin F. Butler, known as "Beast Butler" for his heavy-handed

actions in the occupation of Norfolk and New Orleans, was outlawed by President Davis and reviled by all true Southerners. As a military leader he was a failure, but his political influence and his ability as an administrator kept him in positions of prominence almost throughout the war. He ran occupied Norfolk from January 1863 to October 1864, though after May 1864 he was in the field. In Norfolk he confiscated houses and even churches at will, if the occupants had family members in "Dixie" (the unoccupied Confederacy), or if they were suspected of Southern sympathies. Even after he left the area, his repressive policies were continued by his protégés, Generals Weitzel and Shepley, who succeeded him. As commander of the Army of the James in 1864 he allowed himself to be "bottled up" by Beauregard at Bermuda Hundred, and his expedition against Fort Fisher at the end of the year was an abject failure. After the war he devoted himself to his extensive legal practice and to politics, being elected governor of Massachusetts in 1882.

62. Robert Barraud Taylor was William E. Taylor's eldest son (b. 1839), and a Norfolk friend of Walter Taylor's. At war's beginning he was elected first lieutenant of Co. A, Sixth Virginia Infantry, and regimental adjutant. In August he was made captain of Co. C; then in May 1862 he became the major of the regiment. As major, then as lieutenant colonel, he followed General Mahone to Appomattox. After the war he went on to become a prominent physician.

63. Lilianne or Lelia Baker (b. 1839) married Robert Taylor October 7, 1863. She was the younger sister of May and Mary Baker (see chap. 2, n. 7).

64. This Charlotte is not the city in North Carolina but Charlotte Court House, Virginia, about seventy-five miles southwest of Richmond. John A. Selden, eldest brother of Bettie's mother, had fled there when the Federals occupied his plantation, "Westover," on the lower James, in May 1862. He spent the summer at Amelia Springs, then bought a plantation near Charlotte, and moved in by December. Thus Bettie's cousin John Selden Jr. was going to his parents' home for Christmas. John A. Selden to Martha S. Saunders, March 31 and December 20, 1862, WHT Papers.

65. "Miss Immie" is Imogen Thompson Loyall (1836–79), a Norfolk woman and older contemporary of Taylor's. Just before the war she married Commander Benjamin Loyall, CSN, a close family friend of the Saunderses. She settled in Charlotte during the war and became close to the John Selden family, including their daughter Maria.

After Immie died Loyall married Taylor's little sister Nina.

66. Thomas Mann Randolph Talcott (b. 1838) began the war as a captain of engineers, helping with the defense of Norfolk, but in March 1862 he joined Lee's staff as a major and AAG. He was promoted lieutenant colonel, then, in June 1864, colonel of a regiment of engineers. He

became a lifelong friend of Taylor's, and was a pallbearer at his funeral. Taylor's funeral notice, WHT Papers.

67. "Runy" (usually "Rooney") Lee was R. E. Lee's second son, William Henry Fitzhugh Lee. He was colonel of a cavalry regiment, then twice promoted to become the youngest major general in the C.S. Army. At the writing of this letter he was a prisoner of war, having been wounded at Brandy Station (June 1863) and captured shortly thereafter. His wife Charlotte died in December, having never recovered from the shock of seeing her wounded husband snatched from his bed and borne off to captivity. He was finally released in March 1864. Flood, *Lee, the Last Years,* 37, 127.

68. Ellen Beall was a Richmond friend of Bettie's, not otherwise identified.

69. In December 1863 Butler promulgated an order that Norfolk civilians must take an oath of allegiance to the United States. Whether or not to comply became the great issue in Norfolk. Those who took it were regarded as traitors by those who did not.

70. W. N. Starke did obtain his majority May 11, 1864, to rank from Feb. 19. All appointments of officers required the approval of the Confederate Senate.

71. As previously noted (n. 28), Venable remained on the staff throughout the war.

72. George and Wick are Taylor's two little brothers, George Washington Taylor, aged eleven, and Wickham Taylor, aged twelve.

73. Lewis D. Crenshaw was a wealthy Richmond resident and a Saunders family friend. Taylor family tradition is that Bettie Saunders stayed with the Crenshaws during the war. Perhaps she did between May 1862 and August 1863, but thereafter Taylor's letters show that she was living in her own place with "Coz Mary." Nevertheless she was a frequent visitor, as the present passage implies, and stayed with them when Coz Mary was away. The list of Taylor's pallbearers suggests that the Taylors remained friends with the Crenshaws (and their boarders the Pettys) till the end of their days.

   Mr. Crenshaw is often referred to in the letters as "Mr. C."

Chapter 3: In Camp at Orange

1. Charles Marshall was the other longtime personal staffer of R. E. Lee, along with Taylor, Venable, and Chilton. He joined the staff as major and ADC March 1862. He was promoted lieutenant colonel in May 1864, and had the honor of being the only officer to accompany Lee to the McLean house at Appomattox, to meet Grant for the surrender.

2. As previously noted, Taylor had been made a lieutenant colonel on January 15, 1864.

3. Miss Lee is one of Lee's daughters—Mary, Agnes, or Mildred.
4. Miss Bettie Brander is evidently a Richmond belle—possibly the sister of Captain Thomas A. Brander (b. 1839, in Richmond), commander of Letcher's battery.
5. Baynie is Baynham Baylor Tunstall (b. 1840), the older sister of Alec Tunstall, and oldest child of Dr. Robert B. Tunstall. She was the girlfriend of Taylor's brother Rob ("R. T."), but was trapped in Norfolk for the duration. They were married January 1866.
6. As colonel of the Eighteenth Massachusetts, James Barnes took part in the Peninsula campaign and was made a brigadier general in November 1862. Wounded at Gettysburg, he was posted to garrison and prison duty for the remainder of the war. Evidently at this time he was a subordinate of Butler in Norfolk.
7. Lunsford L. Lomax was colonel of the Eleventh Virginia Cavalry until Gettysburg, after which he commanded a cavalry brigade under Fitzhugh Lee. He became a major general in November 1864, for a time commanding Early's cavalry. After the war he served as president of the Virginia Polytechnic Institute, and when he died in 1913, he was the last but one of the Confederate major generals.
   "Robinson river" is actually Robertson River (see map 3).
8. John C. Breckinridge, who was vice president under Buchanan and a U.S. senator, fought in the West at Shiloh, Vicksburg, Chickamauga, and Missionary Ridge. Transferred to the eastern theater, he accompanied Early in his raid on Washington in 1864. Following Cedar Creek, he rejoined Lee, then was appointed Secretary of War in 1865.
9. All these people are Selden first cousins of Bettie. Miles, Lizzie, Mrs. Heth, and Mrs. Rodman (recently escaped from Norfolk without her husband) are all siblings. Coz John is from another brood.
10. J. Calvert Petty was the oldest child and only son of Hannah Petty. He had just turned seventeen and was seeking to join the army. He eventually joined the Norfolk Light Artillery Blues, which followed Lee in all the campaigns of 1864 and 1865. He surrendered at Appomattox as the quartermaster sergeant of the Blues.
11. Colonel J. J. Garnett was indeed removed from his command (see chap. 1, n. 90), but John Saunders was assigned to a position in Savannah. He was not happy there and continued to pester Taylor for a post in the Army of Northern Virginia, but his hopes were never realized.
12. On February 6 the Federals crossed the Rapidan in strength to probe the Confederate position south of the river. That night they returned to the north bank.
13. W. Palmer Saunders (b. ca. 1843) was the youngest of Bettie's brothers to serve in the war. In August 1861 he was appointed Acting Midshipman, CSN. Until September 1862 he was either serving in the

water defenses of Norfolk and Richmond or in training on the school ship *Patrick Henry* at Richmond. For the next fifteen months he was posted as midshipman to the CSS *Chicora* in Charleston Harbor, where he witnessed the assault on Fort Wagner (chap. 1, n. 99). Throughout he was agitating unsuccessfully for appointment to a seagoing cruiser or some other action post. In December 1863 he returned to the *Patrick Henry*, but weeks later was selected by Commander John Taylor Wood to serve on an expedition against Union gunboats at New Berne, North Carolina. At last he saw action, but already, at the very time Taylor was penning these words, Palmer was dead. S. P. Mallory to Palmer Saunders, August 14, 1861, WHT Papers; Captain Frank Buchanan CSN to Palmer Saunders, December 19, 1861, WHT-SH; B. Forrest to Palmer Saunders, September 3, 1862, WHT-SH; Palmer Saunders to Martha S. Saunders, December 11, 1863, WHT Papers; John Taylor Wood to Martha S. Saunders, February 7, 1864, WHT Papers.

14. Despite the successful naval operation, the Confederate Army's attempt to recapture New Berne failed.

15. Before the war (in 1853 and 1858), Joseph C. Ives, as a lieutenant of U.S. Army Engineers, was a pioneer explorer of Arizona and Southern California. He joined the C.S. Army and from November 1861 to March 1862 was captain and chief engineer on Lee's staff. He was promoted in April to lieutenant colonel and made an aide to President Davis, his post at this time, and to the end of the war. Smith, "Mormon Exploration."

16. In this case the "sister" is young Pattie, with whom Walter had a joking romantic relationship.

17. Norwood, along with Howard's Neck and Elk Hill, was the third country place frequented by Walter and his friends on leave. This plantation was not in Goochland, but in Powhatan County across the James, about halfway down to Richmond from "the Neck." (See map 2 and fig. 11.) It was an ancestral Heth estate, owned by Nancy R. K. Selden, second wife of Miles Cary Selden, Sr. His grown children, Bettie's cousins Miles, Lizzie, Mrs. Heth, Mrs. Rodman, etc., all made their stepmother's home their own during the war years. Christian and Massie, eds., *Homes and Gardens in Old Virginia*, 125–27.

18. Colonel of the First Maryland Infantry (C.S. Army), then a brigadier, Arnold Elzey took part in Jackson's Valley campaign in 1862. Critically wounded during the Seven Days, on his partial recovery he was promoted major general and given command of the Department of Richmond, where he organized a local defense brigade of government clerks and employees.

19. Benjamin F. "Beast" Butler had ordered a raid against Richmond for the purpose of releasing Federal prisoners held there. The expedition, which

failed, involved the skirmish at Bottom's Bridge on the Chickahominy described by Taylor.

20. Stephen Dodson Ramseur, a North Carolinian, graduated from West Point in the class of 1860, commanded the Forty-ninth North Carolina Infantry, and rose rapidly in the Army of Northern Virginia, where he had the reputation of being one of the best fighters as brigade and division commander. He became the youngest graduate of West Point to attain the rank of major general in the Confederate army. At Cedar Creek on October 19, 1864, he was wounded for the fourth time, this time mortally. Sheridan had him brought to his headquarters at Belle Grove, a nearby plantation, where Ramseur expired the next day, surrounded by his former West Point classmates. Gallagher, *Stephen Dodson Ramseur*, 48–49 and passim.

    Mrs. Ramseur, nee Ellen "Nellie" Richmond, was a Taylor acquaintance.

21. "Bob" is Robert Taylor, husband of Lelia (see chap. 2, nn. 62–63).

22. George Edward Tayloe (b. Roanoke, Virginia, 1838) graduated V.M.I. in 1858, and was thus a schoolmate of Taylor. At this point in the war he was lieutenant colonel of the Twenty-second Virginia, becoming a full colonel January 1865. His bride was Delia Smith Willis.

23. Bettie's brother, Palmer, was killed February 2, 1864, in an attack on the Federal gunboat *Underwriter* in the Neuse River near New Berne, North Carolina, which resulted in the capture of the vessel. In his report of the affair, Stephen Mallory, Confederate Secretary of the Navy, referred to Palmer Saunders as "a gallant and promising" young officer, "who fell in a hand-to-hand conflict on the enemy's decks." *O.R.N.*, vol. 9, 454. Commander Benjamin P. Loyall to Martha S. Saunders, February 6, 1864, WHT Papers; William Sheppardson to Bettie Saunders, April 11, 1864, WHT Papers.

24. This is Commander John Taylor Wood, CSN, who also held the equivalent army rank of colonel. He led several similar expeditions against Union gunboats, and later in 1864 commanded the cruiser *Tallahassee*.

25. Along with the war and his love for Bettie, Walter's deep religious sensibility is a theme of these letters. In the context of this deeply religious response to the news of Palmer's death, it seems appropriate to append an excerpt from a letter recording Palmer's burial. The letter, dated "C.S.S. 'Raleigh,' Wilmington, April 11, 1864" is to Bettie Saunders from Assistant Surgeon William Sheppardson, CSN, an Alabaman and the medical officer on the *Underwriter* expedition. WHT Papers.

    I was sent up to Swift Creek Village with the wounded, and took his body along with me. The next day quite a number of the people of the neighborhood came in and I announced to them the funeral would take place that evening at 4 p.m. Hearing there was a Protestant minister in the settlement I sent for him to officiate; but he declined, fearing the Yankees would revenge themselves upon him when we were gone. I had a coffin made, put him in it myself (for I had no one to assist me), had a grave dug in a family inclosure nearby, and announced, as before, the hour of the funeral. Quite a number of people assembled, and followed us to the grave. I had my prayer book with me, and read the Catholic service for the dead, after which a friend and myself knelt by the grave and in silence offered up the prayers of our church. The people around seemed much impressed: the women wept. I saw the grave closed and carefully marked, and then we walked sadly back to the temporary hospital I had established. I was very sorry I was unable to procure a clergyman of his own faith; for I knew it would be much more gratifying to his friends. I hope, however, the part I took may be understood as coming from the heart, prompted entirely by the strong religious feelings which ever belong to those zealous in my own peculiar faith. For your sake I would have had it otherwise: for my own I am better satisfied as it was. (William Sheppardson to Bettie Saunders, 11 Apr. 1864, WHT Papers)

26. About half of Taylor's letters to Bettie Saunders for which envelopes survive are addressed c/o Thomas Selden, Richmond Arsenal, no doubt in order that they might be delivered by military couriers. In the Selden genealogies the best candidate for this man is Thomas Selden (b. 1826), Bettie's first cousin and son of John A. Selden of "Westover" and Charlotte; but there are indications in the letters that he is the younger brother of Mary Selden Knox ("Coz Mary"); the genealogy, which is sketchy for her branch of the family, lacks such a brother. Selden, *Samuel Selden*, 248.
27. Here Taylor is quoting Hebrews 2:6 (KJV).
28. No such "doleful" letter can be identified: perhaps Bettie destroyed it. The regular Sunday letter which Walter should have written January 3, before he went on his January leave, is missing.
29. Colonel Chilton.
30. B. B. is Bettie Brander.
31. In February 1864 Davis appointed Bragg chief military advisor to the president.
32. Lieutenant General "Fighting Dick" Ewell, commander of the Second Corps and ranking officer in Lee's absence.
33. "Old Turner" is most likely William Mason Turner, Assistant Surgeon, CSN, stationed at Richmond and evidently Bettie's immediate boss. In an exchange of letters concerning Palmer, Bettie calls him "Cousin

William." His sister Ellen later married Bettie's brother John. William Mason Turner to Bettie Saunders, March 4, 1864, WHT Papers; Bettie Saunders to William Mason Turner, March 20, 1864, WHT Papers.

34. The reference is to 2 Corinthians 11:23, "Are they ministers of Christ? (I speak as a fool) I am more. . . ."

35. Walter here recalls two visits to the Treasury Building where Bettie worked signing notes, November 1862 to November 1863. The first visit, when she rejected him, was most likely in early 1863. The second visit, when she was friendly and wished to go on rides with him, was during his furlough of September to October 1863, when they became engaged.

36. Bob T. is Robert Taylor (see chap. 2, n. 62). Fluvanna is the Virginia county immediately west of Goochland.

37. For Preston see chap. 2, n. 32. Taylor's comment here is uncharacteristic.

38. Promoted lieutenant general May 31, 1864, Jubal A. Early took command of the Second Corps of the Army of Northern Virginia from an ailing Ewell. Shortly thereafter Lee dispatched him on the raid against Washington. Later he was defeated in the Valley by Sheridan's overwhelming numerical superiority. At the end of the war, he temporarily fled to Mexico. On his return he became the first president of the Southern Historical Society, whose *Papers* have long been considered among the most important sources on the Civil War. He died in 1894, an unreconstructed rebel to the end.

39. On Sunday, February 28, 1864, Kilpatrick left his camp at Stevensburg north of the Rapidan with 3582 men, six guns of the U.S. Horse Artillery, eight caissons, three wagons, and six ambulances, for a long-expected raid on Richmond. His advance party of some 500 troopers was commanded by Colonel Ulric Dahlgren. As a diversion incident to the main raid Sedgwick's Sixth Corps occupied Madison Courthouse, and Custer's cavalry advanced almost to Charlottesville. On Monday, February 29, Dahlgren cut the Virginia Central Railroad just after Lee's train had passed. The raiders were repulsed at the Richmond defenses and Dahlgren was killed.

40. The Dahlgren raid.

41. Tom Selden at the Richmond Arsenal.

42. This is Colonel Chilton, who was about to leave the staff.

43. Having failed to penetrate the Richmond defenses, most of the raiders escaped eastward toward the Peninsula. Dahlgren, himself, was ambushed and killed.

44. Chilton had been confirmed by the Senate as brigadier general February 16, 1864, to rank from December 21, 1863. He had first been recommended for this promotion in March 1863, to rank from October 20, 1862.

    He soon reconsidered, accepted the promotion, and was transferred.

He was not replaced as chief of staff, so Taylor's worries about a new boss were needless.

45. Rev. Rodman had signed Butler's loyalty oath, an act that may have helped precipitate his forced resignation as pastor of Christ Church, Norfolk, the following April 9, in favor of Rev. Okeson.

    The Sharp clan was headed by William W. Sharp, attorney and bank president. They lived across town from the Taylors, and were most likely members of St. Paul's Church, closed by order of Butler and combined with Christ Church. If so, they had an interest in removing Rodman and installing their own minister, Rev. Okeson, as pastor of the combined parishes (see chap. 1, n. 42). Altar Guild, *St. Paul's Church*, 31, 37–38, 41.

46. This is Major John A. Harman, who was Stonewall Jackson's quartermaster from May 1861, becoming chief quartermaster of Jackson's Second Corps. He stayed in this post as the corps passed into the hands of Ewell (May 1863) and Early (June 1864), to the end of the war.

47. Theodoric A. Williams, a bookkeeper in Norfolk in 1860, enlisted in Co. G, Sixth Virginia, as a private. He was promoted to sergeant major of the regiment, then to lieutenant of Co. K, his position from 1862 to Appomattox.

48. Sally Mitchell is not in the Norfolk records; she may have been a Richmond friend of Bettie's.

49. Captain Robert W. Bowden (b. 1808) was a cashier in a Norfolk bank until 1859, but appears to have died before the 1860 census. He was the father of Maggie Bowden Nash.

50. This is Bishop John Johns (1796–1876), bishop of the Episcopal Diocese of Virginia from 1862 to 1876. Brydon, *Highlights*, 46–47.

51. Lee, accompanied by Longstreet, conferred with Davis regarding proposals for the invasion of Tennessee or Kentucky. Bragg was also in Richmond, but Johnston and Beauregard were not present.

52. Colonel L. B. Northrop, the controversial commissary general of the Confederacy, was finally relieved February 15, 1865, as the war was drawing to a close. Much criticized, he faced the almost insurmountable task of feeding not only the Confederate armies but the tens of thousands of Union prisoners as well.

    Longstreet's Corps, then wintering in East Tennessee, was returned to the Army of Northern Virginia in April.

53. This is Emperor Napoleon III of France (1851–70).

54. When Grant was moved east to be commander in chief, W. T. Sherman did assume command of the Federal forces in the West. After his successful Atlanta campaign and March to the Sea, Sherman appears

frequently in the Taylor letters as he advanced north through the Carolinas toward Virginia in 1865.

55. Littimer is a valet in Dickens' *David Copperfield*. In chapter 21 David says of Littimer, "I felt particularly young in this man's presence." Dickens, *David Copperfield*, 244.

56. The two aides are Venable and Marshall.

57. Rev. John H. D. Wingfield, pastor of Trinity Episcopal Church in Portsmouth (adjacent to Norfolk), refused to take Butler's loyalty oath, was arrested, imprisoned, then forced to work on the streets in a chain gang to pay the costs of his imprisonment. His church was confiscated and used as a hospital for black troops. In March, after three months, Wingfield, a broken man, agreed to take the oath, and moved away to Baltimore upon his release.

      Rev. Dr. George D. Armstrong, a Presbyterian minister of Portsmouth, did take the oath. He was the author of a proslavery book and a particular target of Butler's. Butler decided that his oath was insincere, on the basis of reported anti-Northern remarks and his refusal to pray for Lincoln in his church. So he also ended up in jail and, in March, on the chain gang—no doubt filling the slot vacated by Wingfield. Marshall, *Private and Official Correspondence*, vol. 3, 510, 564; vol. 4, 54–56.

58. Page is Taylor's younger brother, Lucien Page Taylor. Born 1844, he took no part in the war.

59. This is Robert B. Baylor (b. 1839), one of Taylor's Norfolk contemporaries. He enlisted as a private in Co. G, Sixth Virginia, and was captured at Burgess Mill October 27, 1864. After the war he became a physician.

60. Aunt Alex is Sarah Alexina Taylor Page (1819–1902), the younger sister of Taylor's father and the wife of Brigadier General Richard Page. After the evacuation of Norfolk she moved with her family to Petersburg.

61. John C. Taylor was working as a staffer in Richmond, but it is uncertain which was "his" general. Their uncle, General Richard Page, had offered John a position as his ADC in Mobile. John accepted the offer (see n. 62).

      General Order No. 27, March 2, 1864, of the Adjutant and Inspector General's Office (National Archives) concerns placing soldiers in units from their home states, and does not touch the status of generals. Taylor may have got the order number wrong.

62. Richard Lucien Page (1811–1905) was a first cousin of General Lee's, as well as Taylor's uncle by marriage. He entered the U.S. Navy as a midshipman in 1824 and rose to commander by 1855. Most of his tours of duty after 1839 were in Norfolk, and in 1841 he married Alexina Taylor. In 1860–61 he served as naval aide to Governor Letcher of

Virginia. Upon secession he was appointed commander, CSN, and ordnance officer of Norfolk. When Norfolk was evacuated he moved the ordnance operations of the Norfolk Navy Yard to Charlotte, North Carolina, and commanded there until March 1864. Thereupon he was assigned the rank of brigadier general C.S. Army, and given charge of the sea defenses of Mobile. At "Uncle Page's" request John Taylor served two tours as his aide, April 1861 to May 1862, and March to August 1864.

63. Miss Mollie was a cousin of Bettie's, probably Mary Ann Selden (b. 1836), one of the John A. Selden family.

64. Taylor alludes here to Lieutenant John Hobson, who held the undemanding post of Goochland County recruiting officer from January to May 1864. During this time he lived at home.

65. Zebulon B. Vance, War Governor of North Carolina 1862–65. On May 4, 1861, at the outbreak of hostilities, he was elected captain of the Ashville Rough and Ready Guards of the Fourteenth North Carolina Regiment. Subsequently he became colonel of the Twenty-Sixth North Carolina, which he commanded during the Seven Days fighting outside of Richmond. As governor, he jealously guarded the supremacy of the civil authorities of the state, at times proving a thorn in the side of Jefferson Davis. After the war he served in the United States Senate from 1879 until his death in 1894. See Dowd, *Life of Zebulon B. Vance.*

66. During the winter religious revivals were sweeping the camps, and thousands of soldiers were converted. J. Jones, *Christ in the Camp,* 312–52.

67. Lydia Sylvester Taylor had two brothers, Richard (b. 1829) and Keeling (b. 1842). Keeling, only two years her junior, was most likely her favorite. A "buffalo" was a southern deserter or fugitive from the draft.

68. The devil, for Julia, is President Lincoln.

69. Traditionally the Episcopal church has a communion service the first Sunday of the month, with "morning prayer" on the other Sundays. The latter service includes a required prayer "for the President of the United States, and all those in authority." The text includes these lines: "Most heartily we beseech Thee, with Thy favor to behold and bless Thy servant the President of the United States . . . grant (him) in health and prosperity long to live," etc. So reads the "hateful northern service." The Confederate service was identical, except that "Confederate States" was substituted for "United States." Butler required all ministers to say "United States" or lose their parishes. Protestant Episcopal Church, *Book of Common Prayer,* 17.

70. Julia refers here to her and Duncan's parents, Duncan Robertson, Sr. (1800–1887) and Julia A. F. Robertson (1804–86). The only other member

of the family was Julia's older sister Helen Sheffield (1830–1912). Maybe she and her husband George are "the children" referred to.

71. Willoughby is not identified.

72. Mary Newton is Georgeanna Newton (b. 1837), and "White" Jones is Lieutenant John Pembroke Jones, CSN. Georgeanna is the eldest daughter of Cincinnatus and Martha Newton, members of a large and old Norfolk family. J. Pembroke Jones, also a Norfolker, was in the U.S. Navy before the war. During much of the war he was stationed in Georgia, commanding first the tug *Resolute* and then the ironclad *Georgia*. At this time (spring 1864) he commanded the ironclad *Raleigh* at Wilmington.

73. The code terms and initials in the preceding passage have been identified from internal evidence and evidence from other letters. The only individual not identified in previous notes is Ellie Henderson. This is possibly a son of James L. Henderson, a commander in the CSN, who as a U.S. naval officer lived next door to the Robertsons before the war. Harrison, "Sheridan's Raiders," 286, 291.

74. Only one corps had in fact joined Grant: Burnside's Ninth Corps. See n. 83.

75. The wife of the uxorious Theodoric Williams was from Leesburg, Virginia, a town thirty-five miles northwest of Alexandria, near the Potomac. Except during Lee's brief invasions of the North, this part of Virginia was always behind enemy lines.

76. Colonel Robert Ould (1820–81) had been since 1862 chief of the Bureau of Exchange of Prisoners. Colonel John E. Mulford was his Federal counterpart.

   The prisoner exchange cartel broke down in 1864 because the Union could spare its captured men, whereas the man-poor Confederacy would be hurt by the cessation of exchanges. Nevertheless they did continue on a limited basis. Miller, *Photographic History,* vol. 7, 101, 103.

77. See n. 50 for the bishop.

78. M. Gay is not identified. No Gay family appears on Norfolk census rolls.

79. This is most likely Captain W. N. Starke.

80. Martin Luther Smith (1819–66), West Point 1842, entered the C.S. Army as a major, was colonel of the Twenty-first Louisiana for a while, then was promoted brigadier and major general during 1862. He was in charge of the fortifications at New Orleans and at Vicksburg. He served as Lee's chief engineer only from April to July 1864, then took charge of the defenses of Mobile.

   Lee had suggested his eldest son, Custis, for the position, but tactfully presented two other names, one of which was General Smith. The latter was chosen by the Secretary of War.

81. At Winchester on April 8, 1864, two companies of Confederate cavalry, estimated at 100 men, attacked a Federal detachment of 107 troopers from the Sixth and Seventh West Virginia Cavalry and 44 from the Fourteenth Pennsylvania Cavalry. The Union force was commanded by Major Hanson W. Hunter of the Sixth West Virginia. In his report he stated that "the advance of the rebels was so rapid and spirited" that he was compelled to give way. His superiors, however, took a different view of the affair, accusing Hunter of "criminal carelessness" and the "disgraceful and dastardly flight of 151 men before less than 100 rebels." As an indication of his perfidy it was stated, in a delightful touch, that "The Union women who witnessed the affair wept in shame." The Northern loss in prisoners was twenty-seven. Hunter was duly arrested and his commanding officer, Brigadier General Averell, was instructed by Major General Sigel "to cause charges to be preferred against him, preparatory to his trial by court-martial." Eventually Hunter was discharged upon expiration of service, August 18, 1864. *O.R.*, vol. 33, 262–65, 833, 836.

82. Rev. Dr. George Peterkin, rector of St. James Episcopal Church, Richmond, and father of Taylor's friend Lieutenant George Peterkin. Peterkin, *Handbook,* 255.

83. Following the debacle at Fredericksburg in December, 1862, Burnside was superseded in command of the Army of the Potomac by Hooker and transferred to the West, where he was given command of the Department of the Ohio. There he was instrumental in holding East Tennessee for the Union and repulsed Longstreet's attempt to capture Knoxville in November, 1863. Early in 1864 he was transferred back to the East and charged with recruiting his old Ninth Corps, whose numbers had dwindled to less than four thousand men present for duty. As a mobilization center he selected Annapolis, Maryland. This corps was "the troops from the West concentrated at Annapolis." The corps, during the winter, was substantially increased in strength though hardly to the extent of the fifty thousand men originally proposed by the War Department. As Grant prepared for the spring campaign of 1864, he advised Burnside to be ready to move from Annapolis with his corps by April 20. When the corps left on the 27th and reached Virginia, Grant assigned it temporarily the task of defending his supply line, the Orange and Alexandria Railroad, Burnside establishing his headquarters at Warrenton Junction. Marvel, *Burnside,* 222, 338–47; Grant, *Personal Memoirs,* vol. 2, 140.

84. Brigadier General Judson Kilpatrick (U.S. Army) was in command of the Third Cavalry Division, a portion of which he had sent under Colonel Dahlgren toward Richmond in February 1864. Born 1836, he graduated West Point 1861, and was promoted brigadier April 1863. Subsequent to

the Dahlgren raid he joined Sherman in the Atlanta campaign and was seriously wounded at Resaca. He commanded Sherman's cavalry in the latter's March to the Sea. A controversial character, he had a reputation as a Don Juan, and when Hampton's cavalry surprised his headquarters early one morning during the campaign in the Carolinas, he is alleged to have been in the embrace of a woman and to have escaped in his underwear.

85. The report proved unfounded, for Warren, with the U.S. Fifth Corps, was still at Culpeper Court House as late as May 1, expecting orders hourly to move forward. Nevins, ed., *Diary of Battle*, 365.

86. Tom is most likely Tom Selden, who worked at the Richmond Arsenal. Mr. Adams would be a coworker.

87. That is to say, back with the Army of Northern Virginia.

88. The Confederate victory at Sabine Crossroads or Mansfield, Louisiana, occurred on April 8, 1864.

89. Rev. Charles Minnegerode was rector of St. Paul's Episcopal Church in Richmond, and most likely Bettie Saunders's pastor at the time. Taylor would also have known him well, as he served as rector of Christ Church, Norfolk, 1853–56. At war's end he was to officiate at their wedding.

90. Nathan Bedford Forrest captured Fort Pillow on the Mississippi on April 12, 1864. He was accused of "massacring" the black troops of the defending force. Regarded by many as the greatest cavalry commander the war produced, the feats of Forrest's independent commands in the West during 1863 and 1864 became legendary. He was made a lieutenant general in 1865.

   The capture by Hoke of Plymouth, on the North Carolina coast, the first major success in the area for a long time, occurred April 20, 1864. Robert F. Hoke was a North Carolinian who served with the Army of Northern Virginia from the Seven Days to Chancellorsville. He was severely wounded in Early's attack on Marye's Heights during the latter battle and was recalled to North Carolina, where his forces captured Plymouth. Promoted major general, he rejoined Lee with his division for the defense of Petersburg.

91. See n. 57, for the case of Rev. Armstrong.

92. For Rev. Rodman's troubles, see n. 45.

93. See n. 72, for identification of this couple.

94. Two Wilmers are celebrated in the annals of the Episcopal church in Virginia: Rev. Richard H. Wilmer, who assumed the see of Alabama in 1862, and Rev. Dr. Joseph P. D. Wilmer, who became bishop of Louisiana after the war. This is presumably the latter. He had been pastor of St. Paul's church in Norfolk briefly in 1838. Altar Guild, *St. Paul's Church*, 41; Agee, *Facets of Goochland*, 121.

95. Burnside took his Ninth Corps from Annapolis to join Grant in late April.

96. Taylor apparently refers to the command of all the armies of the Confederate States. Lee was not given such a post until February, 1865, too late to have much bearing on the outcome of the war.

97. The preceding passage is further indication that the watershed with Bettie occurred during Walter's early fall leave of 1863.

98. Here we learn that Coz Mary works at the Treasury Department, Bettie's former place of employment, and that her home is Columbia, South Carolina. According to the genealogies, Mary Knox had three sisters, an older one named Bettie, and two younger, Eliza and Marie. Selden, *Samuel Selden*, 233.

99. Apparently Bettie has taken a second job at the Conscript Bureau.

Chapter 4: The Wilderness to the Crater

1. With his irrepressible optimism Taylor puts a rosier glow on the outcome of the battles than the facts justified.

2. Bella was wounded, so that Taylor had to change horses (see intro., p. 18), but she recovered, and Taylor was riding her again by August.

3. At the head of the York River.

4. On May 24, Lee suffered a violent intestinal attack brought on, Freeman thought, by bad food and long hours. Freeman, *R. E. Lee*, vol. 3, 356.

5. Breckinridge, after his victory over Sigel at New Market in the Valley, had joined Lee with some 2,400 infantry.

6. Edward (Ned) Willis (b. 1840) attended West Point, but left to become adjutant of the Twelfth Georgia in July 1861. He was on Stonewall Jackson's staff in late 1862, but returned to lead the Twelfth Georgia as a lieutenant colonel. He was promoted full colonel in January 1863. During the whole campaign of May 1864 he commanded Pegram's brigade until he was mortally wounded at Bethesda Church, dying May 31. He is said to have been recommended for promotion to brigadier general, but he died before his commission reached him.

7. In his letter Taylor makes no mention of Grant's decisive repulse at Cold Harbor June 3, 1864.

8. General David Hunter's army then invading the Shenandoah Valley. He was finally turned back at Lynchburg after a brutally destructive raid that included the burning of V.M.I.

9. Philip H. Sheridan, formerly an infantry general under Grant in the West, was made commander of all the cavalry by Grant when he became commander in chief in April. On June 7 his cavalry corps launched a major raid on the Virginia Central Railroad, as Major

General David Hunter began moving up the Shenandoah Valley. In a bold division of force Lee dispatched the bulk of his cavalry under Hampton and Fitz Lee to intercept Sheridan. Though outnumbered two to one, Hampton, in the phrase of Freeman, defeated Sheridan "handsomely" at Trevilian Station on June 11–12, removing the threat of a junction between Hunter and Sheridan, who retreated to the White House, on the Pamunkey, preparatory to crossing the James to join Grant. Later, Sheridan achieved total victory over Early in the Valley, in March 1865, after a six month campaign. Freeman, *R. E. Lee,* vol. 3, 405; see also Starr, *Union Cavalry in the Civil War,* vol. 2, 57–67.

Note that here "cousin John" is John Hobson.

10. Lieutenant Colonel Briscoe G. Baldwin, after serving as major and AAG to General Rodes in 1862 and briefly commanding an arsenal, was selected as Lee's ordnance officer, with the rank of lieutenant colonel, in November 1862. He replaced E. P. Alexander who moved up to the command of the First Corps artillery. Baldwin remained on Lee's staff till the end of the war.

11. Taylor has Grant on the Peninsula, north of the James River, even though the day before Grant had begun to shift his army south of the James, thus threatening Petersburg.

12. It is surprising that Taylor makes no mention of the extremely narrow margin by which Petersburg, with its vital rail connections, was saved from capture on June 15–16.

13. John Saunders's assignment in Savannah had ended, and he was heading north to Richmond.

14. Violet Bank, the Shippen family place, just north of the Appomattox River, was to be Lee's headquarters for over three months during the siege of Petersburg.

15. Thus Grant's first attempt to extend his lines westward to the south of Petersburg and seize the railroad to Weldon, North Carolina, was frustrated.

16. In compliance with Meade's instructions, Brigadier General James H. Wilson, with the Third Division of Sheridan's cavalry corps, set out June 22, 1864, on a raid against the Southside and Richmond and Danville Railroads. After destroying considerable portions of the track of both roads and wrecking the junction of the two at Burkeville, Wilson found the bridge of the Danville road over the Roanoke River at Roanoke Station strongly guarded. In consequence he retreated by a southerly route, designed to bring his men back to the Weldon Railroad near Reams Station. There, however, Lee had set a trap for the raiders. Caught between the converging columns of Hampton's and Fitz Lee's cavalry and Mahone's infantry, Wilson was routed, losing 1000 prisoners, thirteen guns, his wagon train and the loot seized on the raid.

Sheridan, *Personal Memoirs*, vol. 1, 438–45, 454; for a detailed account of Wilson's raid see Starr, *Union Cavalry*, vol. 2, 179–207.

    Mr. Gordon is most likely a landowner near Burkeville.

17. Rev. Platt was a local Petersburg Episcopal minister. We learn in a later letter that his church was called St. Paul's, not to be confused with St. Paul's in Richmond or Norfolk.

18. Many Norfolk families (including the Saunders family) had evacuated when the Federal forces occupied the city in May 1862, and not a few (including Taylor's) had escaped since. Though Taylor longed for an end to their exile, he never allowed himself to think that only a Southern surrender would make it possible.

19. Mr. Crenshaw's patient was Colonel Baldwin (see n. 10). Baldwin survived, as a later letter attests. This brother was likely John Brown Baldwin, a Virginia congressman at this time, but also a colonel of home reserves.

20. Robertson Taylor had been wounded at the Wilderness, May 6, 1864. He never returned to active duty.

21. E. Porter Alexander was chief of artillery of the First Corps of the Army of Northern Virginia. He was previously on Lee's staff as chief of ordnance (June to November 1862). At Gettysburg, it was his guns which opened the action on the third day, prior to Pickett's charge. Long after the war in 1907 he published *Military Memoirs of a Confederate*, regarded as one of the finest works of its kind.

22. I.e., Jubal Early's raid threatening the Federal capital.

23. Raphael Semmes, commander of the celebrated raider, CSS *Alabama*, was the beau ideal of a commerce destroyer, outwitting and running down his opponents time after time. During his career on the high seas he captured eighty-two merchantmen valued at more than $6,000,000, virtually exterminating the United States carrying trade. The *Alabama* was finally brought to bay and sunk off Cherbourg on the French coast by the U.S.S. *Kearsarge* on June 19, 1864. Semmes was rescued and, on his return to the Confederacy, was assigned as a rear admiral to the command of the tiny James River squadron. When Richmond was evacuated in April, 1865, he turned his men into a naval brigade, which he surrendered at Greensboro, North Carolina, as part of Johnston's army. Johnson and Malone, eds., *Dictionary of American Biography*, vol. 16, 579–82.

24. There were two naval Sinclair brothers in Norfolk: Commander Arthur Sinclair (b. 1810) and Lieutenant George Terry Sinclair (b. 1817). Arthur (whose wife Lelia was evidently a relation of Taylor's) had three sons old enough to go to war: Arthur (b. 1837), William (b. 1841), and George T. (b. 1843). The father and all three sons joined the Confederate Navy. Terry Sinclair (and his wife Mary) had one son, William (b. 1848), old

enough to join up and be a midshipman late in the war. In any case, it is Mrs. Terry Sinclair's sixteen-year-old son Willie who is listed as lost. It turns out later that Captain Arthur and his son Lieutenant Arthur (whom Taylor inquires about here) were also lost (see chap. 6, n. 12).

25. This is Dr. Francis L. Galt (1833–1915), Surgeon, CSN (ex-USN). As his dates show, he in fact survived the sinking of the *Alabama*.

26. Walter appears to be reading through Bettie's last letter, responding to whatever catches his eye—thus the offhand query about Tom Taylor's mother-in-law sandwiched in between serious discussions of the *Alabama* and Early. There is a Lieutenant Thomas Taylor, ADC to General Hampton, who might be the man mentioned, but there are several other possibilities.

27. I.e., St. Paul's, Richmond, where he had no doubt attended services with Bettie, and Christ Church, Norfolk.

28. Mag is Margaret Bowden Nash (see chap. 1, n. 67). This Lizzie is Eliza Waller Blacknall (b. about 1838), daughter of Dr. George Blacknall, USN/CSN (who had died in January 1862); she was one of Walter and Bettie's Norfolk set. Liz's widowed mother Emma, with Liz and her three little sisters, moved at the evacuation to "Tower Hill," a plantation in Sussex County, southeast of Petersburg, which was Emma's childhood home and now belonged to her brother, Captain William N. Blow, C.S. Army. Emma Blacknall to Martha S. Saunders, January 8, 1864, WHT Papers.

29. Probably the rumored death of Grant.

30. Brigadier General Henry A. Wise, an irascible character whose military career was undistinguished, served with Lee in West Virginia in 1861 and with Beauregard at Charleston. In 1864 he was in Anderson's corps at Drewry's Bluff. A former Governor of Virginia, he was a brother-in-law of General Meade: Meade and Wise had indeed married sisters from Philadelphia.

31. Taylor's contempt for these rumors is ironic. In fact the Federals *were* mining under the Confederate works at Petersburg. When they exploded their mine, it resulted in the famous "Crater" and the battle therein (July 30, 1864).

32. "Tower Hill" was the wartime residence of the Blacknalls (see n. 28). It was on the Nottoway River about thirteen miles southeast of Stony Creek Station, right on the route of Wilson's retreat to the James (see map 1). Lizzie Blacknall's news was rather out of date—the Wilson raid occurred in June (see n. 16). Emma Blacknall to Martha S. Saunders, January 8, 1864, WHT Papers; *O.R. Atlas*, plate 74, no. 1; Stephenson, *Old Homes in Surry and Sussex*, 53–55.

33. Again, the mining was all too real, as Taylor would discover in five days.

34. Taylor doubtless refers to the battle of Atlanta, fought July 22, 1864. Hood's "success" was illusory, for, in fact, he failed in his objective of turning and defeating the left wing of Sherman's army threatening Atlanta.

John B. Hood distinguished himself as regimental, brigade, and division commander of the Army of Northern Virginia in all its campaigns through Gettysburg, where he was severely wounded in the arm. He accompanied Longstreet to the West in September 1863 and lost a leg in the fighting at Chickamauga. Appointed lieutenant general after the battle, he commanded a corps of the Army of Tennessee under Joseph E. Johnston during the Atlanta campaign, and when the latter was relieved of command, Hood replaced him as a full general (with temporary rank). After the fall of Atlanta he led the Army of Tennessee on its disastrous Nashville campaign in the closing months of 1864.

35. On July 20, 1864, at Stephenson's Depot, six miles north of Winchester, Ramseur, without adequate reconnaissance, attacked the enemy force. Two of his regiments in Lewis's brigade behaved badly and were routed with a loss of four guns and some 250 men. Gallagher, *Stephen Dodson Ramseur*, 130–35.

36. Though an intense believer, Taylor rarely condemned others for their "godlessness"—in keeping with the Christian precept to "judge not." He charitably refrained from "I told you so's" when Early's entire command was annihilated a few months later.

37. The battle of the Crater, July 30, 1864.

38. Elsewhere in the letters the name is spelled out as Mr. Macreary. He is the landlord of the house in Richmond in which Bettie lived from October 1863 to March 1865.

39. Kate Wilson's brother is most likely Lieutenant St. Julien Wilson, Company C, Sixty-first Virginia, who was mortally wounded at the Crater and died the next day. Howard S. Wright, son of a Norfolk street inspector, was fourth sergeant of Company G and later regimental ensign of the Sixth Virginia. His wounds were mortal. The two Hills are Third Corporal John T. Hill and Corporal Chandler W. Hill, both of Company G, Sixth Virginia. Both men recovered and Chandler Hill went on to the end at Appomattox. Captain Wood Williams led Company E of the Sixth Virginia. Duncan Robertson, Harry Williamson, Alec Tunstall, and Robert Taylor have been identified in previous notes.

40. See chap. 2, n. 55.

41. John Saunders was to report to Chilton in Richmond July 25. Thereupon Chilton assigned him to several inspection tours of military facilities in the Carolinas and Georgia.

Brigadier General Richard Page was commander of Fort Morgan, south of Mobile; John C. Taylor was his aide. Fort Morgan was besieged by Admiral Farragut from August 5, when Farragut forced an entrance into Mobile Bay and virtually destroyed the Confederate flotilla opposing him. Page held out in a heroic defense until August 23.

42. Chimborazo was a famous hospital near Richmond, of vast size for its day.

43. Major Alexander Stark's two younger sisters were Mary, aged twenty-one, and Helen, aged nineteen.

44. Probably Tom Selden, Taylor's postal intermediary at the Richmond Arsenal.

45. On August 14, Field's division of the First Corps was attacked in its position north of the James. Going to Chaffin's Bluff in person the next morning, Lee ordered up two brigades from the Petersburg front and made other dispositions to meet the threat. The next day Field's front was temporarily broken, but a counterattack recovered the works and the crisis ended as quickly as it had arisen.

46. See chap. 1, n. 80.

47. See chap. 2, n. 19.

48. Colonel John S. Mosby, the celebrated Rebel partisan, had an independent command 1864–65. He operated from a base behind enemy lines in northern Virginia. His attack was not followed by a major Confederate victory in the Valley.

49. For Chimborazo see n. 42. Harry Williamson had four sisters, Anne, Sarah, Virginia, and Elizabeth. Elizabeth, the wife of Dr. Robert B. Tunstall, is most likely the one at Chimborazo. Dr. Paige is not further identified.

Chapter 5: Stalemate at Petersburg

1. Chaffin's Bluff was on the north bank of the James River about ten miles downstream from Richmond (see map 4). It was a key position in the Richmond defenses.

2. A brilliant student at West Point, W. H. C. Whiting was given a battlefield promotion to brigadier general at First Manassas by President Davis. As an engineer he played a leading role in making Ft. Fisher, near Wilmington, such a formidable fortress. When it fell in 1865 he was wounded, taken prisoner, and brought to Ft. Columbus in New York harbor where he expired some two months later, said to be the last general officer in the Confederate army to die of his wounds. Somewhat unstable, he was accused of drinking.

3. Walter had agreed to delay their wedding until after the war; here he is asking whether Bettie would consider an armistice to be equivalent to war's end.

4 Brigadier General William N. Pendleton, chief of artillery of the Army of Northern Virginia. An Episcopal minister in civil life, he was an intimate friend of Robert E. Lee, who served on the vestry of his church in Lexington, Virginia, after the war.

5. In chapter 2 of Dickens' *Oliver Twist* is the famous scene where the starving young Oliver has the temerity to ask for seconds of gruel at the poor house. Dickens, *Oliver Twist*, 13.

6. One of the three railroads leading south and west from Petersburg, this one runs due south to cross the Roanoke River at Weldon, North Carolina. In the battles for the Weldon Railroad from August 18 to 25 the Federals lost over 8,000 men (killed, wounded, and missing), mainly at Globe Tavern and Reams Station.

7. At which General McClellan was nominated as the Democratic Party's candidate for the presidency.

8. Regarding John Saunders, see chap. 4, n. 41.

9. Fort Morgan had fallen to the Federals on August 23. John C. Taylor remained a prisoner of war until April 1865.

10. Atlanta was surrendered to Sherman September 3, 1864.

11. John C. Fremont, pathfinder in the far West and Republican nominee for president in 1856, was appointed by Lincoln a major general in the Regular Army in 1861 and placed in command of the Department of the West in St. Louis. His most important active service in the field was in the Valley campaign of 1862, where he proved no match for Stonewall Jackson. Fremont in 1864 was the nominee of a new third party, the Radical Democracy, made up of extreme Radical Republicans.

12. Psalm 18:27, Cranmer version. This translation is used only in the psalter at the back of the Episcopal prayer book, a treasured copy of which was surely among Taylor's effects. Protestant Episcopal Church, *Book of Common Prayer*, 371.

13. John Bowdoin Cocke (1836–89), V.M.I. class of 1856, was the son of General Philip St. George Cocke (d. 1861). His parents' home, "Belmead," was on the south bank of the James, in Powhatan County, above Norwood.

14. Bettie was rooming on her own at this point. Her period of independence was brief, however, as Cousin Mary moved back in with her in November.

15. Bettie has evidently turned down Walter's suggestion that they wed after the hoped-for armistice.

16. The photograph is a cluster of individual portraits rather than a group shot. It is reproduced here in the illustrations (fig. 9).

17. Mr. Gibson like Mr. Platt is a local Petersburg Episcopal minister.

18. An observation that reflects Walter's at times unreasoning optimism (and his desire to spare Bettie anxiety), rather than the true state of

affairs. The Weldon Railroad had been lost, the Confederate line was being stretched almost to the breaking point, and, in Freeman's words, "the fortunes of war, which in this case were but another name for numerical inferiority, were running strongly against Lee." Freeman, *R. E. Lee,* vol. 3, 491.

19. Judge John A. Meredith of Richmond had ordered a man discharged from the army on the grounds that he was a justice of the peace. Endorsing over to Lee documents pertaining to the case, Taylor wrote, "Plenty of your able-bodied fellows will be elected magistrates and thus get out of service. With enrolling officers to exempt and detail and judges to discharge we are in a sad way." *O.R.,* ser. 2, vol. 4, pt. 3, 660.

20. City Point was the site of Grant's supply base on the James River below Richmond.

21. Wade Hampton, in his so-called "Beefsteak Raid" to the rear of Grant's supply base at City Point, brought off 2486 beeves for the hard pressed Confederate commissary—helpful, but hardly compensation for the loss of the Weldon Railroad. Boykin, *Beefsteak Raid.*

22. The Howlett house was located near Drewry's Bluff just south of the James River at the left or northern end of the Howlett Line that stretched south to the Appomattox River. From the river the lines continued south and west around Petersburg to the Weldon Railroad. (See map 4.) Walter thus is claiming that the entire Confederate line south of the James is awaiting Bettie's arrival.

23. This is the obnoxious W. N. Starke, not Alexander "Sandy" Stark.

24. Brigadier General Walter H. Stevens was chief engineer of the Army of Northern Virginia from August 28, 1864 to the end, replacing M. L. Smith. Born in New York, Stevens was a West Pointer (1848) but resigned from the U.S. Army to become a captain of engineers for the South. In 1862 he was briefly chief engineer on Lee's staff, as a major. Since then, he had been a colonel in charge of building Richmond's defenses, until he took up his prior post again, with the rank of brigadier.

25. Legislation to enroll blacks in the army was adopted by the Confederate Congress and signed by President Davis March 13, 1865, too late to be of any effect.

26. Among the prisoners taken at Fort Harrison (see n. 27) was Taylor's brother, Major Richard C. Taylor, who was badly wounded. Another was Lieutenant Colonel John Minor Maury, the commander of the Chaffin's Bluff defenses. Born in 1825, he served in the U.S. Navy from 1848 to 1861. He entered the Confederate Navy but transferred to the Army in August 1861, to become a captain of artillery. In August 1862 he was promoted lieutenant colonel and given his present assignment.

He was not released from prison until July 1865.

The third prisoner mentioned, Jack Ellerson, has not been identified.

27. Fort Harrison, one of the main bastions of the Confederate defense line north of the James River, was captured by Federal forces September 29, 1864. Ruins of the fort and portions of the adjacent lines have been preserved and are open to the public.

28. "The Springs" is Amelia Springs, about fifty miles west of Petersburg in western Amelia County. In a letter John A. Selden writes of renting the whole hotel there for his family for the month of April 1862. The Springs were likely the traditional watering place for the John Selden family. Mrs. Rodman, of the Miles Selden family, was no doubt visiting her first cousins there. Miles, her brother, is planning a visit to their family home at Norwood. "Jones" is unidentified. John A. Selden to Martha S. Saunders, March 31, 1862, WHT Papers.

29. Williams C. Wickham was with Jeb Stuart in all of his important battles, as colonel of the Fourth Virginia Cavalry. He was made a brigadier general September 1, 1863, but resigned his commission November 9, 1864, and served the latter part of the war in the Confederate Congress. He had a distinguished railroad career after the war as president of the Virginia Central and subsequently the Chesapeake & Ohio.

30. Alexander S. "Sandy" Pendleton was the son of Lee's friend and minister General W. N. Pendleton (see n. 4); his wife was Kate Corbin Pendleton. Colonel Pendleton had served on Jackson's staff as adjutant and was a great favorite of Stonewall's. Mortally wounded September 22, 1864, during Sheridan's decisive victory over Early at Fisher's Hill in the Valley, he left his young wife and a son, born after his death.

31. Mrs. Heth is Miles's sister.

32. Miss Sue is called Sue Randolph in other letters. Otherwise she is unidentified.

33. Captain Iredell has not been identified. From portions of letters 83 (chap. 5) and 107 (chap. 6) not included in this volume we learn that Captain Thomas had been convalescing from wounds in Richmond, and that he was being regularly visited by Bettie's friend Ellen Beall. Wounded in early October, he was still invalided in March 1865. Lacking his first name, we cannot identify him.

34. "Miss Ellen" is Ellen Beall, "French" is Maggie French, according to other letters. Miss Mattie is mentioned only here. They may all be Bettie's fellow clerks at the Surgeon General's Office. Dr. Williams is Surgeon Thomas H. Williams, C.S. Army. He began the war as a medical officer with Beauregard, but after August 1863, was stationed in Richmond.

35. Hunter Saunders at this point was an aide to General A. L. Long, who commanded General Early's artillery. Captain John M. Gregory was

Long's ordnance officer. Captain Mann Page was a brigade inspector with Early's Second Corps.

36. Major Wood is an unidentifiable Richmond staffer. Note the complex arrangements Walter is willing to make for Bettie's friends and relatives. Not only is a courier assigned to take charge of Hunter's package, but three officers and another man are dragooned into helping: first Wood takes the package from the courier. A soldier will pick it up from him and transport it to Mann Page in the Valley. Page will get it to Captain Gregory, who will deliver it at last to Private Saunders.

37. Ramseur was killed October 19, 1864 at Cedar Creek. Gallagher, *Stephen Dodson Ramseur*, 165.

38. John Withers worked at the Adjutant General's Office in Richmond from September 1861 on, first as a major and after 1863 as a lieutenant colonel.

39. At Burgess Mill, October 27, 1864, a Federal thrust toward the Southside Railroad was turned back by Confederate forces. Mahone's old brigade, including the Sixth Virginia, was in the thick of the fighting.

40. "Keswick" is the home place of Bettie's uncle, Dr. William Allen Selden, Martha Saunders's third brother. It is in the northeastern corner of Powhatan County, on the south side of the James. (See map 2 and fig. 12.) Dr. Selden was an army surgeon stationed in Richmond. Ryan, " 'Keswick'—in Powhatan," 56–61.

41. For the first time in the letters Walter refers to Bettie as his future wife. Yet not even in the last letter before the wedding (let. 110) does he dare spell out the word.

42. This is the Beasley house on High Street, to which headquarters were moved November 1. They remained there only a few weeks: about November 25 Taylor moved them again to "Edge Hill" (see let. 91).

43. After two months Taylor has received prints of the photo he sat for in early September (see n. 16 and fig. 9). In occupied Norfolk, Julia might be considered a "threat to national security" if she were discovered with a photo of Lee's staff in her possession.

44. See chapter 4, n. 38.

45. Edward P. Galt (b. 1845) is the son of Alexander Galt (1793–1855), postmaster of Norfolk. He appears to be a recent arrival in Petersburg.

46. The "north side" is the Chaffin's Bluff area on the north side of the James, where Walter was stationed during the month of October. There he was only ten miles from Richmond, and was able to visit Bettie every week. On the other hand, during six months in Petersburg (thirty miles south of Richmond) he has been able to get to Richmond only once or twice, and has never connected with Bettie. (See map 4). Thus his longing for the north side.

47 Back in December 1863 (see let. 37) Ellen Beall asked for autographed documents of Lee and Jackson. Perhaps Taylor ended up organizing a whole scrapbook for her.

48. The freewheeling blockade runner, Major Ben Ficklin, wrote his friend, General Heth, in the winter of 1864–65, that if the latter would send a wagon to Wilmington he would fill it up with good things. "I did so," recalled Heth. "The wagon was loaded with canned goods, coffee, tea, sugar, hams, twenty gallons of brandy, and the same amount of whiskey, a dozen boxes of fine cigars, etc. By the same wagon he sent me a black horse which was the admiration of the army." Morrison, ed., *Memoirs of Henry Heth*, 192–93.

49. Once again, Mrs. Harriet S. Heth and Lizzie Selden were sisters, first cousins of Bettie.

50. Rev. Patterson has not been identified.

51. "Coz M" is Moses Robertson. He left Norfolk for Liverpool in early 1864. In April his seat on the board of Christ Church was declared vacant, due to his absence abroad. His wife Annie had joined him by September. It is unclear how he is related to Taylor.

52. There was a skirmish at Stony Creek Station on the Weldon Railroad, December 1, 1864.

53. Archibald Gracie was colonel of the Forty-third Alabama, then a brigade commander at Chickamauga. One day in November, 1864, Lee carelessly stood up on the parapet of a trench in Gracie's presence on the Petersburg lines. Realizing the danger from sharpshooters, Gracie threw himself between Lee and the enemy. Both were pulled back over the works before either was hit. But on December 3, Gracie was killed in the Petersburg trenches by a fragment of shrapnel, while observing the enemy through a telescope.

54. On December 7, 1864, the Federals undertook a raid down the Weldon Railroad. Hampton and his cavalry were dispatched in pursuit and Hill's corps ordered in support. The Union troops reached Belfield but were unable to cross the Meherrin River or destroy the bridge there. They succeeded, however, in tearing up some sixteen miles of track. On the way back they were harassed by Hampton, who took some prisoners, but Hill was unable to overtake the raiders and they returned unpunished.

55. Bettie Page (b. 1846) was the oldest child of Alexina and General Richard Page. The General had been a prisoner of war since August, and would continue to be until the following July. His family, evacuees from Norfolk, had set up housekeeping in Petersburg. Bettie, who was just at "coming out" age, was surrounded by young military admirers, and clearly Walter also found his vivacious young cousin attractive.

56. Starke is W. N. Starke (chap. 2, n. 9), and Jno Cocke is John B. Cocke (chap. 5, n. 13). Buck Cooke is Giles Buckner Cooke of Portsmouth, his father being the postmaster there. He was born 1838 and graduated V.M.I. in the class of 1859, one class behind Taylor. He served as ADC or AAG to Generals Philip St. George Cocke, Bragg, Samuel Jones, and Beauregard, being promoted major April 1863. In November 1864 he joined Lee's staff as AA and IG. After the war, he entered the ministry, being ordained an Episcopal minister in 1874. He was a friend of Taylor's from boyhood till death. Funeral notices, W. H. Taylor funeral, WHT Papers.

57. "The dear Captain" is Julia's code name for Bettie.

58. "Tower Hill," the Blacknall residence in Sussex County, was in the path of the December 7 Federal raid down the Weldon Railroad (n. 54). Lizzie Blacknall, twenty-four, the only grown child of her widowed mother, must have had to cope with the invading troops. This was the second time Tower Hill had been pillaged in six months (see chap. 4, n. 32).

59. Mrs. Wells was a Petersburg hostess, cousin to Taylor's friend Maggie Nash.

60. Taylor's great experiment of attempting to "keep the sabbath holy" by not working on Sunday, begun in April (see chap. 3, lets. 54, 56, 57), no doubt failed once the campaign season was under way. Yet he was still attempting to at least work *less* on Sundays.

61. The mistress of Elk Hill was Elizabeth Williamson Harrison (see chap. 2, n. 16).

62. In all probability the salute was prompted by the decisive Northern triumph in the battle of Nashville, December 15, 1864.

63. Taylor surmised correctly: Butler's abortive attack on Fort Fisher (which defended Wilmington, the Confederacy's last major port) occurred December 23–25, 1864, days after the writing of this letter. Gragg, *Confederate Goliath*, 44–53, 62–98.

64. Most likely it was Lizzie Blacknall who was chosen Queen. Captain Atwell is W. H. Atwell, of the Seventh Tennessee, on General Heth's staff.

65. Mr. Rodman's only "home" now is his father-in-law's house, Norwood. Lizzie Selden is his young sister-in-law (about twenty). She was to marry Thomas Rodman (his brother?) in 1868.

    Whether Rodman ever actually served in the army is uncertain.

66. Cousin John A. Selden, Jr., at this point was ordnance officer of Cutshaw's artillery battalion, which remained with Early in the Valley until late January. Jennings Wise, *Long Arm of Lee*, vol. 2, 920; Brock, "Paroles of the Army of Northern Virginia," 17.

67. Surgeon J. S. D. Cullen (since February 1863) was medical director of Longstreet's First Corps.
68. Mrs. Kittie Hobson recently had a baby boy, which she named Mahew, after her brother-in-law, a war casualty (see let. 31).
69. Maria Octavia was the youngest daughter (b. 1845) of John A. Selden, who had made his home near Charlotte Courthouse, Virginia, since 1862.

Chapter 6: Edge Hill to Appomattox

1. Walter was finally given a two-week furlough, starting about January 10, 1865, which he apparently extended a week to about February 1. The lack of any letters for some three weeks before the furlough suggests that he was able to see Bettie in Richmond at least briefly then, and he may have seen her again at the end of January. Yet the bulk of his furlough was spent among her family and friends at Norwood, Elk Hill, and Howard's Neck, while she remained in Richmond.
2. Charlie is Charles Selden (b. 1847), the youngest of the Miles Selden family. He had enlisted in the Fourth Virginia Cavalry as a private the previous November, on his seventeenth birthday, and had already seen action with Early in the Valley. He escaped Appomattox with other cavalrymen and headed for North Carolina. He was paroled in Richmond in June and made his way to Texas. He eventually returned to Virginia, married, and became a railroad executive.
3. Lillie and Cannon as well as baby Mahew are Kittie and John Hobson's children. Lillie (Mary M. in the records) is about six and Cannon about four. Mary is Bettie's youngest sister, aged about thirteen.
4. This is Dr. William Allen Selden (b. 1808), youngest brother of Miles C. Selden, Sr., and John A. Selden of Norwood and Charlotte, respectively. His house is "Keswick" (see chap. 5, n. 40).
5. Mollie and Maria are two of Bettie's Selden cousins from Charlotte, Virginia (see chap. 2, n. 2; chap. 3, n. 63).
6. Young Dr. Clarence Garnett was about to marry Mary W. Garnett after a long courtship (see chap. 1, n. 43; and chap. 2, n. 40).
7. The scene of action was Hatcher's Run. The battle, February 5–6, 1865, resulted in a slight further extension of the Federal left towards the two vital supply lines still in Confederate hands—the Southside and the Richmond and Danville Railroads.
8. Major General George H. Thomas, whose Army of the Cumberland had virtually destroyed Hood's Army of Tennessee in December 1864, did not come east to reinforce Grant.

   Though born in Virginia, Thomas remained loyal to the Union. He fought at Shiloh, and at Stone's River, and his stubborn stand on

300

Snodgrass Hill saved the Northern army at Chickamauga, winning for him the sobriquet, "The Rock of Chickamauga." He commanded the Army of the Cumberland in the Atlanta campaign. When Sherman departed from Atlanta on his March to the Sea, he left Thomas to deal with Hood's army. Thomas defeated the latter decisively at Franklin and Nashville.

9. Another example of Taylor's unwillingness to face reality.

10. Lieutenant Colonel Frederick W. Sims, chief of the Railroad Bureau, was often referred to as superintendent of railroad transportation. The Chief Quartermaster General was Alexander R. Lawton of Georgia, former brigadier in the Army of Northern Virginia. Seriously wounded at Sharpsburg, he was given command of the Quartermaster General's Department in the fall of 1863. Execution of the Railroad Act was in the hands of the Quartermaster Department. The individual referred to by Taylor as "the Inspector" was, in all probability, Lieutenant Colonel Henry E. Peyton, Assistant Adjutant and Inspector General, a member of Lee's staff at the time. Black, *Railroads of the Confederacy*, 166–69.

11. General John Pegram of Richmond is not to be confused with Captain John C. Pegram of Norfolk (chap. 1, n. 64). General Pegram (1832–65), West Point 1854, resigned a lieutenant's commission in the U.S. Army to join the C.S. Army, and was quickly promoted to lieutenant colonel. He was with Kirby Smith on the invasion of Kentucky in 1862, and commanded a brigade of cavalry at Murfreesboro, and a division of Forrest's corps at Chickamauga. Transferred back to the Army of Northern Virginia he was given an infantry brigade in Early's division of the Second Corps. He was wounded in the Wilderness and subsequently served in the Valley, taking over Rodes's division on the death of the latter at Winchester. He was promoted major general. Back with Lee on the Petersburg front he was killed at Hatcher's Run.

   On January 18, 1865, St. Paul's Episcopal Church in Richmond was crowded for the fashionable wedding of the renowned Baltimore beauty, Hetty Cary, to the dashing John Pegram. Just three weeks to the day later, in the same spot, the bride knelt by the coffin of her husband. He was killed February 6, the day after Taylor wrote this letter. Korn, *Pursuit to Appomattox*, 19.

12. See chap. 4, n. 24, for the Sinclair family. No doubt Taylor received this new information from Semmes himself, during the visit noted at the start of this letter. Lelia Thompson Sinclair was the wife of Captain Arthur and mother of young Arthur Sinclair, both lost at sea.

13. On February 6, 1865, Robert E. Lee was approved General in Chief of the military forces of the Confederate States.

14. Vastly outnumbered by Sherman's army that was rapidly advancing northward through the Carolinas, Joseph E. Johnston had suggested that

Lee bring a portion of the Army of Northern Virginia to North Carolina, so that they could face Sherman together, hopefully destroy or cripple him, and then, united, return to face Grant in Virginia. Govan and Livingood, *Different Valor*, 352.

15. Cousin Kittie and Mrs. Hobson are the same person. In the context of her close relation to Bettie, Walter refers to her informally, but as his hostess she becomes "Mrs."

16. Walter's urging that Bettie make plans for the eventuality belies his insistence that Richmond will not fall. His statements here come perhaps less from naive optimism than from his determination to spare Bettie anxiety about the war. As it turned out, the imminence of Richmond's fall and the prospect of her consequent vulnerability were what induced her to accept Walter's plea that they be married without delay.

17. This is most likely Jane Douthat Selden (b. 1831) of "Weyanoke," Charles City County, on the Peninsula. She was the second wife of Dr. William Selden, a man twenty-three years her senior (see n. 4). Indications are she was briefly using Bettie's place as a pied-à-terre in Richmond.

18. Partly because of lack of forage in the Valley, much of Early's artillery was shipped by rail via Gordonsville or Lynchburg to the Richmond defenses, at the end of January. Selden's unit, Cutshaw's battalion, was included in this move.

    Early himself, with a handful of cavalry, did not return to Richmond until the middle of March. Jennings Wise, *Long Arm of Lee*, 919–20; Early, *Autobiographical Sketch*, 466.

19. See n. 7. The battle of Hatcher's Run near Dinwiddie Court House occurred February 5–6, 1865, during the worst weather of a bad winter. The military results were negligible, but the men in the ranks suffered severely from hunger and exposure.

20. From the Hampton Roads conference, which had come to nothing. Lincoln held firm for restoration of the Union, and Davis, just as adamantly, insisted on independence for the South.

21. Jennie is Virginia P. Barron (1844–88) of the prominent Norfolk seafaring family. She was something of an orphan, as her mother had died in the yellow fever of 1855, and her father, Captain Samuel Barron, CSN, was spending the war in Paris as a Confederate agent. She had one older brother, Samuel, Jr., a lieutenant in the Navy. Captain Edward R. Baird was from Essex County, on the Rappahannock northeast of Richmond. He was an aide to General Pickett through most of the war. Taylor's judgment notwithstanding, they were soon married.

22. If Bettie Saunders had in fact visited Petersburg without coming to see Taylor, in the face of his desperation to be with her, such insensitivity

toward him is hard to square with the happiness of their married relationship, to which all witnesses attest. Let us assume Taylor's sources were in error.

Calvert Petty was evidently expected home on leave.

23. Lee retained command of the Army of Northern Virginia; Johnston was given command in the Carolinas.

24. Actually there were three corps, the remnants of Stewart's, Cheatham's, and S. D. Lee's corps of the Army of Tennessee, the latter now under the command of Carter Stevenson. In all they represented less than 5,000 men. Horn, *Army of Tennessee*, 422–26.

25. On the very day of this letter, Beauregard instructed Hardee to evacuate Charleston. On February 17 the evacuation took place. Five days later, without having engaged Sherman, Beauregard was replaced by Johnston.

26. The Confederate Congress was at this time debating the question of conscripting blacks into the army (see chap. 5, n. 25). Taylor is astute to realize that such a soldiery is essentially incompatible with slavery.

27. Walter Taylor's brothers Dick, captured at Fort Harrison September 29, 1864, and John, captured at Fort Morgan August 23, 1864, were both scheduled to be exchanged. Bettie recalled that they arrived in Richmond just before its fall, in time for her and Walter's wedding (see appendix 1).

28. "Our flock" is Taylor's mother and younger brothers and sisters. Lincolnton is about thirty miles northwest of Charlotte, North Carolina.

29. For months Lee had been warning the administration that Richmond might have to be abandoned.

30. Lee's respect for constituted authority was well known. He deferred in important matters of policy to the president, who, under the terms of the Confederate Constitution, was commander in chief of the armed forces.

31. On February 22, Lee, with the reluctant acquiescence of President Davis, put Joseph E. Johnston in charge of operations in the Carolinas.

32. A sheer flight of fancy at this stage on the part of Taylor.

33. In the last months of the war Custis Lee commanded a Richmond defense force made up of clerks and other government employees. Freeman in *R. E. Lee*, vol. 3, 537–38, places him with Lee at his Richmond house. Evidently up to that time he was able to assist his father on his Richmond visits. After that, perhaps because his presence was required on the front lines, he was no longer in town and unavailable.

On the retreat to Appomattox he was attached to Ewell's Corps and captured at Sayler's Creek on April 6, 1865.

34. After chiding Bettie for restraining her expressions of affection, Walter all but admits, by his hesitation, that he has been less than candid in his own letters in expressing his true views of the state of the Army and the Confederacy.

35. As Taylor later all but spells out, his outrage at deficient "leaders" is directed primarily at President Davis (let. 110).
36. On March 2 Sheridan had overwhelmed the remnants of Early's forces in the Valley at Waynesboro. He was now free to join Grant, thus lengthening even further the already hopeless odds faced by Lee.
37. Bettie had such an iron determination to keep her feelings for Walter hidden that she often appears hard-hearted indeed. Her obsession with privacy has, as we see here, robbed posterity of her side of the correspondence, which would have shed light on many obscure passages in the Taylor letters. We are thankful that she at least preserved his letters—or in any case most of them (see chap. 3, n. 28).
38. En route from the Shenandoah to join Grant at Petersburg, Sheridan's cavalry passed through Goochland County. He was based at Columbia, just west of the Goochland line, on March 9, and from there his raiders ravaged western Goochland. On March 11 he moved on to Goochland Courthouse, remaining there for two days to plunder the central part of the county.

    A long letter of Mrs. E. W. Harrison, hostess of Elk Hill, has been published, describing in great detail the impertinence, thievery, pillaging, and brutality of the Northern troops who passed through her plantation on March 9. She also mentions that they occupied "Mr. Hobson's place" (Howard's Neck) that same day, leading away "all the negroes" (p. 287). She adds, "Mr. John Hobson's horses and mules were taken but nothing else. Kittie succeeded in getting her bacon and valuables across the river" (p. 292). Harrison, "Sheridan's Raiders," 285–94.
39. Grant had communicated to Lee that authority to discuss the subject of peace rested solely with President Lincoln. He, therefore, turned down Lee's suggestion of an interview.
40. At the battle of Averasborough on March 16 Lieutenant General William J. Hardee briefly checked a portion of Sherman's advancing army. Outflanked, he withdrew during the night and resumed the retreat. Hardee was a corps commander in the Army of Tennessee in the Atlanta campaign of 1864, known to the troops as "Old Reliable." After President Davis, in an ill-fated move, replaced Johnston as commander of the Army of Tennessee with John B. Hood, Hardee had a stormy and often bitter relationship with the latter. On September 28, 1864, at his own request, Hardee was relieved of command of his corps and ordered to proceed to Charleston and assume command of the Department of South Carolina, Georgia, and Florida. There, under Beauregard's overall direction as commander of the Military Division of the West, he succeeded in evacuating the garrison of some 10,000 men from Savannah before the city fell to Sherman in December 1864. He proceeded to Charleston, remaining there until Sherman's march

northward through the Carolinas outflanked the city and caused its evacuation February 17, 1865. Subsequently Hardee rejoined Beauregard on the retreat in North Carolina and continued to serve under him, until Beauregard himself was replaced by Joseph E. Johnston. Williams, *P. G. T. Beauregard*, 236–56; also see Nathaniel Hughes, *General William J. Hardee*; Roman, *Military Operations of General Beauregard*, vol. 2, 312.

41. A false report. Sherman needed no reinforcements.
42. So Walter finally proposes immediate marriage, but only for the purpose of her protection and with apologies for his "selfishness." Despite her previous reserve, Bettie responded with alacrity (see n. 54), and they were married two weeks from the date of this proposal.
43. Aunt Alex Page lives in Petersburg (see chap. 5, n. 55). Her notion that Petersburg would be a refuge after the fall of Richmond is a little naive. Apparently Taylor's mother has decided to stay in Richmond, but his sister Mary Lou demurs. Recall that under similar circumstances three years before, his mother had decided to stay in Norfolk, while Mary Lou left.
44. On the very eve of marriage and after 100 letters—and then only by "a slip of the pen"—Bettie finally addresses Walter as "dear W."
45. Maria O. Selden (now nineteen) has been visiting her cousin Bettie in Richmond. She may be planning to pass through Petersburg on her way home to Charlotte County.
46. Butler had been transferred from the southeast Virginia theater late in 1864 (in order to attack Fort Fisher), and left the administration of Norfolk to his "minions," Generals Weitzel and Shepley. Brigadier General George F. Shepley was Weitzel's chief of staff. Originally colonel of a Maine infantry regiment, as Butler's protégé he became post commander of New Orleans, then military governor of Louisiana. Voted out of office in a "free" election, he came up to Norfolk in the spring of 1864 to take over administrative duties when Butler went into the field. In April 1865 he was made military governor of occupied Richmond until July, when he resigned.

    Sallie Bloodgood, presumably a Norfolk woman, has not been identified.
47. Sheridan's forces reached White House on the Pamunkey on March 19.
48. Dr. T. H. Williams (see chap. 5, n. 34), Bettie's superior at the Surgeon General's Office, has apparently informed her of an evacuation plan for SGO personnel.
49. In December Mr. Macreary, Bettie's landlord, gave her notice that he was selling his house (let. 94, in a deleted passage). Bettie moved out about March 1 and stayed with the Crenshaws a while, intending to move into new rooms.

    Evidently, the move never took place, as she was still living with the Crenshaws on April 2; the couple in fact did "adjourn to Mrs.

Crenshaw's sitting room" for their wedding ceremony. (See appendix 1.)

50. As Lee's aide Taylor was constantly bombarded by requests for favors from friends and relatives. Dealing with Bettie Saunders's relatives (here her cousin by marriage John Hobson) was especially difficult for him. Here Taylor proposes going to Lee, and through him to General Fitz Lee, who as commander of the cavalry corps, had authority over John Hobson's unit, the Fourth Virginia Cavalry.

    Be it to an aide or a general, family connections were the lubricant that enabled the Army of Northern Virginia to function—at least so it appears from these letters.

51. John Saunders married Ellen Burne Turner a few days before Walter and Bettie were wed. Taylor's courtship was not the only one hastened to a climax by the prospect of Federal conquest.

52. A perhaps unconscious allusion to "these are the times that try men's souls"—and aptly enough. Tom Paine wrote that line in December 1776, at a low point in the fortunes of the Continental Army, just before Washington "crossed the Delaware" to victory at Trenton. Taylor still hoped Lee could work a similar miracle.

53. Although Walter now knows that Richmond will have to be evacuated, he is still unable to imagine the end of the Army of Northern Virginia, and the Confederacy, that would quickly follow. Nor could he entertain the hope that he and Bettie could find happiness in a Virginia forcibly rejoined to the Union—as was to be the case.

54. Walter has received Bettie's consent to his marriage proposal (n. 42). Her acceptance was conditioned on the fall of Richmond. Indeed they waited to marry until April 2, the night before the Federals occupied the city. The separation he now envisages is after their wedding, when he would leave her in Richmond, while he rejoined the army. Such a separation did occur, but for less than two weeks. Taylor arrived back in Richmond with General Lee on April 15, six days after Appomattox.

55. President Davis. (See n. 35)

56. Taylor did receive permission to go to Richmond and marry Bettie Saunders. He was absent from his post probably less than twenty-four hours.

57. Six days before his wedding, Taylor still cannot spell out "wife," though he ventures to supply the first letter.

58. For John Saunders's wedding, see n. 51.

59. The attack on Fort Stedman, March 25, 1865. After an initial success, this final, desperate attempt to break the Union line, stretching thirty-seven miles from White Oak Swamp to Hatcher's Run, failed. (See map 4.)

Bibliography

Manuscript Sources

Eleanor S. Brockenbrough Library, Museum of the Confederacy, Richmond, Virginia. Letter of Robert E. Lee to Taylor, June 17, 1865.

National Archives, Washington, D.C. Confederate States Army, General Order No. 27, RG 109 (microfilm).

National Archives Branch Depository, Laguna Niguel, California. United States Census, 1850, 1860, 1870, Virginia, RG 29, Pub. Nos. M432, M653, M593 (microfilm).

Norfolk Public Library, Norfolk, Virginia. Christ Church Papers, Christ Church (Norfolk) Vestry Minutes 1828–1905 (microfilm). Saunders Family Papers. Walter Herron Taylor Papers.

Preston Library, Virginia Military Institute, Lexington, Virginia. Virginia Military Institute Archives. Letters. Class Reports.

Stratford Hall, Westmoreland County, Virginia. Walter H. Taylor Papers.

Virginia Historical Society, Richmond, Virginia. Joseph S. Bryan Papers. Chamberlayne Family Papers. John Singleton Mosby Papers.

Books

Agee, Helene Barret. *Facets of Goochland (Virginia) County's History.* Richmond: Dietz Press, 1962.

Alexander, E. Porter. *Military Memoirs of a Confederate.* New York: Charles Scribner's Sons, 1907.

Altar Guild of St. Paul's Church. *St. Paul's Church, 1832.* Norfolk, Va.: Altar Guild of St. Paul's Church, 1934.

Basso, Hamilton. *Beauregard, the Great Creole.* New York: Charles Scribner's Sons, 1933.

Bernard, George S., ed. *War Talks of Confederate Veterans.* Petersburg, Va.: Fenn and Owen, 1892.

Bigelow, John, Jr. *The Campaign of Chancellorsville.* New Haven, Conn.: Yale University Press, 1912.

Black, Robert C., III. *The Railroads of the Confederacy.* Chapel Hill, N.C.: University of North Carolina Press, 1952.

Blake, Nelson Morehouse. *William Mahone of Virginia.* Richmond: Garrett and Massie, 1935.

Boykin, Edward. *The Beefsteak Raid.* New York: Funk and Wagnalls, 1960.

Brydon, G. Maclaren. *Highlights along the Road of the Anglican Church*. Richmond: Virginia Diocesan Library, 1957.

Casdorph, Paul D. *Lee and Jackson—Confederate Chieftains*. New York: Paragon, 1992.

Chamberlain, Joshua L. *The Passing of the Armies*. New York: G. F. Putnam, 1914.

Chamberlaine, William W. *Memoirs of the Civil War*. Washington: Bryon S. Adams, 1912.

Chamberlayne, C. G., ed. *Ham Chamberlayne—Virginian*. Richmond: Dietz Printing, 1933.

Christian, Frances Archer, and Susanne Williams Massie, eds. *Homes and Gardens in Old Virginia*. Richmond: Garrett and Massie, 1950.

Clark, Walter, ed. *Histories of the Several Regiments and Battalions from North Carolina in the Great War, 1861–65*. 5 vols. Raleigh, N.C.: Nash Brothers, 1901.

Coddington, Edward P. *The Gettysburg Campaign*. New York: Charles Scribner's Sons, 1968.

Confederate States of America. *Journal of the Congress of the Confederate States of America, 1861–1865*. 7 vols. Washington, D.C.: Government Printing Office, 1904–5.

Connelly, Thomas L. *The Marble Man*. New York: Knopf, 1977.

Cooke, Giles B. *Just Before and After Lee Surrendered to Grant*. Houston: Houston Chronicle, 1922.

Corbin, Richard W. *Letters of a Confederate Officer to His Family in Europe during the Last Year of the War of Secession*. Paris: Neal's English Library, 1913.

Cox, William R. *Address on the Life and Character of Stephen D. Ramseur*. Raleigh, N.C.: E. M. Uzzell, 1891.

Craigie, William A., and James R. Hulbert, eds. *A Dictionary of American English on Historical Principles*. 4 vols. Chicago: University of Chicago Press, 1938–44.

Daniel, Frederick S. *Richmond Howitzers in the War*. Richmond, 1891.

Dashiell, T. Grayson. *A Digest of the Proceedings of the Conventions and Councils in the Diocese of Virginia*. Richmond: William Ellis Jones Publisher and Printer, 1883.

Davis, Burke. *Gray Fox: Robert E. Lee and the Civil War*. New York: Rinehart, 1956.

Davis, Jefferson. *The Rise and Fall of the Confederate Government*. 2 vols. New York: Appleton, 1881.

Dawson, Francis W. *Reminiscences of Confederate Service, 1861–1865*. Charleston, S.C.: News and Courier, 1882.

Dickens, Charles. *Oliver Twist*. 1837–39. Reprint, London: Everyman's Library, 1970.

Bibliography

_____. *Martin Chuzzlewit*. 1843–44. Reprint, Oxford: Oxford University Press, 1984.

_____. *David Copperfield*. 1849–50. Reprint, Cutchogue, N.Y.: Buccaneer Books, 1976.

Dowd, Clement. *Life of Zebulon B. Vance*. Charlotte, N.C.: Observer Printing and Publishing House, 1897.

Dowdey, Clifford. *Lee's Last Campaign*. Boston: Little, Brown, 1960.

_____. *Lee*. Boston: Little, Brown, 1965.

_____. *The Seven Days*. New York: Fairfax, 1981.

Dowdey, Clifford, and Louis H. Manarin, eds. *The War Time Papers of R. E. Lee*. Boston: Little, Brown, 1961.

Early, Jubal A. *A Memoir of the Last Year of the War for Independence in the Confederate States of America*. Lynchburg, Va.: Charles W. Button, 1867.

_____. *Autobiographical Sketch and Narrative of the War Between the States*. With notes by R. H. Early. Philadelphia: J. B. Lippincott, 1912.

Evans, Clement A., ed. *Confederate Military History, Extended Edition*. 19 vols. 1899. Reprint, Wilmington, N.C.: Broadfoot, 1987.

Flood, Charles Bracelen. *Lee, the Last Years*. Boston: Houghton Mifflin, 1981.

Freeman, Douglas Southall. *R. E. Lee, a Biography*. 4 vols. New York: Charles Scribner's Sons, 1934–35.

_____. *The South to Posterity*. New York: Charles Scribner's Sons, 1939.

_____. *Lee's Lieutenants*. 3 vols. New York: Charles Scribner's Sons, 1942–44.

Fremantle, A. J. L. *Three Months in the Southern States, April–June, 1863*. London: William Blackwood, 1863.

Gallagher, Gary W. *Stephen Dodson Ramseur, Lee's Gallant General*. Chapel Hill, N.C.: University of North Carolina Press, 1985.

Gordon, John B. *Reminiscences of the Civil War*. New York: Charles Scribner's Sons, 1903.

Govan, Gilbert E., and James W. Livingood. *A Different Valor*. New York: Bobbs-Merrill, 1956.

Gragg, Rod. *Confederate Goliath: The Battle of Fort Fisher*. New York: Harper Collins, 1991.

Grant, U. S. *Personal Memoirs of U. S. Grant*. 2 vols. New York: Charles L. Webster, 1885–86.

Hagood, Johnson. *Memoirs of the War of Secession*. Columbia, S.C.: The State, 1910.

Harrison, Constance Cary. *Recollections Grave and Gay*. New York: Charles Scribner's Sons, 1911.

Harrison, Walter. *Pickett's Men*. New York: D. Van Nostrand, 1970.

Henderson, G. F. R. *Stonewall Jackson and the American Civil War*. 2 vols. London: Longmans Green, 1898.

Hoke, Jacob. *The Great Invasion of 1863*. Dayton, Ohio: W. J. Shuey, 1887.

Horn, Stanley F. *The Army of Tennessee* Norman, Okla · University of Oklahoma Press, 1953.

Hughes, Nathaniel Cheairs, Jr. *General William J. Hardee*. Wilmington, N.C.: Broadfoot, 1987.

Hughes, Robert M. *General Johnston*. New York: Appleton, 1893.

Johnson, Allen, and Dumas Malone, eds. *Dictionary of American Biography*. 20 vols. New York: Charles Scribner's Sons, 1928–36.

Johnston, David E. *The Story of a Confederate Boy in the Civil War*. Portland, Ore.: Glass and Prudhomme, 1914.

Johnston, Joseph E. *Narrative of Military Operations during the Late War between the States*. New York: Appleton, 1882.

Jones, J. William. *Personal Reminiscences of Gen. Robert E. Lee*. New York: Appleton, 1876.

_____. *Christ in the Camp*. Richmond: B. F. Johnson, 1887.

Jones, Katherine M. *Ladies of Richmond*. New York: Bobbs-Merrill, 1962.

Jones, Samuel. *The Siege of Charleston*. New York: Neale, 1911.

Korn, Jerry, and the editors of Time-Life Books. *Pursuit to Appomattox, the Last Battles*. Vol. 25 of *The Civil War*. Alexandria, Va.: Time-Life Books, 1987.

Krick, Robert K. *Lee's Colonels*. Dayton, Ohio: Press of Morningside Bookstore, 1979.

Lee, Fitzhugh. *General Lee*. New York: Appleton, 1894.

Lee, Robert E., Jr. *Recollections and Letters of General Robert E. Lee*. New York: Doubleday, Page, 1904.

Long, A. L. *Memoirs of Robert E. Lee*. New York: J. M. Stoddart, 1887.

Long, E. B. *The Civil War Day by Day*. New York: Doubleday, 1971.

Longstreet, James. *From Manassas to Appomattox*. Philadelphia: Lippincott, 1896.

McCarthy, Carlton, ed. *Contributions to a History of the Richmond Howitzer Battalion*. 4 pamphlets. Richmond: Carlton McCarthy, 1883–86.

McClellan, H. B. *The Life and Campaigns of Major General J. E. B. Stuart*. Boston: Houghton Mifflin, 1885.

McGuire, Judith W. *Diary of a Southern Refugee*. Richmond: E. J. Hale and Son, 1889.

McKim, Randolph H. *A Soldier's Recollections*. New York: Longmans Green, 1910.

Marshall, Jessie Ames. *Private and Official Correspondence of Gen. Benjamin F. Butler, during the Period of the Civil War*. 5 vols. Norwood, Mass.: Plimpton Press, 1917.

Marvel, William. *Burnside*. Chapel Hill, N.C.: University of North Carolina Press, 1991.

Meredith, H. Clarkson. *Some Old Norfolk Families*. Norfolk, Va.: Tidewater Typography, 1976.

Bibliography

Miller, Francis Trevelyan. *The Photographic History of the Civil War.* 10 vols. New York: Review of Reviews, 1911.

Morris, Whit. *The First Tunstalls in Virginia.* San Antonio, Tex.: Clegg Company, 1950.

Morrison, James L., Jr., ed. *The Memoirs of Henry Heth.* Westport, Conn.: Greenwood Press, 1974.

Mosby, John S. *Stuart's Cavalry in the Gettysburg Campaign.* New York: Moffatt, Yard, 1908.

Murfin, James V. *The Gleam of Bayonets: The Battle of Antietam and R. E. Lee's Maryland Campaign, September 1862.* Baton Rouge: Louisiana State University Press, 1965.

Nevins, Allan, ed. *A Diary of Battle: The Personal Journals of Colonel Charles S. Wainwright 1861–1865.* New York: Harcourt Brace, 1962.

Norfolk City Directories:

Forrest, William S., ed. *The Norfolk Directory for 1851–1852.* Norfolk, 1851.

Fershaw, W. Eugene, ed. *Vickery's Directory for the City of Norfolk.* Norfolk: Vickery, 1859.

Norfolk City Directory, 1860. Norfolk, 1860.

Owen, William M. *In Camp and Battle with the Washington Artillery of New Orleans.* Boston: Ticknor, 1885.

Page, Thomas Nelson. *Robert E. Lee—Man and Soldier.* New York: Charles Scribner's Sons, 1911.

Pemberton, John C. *Pemberton, Defender of Vicksburg.* Chapel Hill, N.C.: University of North Carolina Press, 1942.

Peterkin, Bishop George. *A Handbook for the Use of the Members and Friends of the Protestant Episcopal Church.* Wheeling, W. Va.: Wheeling News Lithography, 1911.

Pickett, Lasalle Corbell. *Pickett and His Men.* Atlanta: Foote and Davies, 1899.

Porter, John W. H. *A Record of Events in Norfolk County, Virginia.* Portsmouth, Va.: Fiske, 1892.

Potts, Frank. *The Death of the Confederacy.* Ed. D. S. Freeman. Richmond: [privately printed], 1928.

Protestant Episcopal Church in the U.S.A. *The Book of Common Prayer.* New York: Oxford University Press, 1898.

Putnam, Sarah. *Richmond During the War.* New York: G. W. Carleton, 1867.

Rhoades, Jeffrey L. *Scapegoat General.* Hamden, Conn.: Archon Books, 1985.

Riley, Franklin P. *General Robert E. Lee after Appomattox.* New York: Macmillan, 1922.

Roman, Alfred. *Military Operations of General Beauregard.* 2 vols. New York: Harper and Bros., 1884.

Ropes, John C., and William R. Livermore. *The Story of the Civil War* 3 vols. New York: G. P. Putnam's Sons, 1894–1913.

Royall, William L. *Some Reminiscences.* Washington, D.C.: Neale, 1909.

Bibliography

Selden, Jefferson S., Jr. *Samuel Selden the Immigrant and His Wife Rebecca Yeo Selden*. Hampton, Va.: J. S. Selden, 1980.

Shaver, Lewellyn A. *A History of the Sixtieth Alabama Regiment.* Montgomery, Ala.: Barrett and Brown, 1867.

Shearer, Benjamin F., and Barbara S. Shearer. *State Names, Seals, Flags, and Symbols, a Historical Guide*. New York: Greenwood, 1987.

Sheridan, Philip H. *Personal Memoirs*. 2 vols. New York: Charles L. Webster, 1888.

Sifakis, Stewart. *Who Was Who in the Confederacy*. New York: Facts on File, 1988.

Smith, Francis H. *History of the Virginia Military Institute*. Lynchburg, Va.: J. P. Bell, 1912.

Starr, Stephen Z. *The Union Cavalry in the Civil War*. 3 vols. Baton Rouge: Louisiana State University Press, 1981.

Stephenson, Mary A. *Old Homes in Surry and Sussex*. Richmond, Va.: Dietz Press, 1942.

Stewart, William H. *A Pair of Blankets*. New York: Broadway, 1911.

Stiles, Robert. *Four Years under Marse Robert*. Washington, D.C.: Neale, 1903.

Street, Julian. *American Adventures*. New York: Century, 1917.

Symonds, Craig L. *Joseph E. Johnston*. New York: W. W. Norton, 1992.

Taylor, Walter H. *Four Years with General Lee*. New York: Appleton, 1878.

_____. *General Lee, 1861–65*. Norfolk, Va.: Nusbaum, 1906.

U.S. Department of the Navy. *Official Records of the Union and Confederate Navies in the War of the Rebellion*. 30 vols. Washington, D.C.: Government Printing Office, 1894–1922.

U.S. War Department. *The War of the Rebellion: A Compilation of the Official Records of the Union and Confederate Armies*. 128 vols. Washington, D.C.: Government Printing Office, 1880–1901.

_____. *Atlas to Accompany the Official Records of the Union and Confederate Armies*. Washington, D.C.: Government Printing Office, 1891.

V.M.I. Alumni Association. *The Register of Former Cadets of Virginia Military Institute*. Lexington, Va.: V.M.I. Alumni Association, 1989.

Wakelyn, Jon L. *Biographical Dictionary of the Confederacy*. Westport, Conn.: Greenwood Press, 1977.

Walker, C. Irvine. *The Life of Lieutenant-General Richard Heron Anderson*. Charleston, S.C.: Art Publishing, 1917.

Warner, Ezra J. *Generals in Gray*. Baton Rouge: Louisiana State University Press, 1959.

_____. *Generals in Blue*. Baton Rouge: Louisiana State University Press, 1964.

Wells, Edward L. *Hampton and his Cavalry in '64*. Richmond: B. F. Johnson, 1899.

White, Henry A. *Robert E. Lee and the Southern Confederacy*. New York: G. P. Putnam's Sons, 1897.

Wight, Richard C. *The Story of Goochland*. Richmond, Va.: Richmond Press, 1943.

Williams, T. Harry. *P. G. T. Beauregard*. Baton Rouge: Louisiana State University Press, 1954.

Winston, Robert W. *Robert E. Lee—A Biography*. New York: Grossett and Dunlap, 1934.

Wise, George. *History of the Seventeenth Virginia Infantry*. Baltimore: Kelly, Piet, 1870.

Wise, Jennings Cropper. *The Long Arm of Lee*. 2 vols. Lynchburg, Va.: J. P. Bell, 1915.

Wise, John S. *The End of an Era*. Boston: Houghton Mifflin, 1901.

Woodward, C. Vann. *Mary Chestnut's Civil War*. New York: Yale University Press, 1981.

Wright, General Marcus J. *List of Staff Officers of the Confederate States Army, 1861–1865*. Washington, D.C.: Government Printing Office, 1891.

_____. *General Officers of the Confederate Army*. New York: Neale, 1911.

Young, James C. *Marse Robert—Knight of the Confederacy*. New York: Rae D. Henkle, 1929.

Articles

"The Association of the Army of Northern Virginia." *S.H.S.P.* 2 (1876): 159.

Bidgood, Joseph V. "List of General Officers and their Staffs in the Confederate Army." *S.H.S.P.* 37 (1910): 156–83.

"Book Notice, *Four Years with General Lee*, by Col. W. H. Taylor." *S.H.S.P.* 5 (1878): 95–96.

Brock, R. A., ed. "Paroles of the Army of Northern Virginia Surrendered at Appomattox C.H., Va., April 9, 1865." *S.H.S.P.* 15 (1887): 1–508.

Colston, Frederick M. "Efficiency of General Lee's Ordnance." *C.V.* 19 (1911): 22–26.

"Col. Walter H. Taylor A.A.G. (*Richmond News-Leader*, [n.d.])." *S.H.S.P.* 41 (1916): 82–87.

Cooke, Giles B. "Col. W. H. Taylor, A.A.G. Army of Northern Virginia: An Appreciation." *C.V.* 24 (1916): 234–35.

Freeman, R. W. "That Appletree at Appomattox." *C.V.* 19 (1911): 521.

"Gen. G. W. C. Lee." *C.V.* 21 (1913): 178.

Harrison, E. W. "Sheridan's Raiders." *William and Mary College Quarterly* 17 (1908–9): 285–94.

Hemphill, Robert R. [Untitled communication on Orr's Rifles]. *C.V.* 7 (1899): 463–64.

Hubard, R. T. "Operations of General J. E. B. Stuart before Chancellorsville." *S.H.S.P.* 8 (1880): 249–54.

Bibliography

Jones, J. William. Review of *Four Years with General Lee*, by Walter H Taylor
S.H.S.P. 5 (1878): 95-96.

Longstreet, James. "The Battle of Gettysburg." *S.H.S.P.* 5 (1878): 257–70.

McIntosh, Charles F. "The Proby Family of England and of Hampton and
Norfolk, Virginia." *V.M.H.B.* 22 (1914): 217–20, 322–28.

"Medallion of Gen. R. E. Lee and Staff." *C.V.* 16 (1908): 486–87.

Meyer, Emanuel. "Walter Herron Taylor and His Era." M.A. thesis, Old
Dominion University, Norfolk, Virginia, 1984.

"The Monument to General Lee." *S.H.S.P.* 17 (1889): 187–335.

"Our Executive Committee." *S.H.S.P.* 8 (1880): 575.

Review of *General Lee, His Campaigns in Virginia 1861–1865*, by W. H. Taylor.
C.V. 16 (1908): 536.

Ryan, E. L. " 'Keswick'—in Powhatan." *V.M.H.B.* 48 (1940): 56–61.

"Sketch of the Lee Memorial Association." *S.H.S.P.* 11 (1883): 388–417.

Smith, James Power. "With Stonewall Jackson." *S.H.S.P.* 43 (1920): 1–110.

Smith, Melvin T. "Mormon Exploration in the Lower Colorado River Area."
In *The Mormon Role in the Settlement of the West*, ed. Richard H. Jackson,
29–49. Provo, Utah: Brigham Young University Press, 1978.

Spence, E. Leslie. "Taking a Brother's Body from the Battlefield." *C.V.* 5
(1897): 484–85.

Talcott, T. M. R. "The Appomattox Apple Tree Once More." *S.H.S.P.* 12
(1884): 573.

_____. Review of *Stuart's Cavalry in the Gettysburg Campaign*, by John S.
Mosby. *S.H.S.P.* 37 (1909): 21–37.

Taylor, Bettie Saunders. "My Wedding." Pamphlet published for the benefit
of the Norfolk Protestant Hospital. Norfolk, 1912. WHT Papers.

Taylor, Nettie Dean. "The Florence Nightingale of the South." *C.V.* 6 (1898):
480–81.

_____. "Worthy Honor to Miss Sallie Tomkins of Virginia." *C.V.* 7 (1899):
358.

Taylor, Walter H. "Causes of Lee's Defeat at Gettysburg." *S.H.S.P.* 4 (1877):
80–87, 124–39.

_____. [Letter to Gen. James Longstreet, April 28, 1875]. *S.H.S.P.* 5 (1878):
75–76.

_____. "Numerical Strength of the Armies at Gettysburg." *S.H.S.P.* 5 (1878):
239–46.

_____. "The Campaign in Pennsylvania." In *The Annals of the War*, ed. The
Publishers of the *Philadelphia Weekly Times*, 305–18. Philadelphia: Times
Publishing, 1879.

_____. "The Battle of Sharpsburg." *S.H.S.P.* 24 (1896): 267–74.

_____. "Lee and Longstreet." *S.H.S.P.* 24 (1896): 73–79.

_____. "Flash-lights from Headquarters of the Army of Northern Virginia,
CSA." Undated ms. in WHT-SH, ca. 1900.

Bibliography

"Unveiling of the Soldiers' and Sailors' Monument." *S.H.S.P.* 22 (1894): 336–80.

"Unveiling of the Statue of General A. P. Hill." *S.H.S.P.* 20 (1892): 352–95.

Venable, Charles S. " 'General Lee to the Rear'—The Incident with Harris' Mississippi Brigade." *S.H.S.P.* 8 (1880): 105–10.

———. "The Campaign from the Wilderness to Petersburg." *S.H.S.P.* 14 (1886): 522–42.

Walker, Carrol H. "Colonel Walter H. Taylor, C.S.A." *Military Collector and Historian* 12 (1960): 39–40.

White, William S. "A Diary of the War, Rolls of Third Company Richmond Howitzers." In *Contributions to a History of the Richmond Howitzer Battalion, Pamphlet No. 2.*, ed. Carlton McCarthy. Richmond: Carlton McCarthy, 1883.

Wilbourn, R. E. "Wounding of General Jackson." *S.H.S.P.* 6 (1878): 266–75.

Wilcox, Cadmus M. *"Four Years with General Lee—A Review." S.H.S.P.* 6 (1878): 71–77.

Index

Ranks given are the highest held during the war. Officers and men listed were in the Confederate Army, unless designated (CSN), (USA), or (USN).